Life *among the* savages
Raising demons

Life *among the* savages

Raising demons

SHIRLEY JACKSON

Quality Paperback Book Club
New York

Life *among* *the* savages

Portions of this book have appeared in other forms in *Charm, Collier's, Good Housekeeping, Harper's, Mademoiselle, Woman's Day, Woman's Home Companion*. The section which was originally published as "Charles" in *Mademoiselle* and *The Lottery* is included here at the particular request of my older son.

For the Children's Grandparents

ONE

OUR HOUSE IS old, and noisy, and full. When we moved into it we had two children and about five thousand books; I expect that when we finally overflow and move out again we will have perhaps twenty children and easily half a million books; we also own assorted beds and tables and chairs and rocking horses and lamps and doll dresses and ship models and paint brushes and literally thousands of socks. This is the way of life my husband and I have fallen into, inadvertently, as though we had fallen into a well and decided that since there was no way out we might as well stay there and set up a chair and a desk and a light of some kind; even though this *is* our way of life, and the only one we know, it is occasionally bewildering, and perhaps even inexplicable to the sort of person who does not have that swift, accurate conviction that he is going to step on a broken celluloid doll in the dark. I cannot think of a preferable way of life, except one without children and without books, going on soundlessly in an apartment hotel where they do the cleaning for you and send up your meals and all you have to do is lie on a couch and—as I say, I cannot think of a preferable way of life, but then I have had to make a good many compromises, all told.

I look around sometimes at the paraphernalia of our living—sandwich bags, typewriters, little wheels off things—and marvel at the complexities of civilization with which we surround ourselves; would we be pleased, I wonder, at a wholesale elimination of these things, so that we were reduced only to necessities (coffeepot, typewriters, the essential little wheels off things) and then—this happening usually in the springtime—I begin throwing things away, and it turns out that although we can live agreeably without the little wheels off things, new little wheels turn up almost immediately. This is, I suspect, progress. They can make new little wheels, if not faster than they can fall off things, at least faster than I can throw them away.

I remember the morning, long ago, when the landlord called. Our son Laurie was three and a half, and our daughter Jannie was six months old, and I had the lunch almost ready and the diapers washed, along with the little shirts and the nightgowns and the soakers and the cotton blankets, and they were all drying on the line (and I don't care what *any*one says, that's a morning's work, when you consider that I had also made brownies and emptied the ashtrays) and then the landlord called. He was a kindly man, and a paternal one, so that he asked first about my health, and my husband's health, and then he asked how was our boy? and how was the baby? and when I said that we were all fine, fine, he said that of course we were aware that our lease was up? I said well, no, we hadn't really known that our lease was up. So he said well, he supposed that we hadn't looked at the lease recently and I (wondering if that was the paper Laurie had torn up and eaten) said that it had been quite a while, really, since we sat down together and read over our lease. That was too bad, he said. Wasn't it, I said. Because, he said, his voice gentle, the apartment had been rented to someone else. After a minute I said rented? to someone *else?* Then I laughed and said what were *we* supposed to do—move? He said well, yes, we were supposed to do just that.

"Naturally," he went on, "we could evict you if we wanted to."

"You could?" I was thinking of letters to the president, appeals for the sake of our two small children. "We'd much rather you'd just move out," he said.

"But where?"

He laughed genially. "Ask me another," he said. "Apartments are mighty tough to find these days."

"I suppose we could take a look around," I said dubiously. Letters, I was thinking, sue them for the piece of plaster that fell on my husband while he was shaving: lawyers.

"We'll expect to take possession around May first," he said.

"Today is March twenty-fifth," I said.

"That's right," he said. "Rent almost due," and he laughed again.

The next day we got a letter saying that it was "first notice of warning to evict." I began to think in terms of pouring boiling oil from the windows and barricading the doors with the dining room table. What made both of us even angrier was the fact that we had never had any intention of renewing our lease, but had planned vaguely on moving as soon as we found another place. "The very idea," I told my husband indignantly, "renting this apartment to someone else without fixing that broken step. The one on the stairs."

"Leave a note for the new people about the cockroaches," my husband advised. He also advised strenuously against bringing suit for some undetermined reason (the piece of plaster? the neighbor's radio?) and said, patting me on the shoulder, that he knew how anxious I had been to find another place.

Our fondest dream had been to move to Vermont, to a town where a couple we knew had settled and from which they had written us glowing accounts of mountains, and children playing in their own gardens, and clean snow, and homegrown carrots, and now suddenly it looked overwhelmingly as though we moved either to Vermont or to a tent in the park. I called half a dozen city agents, and they all laughed as gaily as our landlord had laughed; "Got any relatives you could move in with?" one of them asked me.

Finally, two hardy adventurers making for unexplored territory, we left the children with their grandparents, got ourselves and our suitcases and our overshoes onto a train at the station, and set out, an advance scouting party, for the small town where our friends lived, and where the mountains were so high and the snow so clean. There was no doubt, we discovered, about the snow. Our city overshoes went in over their heads as we stepped off the train, and for the three days we were there we both went constantly with damp feet and small bits of ice melting against our socks.

One nice thing was, there were lots and lots of houses available. We heard this from a lady named Mrs. Black, a motherly old body who lived in a nearby large town, but who knew, as she herself pointed out, every house and every family in the state. She took us to visit a house which she called the Bassington house, and which would have been perfect for us and our books and our children, if there had been any plumbing.

"Wouldn't take much to put *in* plumbing," Mrs. Black told us. "Put in plumbing, you got a real nice house there."

My husband shifted nervously in the snow. "You see," he said, "that brings up the question of . . . well . . . money."

Mrs. Black shrugged. "How much would *plumbing* cost?" she demanded. "You put in maybe twelve, fifteen hundred dollars, you got a real nice house."

"Now look, if we had fifteen hundred dollars we could give an apartment superintendent—" my husband began, but I cut in quickly, "You must remember, Mrs. Black, that we want to *rent*."

"Rent, did you?" said Mrs. Black, as though this proved at last that we were mere fly-by-nights, lookers at houses for the pleasure of it. "Well, if *I* was you folks, small children and all, well, *I*'d buy."

"But money—" my husband said.

"Money?" said Mrs. Black scornfully. "Two, three thousand dollars." She thought. "On the other hand," she said brightly, "if you was to fix it up *yourselves*—set in the plumbing, do a little painting, fix a few things maybe, you might cut your price down considerable."

She was looking directly at my husband as she said this, and he smiled weakly and nodded, obviously for that brief moment taken in by the notion that he might himself set in the plumbing. "You got to *figure*," Mrs. Black pursued, "you put down maybe two, three thousand dollars, you get a first mortgage from Henry Andrews down to the bank, you sign to put in a few improvements—all you got to figure *there* is title, I think, and maybe equity, Henry Andrews can tell you just exactly *what*. Taxes, o'course. Insurance, you'd want, and then you figure heat and electric, and maybe you could get Bill Adams to put in the plumbing for you for less on account it's his wife's sister owns the house, and there you are. Ten, fifteen years, you got a real nice house here, and you *own* it. Other way, you'd still be paying rent."

"But money—" my husband said.

Mrs. Black continued smoothly, "Other hand," she said, "you might like the McCaffery house. Now *there's* one with plumbing."

The McCaffery house may have had plumbing for all we ever knew; we could not get to it because the dirt road leading up to the top of the hill where the house sat was impassable with snow. "Have to clear *this* out some," Mrs. Black said, as we all stood at the bottom of the hill looking up at the house.

A Mr. Miller, who wore a leather jacket and a cap with earmuffs, took us to see the Donald house. This was a pretty place, set in an acre of marsh, but we unreasonably required a furnace, which Mr. Miller figured we ought to be able to put in for maybe two, three thousand. "Heat it with stoves, *I* would," he said. "Don't cost's much to run's a furnace."

"Money—" my husband said.

"Might be," Mr. Miller said, looking doubtfully at my husband, "might be you're handy-like around a house?"

Mr. Faber, who wore checked hunting pants and rolled his own cigarettes, showed us the Grant house, which had only three rooms and a lovely garden, and the Exeter house, which was big and rambling and heated and even had plumbing. "Real nice house here," Mr. Faber said as we stood, wondering, in the panelled dining room. "Priced at fifty thousand, but he ought to come down some on *that*."

"Fif—" said my husband.

"Well," Mr. Faber said sadly, "I didn't suppose you cared to go *that* high, but I figured you'd enjoy *seeing* it."

Mrs. Black, who picked us up again at nine the next morning, took us to see the Hubbard house, which had been made over from an old farmhouse, and had lovely floors and high ceilings and fireplaces and clean colored walls and even a garage, but no bedrooms. "The living room *alone* is seventy foot," Mrs. Black said. "Studio type house, you might say." She hesitated. "Matter of three, four thousand to build on a wing," she suggested hopefully.

"But we want to *rent*," I said, wailing. "We don't want to put things in and build things on and plough things out, we want to rent a house that's all put together *before* we move in."

Mrs. Black sighed. "There's a nice place, the Exeter house," she said at last. "Real big, suit you folks fine. Priced at—"

By the end of the second day we had even looked at a barn which someone had thought he might just rent out, but there were two cows and a tractor in that, and even Mrs. Black's optimistic suggestion that we could easily make up the stalls into bedrooms for the children could not encourage us.

"Well," Mrs. Black said as she said goodbye to us in

front of our friends' house, "I guess you folks are pretty lucky you got a place to live in the city."

Wearily, that evening, we sat in the comfortable living room of our friends' house, sheltered beneath a roof, securely, though temporarily, housed, and tried frantically to plan. It was April second, we had had our second notice of warning to evict, and we had begun to think wildly of renting a trailer, or having the children live with their grandparents, or borrowing a tent and a canoe and exploring the Great Lakes.

"Exeter," my husband said, miserably, "Exeter, McCaffery, Grant. Bassington, Hubbard, Donald. McCaffery, Bassington, Donald, Grant. Exeter, Hubbard—"

"We just can't *live* in a house without plumbing," I said.

"Or a furnace," my husband said. "McCaffery, Hubbard—"

"Maybe we *could* get an extension from our landlord," I said without hope. "Maybe if he knew how hard we tried he might let us have a few weeks more."

Our friends sat, shaking their heads sympathetically, although their own home was paid for and firmly fixed upon its foundations, with its furnace working smoothly and its plumbing in repair.

"If we only had some *money*," my husband said and everyone sighed.

We had to take the train home the next day, and on the way to the station I stopped in at the one grocery in town for cigarettes. After I had paid him the grocer said, "Couldn't find a place, I guess."

"No," I said, surprised, although I was to learn later that the grocer not only knew our housing problems, but the ages and names of our children, the meat we had been served for dinner the night before, and my husband's income.

"To bad you weren't interested in the Fielding place," the grocer said.

"We didn't even hear about it," I said.

"Would have called you," the grocer said, "but Mae Black, *she* said you only wanted to buy. Not for sale, the Fielding house."

"What's it like?"

The grocer waved his hand vaguely. "Old," he said. "Been in the family a long time." He accepted a nickel from a small boy, helped him take the wrapper off a popsicle, and said, "Whyn't you call old Sam Fielding? I bet he'd be real glad to take you over there."

There was only one train a day from the town. If we stopped long enough to look at the Fielding house we would not be able to leave until tomorrow; I hesitated, and the grocer said, "Won't do any harm to *look*, anyway."

I went outside and put my head in through the window of the car where my husband was waiting with our host and hostess. "Ever hear of a house called the Fielding house?" I asked.

"The *Fielding* house?" said our hostess, and our host said, "What on earth do you want with *that?*"

"What's the matter with it?" I asked.

"Well," said our hostess, "it's a thousand years old, I think."

"A million," said our host. "It's . . ." He gestured helplessly. "It's got these big white pillars across the front," he said.

"Is there a house in back of the pillars?" my husband asked. "Because if there is, and it has plumbing and a furnace and bedrooms and they'll rent it to us, we're going to be living there."

The Fielding house was a very old house about a mile out of town. It was the oldest in its neighborhood and the third oldest in the township; we had passed it, we realized with something of a shock, several times when we drove with Mrs. Black or Mr. Miller or Mr. Faber to look at other houses. It had been built—I looked it up in the town history shortly after we moved in, when I was vainly trying to come to terms with it—about eighteen-twenty, by a doctor named Ogilvie, who set it up as a manor house in the center of a great farm. The classical revival was upon the county then, and Doctor Ogilvie modeled his house after, presumably, a minor Greek temple; he set up the four massive white pillars across the front, threw wings out to both sides and then, with true New England economy, left the house only one room deep behind its impressive facade. When the Ogilvie family died off or moved away, as it did shortly after the house was built, it passed into the hands of a family named Cortland, who sold off most of the farm land and changed Doctor Ogilvie's woodshed into a summer kitchen. The Cortlands eventually sold the house to a family named Fielding, who promptly bought back all the surrounding land, now somewhat built up with houses, rented the houses out, set up a lumber mill on the river that used to run across Doctor Ogilvie's farm, and hired their tenants as employees. It seemed from the town records that the original Fielding had been a farm hand for Doctor Ogilvie, and the family no doubt had their eyes on the place even then. As the town developed the Fieldings became wealthier, and eventually the final generation of authentic Fieldings died off in the house and the entire property went to three cousins, all of whom lived in severely modern houses in neighboring towns, doing handsomely on their interests in the lumber mill.

When the manor house was put up for rent it was as though a vital part of the town had slid imperceptibly into the river, and a great coolness arose between the Fielding heirs and the Bartletts, who owned the second oldest house in town. During the worst housing shortages, when the lumber mill was going full blast night and day, the old manor house on top of the hill stayed empty, its white pillars sagging and its driveway choked with dead leaves or smooth with unmarked snow. When we saw it first it looked faintly ridiculous, and even the fences on either side and along the front leaned a little bit away from it, without actually renouncing it, as though they deplored it privately and yet wanted to present a unified front to the world of inhabitants. Sam Fielding was the only one of the Fielding cousins who retained the family name and so it had apparently been felt that he was the logical one to show us the house; he was a small quiet old man with the slow voice of the thoughtful Vermonter, and he stood with us at the foot of the. lawn and he and my husband and I stared silently up at the huge pillars, the spread wings, the iron weather vane which stared mutely back at us.

"That's it," said Mr. Fielding undeniably. "I'd like to get *some* use out of it." He looked away quickly, as though avoiding an accusing glance from the house. "Good house," he added.

"It looks so . . ." I hesitated. "Imposing," I said finally.

"Imposing," Mr. Fielding agreed. He declined a cigarette from my husband and took out a cigarette of his own; it was the same brand, but it was his own. "Clean it up some," he said, nodding his head at the house.

"May we go inside?" I asked. "If we *were* interested in the house, I'd rather like to see the inside."

"Door's open," Mr. Fielding said.

We hesitated, my husband and I. Mr. Fielding settled himself comfortably on a tree stump and crossed his legs. "Door's open," he said again.

Together my husband and I made our way to the front door, avoiding just in time the broken step that led onto the porch. Once among the pillars the sense of the house came upon one with a rush; here was a *house,* as compared with the makeshift McCafferies and Exeters. My husband tried the front door tentatively, and it swung open. Gingerly, watching out for broken floorboards, we went inside, into a wide hall shadowed by the pillars and backed by a straight, lovely, colonial stairway; somewhere to our right were a carpet flooded with red cabbage roses and a harmonium, under dark old pictures which seemed to lean forward a little to watch us, surprised; we went into a kitchen where a monumental ironwork stove threatened to fall on us, and in the kitchen there was a table thick with dust and on it were a dusty cup and a plate with two solid, ancient doughnuts on it. There was a chair pushed a little away from the table.

"I'm sorry we stayed," I said to my husband earnestly, my hands shaking as I looked at the two hideous doughnuts, "we interrupted their lunch, let's leave right away."

"If it weren't the only house in town . . ." he said, but he followed me rapidly outside.

Mr. Fielding rose to meet us as we came back down between the pillars, and when we were near him he said, "Weather's closing in. Snow before morning." He escorted us solemnly to the station, discussing the weather, and as our train came in he remarked, "Fix her up some, then, before you folks come in the spring."

"Tell me," I said, "how long since anyone's been *in* that house?"

"Not since the old man died," he said. "Four year I figure that might be."

"But to straighten it up?" I insisted. "Look over his things, or anything?"

"Never really figured it would rent," he said thoughtfully. "No sense rushing things."

He waved to us kindly when we got onto the train. During most of that next two weeks I held firmly to the impractical conviction that I didn't *care* if it was the last house in the town, or in the world for that matter, and I didn't *care* if it meant living in the park, I was not going to live in a house with two petrified doughnuts. The following week, however, we received a letter from Mr. Fielding, saying that the house was being fixed up, and did we feel that fifty dollars a month was too much rent?

"You seem to have taken the house," I said unjustly to my husband.

"It's probably because we went inside," he said. "No one else has ever gone inside, and that probably constitutes a lease."

A week later we received another letter from Mr. Fielding, saying that the house was all ready for us, except for the outside, which would be painted when the weather opened up. Since we had not answered his last letter, he figured that his rent was too high, and did we think we could manage forty?

A strong sense of guilt impelled my husband to write

back immediately saying that fifty dollars a month was fine; "before he *gives* it to us," he told me.

"But I'm not—" I said, realizing that of course I was.

I came up on the train, a day after my husband. I brought with me a wildly excited Laurie, and Jannie, in a basket; and all the way up on the train, crushed in between Laurie and the baby's basket and the suitcases and the sandwiches, I was wondering if anyone had thought to take away the kitchen table and the doughnuts: my husband had promised that if we really couldn't stand it we could try once more to find something in the city. Mr. Fielding was with my husband to meet us at the station, and when I saw Mr. Fielding again the whole clear sense of the house came back to me and I was ready to turn around and go back right then. He smiled at me cheerfully, said, "Afternoon, young fellow," to Laurie, and stared gravely at the baby for a minute; she stared back at him, and then he nodded to me and said reassuringly, "Fixed her up some."

I knew what he meant when I saw the house. It had been literally scraped clean, down to the wood in the walls. Mr. Fielding had put on new wallpaper, rich with great gorgeous patterns, the windows had been washed, the pillars straightened, the broken step repaired, and a cheerful man in the kitchen was putting the last touches of glittering white paint to the new shelving; there was a brand new electric stove and a new refrigerator, the floors had been repaired and varnished, a hornets' nest had been removed from the farthest pillar on the right. The lawn was just beginning to show green, and Laurie ran in and out between the pillars, touching every one, and then, shouting, up and down the straight stairway. In her basket Jannie smiled, looking up at the sky over the trees.

"It's beautiful," I said to Mr. Fielding, almost in tears. "I thought it would look like it did before."

"Needed some work done," Mr. Fielding agreed. Then he nodded at the new kitchen stove and said, "Did the old place good."

Just then our moving van arrived, and the three muscular, brazen fellows who had looked so natural carrying our furniture out of the apartment became abruptly incongruous carrying our small chairs and tables in between the pillars.

"Put in some more plumbing, too," Mr. Fielding said, and departed.

For the first week or so things were completely at cross-purposes. Our furniture, which had been more than adequate for a city apartment, here spread all too thinly among the echoing rooms of the house, and we had to fill out with odd tables and chairs brought from Mr. Fielding and from nearby second-hand shops. The house had grown enormously, I later learned, from Doctor Ogilvie's original structure. The Cortlands had added the summer kitchen, but the Fieldings had added on and on, so that the room which had been the summer kitchen, for instance, and hitched on to the back of the house in the first place, was now smack in the middle, tucked in among larger and sturdier rooms, and was no longer a kitchen at all but only a dark little room which was sometimes difficult to find. We had only three beds and we had six bedrooms, so Mr. Fielding sold us, for fifty cents, a bed that had been only recently taken out of the house and put into one of the capacious barns. We tried to buy the harmonium but the Fieldings had sold it to an antique dealer; we did buy the carpet with the cabbage roses, since it was the only one which would fit into the vast desert of the parlor; we declined, with one voice, the old kitchen table. All these things, the ones that had been in the house before, and other things which had been in similar old houses and knew their ways, fell naturally into good positions in the rooms, as though snatching the best places before the city furniture could crowd in. No matter how much we wanted to set our overstuffed chairs on either side of the living room fireplace, an old wooden rocker that Mr. Fielding had given us insisted upon pre-empting the center of the hearth rug and could not in human kindness be shifted. An old highboy, which was a contemporary of the rocker although it had come from a barn across town, took over the living room corner near the rocker, and the two of them lived there in silent companionship.

After a few vain attempts at imposing our own angular order on things with a consequent out-of-jointness and shrieking disharmony that set our teeth on edge, we gave in to the old furniture and let things settle where they would. An irritation persisted in one particular spot in the dining room, a spot which would hold neither table nor buffet and developed an alarming sag in the floor when I tried to put a radio there, until I found completely by accident that this place was used to a desk and would not be comfortable until I went out and found a spindly old writing table and set a brass inkwell on it.

There was a door to an attic that preferred to stay latched and would latch itself no matter who was inside; there was another door which hung by custom slightly ajar, although it would close goodhumoredly for a time when some special reason required it. We had five attics, we discovered, built into and upon and next to one another; one of them kept bats and we shut that one up completely; another, light and cheerful in spite of its one small window, liked to be a place of traffic and became, without any decision of ours, a place to store things temporarily, things that were moved regularly, like sleds and snow shovels and garden rakes and hammocks. The basement had an old clothesline hung across it, and after the line I put up in the back yard had fallen down for the third time I resigned myself and put up a new line in the basement, and clothes dried there quickly and freshly. We stocked the woodshed, since we had four fireplaces, and my husband discovered an odd pleasure in splitting wood, and the sound of an axe in the woodshed echoed agreeably through the kitchen. One bedroom chose the children, because it was large and light and showed unmistakable height-marks on one wall and seemed to mind not at all when crayon marks appeared on the wallpaper and paint got spilled on the floor. We put bookcases in the little dark room downstairs, and after the second week my husband got so he could find it nine times out of ten.

It *was* a good old house, after all. Our cats slept on the rocking chair; our friends came to call. We accustomed ourselves to trading at certain stores and we bought our cheese locally and we found a doctor and a dog; Laurie entered the community nursery school and learned, as I had, to identify the house by saying "It's the old Fielding house —the one with the pillars." Toward the end of our first year there the painter arrived to do the outside of the house, and he painted it white with green trim, the colors it had always been painted before; indeed, I doubt if he owned any other colors of paint. "Not many houses like *this* nowadays," he told me, smiling benignly down at me from the top of his ladder, "don't find houses *built* like this any more."

I looked from the front porch in through the glass of the front door, seeing the slim line of the stairway and the bright curtains in the dining room. "It's a good old house," I said.

"Can always tell by the cats," the painter said enigmatically.

I found that, where in the city I had always been too busy to do anything at all, I was now making odd things like gingerbread and cabbage salad. Laurie started a crude garden out back, and Jannie took her first step in the dining room. Once I left both of them with our next-door neighbor, and went into the city for a wild two-day shopping trip; when I wandered into our old neighborhood and stood in front of our old apartment house I could only think how small and dirty it looked. "No pillars *there*," I told myself with deep gratification, and wished I could write our old landlord and tell *him*.

So, the house was old when we found it, and noisy when we entered it, and it took very little time for it to fill up. Our children brought in friends and rocking horses and paint brushes, we brought in friends and books and little wheels off things. I learned to make pie crust—although I have not the touch of a born pie-maker, I am afraid. People from the city began driving up for weekends in the nice weather.

Jannie spoke for a long time about a faraway voice in the house which sang to her at night, and we put the Christmas tree in the corner of the living room where the lights shone at night out between the pillars; we raked leaves on the front lawn and went sledding down the hillside. We began to speak slightingly of city-folk.

I have, as I say, never found a way of life preferable to this; its only fault—aside from the back-breaking labor and the vicious pie crusts which refuse to brown—is that it goes on and on, without, it seems, any major change at all. I observe my neighbors and it seems to me that they are content to live on, registering and employing each day but not in the least distinguishing one day beyond another, and, although that is obviously the best way of passing time, it makes, I feel, for little or no excitement. Even a major event (like our hurricane, or the time we had the flood, or that terribly heavy snow when all the electricity was out for three days) tends to become, by the next day, only a remembered landmark—"that was two days, I recollect, before the hurricane, because we had all those raspberries to set out . . ."—and even the last trump will, I am afraid, make no more of an impression on our community (". . . well, now, let's see; that there bugle blowed around about three in the afternoon, and I remember the day because it was the day I w's supposed to hammer on the boards on that there gate, and here it's been maybe six weeks since that ol' bugle, and there hangs the gate right now . . ."). When I think about it, I can only remember the year Laurie was born because I was waiting to get a new winter coat.

One of the most unnerving, and least original, observations I have made about my children is that as these years turn and Christmas inevitably follows the fourth of July and the fourth of July inevitably follows Christmas, they tend to grow older. Every October, for instance, Laurie has a birthday. Every November, incredible as it may sound, Jannie has a birthday; the fact that I also have a birthday every December is unfortunately entirely believable but somehow less heartwarming. When we first came to the house in the country, Laurie was something over three years old, and Jannie was six months, and then suddenly—although I had in the meantime grown a year older, and so had my husband, and we wished one another "Happy Birthday" very properly—Jannie was almost two and had become a legitimate member of the family named Jannie (instead of Baby, or The Baby), and Laurie was just short of five and was clamoring for the right to vote on domestic policies.

The day Laurie started kindergarten he renounced corduroy overalls with bibs and began wearing blue jeans with a belt; I watched him go off the first morning with the older girl next door, seeing clearly that an era of my life was ended, my sweet-voiced nursery-school tot replaced by a long-trousered, swaggering character who forgot to stop at the corner and wave goodbye to me.

He came home the same way, the front door slamming open, his cap on the floor, and the voice suddenly become raucous shouting, "Isn't anybody *here?*"

At lunch he spoke insolently to his father, spilled Jannie's milk, and remarked that his teacher said that we were not to take the name of the Lord in vain.

"How *was* school today?" I asked, elaborately casual.

"All right," he said.

"Did you learn anything?" his father asked.

Laurie regarded his father coldly. "I didn't learn nothing," he said.

"Anything," I said. "Didn't learn anything."

"The teacher spanked a boy, though," Laurie said, addressing his bread and butter. "For being fresh," he added with his mouth full.

"What did he do?" I asked. "Who was it?"

Laurie thought. "It was Charles," he said. "He was fresh. The teacher spanked him and made him stand in a corner. He was awfully fresh."

"What did he do?" I asked again, but Laurie slid off his chair, took a cookie, and left, while his father was still saying "See here, young man."

The next day Laurie remarked at lunch, as soon as he sat down, "Well, Charles was bad again today." He grinned enormously and said, "Today Charles hit the teacher."

"Good heavens," I said, mindful of the Lord's name, "I suppose he got spanked again?"

"He sure did," Laurie said. "Look up," he said to his father.

"What?" his father said, looking up.

"Look down," Laurie said. "Look at my thumb. Gee, you're dumb." He began to laugh insanely.

"Why did Charles hit the teacher?" I asked quickly.

"Because she tried to make him color with red crayons," Laurie said. "Charles wanted to color with green crayons so he hit the teacher and she spanked him and said nobody play with Charles but everybody did."

The third day—it was Wednesday of the first week—Charles bounced a seesaw onto the head of a little girl and made her bleed and the teacher made him stay inside all during recess. Thursday Charles had to stand in a corner during storytime because he kept pounding his feet on the floor. Friday Charles was deprived of blackboard privileges because he threw chalk.

On Saturday I remarked to my husband, "Do you think kindergarten is too unsettling for Laurie? All this toughness and bad grammar, and this Charles boy sounds like such a bad influence."

"It'll be all right," my husband said reassuringly. "Bound to be people like Charles in the world. Might as well meet them now as later."

On Monday Laurie came home late, full of news. "Charles," he shouted as he came up the hill; I was waiting anxiously on the front steps, "Charles," Laurie yelled all the way up the hill, "Charles was bad again."

"Come right in," I said, as soon as he came close enough. "Lunch is waiting."

"You know what Charles did?" he demanded, following me through the door. "Charles yelled so in school they sent a boy in from first grade to tell the teacher she had to make Charles keep quiet, and so Charles had to stay after school. And so all the children stayed to watch him."

"What did he do?" I asked.

"He just sat there," Laurie said, climbing into his chair at the table. "Hi Pop, y'old dust mop."

"Charles had to stay after school today," I told my husband. "Everyone stayed with him."

"What does this Charles look like?" my husband asked Laurie. "What's his other name?"

"He's bigger than me," Laurie said. "And he doesn't have any rubbers and he doesn't ever wear a jacket."

Monday night was the first Parent-Teachers meeting, and only the fact that Jannie had a cold kept me from going; I wanted passionately to meet Charles' mother. On Tuesday Laurie remarked suddenly, "Our teacher had a friend come see her in school today."

"Charles' mother?" my husband and I asked simultaneously.

"Naaah," Laurie said scornfully. "It was a man who came and made us do exercises. Look." He climbed down from his chair and squatted down and touched his toes. "Like this," he said. He got solemnly back into his chair and said, picking up his fork, "Charles didn't even *do* exercises."

"That's fine," I said heartily. "Didn't Charles want to do exercises?"

"Naaah," Laurie said. "Charles was so fresh to the teacher's friend he wasn't *let* do exercises."

"Fresh again?" I said.

"He kicked the teacher's friend," Laurie said. "The teacher's friend told Charles to touch his toes like I just did and Charles kicked him."

"What are they going to do about Charles, do you suppose?" Laurie's father asked him.

Laurie shrugged elaborately. "Throw him out of school, I guess," he said.

Wednesday and Thursday were routine; Charles yelled during story hour and hit a boy in the stomach and made him cry. On Friday Charles stayed after school again and so did all the other children.

With the third week of kindergarten Charles was an institution in our family; Jannie was being a Charles when she cried all afternoon; Laurie did a Charles when he filled his wagon full of mud and pulled it through the kitchen; even my husband, when he caught his elbow in the telephone cord and pulled telephone, ash tray, and a bowl of flowers off the table, said, after the first minute, "Looks like Charles."

During the third and fourth weeks there seemed to be a reformation in Charles; Laurie reported grimly at lunch on Thursday of the third week, "Charles was so good today the teacher gave him an apple."

"What?" I said, and my husband added warily, "You mean Charles?"

"Charles," Laurie said. "He gave the crayons around and he picked up the books afterward and the teacher said he was her helper."

"What happened?" I asked incredulously.

"He was her helper, that's all," Laurie said, and shrugged.

"Can this be true, about Charles?" I asked my husband that night. "Can something like this happen?"

"Wait and see," my husband said cynically. "When

you've got a Charles to deal with, this may mean he's only plotting."

He seemed to be wrong. For over a week Charles was the teacher's helper; each day he handed things out and he picked things up; no one had to stay after school.

"The P.-T.A. meeting's next week again," I told my husband one evening. "I'm going to find Charles' mother there."

"Ask her what happened to Charles," my husband said. "I'd like to know."

"I'd like to know myself," I said.

On Friday of that week things were back to normal. "You know what Charles did today?" Laurie demanded at the lunch table, in a voice slightly awed. "He told a little girl to say a word and she said it and the teacher washed her mouth out with soap and Charles laughed."

"What word?" his father asked unwisely, and Laurie said, "I'll have to whisper it to you, it's so bad." He got down off his chair and went around to his father. His father bent his head down and Laurie whispered joyfully. His father's eyes widened.

"Did Charles tell the little girl to say *that?*" he asked respectfully.

"She said it *twice*," Laurie said. "Charles told her to say it *twice*."

"What happened to Charles?" my husband asked.

"Nothing," Laurie said. "He was passing out the crayons."

Monday morning Charles abandoned the little girl and said the evil word himself three or four times, getting his mouth washed out with soap each time. He also threw chalk.

My husband came to the door with me that evening as I set out for the P.-T.A. meeting. "Invite her over for a cup of tea after the meeting," he said. "I want to get a look at her."

"If only she's there," I said prayerfully.

"She'll be there," my husband said. "I don't see how they could hold a P.-T.A. meeting without Charles' mother."

At the meeting I sat restlessly, scanning each comfortable matronly face, trying to determine which one hid the secret of Charles. None of them looked to me haggard enough. No one stood up in the meeting and apologized for the way her son had been acting. No one mentioned Charles.

After the meeting I identified and sought out Laurie's kindergarten teacher. She had a plate with a cup of tea and a piece of chocolate cake; I had a plate with a cup of tea and a piece of marshmallow cake. We maneuvered up to one another cautiously and smiled.

"I've been so anxious to meet you," I said. "I'm Laurie's mother."

"We're all so interested in Laurie," she said.

"Well, he certainly likes kindergarten," I said. "He talks about it all the time."

"We had a little trouble adjusting, the first week or so," she said primly, "but now he's a fine little helper. With lapses, of course."

"Laurie usually adjusts very quickly," I said. "I suppose this time it's Charles' influence."

"Charles?"

"Yes," I said, laughing, "you must have your hands full in that kindergarten, with Charles."

"Charles?" she said. "We don't have any Charles in the kindergarten."

IT WAS SOON after this meeting—the whole question of Charles having somehow dissipated and become without discussion a forbidden topic—that my husband, moved by some obscure impulse which may or may not have been connected with Charles, bought himself an air gun. I have never really believed that my husband is the Kit Carson type, but it is remotely possible that occasionally a feeling for the life romantic overcomes him; this air gun was large and menacing and he told me, in that terribly responsible voice men get to using when they are telling their wives about machinery, or guns, or politics, that he got it for target practice.

There had been a rat in the cellar, he said; he was sure he had seen a rat when he went down to start the furnace. So, of course, he was going to shoot it. Not trap it or poison it—that was for boys and terriers; *he* was going to shoot it.

For the better part of a Sunday morning he crouched dangerously at the open cellar door, waiting for the rat to show his whiskers, which the rat was kind enough not to do. Our two excellent cats were also staying inside, sitting complacently and with some professional interest directly behind my husband. The rat hunt was broken up when the kitchen door banged open and Laurie crashed in with three friends to see how his father shot the rat. Eventually, I suppose, the rat wandered off, although I do not see how he could conceivably have been frightened by the prospect of being shot. Probably he had never realized until then that he had strayed into a house with cats *and* children. At any rate, my husband and the cats, hunting in a pack, managed to bring down even better game; it must have been about the Tuesday after the rat hunt that our female cat, Ninki, who is something of a hunter, caught a chipmunk. She has done this before and will do it again, although I am sure she will never again ask my husband to sit in with her. The chipmunk she caught that morning—it was about nine-thirty—was not co-operative, and when Ninki brought him into the kitchen, where she usually brings chipmunks with some odd conviction that she must eat them in her own dish, the chipmunk ducked under her paw and raced madly to a rather tall plant on the window sill. The plant was just strong enough to bear the weight of one chipmunk, and Ninki, in a sort of frenzy, hurried into the dining room where my husband was just finishing his coffee and talked him into going into the kitchen to see her chipmunk in the plant. My husband took one look and went for his air gun.

Ninki was able to get onto the window sill, but the plant was tall enough and the pot it stood in shaky enough so that she could not quite reach the chipmunk, who was standing precariously on the very top of the plant. My husband drew a careful bead with the air gun and then found that unless he stepped up and held his weapon against the chipmunk's head, he stood a very good chance of missing the chipmunk, if not actually the cat, who was a large and intrusive target.

By this time, of course, I had put down my coffee cup and was standing in the doorway between the kitchen and the dining room, safely out of range as women should be when men are hunting, and saying things like "Dear, why don't you put a paper bag over it or something and take it outside?" and "Dear, don't you think it would be easier if—"

Ninki was by this time irritated beyond belief by the general air of incompetence exhibited in the kitchen, and she went into the living room and got Shax, who is extraordinarily lazy and never catches his own chipmunks, but who is, at least, a cat, and preferable, Ninki saw clearly, to a man with a gun. Shax sized up the situation with a cynical eye, gave my husband and his gun the coldest look I have ever seen a cat permit himself, and then leaped onto the window sill and sat on the other side of the flowerpot. It made a pretty little tableau: Ninki and Shax sitting on either side of the flowerpot and the chipmunk sitting on top of the plant.

After a minute the chipmunk—feeling rightly that all eyes were upon him—fidgeted nervously, and the plant began to sway. As the chipmunk was very nervous and the top of the plant very supple, soon the top of the plant began to swing from side to side, like a pendulum, so that the chipmunk, going faster and faster, rocked over to one cat and then to the other, grazing a nose of each, while they backed away dubiously. My husband still had his aim on the chipmunk, and *he* began to rock back and forth. When the cats finally realized what was happening, they took turns batting the chipmunk as he swung between them.

All of this happened so quickly that I believe—unless I prefer to move out I have no choice *but* to believe—that my husband pressed the trigger of the air gun without really meaning to, because it is certain that he missed the chipmunk and the cats, and hit the window. The crash sent cats, chipmunk, and Nimrod in all directions—the cats under the table, the chipmunk, with rare presence of mind, out the broken window, and my husband, with even rarer presence of mind, back to the dining room and to his seat at the table. I advanced from my post in the kitchen doorway and picked up the air gun from the floor; then, with what I regard as unique forbearance, I went for the broom and dustpan. All I permitted myself, spoken gently and without undue emphasis, was "Thank heaven Laurie is in school."

I was indulgent enough to return the air gun to my husband after a few days, but I would have thought that Ninki had more sense. Perhaps she never dreamed I would give the air gun back, or perhaps she just thought target practice around the house had been given up as impractical; perhaps, with some kind of feline optimism I cannot share, she believed that the chipmunk episode had been a freak, the sort of thing that might happen to any man confronting an oscillant chipmunk.

So it was not more than a week later that Ninki gave the air gun another chance. It was a cool evening, and I was lying on the couch with a blanket over me, reading a mystery story; my husband was sitting quietly in his chair reading the newspaper. We had just congratulated one another on the fact that it was now too late for casual guests to drop in, and my husband had mentioned three or four times that he thought he might like some of that pot roast in a sandwich before he went to bed. Then we heard Ninki's unmistakably triumphant mighty-hunter howl from the dining room.

"Look," I said apprehensively, "Ninki's got something, a mouse or something. *Make* her take it outside."

"She'll get it out by herself."

"But she'll chase it around and around and around the

dining room and kill it there and—" I gulped unhappily "—eat it. Get it out *now* while it's still alive."

"She won't—" my husband began, when Ninki's triumphant wail broke off with a muffled oath and Ninki herself came hurriedly to the dining room door and stared compellingly at my husband.

"Do you *always* need help?" he asked her crossly. "Seems to me a great big cat like you—"

I shrieked. Ninki lifted her head resignedly, as one whose bitterest views of fate have been confirmed; my husband gasped. Ninki's supper, a full-grown and horribly active bat, was sweeping magnificently down the length of the living room. For a minute I watched it with my mouth open and then, still yelling, buried my head under the blanket.

"My gun," I heard my husband shouting at Ninki, "where is my gun?"

Even under the blanket I could hear the flap of the bat's wings as it raced up and down the living room; I put my knees under my chin and my arms over my head and huddled under the blanket. Outside, they were stalking the bat; I could hear my husband tiptoeing warily down the room, with Ninki apparently right behind him, because he was saying, "Don't *hurry*, for heaven's sake, give me a chance to *aim*."

A hideous thought came to me. "Is it on me?" I said through my teeth, "just tell me once, is it on me, on the blanket? Ninki, *is* it? Is it?"

"Now you just stay perfectly still," my husband said reassuringly. "These things never stay in one place for very long. Why, only the other day I was reading in the paper about a woman who—"

"Is it on the *blanket?*" I insisted hysterically, "on *me?*"

"Listen," my husband said crossly, "if you keep on shaking like that, I'll *never* be able to hit it. Hold still, and I'm sure to miss you."

I do not know what the official world's record might be for getting out from under a blanket, flying across a room, opening a door and a screen door, and getting outside onto a porch with both doors closed behind you, but if it is more than about four seconds I broke it. I thought the bat was chasing me, for one thing. And I knew that, if the bat were chasing me, my husband was aiming that gun at it, wherever it was. Outside on the porch, I leaned my head against the middle pillar and breathed hard.

Inside, there was a series of crashes. I recognized the first as the report of the air gun. The second sounded irresistibly like a lamp going over, which is what it turned out to be. The third I could not identify from the porch, but my husband said later that it was Ninki trying to get out of the way of the air gun and knocking over the andirons. Then my husband spoke angrily to Ninki, and Ninki snarled. Each of them, it seemed, thought the other one had frightened the bat, which had left the blanket when I did, although not half so fast, and was now circling gaily around the chandelier.

"Come on in," my husband said through the door; he tried to open it but I was hanging on from the outside; "Come on in, it won't hurt you. I promise it won't."

"I'll stay out here," I said.

"It's just as frightened as you are," he said.

"It is *not*," I said.

Then he apparently spoke to Ninki again, because he said excitedly, "It's landing; keep away now, you'll be hurt."

There was a great noise of rushing and snarling and shooting, then a long silence. Finally I asked softly, "Are you all right?"

Another silence. "Are you all *right?*" I said.

Another silence. I opened the door a crack and peered in cautiously. My husband was sitting on the couch, beating his hands on his knees. The air gun was on the floor. Ninki and the bat were gone.

"Is it all right to come in?" I asked.

"I don't know," my husband said, looking at me bitterly, "have you got a ticket?"

"I mean," I said, "where's the bat?"

"She's taken it into the dining room," my husband said.

There was a nick in the wallpaper over the couch. In the dining room Ninki was growling pleasurably, deep in her throat. "She went faster than the pellet, is all," my husband said reasonably. "I was just getting ready to aim and she passed me and passed the pellet and hit the bat just as the pellet hit the wall."

"Hadn't you better get it out of the dining room?" I asked.

He began to beat his knees again. I went back to the couch, shook the blanket thoroughly to make sure there had been only one bat on it and that one was gone, and settled down in my chair with my mystery story. After a while Ninki came out of the dining room, nodded contemptuously at my husband, glanced at me and, with a grin at the air gun, got onto my husband's chair and went to sleep on his paper.

I took the air gun and put it on the top shelf of the pantry, where I believe it still is. Now and then it occurs to me that in case of burglars I can take it down to protect the house, but I really think one of the kitchen knives would be safer, if Ninki is not around to take care of me.

It was only the next morning that the man came to fix the glass in the kitchen window, and when Laurie, who was on his reluctant way to school, told the man his father had shot it out with a gun, I laughed cheerily and remarked that boys always had such good stories to cover their own misdeeds. Laurie looked at me in honest indignation, and I told him that he could take a package of gum from the pantry. Although I do not believe in actually encouraging children to tell lies, and do not in any case suppose that one pack of gum can cover up a flagrance like that one, Laurie gave every impression of being satisfied to share a joke about his father. It never occurred to me that the foundations of our parental authority were being slowly shattered until he came home from school some three or four days later with his jacket torn and an air of great innocent suffering. He was half an hour late, and he was accompanied by two of his friends, both of unsavory character; they strode manfully into the house and on into the study where my husband was peacefully doing research for an article on extinct fishes. I heard part of the conversation from upstairs where I was trying to dress Jannie after her nap. With my mind almost unoccupied, I listened without any real attention. "And they threw stones," one of Laurie's friends said in a thin, excited voice; he is somewhat older than Laurie, and he usually tells Laurie's stories for him when Laurie is too modest to tell them for himself, "and they said *terrible* language, and they *hit* Laurie, and *everything*."

"Where were *you* all this time?" my husband asked. I could feel through the floor the righteous indignation mounting in the study. "Where were you two while these boys were hitting Laurie?"

There was a moment of quiet, and then Laurie's voice: "George was behind the tree, and William was running up here to tell you." Laurie apparently stopped to think for a minute. "I didn't run," he added finally, "because I *can't* very well, in these snow pants."

The enemy—I could see them from the upstairs front window—were still lingering outside, backing down the hill slowly, prepared to do further battle. Then I heard the front door slam. My husband issued forth, supported valiantly on either side by Laurie's two friends, while Laurie, with commendable discretion, stayed just inside the front door, yelling, "Here comes my *father!*"

Halfway up the hill, the enemy waited for my husband, and, although I could not hear, I could see them—my husband speaking fiercely and the enemy looking at him with wide, honest eyes. Presently the battle was resolved; my husband turned and stamped back to the house and the enemy went on down the hill, turning at a safe distance to call inaudible insults.

When my husband came inside, I went downstairs to meet him. "Well?" I said.

All of them began talking at once. "And they *hit* Laurie and *every*thing," his talkative friend said; "They even chased *me*," his other friend added.

"And these darn old snow pants," Laurie said at the same time, while over all of them rose the voice of my husband saying, "Ought to be taught better manners. Boy like that deserves a good whipping."

Jannie came down the stairs behind me, asking hopefully, "Was Laurie bad? I'm good, aren't I? Did Laurie do something *new* bad?"

When I had isolated the various political maneuvers into offense and defense, the story went something like this: Laurie and his two friends were walking home from school, entirely without malice, not hurting anybody and minding their own business. As a matter of fact, they stopped quite of their own accord to pick up the books of a little girl who had dropped them into a mud puddle. Furthermore, they were not even thinking any harm, because they were all three most unpleasantly surprised when the largest of the enemy, a boy named David Howell, came up behind them and pulled on the hood of Laurie's jacket. When Laurie said "Hey!"—and we all agreed he was perfectly justified—David spat at him, pronounced half a dozen forbidden epithets, and finally struck him. Laurie's two friends took no active part in the battle, partly because David was bigger than any of them and partly because, as they explained at great length, they felt strongly that it was Laurie's fight and interference would not be sporting. They had come home with Laurie, however, to be his witnesses and to see that justice was done.

"What did you do to David?" I asked my husband.

"I said you'd tell his mother," he said virtuously.

I have seen David's mother, have even spoken to her at P.-T.A. meetings. She is one of those impressive women who usually head committees on supervising movies, taking the entire sixth grade on a tour of one of our local factories, or outlawing slingshots, and I daresay she would be the first person everyone would think of if there should arise an occasion for the mothers to lift the school building and carry it bodily to another location. I felt very strongly, as a matter of fact, that bringing David's mother into this incident was a grave tactical error.

But there were the four of them looking at me trustingly—five, if you count Jannie, who was saying "Poor, poor Laurie," and rubbing his head violently.

"I'll phone her right away," I said, trying to make it sound resolute and threatening. After some unavoidable fumbling with the telephone book I found the Howells' number and finally, with everyone sitting around the phone expectantly, cleared my throat, straightened my shoulders, and briskly gave the number to the operator. After a minute, a strong, no-nonsense voice said "Hello?"

"Hello," I said faintly, "is this Mrs. Howell?"

"Yes," she said. She sounded quite civil, so I changed my mind and said as politely as I could, "Mrs. Howell, I don't know if your boy David has told you about attacking my son Laurie on his way home from school today, but I thought I'd better call you anyway and see if we can't do something about it." Realizing that I had ended a little weakly, I added, "Laurie is *quite* badly hurt."

Laurie looked up, gratified, and nodded. "Tell her I'm dead," he said.

"Mrs. Howell," I said into the phone, scowling at Laurie, "I *do* think that a boy so much bigger than Laurie —a boy so much bigger, as David is—I mean, David is so much bigger than Laurie that I *do* think—"

All this time Mrs. Howell had been silent. Now she said amiably, "I quite agree with you, of course. But I can't quite believe this of David; David is such a *quiet* boy. Is your little boy sure it wasn't David Williams or David Martin?"

"Are you sure it wasn't David Williams or David Martin?" I asked hopefully of the audience beyond the telephone. They all shook their heads violently, and one of Laurie's friends—the one who ran—said enthusiastically, "I know David Howell, and it was him all right. Anyway, he's always doing things like this. Two, three times now, he's hit Laurie. And me, too. He hits everybody."

"It was certainly your David," I said to Mrs. Howell. "They all agree on that. He picked a fight with Laurie on the way home from school and really hurt Laurie *quite* badly."

"Well," she said. "I'll certainly speak to David," she added after a minute.

"Thank you," I said, perfectly content to depart with this empty triumph, but my husband said, "Tell her he was fresh to me, too."

"He was fresh to my husband, too," I said obediently into the phone.

"Really?" Mrs. Howell said, as though David were fresh to her husband all the time and this was no surprise. "Well," she said again, "I'll certainly speak to him."

"Tell her he's hit me lots of times," Laurie said.

"Don't forget the bad words," one of Laurie's friends prompted.

"Make it really forceful," my husband said. "Why should he get away with a thing like this?"

"Will you see that this is stopped once and for all?" I demanded emphatically into the phone.

Her voice sharpened. "I *said* I'd speak to David," she repeated ominously.

"Thank you," I said hastily, and hung up.

We were congratulating one another on our victory when the phone rang. "This is Mrs. Howell," she said when I answered, and her voice had lost much of its civility. "I spoke to David," she went on. "I told you I would. And it seems that David was not entirely at fault." She dwelt on the last few words as though they gave her some fierce pleasure.

"I don't understand," I said. "Laurie was just walking along the—"

"I beg your pardon," she said, still with great relish. "What about the rock he threw at David?"

I looked at Laurie over the top of the phone, and he returned my glance with sober earnestness. "What rock?" I said, and Laurie's gaze did not waver, but an odd sort of reminiscent pleasure crept into his eye.

"Laurie," said Mrs. Howell plainly, "threw a rock and hit David in the head. There's a big big bump. David hadn't done *any*thing up to then. But if your little boy throws rocks, I can hardly blame—"

I retreated abruptly to safer ground. "Surely," I said, "you are not going to say that there is *any* excuse for a bigger boy hitting a smaller boy?"

"I shall certainly speak to David about that," she said stiffly. "But then, when Laurie's father called David a little sneak and said he ought to be horsewhipped—"

"What about what David called Laurie?" I countered tellingly. "It was so bad that Laurie wouldn't dream of repeating it."

Laurie and his two friends immediately said loudly what it was.

"Your husband said David ought to be horsewhipped," she said, not shaken, and almost, I thought, as though he were not actually the first person who had suggested major punishment for David, "and poor little David tried to tell him that Laurie had been throwing rocks. You really *ought* to do something about a child throwing rocks. None of *my* children throw rocks; it's something *I* can't stand. But poor little David—"

"David did so throw rocks," I said. "And if my husband said—"

"I did not say it," my husband said.

"Surely there is no excuse," she said, "for a grown man to pick on a poor little boy."

I backed up again. "What about poor little Laurie?" I asked. "He was *quite* badly hurt. Surely there is no excuse—"

"Poor little David—" she began.

"And my poor little—" I said, and then started again. "My husband, I mean. What about the names they yelled at *him?*"

I was suddenly reminded of the time Mrs. Howell had taken part in a local debate, holding and maintaining with absolute conviction the position that our state should secede from the United States to avoid having its natural resources completely depleted. "Furthermore—" she was saying.

"What a way to bring up a child," I said gently. "What kind of a mother are you?"

My audience, I perceived, was growing restless. Laurie's two friends were putting on their overshoes; Laurie himself had entered into an elaborately casual game with Jannie that had taken them almost to the kitchen doorway, and my husband was sauntering almost noiselessly back to the study.

"Now you listen to me," Mrs. Howell began, her voice rising, "now you listen to me—"

I hung up gracefully and followed Laurie into the kitchen.

"Laurie," I said sternly, "did you throw a rock at David?"

Laurie pondered, frowning, his head on one side and one finger thoughtfully tapping his cheek. "I forget," he said at last.

"Try to remember," I said threateningly. Laurie shook his head in despair. "I just forget," he said.

I went to the study door. "Did you call David a little sneak?" I demanded.

My husband looked up from his article on extinct fishes. "A little what?" he said.

"A little sneak."

"Don't be ridiculous," my husband said. "Why would I

call what's-his-name a little sneak?" He turned back to his article. "Are you still worrying about *that?*" he asked.

The phone rang. I strode over and slammed it out of the receiver. "Well?" I said.

"If you think you can just hang up on people just because your son is a little bully and goes around throwing rocks and—"

"If you think you and your half-witted David can get away with picking on every child in the neighborhood just because he's overgrown and stupid—"

"If you would care to—"

"Perhaps *you* would like to—"

We hung up simultaneously. My husband opened the study door and looked out. "Who were you talking to?" he asked.

"Look," I said, "if you'd just take care of your own affairs and let Laurie fight his own battles and not come to me to—"

"I'm good, aren't I?" Jannie said. She came over and pulled at my hand. "I'm *good*, aren't I?"

My husband said loudly, "Let's box for a while, son. Get the gloves." Without looking at me he added, "We'll box out in the woodshed. Then," he said thoughtfully, "the noise won't bother Mother when she's on the phone."

"Aren't I?" said Jannie urgently. "*Aren't* I?"

I reached for the phone, and then hesitated. It was time to start the potatoes for dinner; I had a quick picture of Mrs. Howell peeling potatoes with one hand while she held a phone with the other, and I heard Laurie yelp as he walked into what was almost certainly a right cross.

"Want to help Mommy make dinner?" I asked Jannie.

Mrs. Howell and I met at the meat counter in the grocery the next morning; she smiled and I smiled and then she said, "How is Laurie today?"

"He seems much better, thanks," I said solemnly. "And David?"

"Fairly well," she said without turning a hair.

"Horrible little beasts," I said.

"Liars, all of them," she said. "*I* never believe a word they say."

We both laughed and turned to regard the meat. "They certainly do eat, though," she said mournfully. "I suppose it's hamburger again today."

"I was thinking about liver," I said.

"Will Laurie eat liver?" she asked with interest. "David won't touch it; do you cook it any special way?"

I REMEMBER THAT during that fall and winter Laurie was still wearing, when I forced him, a pair of red overalls onto which I had embroidered—during a time when I was somewhat more free and had a good deal more time to spend on the pretty little delicacies of life—a "Laurie" in green silk. He wore it to school only once, as I remember, and after that we made a bargain about how if I didn't make him wear it in public he would try to bring himself to it on strictly private occasions. When it began to grow noticeably short on him, without being noticeably worn, I whimsically crossed out the "Laurie" with a green embroidered line, and embroidered "Joanne" underneath, and shortened it along with half a dozen other pair of overalls for Jannie. She wore it during the late spring and early summer, when Laurie first started going to the barber to get his hair cut; she was now wearing the green corduroy jacket Laurie had worn the day we moved. This was when my personal schedule resolved itself into a round of hemlines and chocolate pudding. When I was not shortening or lengthening the one I was stirring the other. The summer saw Jannie inherit a number of pullover shirts, which are fortunately without gender, and thousands of bachelor socks, in preparation for nursery school in the fall. Laurie had a new jacket for school, which we were taught to call a windbreaker rather than a jacket, and his shoes were so huge that I was uncomfortably made aware that he had passed from the lower-priced size into the higher-priced size.

Summers go by so quickly, with a minimum of washing and a maximum of daylight, that we none of us have ever been able to perceive that infinitely cruel moment when the year turns and the days draw in; one morning the children were drinking lemonade in the back yard and talking largely of what they planned to build during the summer, and the next afternoon they were raking leaves and Jannie had lost a sandal in the leaf pile, to be hidden until perhaps next spring. Mothers have their own seasonal occupations; one afternoon I was sitting quietly in the living room, lengthening and shortening overalls in a sort of unworldly account; I had done three pair—one short and two long—when Laurie wandered in and stood in the center of the room, regarding me bleakly. Behind him trailed his dear friends Stuart and Robert, and after a few minutes, about as long as it takes short fat legs to catch up, Jannie plodded in. Our big dog Toby followed *her*. They lined themselves up in the center of the carpet and stood looking at me silently.

I looked up, forcing an expression of bright cheer onto my face. Unasked I said, "You may each have a piece of candy from the dish on the table."

"No, thank you," said Laurie gloomily.

"No, thank you," said Robert.

"No, thank you," said Stuart.

They stood sadly, watching me as I pushed the needle in and out of the cloth.

"No, thanks," said Jannie.

Laurie sighed deeply; so did Stuart and then Robert. I smiled falsely and said, "Would you each like an apple then?"

Laurie shook his head, so did Stuart and Robert and then, finally, Jannie.

"Nothing at all," said Laurie tragically. He paced over and sat down on the couch, and Robert and Stuart followed him. The three of them watched me sewing, and I tried with some embarrassment to hide what I was doing.

Toby still sat in the middle of the floor, looking with perplexed eyes first at me and then at the boys.

"Would you like to run down to the store and get some ice cream for all of us?" The boys shook their heads, as one man.

Jannie sat down solidly on the floor next to Toby and asked me, "Are you fixing Laurie's overalls?"

"Why, I certainly am," I said gaily.

"For school tomorrow?" Jannie asked.

There was a long silence. Then Laurie said, "Aaaaaah, *keep* quiet," to Jannie.

"What you talking about it for?" Stuart demanded.

"Old big-mouth Jannie," Robert said.

"Never mind, boys," I said. "You've had a fine summer."

"But *school*," Laurie said, as one to whom a vast injustice has been done.

"I know," I said. "Would you each like a cookie?"

"Naw," Laurie said.

"Why'n earth they want us to go to school *any*way?" Stuart demanded.

"Old first grade," Robert said.

"Why," I said treacherously, "first thing you know you'll be having a wonderful time in school. You've just forgotten what school is *like*."

"*No*, we haven't," Robert said.

"*I* used to *love* school," I said.

This was a falsehood so patent that none of them felt it necessary to answer me, even in courtesy. They sat and stared at me instead.

"Why don't you do something—play, or something?" I asked. "Then you'd forget all about it."

"We could play school," Jannie suggested. "Why don't we play school?"

She was silent as the three faces turned evilly towards her.

"We could ride our bikes," Robert said unenthusiastically.

"*Why* don't you?" I said, with great animation. "That would be *fun*."

"We could have a war," Stuart said.

"We could play store," Laurie said.

"We could play school," Jannie said.

"Listen," Stuart said, "we could be Indians and Jannie could be our prisoner . . ."

"We could tie her up," Laurie said, looking at his sister speculatively.

"I will be your prisoner," Jannie said cheerfull, "and you must all tie me up and be Indians."

"No, *listen*," Robert said. Activity came to all three of them at once. Robert rolled off the couch and ran into the hall, and the other two followed. After a minute Jannie hoisted herself off the floor and went along too. Toby, opening one eye, sighed deeply and got up; he had just started across the floor when the three boys and Jannie came hurrying back.

"Listen," Laurie said to me excitedly, "we're going to make a show. You're going to be the audience, and you got to go out in the kitchen while we get ready."

It was the last day of vacation; I put my needle carefully through the hem I was sewing and folded all the overalls and set them aside. Laurie and Robert pushed me out into the kitchen, where I took a handful of cookies and sat down, munching, to wait.

After about five minutes and much loud consultation they called me back and sat me down on the couch. Then Stuart sat in the chair I had vacated and took up the newspaper.

"I'm supposed to be reading the paper," he told me condescendingly.

Laurie and Robert and Jannie and Toby were in the dining room; I could hear them arguing. Finally there was a knock on the dining room door and Stuart put down his paper and said, "Come in." Laurie entered, wearing his cowboy hat, his spurs, his gun, his cowboy vest, his neckerchief, his lasso, and his boots. "Hi, pardner," he said.

"Hi, pardner," Stuart said.

Laurie sat down in the chair across from Stuart, and he and Stuart regarded one another intently.

"How are you, pardner?" Laurie enquired at last.

"Oh, I'm fine, pardner," Stuart said. They giggled

slightly and then Stuart, with a large expansive gesture, said, "Have some candy, pardner."

"Thanks, pardner, don't mind if I do," Laurie said. He swaggered over to the table, helped himself to a piece of candy, and went back to his chair. He finished the candy, licked his fingers and then, with a loud and dramatic groan, grasped his stomach and rolled off the chair onto the floor, where he lay still groaning. "See," he said, raising his head to look at me, "the candy was poisoned."

"I see," I said. "Very effective."

Laurie subsided, and there was a long pause, during which Stuart began to fidget, looking at the candy dish. Then finally he said, "Robert, come *on,*" and Robert said from the dining room, "Okay, I'm *coming.* I got to get my *gun* on, don't I?"

Then there was another knock on the dining room door, and Stuart said "Come in."

Robert came in, said "Hi, pardner," and sat down.

"Hi, pardner," Stuart said. "Have a piece of candy."

"Don't care if I do," said Robert. He took his candy, swallowed it whole, and then fell groaning on top of Laurie.

"Now me," Jannie howled from the dining room, and she hurried in, said "Hi, pardner," over her shoulder to Stuart, and took a piece of candy. "Can I have two?" she asked me, and I shook my head no. She ate her candy, groaned shrilly, and sat on Robert.

"Guess I'll have a piece of candy too," Stuart said. He fell groaning onto the heap on the floor.

I began to applaud, and Laurie put his head up and said, "*That's* not the end."

"Sorry," I said. I started to take a piece of candy, remembered in time that it was poisoned, and drew back my hand.

Laurie disengaged himself from the pile on the floor. "Now the stagecoach," he said.

The others got up and dusted themselves off. Everybody retired to the dining room, and I waited.

Finally Laurie reappeared, leading Toby by the collar. "I'm the good cowboy," he explained to me. "I'm Hopalong Cassidy and I—"

"*I'm* Hopalong Cassidy," Robert's voice rose protestingly from the other room.

"I'm Roy Rogers," Laurie continued smoothly, "and this is the stagecoach and I'm riding along with it."

"What's the stagecoach?" I asked, confused.

"Toby is," Laurie said. Toby glanced at me in mild apology. "See," Laurie said, "the gold is in the stagecoach and the bad guys are going to try and get it, but me and my gang, we're riding close along . . ." He began to hurry Toby across the room, making galloping cowboy noises, while Toby stumbled reluctantly along behind him.

"Good dog," I said reassuringly, and Toby put his head down and galloped resolutely. "Good dog," I said.

As they passed the dining room door for the second

time the horde of bandits fell upon them. Stuart and Robert brandished their guns, shouting fearfully and making simultaneous sounds of horse hooves and gunfire. Jannie, a small stout cowboy in a flapping hat, carrying a water pistol, followed fiercely, saying "Bang," with outlaw abandon.

"We got ya covered," Hopalong Cassidy remarked. Roy Rogers, undaunted, took cover behind a chair, while the stagecoach trotted hastily over to the couch and tried to get into my lap.

Stuart and Robert had now taken cover also, one in the dining room doorway, the other in the angle of the fireplace. They were shooting across the room, taking careful aim and exposing themselves rashly before leaping back into hiding.

Jannie sat down in the middle of the floor and began to take off her sandals. "Something in my shoe," she told me. "Wait a minute, boys, till I get my shoe fixed."

"Get into a safe place," Laurie shouted at her, "you want to get killed, woman?"

"Bang," Jannie said, aiming her water pistol at him. "Bang," she said, at Stuart, and "Bang" at Robert. "I killed you all three," she said. "Now I can fix my shoe."

Laurie began to inch out from behind the chair until he was standing free of it. "Reach," he said suddenly. "Drop them guns."

Obediently, Stuart and Robert dropped their guns and raised their hands. Laurie walked over, gun ready, and frisked them both. Then he shot them. They both fell, dying fearfully. Robert raised himself on one elbow and said, "Joe, Joe."

"What, Joe?" Laurie said, turning.

"Get the guys that did this, Joe," Robert said.

"I shore will, Joe," Laurie said. He turned thoughtfully and shot Jannie, who looked up, surprised. "I said I was fixing my *shoe*," she said irritably.

"Y'got it anyway," Laurie said.

"Okay," said Jannie. She fell obligingly over onto her side and went on putting on her shoe that way.

"Well," I said, applauding again, "this has certainly been an exciting—"

"Listen," Laurie said earnestly, "this is only our *practice*. You're only seeing the *practice*, so far."

"We're going to do a real play when we finish our *practice*," Stuart confirmed.

"Reach," Laurie said to him.

"I won't," Stuart said pettishly. "Why do *I* always have to be the guy that reaches?"

"Keep them hands up," Laurie ordered. Robert stole up behind him and put a gun into his back. "*You* reach," Robert said.

Laurie dropped his gun and Stuart picked it up. Robert shot Stuart and Laurie and they both fell groaning.

"Who's the good guy," Stuart asked suddenly. "I forget."

"I'm Gene Autry," Laurie said.

"I'm Roy Rogers," Robert said.

"*I'm* the good guy, then," Stuart said with satisfaction. "Reach."

Stuart shot Robert and Laurie

"Listen," Laurie said from the floor, "we don't *die* right. We ought to roll more."

"Sometimes we ought to get dragged by our horses," Robert added.

"Reach!" Jannie said suddenly. Stunned, Gene Autry, Roy Rogers, and Hopalong Cassidy turned; Jannie had them all covered with her water pistol.

"It's a *dame*," Stuart said.

"A cowgirl," Robert amplified.

"It's Jesse James," Laurie said. "Now you must shoot us all, Jan."

"Bang, bang, bang," Jannie said, and the heroes fell, rolled, goaned, and were even dragged a little by their horses.

While they were still groaning I stole away, back into the kitchen, where I poured four glasses full of fruit juice and put cookies on a plate. When I came back into the living room the actors were dusting themselves off.

"That was a great show," I said.

"We'll do a *real* one tomorrow," Laurie said. Then his face fell. "I forgot," he said.

I thought briefly and comfortably of the quiet mornings, the long lovely afternoons, the early bedtimes.

"Well," I said, with immense heartiness, "it will be summer again before we all know it."

"A WHAT?" said Jannie.
"What *for?*" said Laurie.

EVERYONE ALWAYS SAYS the third baby is the easiest one to have, and now I know why. It's the easiest because it's the funniest, because you've been there twice, and you know. You know, for instance, how you're going to look in a maternity dress about the seventh month, and you know how to release the footbrake on a baby carriage without fumbling amateurishly, and you know how to tie your shoes before and do knee-chests after, and while you're not exactly casual, you're a little bit off-hand about the whole thing. Sentimental people keep insisting that women go on to have a third baby because they love babies, and cynical people seem to maintain that a woman with two healthy, active children around the house will do *any*thing for ten quiet days in the hospital; my own position is somewhere between the two, but I acknowledge that it leans toward the latter.

Because it *was* my third I was spared a lot of unnecessary discomfort. No one sent us any dainty pink sweaters, for instance. We received only one pair of booties, and those were a pair of rosebud-covered white ones that some- one had sent Laurie when he was born and which I had given, still in their original pink tissue paper, to a friend when *her* first child was born; she had subsequently sent them to her cousin in Texas for a second baby and the cousin sent them back East on the occasion of a mutual friend's twins; the mutual friend gave them to me, with a card saying "Love to Baby" and the pink tissue paper hardly ruffled. I set them carefully aside, because I knew someone who was having a baby in June.

I borrowed back my baby carriage from my next-door neighbor, took the crib down out of the attic, washed my way through the chest of baby shirts and woolen shawls, briefed the incumbent children far enough ahead of time, and spent a loving and painstaking month packing my suitcase. This time I knew exactly what I was taking with me to the hospital, but assembling it took time and even- tually required an emergency trip to the nearest metropo- lis. I packed it, though, finally: a yellow nightgown trimmed with lace, a white nightgown that tied at the throat with a blue bow, two of the fanciest bed-jackets I could find—that was what I went to the city for— —and then, two pounds of homemade fudge, as many mystery stories as I could cram in, and a bag of apples. Almost at the last minute I added a box of pralines, a bot- tle of expensive cologne, and my toothbrush. I have heard of people who take their own satin sheets to the hospital, but that has always seemed to me a waste of good suit-case space.

My doctor was very pleasant and my friends were very thoughtful; for the last two weeks before I went to the hospital almost everyone I know called me almost once a day and said "Haven't you gone *yet*?" My mother- and father-in-law settled on a weekend to visit us when, according to the best astronomical figuring, I should have had a two-week-old baby ready to show them; they arrived, were entertained with some restraint on my part, and left, eyeing me with disfavor and some suspicion. My mother sent me a telegram from California saying "Is everything all right? Shall I come? Where is baby?" My children were sullen, my husband was embarrassed.

Everything was, as I say, perfectly normal, up to and including the frightful moment when I leaped out of bed at two in the morning as though there had been a pea under the mattress; when I turned on the light my husband said sleepily, "Having baby?"

"I really don't know," I said nervously. I was looking for the clock, which I hide at night so that in the morning when the alarm rings I will have to wake up looking for it. It was hard to find without the alarm ringing.

"Shall I wake up?" my husband asked without any sign of pleased anticipation.

"I can't find the *clock*," I said.

"Clock?" my husband said. "Clock. Wake me five minutes apart."

I unlocked the suitcase, took out a mystery story, and sat down in the armchair with a blanket over me. After a few minutes, Ninki, who usually sleeps on the foot of Laurie's bed, wandered in and settled down on a corner of the blanket by my feet. She slept as peacefully as my husband did most of the night, except that now and then she raised her head to regard me with a look of silent contempt.

Because the hospital is five miles from our house I had an uneasy feeling that I ought to allow plenty of time, particularly since neither of us had ever learned to drive and consequently I had to call our local taxi to take me to the hospital. At seven-thirty I called my doctor and we chatted agreeably for a few minutes, and I said I would just give the children their breakfast and wash up the dishes and then run over to the hospital, and he said that would be just fine and he'd plan to meet me later, then; the unspoken conviction between us was that I ought to be back in the fields before sundown.

I went into the kitchen and proceeded methodically to work, humming cheerfully and stopping occasionally to grab the back of a chair and hold my breath. My husband told me later that he found his cup and saucer (the one with "Father" written on it) in the oven, but I am inclined to believe that he was too upset to be a completely reliable informant. My own recollection is of doing everything the way I have a thousand times before—school-morning short cuts so familiar that I am hardly aware, usually, of doing them at all. The frying pan, for instance. My single immediate objective was a cup of coffee, and I decided to heat up the coffee left from the night before, rather than taking the time to make fresh; it seemed brilliantly logical to heat it in the frying pan because anyone knows that a broad shallow container will heat liquid faster than a tall narrow one like the coffeepot. I will not try to deny, however, that it *looked* funny.

By the time the children came down everything seemed to be moving along handsomely; Laurie grimly got two glasses and filled them with fruit juice for Jannie and himself. He offered me one, but I had no desire to eat, or in fact to do anything which might upset my precarious balance between two and three children, or to interrupt my morning's work for more than coffee, which I was still doggedly making in the frying pan. My husband came downstairs, sat in his usual place, said good-morning to the children, accepted the glass of fruit juice Laurie poured for him, and asked me brightly, "How do you feel?"

"Splendid," I said, making an enormous smile for all of them. "I'm doing wonderfully well."

"Good," he said. "How soon do you think we ought to leave?"

"Around noon, probably," I said. "Everything is fine, really."

My husband asked politely, "May I help you with breakfast?"

"No, indeed," I said. I stopped to catch my breath and smiled reassuringly. "I feel *so* well," I said.

"Would you be offended," he said, still very politely, "if I took this egg out of my glass?"

"Certainly not," I said. "I'm sorry; I can't think how it got there."

"It's nothing at all," my husband said. "I was just thirsty."

They were all staring at me oddly, and I kept giving them my reassuring smile; I *did* feel spendid; my months of waiting were nearly over, my careful preparations had finally been brought to a purpose, tomorrow I would be wearing my yellow nightgown. "I'm *so* pleased," I said.

I was slightly dizzy, perhaps. And there *were* pains, but they were authentic ones, not the feeble imitations I had been dreaming up the past few weeks. I patted Laurie on the head. "Well," I said, in the tone I had used perhaps five hundred times in the last months, "Well, do we want a little boy or a little boy?"

"Won't you sit down?" my husband said. He had the air of a man who expects that an explanation will somehow be given him for a series of extraordinary events in which he is unwillingly involved. "I think you ought to sit down," he added urgently.

It was about then that I realized that he was right. I ought to sit down. As a matter of fact, I ought to go to the hospital right now, immediately. I dropped my reassuring smile and the fork I had been carrying around with me.

"I'd better hurry," I said inadequately.

My husband called the taxi and brought down my suitcase. The children were going to stay with friends, and one of the things we had planned to do was drop them off on our way to the hospital; now, however, I felt vitally that I had not the time. I began to talk fast.

"You'll have to take care of the children," I told my husband. "See that . . ." I stopped. I remember thinking with incredible clarity and speed. "See that they finish their breakfast," I said. Pajamas on the line, I thought, school, cats, toothbrushes. Milkman. Overalls to be mended, laundry. "I ought to make a list," I said vaguely. "Leave a note for the milkman tomorrow night. Soap, too. We need soap."

"Yes, dear," my husband kept saying. "Yes dear yes dear."

The taxi arrived and suddenly I was saying goodbye to the children. "See you later," Laurie said casually. "Have a good time."

"Bring me a present," Jannie added.

"Don't worry about a thing," my husband said.

"Now, don't you worry," I told him. "There's nothing to worry about."

"Everything will be *fine*," he said. "Don't worry."

I waited for a good moment and then scrambled into

the taxi without grace; I did not dare risk my reassuring smile on the taxi driver but I nodded to him briskly.

"I'll be with you in an hour," my husband said nervously. "And don't worry."

"Everything will be *fine*," I said. "Don't worry."

"Nothing to worry about," the taxi driver said to my husband, and we started off, my husband standing on the lawn wringing his hands and the taxi tacking insanely from side to side of the road to avoid even the slightest bump.

I sat very still in the back seat, trying not to breathe. I had one arm lovingly around my suitcase, which held my yellow nightgown, and I tried to light a cigarette without using any muscles except those in my hands and my neck and still not let go of my suitcase.

"Going to be a beautiful day," I said to the taxi driver at last. We had a twenty-minute trip ahead of us, at least —much longer, if he continued his zig-zag path. "Pretty warm for this time of year."

"Pretty warm yesterday, too," the taxi driver said.

"It *was* warm yesterday," I conceded, and stopped to catch my breath. The driver, who was obviously avoiding looking at me in the mirror, said a little bit hysterically, "Probably be warm tomorrow, too."

I waited for a minute, and then I was able to say, dubiously, "I don't know as it will stay warm *that* long. Might cool off by tomorrow."

"Well," the taxi driver said, "it was sure warm *yesterday*."

"Yesterday?" I said. "Yes, that was a warm day."

"Going to be nice today, too," the driver said. I clutched my suitcase tighter and made some small sound—more like a yelp than anything else—and the taxi veered madly off to the left and then began to pick up speed with enthusiasm.

"Very warm indeed," the driver babbled, leaning forward against the wheel. "Warmest day I ever saw for the time of year. Usually this time of year it's colder. Yesterday it was *terribly—*"

"It was not," I said. "It was freezing. I can see the tower of the hospital."

"I remember thinking how warm it was," the driver said. He turned into the hospital drive. "It was so warm I noticed it right away. 'This is a warm day,' I thought; that's how warm it was."

We pulled up with a magnificent flourish at the hospital entrance, and the driver skittered out of the front seat and came around and opened the door and took my arm.

"My wife had five," he said. "I'll take the suitcase, Miss. Five and never a minute's trouble with any of them."

He rushed me in through the door and up to the desk. "Here," he said to the desk clerk. "Pay me later," he said to me, and fled.

"Name?" the desk clerk said to me politely, her pencil poised.

"Name," I said vaguely. I remembered, and told her.

"Age?" she asked. "Sex? Occupation?"

"Writer," I said.

"Housewife," she said.

"Writer," I said.

"I'll just put down housewife," she said. "Doctor? How many children?"

"Two," I said. "Up to now."

"Normal pregnancy?" she said. "Blood test? X-ray?"

"Look—" I said.

"Husband's name?" she said. "Address? Occupation?"

"Just put down housewife," I said. "I don't remember *his* name, really."

"Legitimate?"

"What?" I said.

"Is your husband the father of this child? Do you *have* a husband?"

"Please," I said plaintively, "can I go on upstairs?"

"Well, *really*," she said, and sniffed. "You're *only* having a baby."

She waved delicately to a nurse, who took me by the same arm everybody else had been using that morning, and in the elevator this nurse was very nice. She asked me twice how I was feeling and said "maternity?" to me inquiringly as we left the elevator; I was carrying my own suitcase by then.

Two more nurses joined us upstairs; we made light conversation while I got into the hospital nightgown. The nurses had all been to some occupational party the night before and one of them had been simply a riot; she was still being a riot while I undressed, because every now and then one of the other two nurses would turn around to me and say, "Isn't she a riot, honestly?"

I made a few remarks, just to show that I too was light-hearted and not at all nervous; I commented laughingly on the hospital nightgown, and asked with amusement tinged with foreboding what the apparatus was that they were wheeling in on the tray.

My doctor arrived about half an hour later; he had obviously had three cups of coffee and a good cigar; he patted me on the shoulder and said, "How do we feel?"

"Pretty well," I said, with an uneasy giggle that ended in a squawk. "How long do you suppose it will be before—"

"We don't need to worry about *that* for a while yet," the doctor said. He laughed pleasantly, and nodded to the nurses. They all bore down on me at once. One of them smoothed my pillow, one of them held my hand, and the third one stroked my forehead and said, "After all, you're *only* having a baby."

"Call me if you want me," the doctor said to the nurses as he left, "I'll be downstairs in the coffee shop."

"*I'll* call you you if I need you," I told him ominously, and one of the nurses said in a honeyed voice, "Now, look, we don't want our husband to get all worried."

I opened one eye; my husband was sitting, suddenly, beside the bed. He looked as though he were trying not to scream. "They *told* me to come in here," he said. "I was trying to find the waiting room."

"Other end of the hall," I told him grimly. I pounded on the bell and the nurse came running. "Get him out of here," I said, waving my head at my husband.

"They *told* me—" my husband began, looking miserably at the nurse.

"It's alll111 right," the nurse said. She began to stroke my forehead again. "Hubby belongs right here."

"Either he goes or I go," I said.

The door slammed open and the doctor came in. "Heard you were here," he said jovially, shaking my husband's hand. "Look a little pale."

My husband smiled weakly.

"Never lost a father yet," the doctor said, and slapped him on the back. He turned to me. "How do we feel?" he said.

"Terrible," I said, and the doctor laughed again. "Just on my way downstairs," he said to my husband. "Come along?"

No one seemed actually to go or come that morning; I would open my eyes and they were there, open my eyes again and they were gone. This time, when I opened my eyes, a pleasant-faced nurse was standing beside me; she was swabbing my arm with a piece of cotton. Although I am ordinarily timid about hypodermics I welcomed this one with what was almost a genuine echo of my old reassuring smile. "Well, well," I said to the nurse. "Sure glad to see *you*."

"Sissy," she said distinctly, and jabbed me in the arm.

"How soon will this wear off?" I asked her with deep suspicion; I am always afraid with nurses that they feel that the psychological effect of a hypodermic is enough, and that I am actually being innoculated with some useless, although probably harmless, concoction.

"You won't even notice," she said enigmatically, and left.

The hypodermic hit me suddenly, and I began to giggle about five minutes after she left. I was alone in the room, lying there giggling to myself, when I opened my eyes and there was a woman standing beside the bed. She was human, not a nurse; she was wearing a baggy blue bathrobe. "I'm across the hall," she said. "I been hearing you."

"I was laughing," I said, with vast dignity.

"I heard you," she said. "Tomorrow it might be me, maybe."

"You here for a baby?"

"Someday," she said gloomily. "I was here two weeks ago, I was having pains. I come in the morning and that night they said to me, 'Go home, wait a while longer.' So I went home, and I come again three days later, I was having pains. And they said to me, 'Go home, wait a while longer.' And so yesterday I come again, I was having pains. So far they let me stay."

"That's too bad," I said.

"I got my mother there," she said. "She takes care of everything and sees the meals made, but she's beginning to think I got her there with false pretenses."

"That's too bad," I said. I began to pound the wall with my fists.

"Stop that," she said. "Somebody'll hear you. This is my third. The first two—nothing."

"This is *my* third," I said. "I don't care who hears me."

"My kids," she said. "Every time I come home they say to me, 'Where's the baby?' My mother, too. My husband, he keeps driving me over and driving me back."

"They kept telling me the third was the easiest," I said. I began to giggle again.

"There you go," she said. "Laughing your head off. I wish *I* had something to laugh at."

She waved her hand at me and turned and went mournfully through the door. I opened my same weary eye and my husband was sitting comfortably in his chair. "I said," he said saying loudly, "I said, 'Do you mind if I read?'" He had the New York Times on his knee.

"Look," I said, "do I have anything to read? Here I am, with nothing to do and no one to talk to and you sit there and read the New York Times right in front of me and here I am, with nothing—"

"How do we feel?" the doctor asked. He was suddenly much taller than before, and the walls of the room were rocking distinctly.

"Doctor," I said, and I believe that my voice was a little louder than I intended it should be, "you better give me—"

He patted me on the hand and it was my husband instead of the doctor. "Stop yelling," he said.

"I'm *not* yelling," I said. "I don't like this any more. I've changed my mind, I don't want any baby, I want to go home and forget the whole thing."

"I know *just* how you feel," he said.

My only answer was a word which certainly I knew that I *knew*, although I had never honestly expected to hear it spoken in my own ladylike voice.

"Stop yelling," my husband said urgently. "*Please* stop saying that."

I had the idea that I was perfectly conscious, and I looked at him with dignity. "Who is doing this?" I asked. "You or me?"

"It's all right," the doctor said. "We're on our way." The walls were moving along on either side of me and the woman in the blue bathrobe was waving from a doorway.

"She loved me for the dangers I had passed," I said to the doctor, "and I loved her that she did pity them."

"It's all right, I tell you," the doctor said. "Hold your breath."

"Did he finish his New York Times?"

"Hours ago," the doctor said.

"What's he reading now?" I asked.

"The Tribune," the doctor said. "Hold your breath."

It was so unbelievably bright that I closed my eyes. "Such a lovely time," I said to the doctor. "Thank you so much for asking me, I can't tell you how I've enjoyed it. Next time you must come to our—"

"It's a girl," the doctor said.

"Sarah," I said politely, as though I were introducing them. I still thought I was perfectly conscious, and then I was. My husband was sitting beside the bed, smiling cheerfully.

"What happened to *you?*" I asked him. "No Wall Street Journal?"

"It's a girl," he said.

"I know," I said. "I was there."

I was in a pleasant, clean room. There was no doubt that it was all over; I could see my feet under the bedspread.

"It's a girl," I said to my husband.

The door opened and the doctor came in. "Well," he said. "How do we feel?"

"Fine," I said. "It's a girl."

"I know," he said.

The door was still open and a face peered around it. My husband, the doctor, and I, all turned happily to look. It was the woman in the blue bathrobe.

"Had it yet?" I asked her.

"No," she said. "You?"

"Yep," I said. "You going home again?"

"Listen," she said. "I been thinking. Home, the kids all yelling and my mother looking sad like she's disappointed in me. Like I did something. My husband, every time he sees me jump he reaches for the car keys. My sister, she calls me every day and if I answer the phone she hangs up. Here, I get three meals a day I don't cook, I know all the nurses, and I meet a lot of people going in and out. I figure I'd be a *fool* to go home. What was it, girl or boy?"

"Girl," I said.

"Girl," she said. "They say the third's the easiest."

TWO

I BELIEVE THAT all women, but especially housewives, tend to think in lists; I have always believed, against all opposition, that women think in logical sequence, but it was not until I came to empty the pockets of my light summer coat that year that I realized how thoroughly the housekeeping mind falls into the list pattern, how basically the idea of a series of items, following one another docilely, forms the only possible reasonable approach to life if you have to live it with a home and a husband and children, none of whom would dream of following one another docilely. What started me thinking about it was the little slips of paper I found in the pockets of my light summer coat, one beginning "cereal, shoes to shop, bread, cheese, peanut butter, evening paper, doz doughnuts, CALL PICTURE." I showed this list to my husband, and he read it twice and said it didn't make any sense. When I told him that it made perfect sense because it followed my route up one side of the main street of our town and down the other side—I have to buy the cereal at a special store, because that's the only one which carries the kind the children like—he said then what did CALL PICTURE mean? and when I explained that it meant I must call the picture-framer before I started out and was in big letters because if I took the list out in the store and found I had forgotten to call the picture-framer I would then have to stop in and see him, he sniffed and said if he managed his filing cabinet the way I managed my shopping. . . . The other list I found in my summer coat pocket started out "summer coat to clnrs."

The fact that I hadn't *taken* my summer coat to the cleaners (oh, those first fall days, with the sad sharpness in the air and the leaves bright so that our road is a line of color, and the feeling of storing-in against the winter, and the pumpkins) does not materially affect my conviction that the kind of progress from one thing to another which makes up a list is deeply logical, if ineffectual. Say to my next-door neighbor that you admire her new kitchen linoleum, and she will tell you, "Do you like it, really? I wanted to get white instead of blue, but it gets dirty so quickly, and then of course John always did like blue best, but of course the cannister set and the kitchen table are lighter blue, and it would have meant replacing *them*, but then the curtains . . ." From here she may go off onto any of several tangents (I am assuming, of course, that she is not interrupted by my telling of my own experiences, or

John's saying how about bringing out some crackers and cheese for everybody, or a child crying somewhere up-stairs), such as the dirt detour; she may give you a list of things which *do* get dirty (" . . . a black linoleum, and do you know it showed every single track . . .") or things which do *not* get dirty (". . . and even though it was really a pale yellow it just wiped off . . ."), or she may become interested in kitchen fixtures (". . . and she had the *prettiest* curtains, but they were sort of odd, I thought, in a *kitchen;* they were . . .") or bathroom fixtures (". . . and they had the same tiles in the bathroom, only these were pink, and the curtains *there* . . .") or even John's likes and dislikes (". . . but of course he won't eat anything with garlic in it, so I have to take all the recipes I get and put in . . .").

I think that may be why my summer coat never got to the cleaners. You can start from any given point on a list and go off in all directions at once, the world being as full as it is, and even though a list is a greatly satisfying thing to have, it is extraordinarily difficult to keep it focussed on the subject at hand. Right at this point, for instance, I was thinking about demitasse cups. I personally prefer a double-sized coffee cup, but with those tiny cups coffee is served so graciously (I see a list here, going on off into tiny spoons, and after-dinner liqueurs, and me in a long gown at the table, and everyone speaking wittily, and the children sweetly asleep in the nursery with an effi-cient Nanny on guard)—so easily (this list includes a maid and a butler to wash the cups and polish the tiny spoons) and so elegantly (years ago my mother promised me a silver coffee service, and then there's always the coffee table we inherited from Great-Aunt Martha, and if my husband would just get to work and sand it down and varnish it . . .) that, infected as I am by the constant desire to change everything, I may give in to the demitasse, after all. What persuaded me to think about demitasse cups at all was a statement made recently by one of my close friends, who said that she personally did not like our big cups for dinner coffee, but preferred a demitasse because she liked her coffee scalding hot. That, of course, sent me off onto several tangents on *her* housekeeping; she is a *very* good friend, and I would not for the world mention to her that the last time we visited there, there was no soap in the bathroom. I am terribly fond of her, but it *is* true that her guest room windows do not open. She is a grand girl, and if she likes her coffee in small cups at my house, she shall have it that way, in spite of the fact that the last time we dined there I found a spider in the salad.

Perhaps—following still another list—if we did have demitasse cups, our after-dinner hour, which is complicated by the presence of children coming out of bathtubs, and children with pressing problems in elementary reading, and dishes on the table waiting to be washed, and dogs and cats clamoring for their supper—perhaps our after-dinner hour would somehow become imperceptibly more gracious; perhaps the children, seeing us endlessly refilling our demitasse cups, would tiptoe thoughtfully away from the dining room door. Perhaps if we had demitasse cups a local couple, who have no children and have exhibited a vast distaste for our hospitality, would come to call. Perhaps, as a matter of fact, if we had demitasse cups, we could overlook the fact that the vast distaste of the local couple was provoked by our short-tempered reception of their resentment of our children. We *should* live more graciously, after all.

Then, naturally, there is the question of the cups themselves. I am immediately tempted to buy them just as cheaply as possible (*there's* a list for you, the prices of things) and have thought of the five and ten (". . . and I got the *sweetest* little cups right there, can you imagine, and even though the cups and saucers came separately I didn't really pay much *more* . . .") but dismissed the idea through pride (". . . and everyone could *tell* because of course those *same* patterns . . ."). I shall have to go off and purchase them in some big store where I have a charge account (". . . a charge account? Let me just tell you what happened to *me* when . . .") and I suspect that I will end up after a day of shopping with four cheap flowered demitasse cups and a set of dishes (I have *so* been needing dishes) and a set of glassware which will be wonderful for the children to use when they have company for breakfast, and while I am in that department I think I ought to look at electric mixers because it is only four months to my birthday.

I tabulated recently a conversation, or double-listing, between two women, one of them me. The conversation began, civilly enough, with a compliment from me about my friend's new slipcover, which she had made herself. We then went rapidly through slipcovers (custom-made, prices of) the value of a sewing machine, the clothes children wore to school, and children's shoes (prices of). She then remarked that she hated to repeat cute things her children had said, but she just *had* to tell me what her daughter said the other day. I retaliated with a really clever story about Jannie. She said that prices were awful, weren't they; the conversation could have ended right there, with both of us crying, but fortunately one of our husbands stepped in with a remark about how we *had* really planned to play bridge, hadn't we? because if we *had*, here were the cards dealt and the chairs ready. We sat down, and she told me about how angry her husband had been the last time we played bridge, because she had reneged twice, and I told her a little sad story about how my husband had opened once with two hearts and I had said two spades and he said three diamonds and there I sat with the king, jack, seven of diamonds and . . . well, *she* told *me* about these people they used to know, and *I* told *her* about these people *we* used to know, and then she said, well, the way some people bring up their children, and I told her about the bad manners of the children of these friends of ours, and she said well, of course, progressive education, and my husband said were we going to play bridge or weren't we?

So then she said that she loved my new blouse and I said I wished I could make things for myself, and she said the stores were awful, weren't they. I told her about how a salesclerk was so rude I walked out without buying anything, and she said that the butcher in our mutual grocery was really terribly mean today about the hamburger. I said that even hamburger was almost out of our range these days and she told me about how prices are up at least two cents a pound since practically yesterday. I told her that I understood that the main reason they had given up school lunches was the cost, and she said that it really cost less to make lunch at home and send it, the way things were these days. I said the only trouble was, Laurie preferred sandwiches made with cold meat, and she said had I tried this new spread made with olives. When I said no, she said that she had also tried a new cake mix and it was marvelous, but of course you really *needed* an electric mixer, and I said my birthday was only four months off. My husband bid three hearts in a loud voice. I bid three spades, and said that I envied her the cookies she made, that my children preferred to stop off for cookies at her house because our cookies were all store-bought. She said shyly that she had made a new kind of lemon meringue tart to serve after our bridge game and my husband said oh, were we playing bridge? Her husband then bid four hearts, she bid four no trump, and I said that I was planning to get a set of demitasse cups.

We played the hand in six spades, and made it easily, but

it turns out that if I *am* going to get an electric mixer I shall have to shop around and get a really good one; she has a friend who used hers once and it fell apart. Of course she got a new one right away from the manufacturers, but my husband believed that if his partner had led anything except the ace of hearts . . . I took the recipe for the lemon meringue tarts, and when I got home I made a new list, which began "lemons, demitasse cups, summer coat to cleaners . . ."

That summer coat was a good one; I had worn it my last two years in college and every summer since. With three small children I perceived clearly what I had suspected when I had only one child, and half-believed when I had only two children—that parents must automatically resign themselves to wearing every article of their own clothing at least two years beyond its normal life expectancy. During the long summers—which are hotter, by the way, than they used to be when I was a child, just as the winters are colder—I can get along nicely on my summer coat and my few surviving cotton dresses, but the winter is another thing; unless I find someone who can fix the pockets of my old fur coat I shall not even be able to carry a handkerchief any more, unless I pin it to the front of me the way I do with Jannie. However, mending a fur coat is so ridiculous in the middle of summer that I have a little list, in my top dresser drawer, which has been there for— I think—two years. "Mend fr coat," it says.

By the time I woke up on a summer morning—the alarm having missed fire again, for the third time in a week—it was already too hot to move. I lay in bed for a few minutes, wanting to get up but unable to exert the necessary energy. From the girls' room, small voices rose in song, and I listened happily, thinking how pleasant it was to hear a brother and two sisters playing affectionately together; then, suddenly, the words of the song penetrated into my hot mind, and I was out of bed in one leap and racing down the hall. "Baby ate a spider, Baby ate a spider," was what they were singing.

Three innocent little faces were turned to me as I opened the door. Laurie, in his cowboy-print pajamas, was sitting on top of the dresser beating time with a coat hanger. Jannie, in pink pajama pants and her best organdy party dress, was sitting on her bed. Sally peered at me curiously through the bars of her crib and grinned, showing her four teeth.

"What did you eat?" I demanded. "What do you have in your mouth?"

Laurie shouted triumphantly. "A spider," he said. "She ate a spider."

I forced the baby's mouth open; it was empty. "Did she *swallow* it?"

"Why?" Jannie asked, wide-eyed. "Will it make her sick?"

"*Jannie* gave it to her," Laurie said.

"*Laurie* found it," Jannie said.

[85]

"But she ate it herself," Laurie said hastily.

I went wearily back into my own room, resisted the strong temptation to get back into bed, and began to dress. The conversation from the children indicated that they, too, were what might be called dressing.

"Put it on Baby," Laurie remarked.

"It's too little," Jannie objected.

"That's all right," Laurie said. "Put it on her anyway."

"She can wear my bluuuuuuuue shirt," Jannie said.

"*That* shirt's no good," Laurie said.

"It is so," Jannie said.

"It is not," Laurie said.

"It is so," Jannie said.

"It is not," Laurie said.

"Children," I called, my voice a little louder than it usually is at only nine in the morning. "Please stop squabbling and get dressed."

"*Laurie* started it," Jannie called back.

"*Jannie* started it," Laurie called.

Hastily I pushed the comb through my hair and hurried down the hall; hurrying made me hotter. I lifted Sally out of her crib and set her on Jannie's bed to dress her, and Laurie and Jannie immediately abandoned their dressing and came to sit on the bed and watch. I changed Sally with the casual speed that comes to mothers of three, decided against putting anything more than a diaper on her, and started downstairs with her under my arm. Behind me Jannie lifted her voice tearfully.

"I can't find my shoooooooes," she howled.

Laurie began to chuckle maliciously. I saw that he was putting Jannie's red sandals on his own feet, reflected briefly and bitterly on the theory that seven-year-olds have good days and bad days, and said briskly, "Just for that, you can put Jannie's shoes on *her* feet, and buckle them for her, too."

I knew immediately what he was going to do, and, with speed, I made a strong tactical retreat downstairs before I could see him do it. In the kitchen it was hotter than ever, and I set Sally in her high chair and began opening windows and doors to get some air. The bright sunlight reassured me; by ten o'clock breakfast would be done with, I would have had my coffee; I might even feel like taking the children swimming, or on a picnic. Acting with all the alertness and vivid grace which I usually bring to the breakfast hour, I filled the coffee pot and set it on the stove, filled Sally's bottle and put it on to heat, and then looked around for Phoebe. Phoebe was our household help, and, being a local girl, she possessed all the native Vermonter's independence of thought and action; she was supposed by me to arrive every morning by eight o'clock and frequently arrived, having clearly established her emancipated state, by nine. This morning there was no sign of her, not even in her favorite spot for mornings when I get up late, which is out on the side porch playing solitaire. I began to set the table irritably.

Laurie came bounding heavily down the stairs, with Jannie's infuriated wail following him.

"Where's Phoebe?" he demanded.

"Not here yet," I said briefly, because I could not trust myself to speak fully. "Dime if you set the table."

Laurie began to sing loudly, and rattled the silverware vigorously. As his singing grew louder, a suspicion grew in me. "Did you brush your teeth?" I asked him.

He sang more sweetly still. "Did you brush your *teeth?*" I said.

The phone rang. Because I was on the wrong side of the table, and hampered by the chairs, Laurie beat me to it by a full five feet.

"Hello?" he said politely, as he has been taught. "This is Laurence." His eyes circled meaningfully around to me and he looked sorrowful. "No," he said sadly, "she's not up yet. She's still asleep."

"Young man," I said ominously, and he backed away so I could not reach the phone. "I'll tell her when she wakes up," he said, and hung up hastily. "I knew you wouldn't want to talk to *her*," he said. "She always talks so long, and you're so busy with breakfast and everything."

"Who?" I asked.

"I'll write it down for you," Laurie said. He took the telephone pad and pencil and began, with his laborious printing. The coffee boiled over, and I fled back into the kitchen. I turned off the coffee, gave Sally her bottle—she is learning to drink her milk from a cup, but insists also upon having her bottle, full, for no better apparent reason than as a weapon with which to brain anyone foolish enough to bring a head near her—and began to break eggs into a bowl. Jannie came downstairs with a clatter, her shoes, as I had known inevitably they would be, on the wrong feet.

"Where's Phoebe?" she said.

"She didn't come today," Laurie said. "Mommy's *terrible* mad. Mommy's probably going to kill her."

"Laurie," I said, but they had already started, "Mommy's going to kill Phoebe, Mommy's going to kill Phoebe."

My husband came downstairs without that spring in his step which is usually associated with daddies coming down to a good nourishing breakfast with their kiddies; he came into the kitchen and glanced around. "Where's Phoebe?" he said.

"Not here," I said.

"Mommy's going to kill Phoebe," the children chanted.

"You'll really *have* to fire that girl," my husband observed. "Good morning, children."

"*Good* morning, Daddy," Jannie said sweetly.

"*Good* morning, Dad," Laurie said manfully.

I turned around. Jannie was balancing the fruit juice glasses one on top of another. Laurie was making a train of knives and forks. Sally finished with her bottle abruptly and threw it on the floor.

"It's hot," my husband remarked. He sat down at the table, rescued a knife and fork from Laurie and a glass of fruit juice from Jannie. "Why do you let the children play with things on the table?" he asked. "Don't they have enough toys of their own?"

I did not feel equal to answering. I put the eggs, the toast, and the coffee on the table and sat down; I could tell by looking that my coffee was going to be too hot and it was perfectly clear that the toast was burned.

"What's this junk?" Laurie said, regarding his plate.

"Once," Jannie observed, through a mouthful of egg, "once there was a little boy and he had no mother or father and he ran out into the middle of the street."

"What happened to him?" Laurie asked with interest.

"He was eaten by a truck," Jannie said demurely.

"*That's* no good," Laurie said.

"It is too," Jannie said.

"It is not," Laurie said.

The phone rang. I was cornered behind Sally's high-chair and Laurie beat me again. "This is Laurence," we could hear him saying precisely. "Who is calling, please?"

He came into the kitchen and addressed his father. "It's Mr. Feeley," he said. "He wants to know can you play poker tonight."

My husband avoided looking at me. "Tell him I'll call him back," he said.

"Once there was a little boy," Jannie said, "and he had no mother or father."

"What happened to him?" I asked dutifully, Laurie being still on the phone.

"He was eaten by a bear," Jannie said. "Can I have some candy when I finish my breakfast?"

Each of the children had a toy filled with candy which sat on the table; they were little glass airplanes, and the candy inside was the sort usually used for cake decoration, tiny little colored balls of sugar. This candy enchanted Jannie, although Laurie was cynically aware that the whole amount contained in the airplane was hardly worth one chocolate-covered pepperment.

"If you eat every single bite of your breakfast," I said, "you may have some of your candy."

"Once there was a little boy," Jannie said, shoving her egg around the plate with the handle of her fork, "and he had no mother or father."

"What happened to him?" Laurie said, sliding into his chair. "He says call back before two," he remarked confidentially to his father.

"He was eaten by a elephant," Jannie said. "Look, no more breakfast."

I lifted her plate and, with a spoon, gathered the egg off the table and put it back onto the plate. "Every bite," I said firmly, "or no candy."

"Once there was a little boy," Jannie said mournfully, "and he had no mother or father."

She waited for a minute, but no one spoke; Laurie was engaged with his toast, I was trying to get Sally's spoon out of her mouth, and my husband was counting the money in his wallet.

" 'Once there was a little boy,' " Jannie said loudly,
" 'and he had no mother or father,' I said."

"What happened to him?" Laurie asked resignedly.

Jannie giggled. "He was eaten by a bicycle," she said.

"Through," Laurie announced suddenly. "See?" He
turned his plate upside down, his milk cup upside down
on top of that, and balanced his fruit juice glass on top of
the whole thing.

"Laurence," his father said absently, "your napkin is
on the floor."

Laurie snatched his airplane full of candy, and retired.
I picked his napkin up off the floor, unloaded the milk cup
and the fruit juice glass, caught Jannie's plate just as it
was sliding off the edge of the table, rescued the spoon
from Sally, and said "More coffee?" to my husband.

He looked deeply into his cup. "Yes, please," he said.

Breakfast was nearly over.

Laurie had emptied his candies into a small bowl, and
was stirring them around vigorously. "Look," he said,
coming around to Jannie's side of the table, "Look, whirlpools."

"I want my candy," Jannie said immediately.

"Look, whirlpools," Laurie said to his father. "Whirlpools," he said to me. An idea struck him suddenly and
he took a handful of the candies and put them on the
tray of Sally's high chair; they rolled back and forth and
Sally regarded them dubiously.

"Eat, Sally," Laurie said. "Eat, eat, eat, eat, eat, eat, eat, eat . . ."

"Laurence," I said feverishly.

"Okay, okay," Laurie said. "Look, Sally. Candy."

He pointed to the small candies and Sally tried experimentally to pick one up. Her fingers were not well enough controlled to take hold of it, and she began to giggle, chasing the candies around the highchair tray.

"Listen," Laurie shouted, "Phoebe's coming."

"Phoebe's coming," Jannie agreed loudly. She began to struggle, and Laurie at the same time tried to gather his airplane and candy together preparatory for a dash at the door. Jannie teetered backward in her chair, Laurie crashed into her, and they both went over, Jannie's plate, with egg, moving gracefully off the table after them.

"Can I have my candy now?" Jannie asked me, looking up hopefully from the floor. "*Laurie* did it."

"Phoebe," Laurie was shouting from the front door, "Mommy's going to *kill* you, and Daddy says—"

The phone rang. This time I made it first, and, breathing hard, I lifted the receiver and said "Hello?"

"Hello?" said a high thin voice. "May I please speak to Laurence?"

PHOEBE WAS THE last, for a long, long time, of my adjuvants. Not that I can't *use* help around the house, but I am, not to put too fine a point on it, the person to whom the almost unemployable slack-jawed mother's helper gravitates as to a natural home. I have never in my life made any pretence at being an efficient housekeeper; I can make a fair gingerbread and I know a thing or two about onion soup, but beyond the most rudimentary sweepings and dustings I am not capable. Not for me the turned sheet, the dated preserve, the fitted homemade slipcover or the well-ironed shirt. Nor do I stack up particularly well in the hired girl department; in our town the employer (obviously a staunch New England type who because of a broken leg or some incurable malady has found it necessary to "get help") is expected to "work along," to check dirt, to remain, at all times, level-headed.

That is why I always end up with people like Phoebe. If she could make chowder or raised doughnuts she would, in our town, have a home of her own. If she had a natural gift for getting things clean, or an instinctive ability at getting three rebellious children into bed, she would be gainfully employed in our nearest big town. If she knew how to do anything right at all, she would not be working for me.

Take Hope, for instance. I always get hold of these people because they answer an ad I put in the paper, and someone apparently read it to Hope. I wanted to phrase the ad in some cute irresistible fashion such as "I am almost helpless around a house. I honestly don't know a *thing* about housework. Isn't there some kind girl who wants to help me, at a moderate salary?" Instead, at a dollar for ten words for three days, what I usually say is "Houseworker wanted. Good ref. Mod. sal. Children. Meals. Laundry. Cleaning."

I always hire the first person who comes, usually without remembering to check on the good ref. This is not only because I am extremely gullible, but at least partially because I am openly terrified of anyone who looks me straight in the eye and speaks emphatically, and these women, looking for jobs at mod. sal. and with no serious intentions whatsoever about Meals. Laundry. Cleaning., alway use a voice of great clarity and strength when talking to me. I am usually not able to say anything at all, or else what I do say comes out entirely wrong, and modest disclaimers turn out to be flat denials—a statement to the effect that no one can cook for my husband except me because he has odd ideas about food turns out to say that I intend to do all the cooking myself, in spite of what my ad said, with the rider that I have a crazy husband who lives exclusively on bread and water.

The only person, by the way, whom I ever escaped in a situation like that was a gentlewoman of about two hundred years who came one day in answer to one of my usual ads; I tried to conduct the interview with gravity, and she answered all my timid questions with modesty and restraint until I mentioned, in the laughing voice that I reserve for controversial subjects, that dishes were a problem in a family the size of ours, particularly, I added, washing them.

"Dishes," she said eagerly, "now, I *love* dishes."

"I suppose you collect them?" I asked, for want of anything better to say.

"Washing dishes," she said. "Now, washing dishes I can't stop. If I don't watch myself—" she cackled delightedly "—I just go on washing dishes over and over and over and over and over and over again, all day long. All day *long*, now," and she cackled again.

I told her I would let her know about the job, and after she had left I telephoned the number she gave me and left a message that I had just had word that my mother was coming to live with me and so I wouldn't need anyone to help around the house.

I passed up that nice old lady, who was essentially agreeable and had at least one cleanly virtue, to hire Hope. Hope disliked washing dishes, but she did them. She wore neat house dresses, although she had a weakness for high-heeled, ankle-strap black sandals around the house. She did not quarrel with my cooking for my husband, although, as it turned out, it was unnecessary; Hope spent most of her time in the kitchen making biscuits which were light and pleasant, and cheese soufflés, and chocolate cakes, and fried chicken. I even checked her good ref. The old lady to whom I spoke was enthusiastic in her praise. "She's a *good* girl," the old lady said insistently—perhaps I feel now, *too* insistently. "You don't need to worry about Hope any, she's a *good* girl. Don't you pay any attention to what you may *hear*—that Hope is a *good* girl."

The only trouble with Hope was that she disappeared at the end of the first week, taking with her her salary, ten dollars she had borrowed from me, and my overshoes. Two days after Hope disappeared I answered a ring at the door, and found standing there a lady of unequivocal firmness and a most suspicious eye. "Is Hope here?" she asked me.

"She is not," I said shortly, not overanxious to dwell lengthily upon the subject of Hope.

"I'm her parole officer," the woman said. "If you know where she is it's your duty to tell me."

"She's got my overshoes, wherever she is," I said, and tried to close the front door, but the parole officer put her shoulder against the frame and said, "It's your civic duty as a citizen to report this matter." After I had told her all about Hope and my overshoes I pointed out that the ten dollars was relatively unimportant but that with this constant wet weather it was hard going without anything on my feet, and asked nervously what chance there was of getting them back.

"*We*'ll get them," she said enigmatically, "they can't get far without stealing a car."

A week later I was invited to the local jail to see Hope, who gave me back my overshoes with an apology for having kept them so long, asked kindly after the children, the cats, and the dog, remarked parenthetically that she had never really gotten to know my husband, and asked me to go five thousand dollars bail for her.

I told her civilly enough that these constant ads in the paper made such a drain on my pocketbook that I had really nothing left for more than household expenses, and asked nicely what she was in for. It turned out to be grand larceny; my overshoes, she said, she had never regarded as anything but a loan; it was a difficulty with a former employer's fur coat which worried her now. I shook hands cordially with the jailer's wife, declined a piece of fresh-made sponge cake, and departed. I sent a carton of cigarettes and some magazines to the jail for Hope about a month later, and got back an earnest letter saying she would be sure to come back to work for us when she got out, and could we wait three years?

Between the time I last saw Hope and the time I got her letter, Amelia had come and gone. Amelia had been recommended to me by a neighbor, with the specific statement that Amelia was not an intelligent girl, but she was able, my neighbor was confident, to do simple household tasks. Amelia washed dishes, but not very clean. She arrived every morning on foot, by a process which required that she inquire at every house in the neighborhood each day before she found ours. She never tried to borrow my overshoes, which I was keeping anyway in the only closet in the house which locked, and I sincerely believe that after working for us for two days she was still unable to find her way from the kitchen to the front door without falling over the furniture.

Like Hope, Amelia had but one major failing. The second day she was with us—which turned out, coinciden-tally, to be the last—she made cookies, spending all one joyous afternoon in the kitchen, droning happily to her-self, fidgeting, cluttering, measuring.

At dinner, dessert arrived with Amelia's giggle and a flourish. She set the plate of cookies down in front of my husband, and my husband, who is a nervous man, glanced down at them and dropped his coffee cup. "Sinner," the cookies announced in bold pink icing, "Sinner, repent."

Phoebe did not stay with us much longer than Amelia had. She was accustomed to arriving mornings on a motor-cycle, but after two weeks her mother called one morn-ing to say that there had been an American Legion con-vention in a nearby city and that Phoebe was now in Kansas City. It was terribly hot all that summer, and I kept thinking about poor old Phoebe in Kansas City on her motorcycle. Perhaps I privately envied the motorcycle, it being a species of abandoned travel with which I am respectably unfamiliar; perhaps the notion of wild noisy motion appealed to Laurie. He asked me one morning later that summer, "Why don't we have a car?" I was stirring chocolate pudding—a talent of the late Phoebe's—at the stove, and he was painting at the kitchen table. Jannie was laboriously dressing her doll on the floor, sing-ing quietly to herself while she stuffed the doll's arms brutally into one of the baby's nightgowns.

"Why don't we have a car?" I repeated absently. "I suppose because no one around here can drive."

"If we had a car," Laurie said, in the tone which I was beginning to recognize as one all seven-year-old boys use to their mothers, as of one explaining a relatively uncomplicated situation to a sort of foolish creature, apt to become sentimental and impertinent unless firmly held in check, "if we had a car, we could ride around."

"But no one around here can drive," I said.

"And we could go anywhere we wanted," Laurie said. "And we wouldn't have to walk, or drive with other people, or take taxis."

"Who would drive us?"

"I could sit in the front seat," Laurie said, "and Jannie and Sally could sit in the back seat." He thought. "And Daddy could ride on the running board."

"What would I be doing?" I asked. "Driving?"

"I want to ride in the front," Jannie said, lifting her head to scowl at her brother. "I want to ride in the front and Laurie in back with Baby."

"I'm going to ride in the front," Laurie said. "I'm older."

"But I'm a girl," Jannie said, undeniably.

"But who would *drive?*" I said.

"Listen," Laurie said to me, a thin edge of contempt in his voice, "can't you drive a *car?*"

"No, I can not."

"Can Daddy?"

"No."

"Can't *either* of you drive?"

"No."

Laurie put his paint brush down and looked at me for a long minute. "Then what *can* you do?" he asked.

"Well," I said, "I can make chocolate pudding, and I can wash dishes, and I can . . ."

"*Any*body can do that," Laurie said. "What *I* mean is, can't you drive a *car?*"

"No," I said sharply, "I can not drive a car. And I do not, furthermore, intend to learn. And I also do not want to hear one more—"

"If we had a car," Jannie said, "I could ride in the front and Laurie could ride in the back with Baby."

"I'm older," Laurie said mechanically. "*You* ride in back."

"I'm a girl," Jannie said.

"Why not let Baby ride in front?" I asked in spite of myself. "She's younger. And she's a girl."

"But if Laurie and I rode in back we would fight," Jannie said.

"That's true," I said. "So why not—" but the chocolate pudding thickened and I had to stop talking.

Jannie began to sing one of her morning songs. "On earth, what are you doing," she sang softly, "on earth, what are you doing? I am going splickety-splot. On earth, what are you doing, on earth, what are you doing? I am going thumpety-thump. We do dig and it does rain." While she sang she rocked her doll, Laurie painted amiably, and I hummed to myself while I poured the pudding into dishes and wondered whether I could get away with chicken soup again for lunch today.

Jannie began her song for the third time, and Laurie set his page aside and asked absently, "Why did you say we don't have a car?"

"We don't have a car," I said wearily, "because both Daddy and I would rather roller-skate."

"Can Daddy drive?" Jannie asked. "Daddy can do anything, can't he?"

I hesitated, not at the moment able to find an answer, and Laurie said, "If we had a car you could take us for rides."

"Now listen to me, both of you," I began with great firmness, but at that moment the baby woke up and as I started upstairs I heard Laurie asking dreamily, "Jannie, what would you do if a snake came and ate you?"

In our family a conversation such as this one about the car does not end, ever. At dinner that night Laurie remarked to his father, "Mommy is going to get a car and drive it around."

"And I'm going to ride in front," Jannie said.

"*I'm* going to ride in front," Laurie said. "I'm—"

"I'm a girl," Jannie said.

My husband regarded me with mild surprise. "A car?" he said, perplexed. "You mean, drive me if I wanted to go for a haircut? And I wouldn't have to—"

"Wait," I said, "wait, wait."

"I'm going to ride in *front*," Laurie said.

"I'm a—"

"*I* am going to ride in front," my husband said flatly.

THE MAN FROM the driving school was named Eric, and he was about eighteen years old and undisguisedly amused at meeting anyone who could not drive a car. When I told him sharply that in his business he must meet quite a few people who could not drive a car he laughed and said that usually people my age did not try to learn new tricks. I eyed the dual-control car he had parked in our driveway and said falsely that I might surprise him by learning faster than he expected. He patted me on the shoulder and said, "That's my girl."

Laurie and Jannie and my husband holding the baby stood on the front porch cheering and waving as I rode off with Eric, crushed into a corner of the seat to avoid touching any of the dual controls, and desperately afraid that if I did the car would go out of control and rocket madly off the road, no doubt killing other innocent people and very probably ending my driving lessons. Laurie and Jannie and my husband holding the baby were again on the front porch cheering, two hours later, when I came back with Eric, dismayed and bewildered and not prepared to take levelly any childish prattle about how we would drive around when we had a car.

I took ten lessons from Eric, including lessons in stopping and starting, making a U turn—that was how I got the dent in the back of the car, but Eric said they were insured against that kind of thing—making right turns and left turns, shifting gears, backing and filling, allemande left, and reeling and writhing and fainting in coils. He neglected to teach me how to turn on the lights and what to do when a funny little noise started somewhere inside. Every time I got out of his car in front of my own house, weak-kneed and with my hands stiffened into a permanent grasp on a steering wheel, I was greeted with cheers and friendly criticism by my faithful family. I completely captivated one of Laurie's friends—a young gentleman from Cub Scouts whose mother and father both know how to drive, and have for years—by running smack into the stone wall at the foot of our garden, something no one else has so far been able to do, since the wall is set approximately seven feet from the driveway and is clearly visible. Evenings, I studied a little book Eric had sold me, which told in graphic detail what to do in case the car skidded out of control, what to do in case the steering wheel came off in my hands (from this I got the vivid impression of running the car like a bobsled, and steering by leaning from side to side), and how to bandage a compound fracture.

My test, which I shall always believe was supposed to be a test of whether or not I could drive a car, I passed seemingly without effort, and with only one bad moment when, told to stop completely halfway up a hill which may well have been Mount‑Everest, I realized that the head inquisitor assumed with infinite amusement that I would be able to start again. He was a very patient man, and waited for several minutes, tapping his fingers gently against the window while I scoured my mind for Eric's directions on starting a car on a hill. ("Swing your wheel sharp? Turn down your lights? Keep one foot on the clutch and one foot on the brake and one foot on the starter . . . ?") "Well?" said the inquisitor, looking at me evilly.

I gestured competently with one hand, keeping the other one locked to the wheel in some obscure belief that only my grip on the wheel kept the car from rolling back down the hill. "State law," I said carelessly. "Child coming, can't start."

He glanced at me briefly and then craned his neck out of the window to see where a boy about twenty was sauntering down the sidewalk. I had hoped to distract his attention, and did, but I then discovered that it is not possible to be surreptitious about starting a stalled car on a hill. I firmly believe that the inquisitor gave me a license only because he was sure I could never start a car and so could never become a substantial menace on the highways.

Meanwhile, it had been decided who was to ride in front (Baby), I had learned to drive, the lessons had been paid for, and I had a little piece of official paper saying that I knew how to drive. We lacked only a car. This was adjusted by a gentleman who, saying he acted only from pure friendship, sold us one of *his* cars. He said he was very reluctant to part with it, particularly at that price, he said it was a better car than any of the new ones on the market, he praised its spark plugs and its birdlike appetite for oil.

"The cigarette lighter doesn't work," I pointed out in a spirit of pure critical inquiry.

"Neither does the clock," said my husband.

"And the fender is sort of caved in," I added.

"Tell you what I'll do," the man said. "I'll pay for the license plates."

"Better get that cigarette lighter fixed right away," my husband told me, as we surveyed our new car. "And the clock. Best to be on the safe side."

"I'll have to find a place to get them fixed," I said.

"Can't be too careful," my husband said.

I got into the car and reasoned out how to start it and drove with great caution, in the middle of the road, to a garage that could be reached without a left turn, and there I talked for quite a while with a young man covered with grease and oil who had "Tony" written across the front of him in big red letters. "Got a nice car there," he said, after I had told him we had just bought it, and what we paid for it, and had added trustingly that I had just learned to drive and had never before owned a car and knew nothing about cars or motors or, as a matter of fact, driving. "You're even going to have to tell me what gas to use," I added laughingly.

Tony nodded soberly. "But you got a real nice car there," he insisted, "for the price you paid, you couldn't get a better one. Needs a little attention, of course." He laughed. "Wouldn't be a car if it didn't," he told me.

"Yes, I know," I said. "The cigarette lighter—"

"You take that clutch, for instance," Tony said. He opened the door and pushed the pedal up and down reflectively. "Now I guess you don't know anything about the clutch, do you?" he asked. I shook my head, and he went on, "Well, it's a funny thing about the clutch. You go along for maybe one, two thousand miles and then all of a sudden . . ." He shrugged expressively. "You got a repair job costs you maybe two, three hundred dollars. Always better to get the clutch fixed in time, saves you money, expense, wear and tear."

"You mean I have to get something fixed?"

He shrugged again. "You don't *need* to, of course," he said. "But you got to look at it this way. You got small children, you're driving them around in the car, you're not going to take chances with *them*."

Nervously I agreed that I was not going to take chances with my small children.

"Well, then," said Tony. "Now brakes are important, too." He pushed the brake pedal down and shook his head sadly. "That guy sold you this car," he said.

"Is this going to be very expensive?" I asked.

"Well, now," Tony said, and laughed. "But let's look

it over and see just exactly what you need. No sense getting something you don't *need*," he said jovially.

From then on, as nearly as I can remember, it was wheel alignment and something called camber or clamber or clabber, and wheel work was always expensive because every single car in the world except the make and model I owned had little adjustable pegs which could be fixed for next to nothing, but when Tony had to work with nonadjustable pegs, well, peg work was always expensive. Body work, too, would always set you back plenty, but it was the lives of my children I was taking in my hands if I let the fenders go.

"You got to regard this as an *investment*," Tony said earnestly. "Now, I wouldn't be treating you fair if I let those spark plugs go, for instance. You'd say I played you a pretty dirty trick if you had to come back a month from now for a big repair bill, you'd say to me, 'Tony, why didn't you fix those spark plugs a long time ago before I had to pay this big repair bill?' You see, it's an investment *now* so's it won't cost you so much *later*. Now take the muffler."

"Muffler," I said. Tony pointed to something under the car which I could not see.

"You see that?" he said. "I guess you didn't notice it before or you would of called it to my attention sooner. Lucky thing I saw it in time, I wasn't looking for anything like *that*."

"What would have happened?" I asked him nervously.

He shook his head. "Can't ever tell," he said. "*Nothing* might have happened—for a while. And then one day you're going up a hill, car full of children . . ." He shook his head again. "And the brake lining," he said. "*And* the ignition system."

I then made one of the bigger mistakes of my life. "How are the tires?" I asked.

Tony laughed. "You call those *tires?*" he demanded. "Why, let me tell you, one day I saw a guy, had his two little children with him, and I said to him—"

TWO WEEKS LATER I had my car back and we had managed to borrow enough extra money to pay the bill, upon which Tony had presumably retired to a little home in the hills to grow hollyhocks. The car looked and acted almost exactly the same except that the tank full of gas I had left in it was down almost to nothing. Tony said that was because they had to drive it in and out of the garage so many times.

I took everybody, including the dog, for a ride, and we went around the block four or five times, congratulating one another upon our new mobility. I discovered that my former usual attitude of timid acquiescence was not consistent with someone who could drive a car, so I fell gradually into a new personality, swashbuckling and brazen, with a cigarette usually hanging out of one corner of my mouth because I had to keep both hands on the wheel. We began to make plans for driving across the country to visit Grandma and Grandpa in California.

Some time later, while I, cigarette in the corner of my mouth, was stirring butterscotch pudding at the stove, and Laurie was glueing a model airplane at the kitchen table and Jannie was making double marshmallow chocolate ice cream pineapple coffee cake at *her* stove, Laurie raised his head and asked, "We've got a car now, haven't we?"

"We have," I said. "Why?"

"Why'd we get a car?" Laurie asked. "We never had one before."

"Daddy still walks for his haircut," Jannie said to her stove.

"That's because he's *scared* to get in the car," Laurie said.

"You know what I wish?" Jannie said. "I wish we had a airplane."

"Hey," Laurie said, interested. "*That* would be good. I could ride on the wing and Baby—"

"*I* could ride on the wing," Jannie said immediately. "I'm—"

"And what would *I* be doing?" I asked in a deadly voice.

They both turned and looked at me, their sweet trusting little faces confident.

AT THIS TIME, Laurie was seven and a half, Jannie was four and a half, and Sally was one and a half. We had been in our big old house for four years, and space which had at one time seemed vast had contracted into little more than enough to hold us and the children and the cats and the dog. We had a car, and we had taken to telling one another that we couldn't imagine how we had ever got along without it. One of the left-hand pillars had begun to tremble during storms, and it was necessary to have it re-enforced.

It was when Jannie was very nearly five that the question of her name became desperately important. When she was born her father wanted to name her Jean and I wanted to name her Anne, and we compromised upon an arbitrary Joanne, although I frequently call her Anne and her father very often calls her Jean. Her brother calls her Honey, Sis, and Dopey, Sally calls her Nannie, and she calls herself, variously, Jean, Jane, Anne, Linda, Barbara, Estelle, Josephine, Geraldine, Sarah, Sally, Laura, Margaret, Marilyn, Susan, and—imposingly—Mrs. Ellenoy. The second Mrs. Ellenoy.

The *former* Mrs. Ellenoy—I have this straight from my daughter—was a lovely woman, mother of seven daughters, all named Martha, and she and Mr. Ellenoy used to be very angry with one another, until one day they grew so *very* angry that they up and killed each other with swords. As a result my daughter is the new Mrs. Ellenoy and has inherited all the Marthas as stepdaughters. When she is not named Jean, Linda, Barbara, Sally, and so on, but is being Mrs. Ellenoy, her daughters are allowed to assume these names, so that there is a constant bewildering shifting of names among them, and it is sometimes very difficult to remember whether you are addressing Janey Ellenoy or a small girl with seven daughters named Martha.

Since there is enough confusion in our house anyway, no one worries excessively about anyone else's name. Laurie has recently taken a flat stand on being called Laurie, and insists upon being addressed as either Laurence or Sir. Sally was named Sarah when she started, got shortened to Sally, and immediately got into trouble with Sally Ellenoy, so now we call the one Baby and the other Sallyellenoy. Baby is unmistakable, as is Dog for the dog, since *his* name is Toby and Baby renamed him Bowowby and Laurence renamed him Trigger and Mrs. Ellenoy generally calls him Child. The two cats look exactly alike, so we call them Kitty, generally. I myself use two names, a maiden name professionally and a married name, and my husband, who is addressed in all variants of father from Pappy to Da, now answers to almost anything, even—being a man not easily thrown off balance—Mr. Ellenoy.

In places where we have specific locations, such as our beds, or the dinner table, it is easy enough for us to address one another by facing the place we want. Equally, particular questions may be identified and caught by the person they most concern, so that something like "Did you know the bank called about that overdraft?" or "Didn't I tell you to change into a clean dress?" or "Do you want to go outside *again?*" or "Did she eat up all her nice cereal?" can easily be answered by the correct character, without all the trouble of trying to remember a name, or the rudeness of pointing. It is only on such a general question as "Well, who hasn't washed for dinner?" that the bitter matter of identification comes up.

I know what they all *look* like, of course. The dog has four feet and is far larger than the cats, who operate as a two-part unit anyway. The boy is dirty and wears a disgraceful pair of blue jeans. The father looks worried and a little bit overwhelmed. The older daughter is larger than the younger daughter, although there is an uncanny shifting of identity there, since the smaller wears the clothes the larger wore a short while before, and they both have blond curls and blue eyes. But as to trying to remember, for instance, which two out of three have already had chicken pox and which one was innoculated for whooping cough and whether any given one of them got all three prescribed injections or one of them got nine, and, worst, which of the Ellenoy girls got spanked for breaking Laurence's six-shooter and who told on her, I go all to pieces.

For example: I glanced out of the kitchen window one Sunday morning and found my older daughter up to her knees in a mud puddle. "Joanne," I said sharply, rapping on the glass in traditional manner with my wedding ring. She turned and smiled and I dried my hands on the dish towel and made for the back door. "What are you doing in that mud?"

My daughter looked at me, amused. "*This* is Mrs. Ellenoy," she said. "*I'm* over there." And she pointed.

One trouble about all this is that it is extraordinarily easy to be taken in by any particular statement.

"Joanne," I said, addressing the empty air where she was pointing, "get out of that mud puddle this minute."

"Get out at once," Mrs. Ellenoy added emphatically. "Joanne, I'm ashamed of you." She turned to me. "I don't know what we're going to do with her," she said. "Joanne," she added again, "you heard your mother. Get out of that mud puddle right now." She nodded reassuringly at me. "She'll be right in," she said. "I'll stay out here and wait for her."

I went back inside, talking to myself, and after a minute Mrs. Ellenoy poked her head in through the kitchen door. "Martha's out here," she said, "and she won't stop crying till you give her a cookie."

"I'm not giving a cookie to any little girl covered with mud," I said.

"*Martha's* not covered with mud," Mrs. Ellenoy said reasonably. "That was bad Anne. Martha's been playing quietly under the apple tree all this time."

There was the frightful moment in the restaurant when all seven Ellenoy girls tried to climb onto Mrs. Ellenoy's lap just as the waitress was putting down a plate of soup. "You *can't* get into my lap now, can't you see I'm having my lunch?" Mrs. Ellenoy said crossly, and the waitress gave me a startled look and retreated, backing directly into Laurence's spurs. There was the black morning the census taker spent at our house, since she arrived before I was dressed and my daughter entertained her until I came down. There was the uncomfortable incident when my daughter trotted in to me and said, "There's a lady outside named Mrs. Harper and she wants to know will you give her a dollar?" and I replied absently, "Tell Mrs. Harper she may take the penny off my desk and not to bother me any more." My daughter told Mrs. Harper and Mrs. Harper went away furious and a little frightened, and I was entered on the P.-T.A. books as refusing to pay my dues.

Or there was this most touching incident which has really exposed my husband; as I say, he is a man not easily thrown off balance.

I glanced into the study the other morning and found my older daughter settling herself on the couch next to her father, who was reading the paper. She had *The Wizard of Oz* under her arm and as I passed by, smiling fondly, she asked her father, "Will you read for a minute to me?" In my subsequent wanderings through the house I frequently passed the study door and heard the comfortable drone of my husband's voice plowing his way toward the Emerald City. Finally, looking in and seeing him still reading aloud, but alone, I said in surprise, "Still reading?"

"I'm reading to Marilyn till Jean gets back," he said, not looking up from the book.

I went outdoors to where my daughter was sitting drawing pictures under the apple tree and said conversationally, "Dad's still reading to Marilyn."

"I know," said my daughter, nodding. "I got too restless so I left."

We played a game of croquet and picked some flowers for the house and ordered the groceries and my husband was still reading.

After a while my daughter went back into the study, said softly, "Move over, Marilyn," and settled down to hear the rest of the book.

"Dad was reading out loud to himself all morning," my son observed as he sat down at the dinner table that evening.

"No, I wasn't," said my husband. "I was reading to Marilyn."

"I thought you were reading to yourself," Laurie said.

"Marilyn doesn't brush her teeth," Mrs. Ellenoy said. "*None* of my girls brush their teeth," she added wistfully, "but all of them were dancing this afternoon. All the girls were dancing in the garden. There was Martha, and Sallyellenoy and Janey and Linda and Margaret—"

"You know what I wish?" Laurie demanded of his father. "I wish I was in Texas right now on a horse."

"—and Estelle and Barbara and Josephine and they were

all dancing," Mrs. Ellenoy continued. "And all us Ellenoys, we were dancing too."

"*Did* you call the bank?" my husband said, raising his voice to be heard.

"All dancing," said Mrs. Ellenoy happily, "all the girls were dancing."

"Mommy," said Sally, thumping crazily on her dish with her spoon, "Daddy, Nannie, Kitty, Mommy, Okay, Goodbye, cookie?"

Jannie sang softly, in a minor counterpoint, "Sally's bottom is dry as a fly, so goodbye, my peekaboo Sally."

Sally had consumed her chicken and her potatoes and was eating her peas one by one with her fingers, Jannie was daintily making designs in her potatoes with the back of her spoon, Laurie waved a chicken leg at his father and said vigorously, "say, *listen*, you know what's funny?" I was remembering the time the waitress backed into Laurie's spurs; sooner or later, I suppose, there must be in every mother's life the inevitable moment when she has to take two small children shopping in one big store. Although I keep telling myself that Laurie and Jannie are not more undisciplined, less poised, than any other two children of their age, I could not, for anything in the world, take them into public view again. Jannie had needed shoes, and Laurie some kind of trousers, made of any material on the order of sheet iron, to wear to school, where apparently the second-graders amuse themselves during the long weary days by cutting holes in one another's clothes with scissors. I felt, erroneously, that it was preferable to buy Jannie's shoes and Laurie's pants in a large department store in the nearest city, rather than relying so entirely upon our small local stores, and it seemed to me that I should have the children with me to try things on. I *have* tried buying shoes for children with an outline of the child's foot traced on paper, but it is never completely satisfactory, aside from the pleasure the child gets out of having his foot traced.

It was a Wednesday morning when I assembled the children, Laurie having been kept home from school because I had a faint idea that Wednesday was the day when the stores were least crowded. I have no idea what persuaded me that the stores were going to be least crowded on Wednesday, although, as it turned out, it hardly mattered, since my children proved to be able to assemble a crowd at any given time on any given day.

We all looked very nice when we started out. Jannie was wearing her best dark red coat, with high blue stockings and a blue beret. Laurie was wearing his suit, which was a little too small for him, his dark blue tie, his spurs, and two pearl-handled revolvers, although I took a firm stand on his not loading them with caps. I was wearing a gray fur coat and the low-heeled shoes which I ordinarily wear around the house, but which I chose to wear shopping this day because low heels seemed more practical for the broken field running I expected to be doing. I had also, with rare good sense, stripped for action in that I carried absolutely nothing—no pocketbook, no gloves, no hat. I assumed, and correctly, that I was going to need all the hands I could get. I had my money in a little purse in my pocket, which I kept feeling nervously to make sure it was still there. I had left simple instructions for my husband on care of Sally ("if she cries, ignore her, unless she seems to be crying because she's in trouble—you'll be sure to recognize the difference—or else she might be crying because she's dropped her little suitcase out of the crib and wants you to pick it up, but be *sure* not to let her have the doll in the blue dress because its arm is broken and if she wants a drink make her take the half-glass of milk in the left-hand lower corner of the refrigerator because that's what she left from breakfast and if she goes in the playpen—") and he had given each of the older children a dime.

We sailed off in fine style, as far as the ·front door, where Jannie flatly declined to move further unless allowed to take along her doll carriage and doll. There was a violent argument; I took the always-losing position of "Either the doll stays home or you do," and Laurie swung on the knob of the front door saying "Come *on*, let's *go*." We got the doll carriage into a bus, finally, and all the way into town Jannie bent over it, crooning to her doll about how no one was going to leave sweet dolly at home while Jannie had anything to say about it; Laurie shot people from the bus window with his pearl-handled revolvers. I made rapid and inaccurate mental calculations about the probable price of lunch and the cost of transporting the doll carriage in taxis. Fortunately, my shopping list was simple: J. shoes; L. pants, and if I *did* happen to be anywhere near a suit department I might take a look at dark suits, the simple kind they don't seem to make any more.

"Move over," Jannie said to me, "you're sitting on Linda."

"*Linda*'s not coming?" I said incredulously.

"Certainly she's coming," Jannie said, "and you're sitting on her."

"You and your old girls," Laurie said, drawing in his head and pointing his gun. "There, I shot her."

A crisis was averted at that moment because the bus stopped in front of the department store where I fondly believed they had shoes in Jannie's size and pants in Laurie's strength and suits in my shade of darkness. We got out of the bus, apologizing, and reached the sidewalk without trouble—quite an accomplishment, with the doll carriage, Linda, and Laurie, who remembered his manners at the last minute, and ran back from the sidewalk to hold the door for me after I had already gotten out, leaving Jannie alone and disconsolate, so that she started sadly down the street alone pushing her carriage, with the crowd separating to make a path for her, and one or two old ladies turning to smile and tell one another that she was sweet, and cute, and adorable.

By the time Laurie and I, shouting, had caught up, Jannie and the doll carriage were almost inextricably caught in a revolving door.

I think, every time I step into a department store with my children, surely, I think, it *is* possible to take children shopping, otherwise, the ten thousand mothers and children surrounding us at this moment are either figments of my imagination, which is perfectly possible, or else actors paid by the store to make itself look busy, which is also perfectly possible, but impractical considering the amount of trade I am likely to bring in with Laurie and Jannie; it *must* be, I keep telling myself, a simple and wholesome business, to buy one's children clothes. Doll carriage, revolvers, and all, we got onto the escalator, a machine which I am absolutely convinced is intent upon trapping small unwary feet or, preferably, well-shod maternal feet, and I said, "Careful, children, please."

"Watch your feet, Linda," Jannie said repeatedly as we went from the first to the second floor, "watch your feet, Marilyn. Susan, watch your *feet.*"

I was carrying the doll carriage by then, under my arm; when I recognized the third, and boy's floor, I said briskly, "All right, we get off here." Doll carriage under my arm, I alighted and used my free hand to swing Jannie off the escalator. Laurie disembarked with a theatrical gesture which found me leaping backward to catch him before he went along with the escalator to whatever submerged and awful depths it departs; "What's the matter with *you?*" Laurie demanded irritably, "scared or something?"

"Linda," Jannie said anxiously, "watch your step getting off the escalator. Susan, be careful. Linda, jump now; Barbara, help Linda; Marilyn, wait for your turn; Margaret—"

"Jannie," I said, "please stop. They can get off by themselves." I was beginning to be aware of a familiar and dreadful feeling: that of being stared at by hordes of people—salesladies, floorwalkers, mothers, immaculate children, and perhaps truant officers. "Come on," I said nervously, and added just in time, "my dears."

I put the doll carriage down and Jannie settled herself behind it, hands on the bar, alert and ready to start. "Linda," she said softly, "all girls, get in line behind me, please."

"We going to get *clothes?*" Laurie demanded, looking about him with vast contempt. "I thought you said *lunch.*"

"A pair of pants for you, dear," I said sweetly. I was tacking the "dear" onto every sentence I spoke for fear someone should hear me. At this moment, just as our procession was ready to get under way, a large, red-faced man in a rumpled brown suit accosted us. "Madam?" he said inquiringly to me.

He was not a floorwalker, he was certainly not a salesclerk; he might just possibly have been some cowboy hero in mufti—although in that case he would probably have addressed himself to my son, where he would be assured of at least some comprehension—and he was not, I discovered by feeling at my pocket, a thief. "This little boy buying clothes?" he asked me, gesturing grandly toward Laurie.

"He is," I said. "Aren't we, dear?" to Laurie.

"Well, Madam," the man went on, smiling alternately at me and—with some tentative geniality—at Laurie, "I represent the Real Western Rancho Clothes for Boys Company. We are meeting boys shopping here, talking to them and to their mothers, trying to find out what boys *really* like in clothes. For instance," he went on, obviously gaining courage as Laurie and I—not being notoriously quick thinkers—only stared blankly at him, "for instance, here is a boy, I can tell right away, who is lively and full of fun and a real Western Rancho type, right out there with the cowhands at chow time—" he squatted down by Laurie and looked Laurie straight in the eye,"—and this critter here *needs* real cowpunching duds. Why, I bet this hombre knows a good suit of clothes when he sees it, don't you pardner?" He gave Laurie's shoulder a friendly shake. "What's this?" he demanded, "your shooting iron?"

Laurie stepped back. "It's a gun," he said. "You think it was a squirrel or something?"

The man laughed commercially, and I said in warning, "Laurie," and added, "dear." "Bright boy," the man said to me. "Now, come along, pardner, and let this here coyote take your picture."

"Do what?" said Laurie.

The man laughed again, and tried to give Laurie a little tug over to where another, unhappy-looking man, this one in an ill-fitting cowboy hat, was standing behind a camera, looking as though he would have been more at ease sitting on a corral fence in front of a dry martini; "You're next, Pancho," the man in the brown suit said insistently to Laurie.

"Hey," Laurie said, holding back. I could tell that he had not yet decided upon his final attitude toward this, but I could have told the man a thing or two about getting a firm grip on a boy's arm (never *below* the elbow). Jannie, who had wandered off down the aisles, pushing her doll carriage and indicating to Linda, Marilyn, Susan, and the rest various interesting sights they passed, now turned and called to me from the other end of the store, "Mommy, Linda wants you to get her this cowboy hat."

"*Cut* it out," Laurie said, pulling away easily.

"That gun loaded?" said the man, grinning. "You aim to shoot, stranger?"

"What?" said Laurie.

The man looked up at me. "He have TV yet?" he asked.

"Yes," I said, "but—"

"Well, what we waiting for, fella?" said the man. "Put your picture in the paper," he said. "All the girls'll see it."

Laurie froze. "Girls?" he said. "What girls?"

"Don't you have a girl friend?" the man said.

"I'm a married man," Laurie said.

"*Laurie*," I said.

"Mommy." The doll carriage smacked against the backs of my knees. "Mommy," Jannie said, "I called you and

[124]

called you and Linda called you too and you didn't answer me. Who's that man talking to Laurie?"

She went over close to the man and stared curiously into his face. "Who're you?" she asked. "Does Mommy know you're talking to Laurie?"

"M'sister," Laurie said; perhaps it was the last shred of courtesy left in him, or perhaps he was just terribly afraid that this stranger might think Jannie a girl friend.

"Well," said the man, "and is this little sister? Do you pull her hair?" he asked Laurie.

"*My* hair?" said Jannie, and laughed shortly. "And this," she added, "is Linda, and this is Marilyn, and this is Susan, and this is Barbara, and this is—Margaret? Where is Margaret?"

"Margaret?" said the man in the brown suit.

"Margaret," Jannie said sharply. She stamped her foot. "Margaret," she said, "you come here at once. How dare you run away like that? You ought to be spanked right now and here. You bad, bad, bad, bad—"

"Jannie," I said helplessly, "please don't scold her. She's so little."

"The more reason she should stay with Linda," Jannie said.

The man in the brown suit, who had been steadily backing away, now rose to his feet and looked long at Laurie and long at Jannie and then, inscrutably, at me. As he turned away, Jannie said, "You can take *my* picture if you want to, and Linda's and Marilyn's and everybody's but Margaret."

A large lady accompanied by a young boy swept past me and grabbed the stranger by the arm. "You the man taking pictures in the paper?" she asked. "Look, you the man?"

"I always wear Western Rancho clothes," said the little boy anxiously; he was wearing a pale blue gabardine suit, with a darker blue shirt and a dark red figured tie, neatly knotted. His shoes were polished, his tie pin glittered. His nails, I could see, were clean, as were his ears. He was wearing a neat cap, which he took off when he addressed the man in the brown suit. I glanced at Laurie; he was staring with his mouth open.

"Hello, boy," Jannie said. She turned to Laurie. "Boy?" she whispered, "or girl?"

"Huh," said Laurie.

"Madam," said the man in the brown suit, "here is a boy, I can tell right away, who is lively and full of fun and a real Western Rancho type, right out there with—"

"In all the papers?" said the woman; she was removing a spot from the boy's face with the corner of her handkerchief.

"Look," said Laurie loudly, "he got dirty, poor thing."

With a certain obscure pride in my son I took him by the back of the collar and hauled him purposefully toward the department where they had pants in his size; I pushed the doll carriage with my other hand while Jannie shepherded Linda, Marilyn, and the rest, with loud, laughing directions. I was also carrying Jannie's beret and her coat —they could not be set on top of the carriage without disturbing sweet dolly—and Laurie's suit jacket, and my own coat. My voice was getting shrill, but I was still doggedly adding "dear" to every sentence.

Once I got Laurie into the department where I wanted him, there was small trouble in getting him to choose a pair of pants. He also chose a gabardine suit much like the one the boy with his picture in the paper had been wearing, priced at $59.95, a complete suit of space cadet armor, priced at $47.00, a very odd fur hat which for some reason he admired, and which would have cost me $7.50, a shaggy suede jacket which was called a Buffalo Bill jacket, and which was priced modestly at $32.50, pants to match $17.00. I one by one eliminated these articles, on the grounds that they were too heavy, too furry, too shaggy, or too expensive. I proffered a bright red bow tie, priced at sixty-nine cents, as a substitute. After some argument, during the course of which I told him he could buy anything he wanted with his father's dime, he was persuaded to take the bow tie or nothing, and the salesman remarked in an aside to me, "*I* don't think these fads will last." Jannie had amused herself during this time by trying on one fur hat after another, to the extreme bewilderment of Linda, Marilyn, and the rest. She also fell into conversation with a harmless old lady who was trying to find a birthday gift for her nephew and who had great difficulty resisting Jannie's invitation to come shopping with us and Mommy would buy her a pair of shoes.

I added the package with the bow tie and two pairs of corduroy pants to the doll carriage, Jannie's coat and beret, Laurie's suit jacket, and my own coat. Fortunately Jannie's shoes were on the same floor; we could not conceivably get into an elevator, and I was most reluctant to get back onto the escalator. In the shoe department, Jannie sat herself down, ranged her girls about her, and, folding her hands peaceably, announced that she intended to have a pair of shiny black shoes with high-heels and pretty straps and sparkles and no toes.

"Shoes for the kiddies?" said the shoe clerk brightly, setting his little stool down before us.

"Just me and my girls," Jannie said. "We all want shoes."

The clerk did not hear this because I was telling him loudly that we wanted something in a solid brown oxford with a good sole. I knew I was going to have to reach a compromise somewhere along this line, and I thought I would start from rock bottom and so, going up, have more bargaining power. When the clerk brought the brown oxford Jannie dismissed it after a brief glance. "That's for my brother," she said, "bring something for *me*."

During the excruciating process of Jannie's buying herself a pair of shoes, Laurie amused himself by counting the number of boxes the clerk brought out, Jannie held steadfastly to the high-heeled black sandal, and I grew very tense and began saying things like "How will you go to *school* without shoes because you are certainly *not* going to have any *shoes* until you start behaving like a little *lady* . . ."

We reached a tearful compromise on a pair of black patent leather shoes, completely impractical, but better, I reassured myself, than the black sandals with the high heels. Jannie remarked, as we left the shoe department, "I'm glad you're not my mommy. My mommy always buys me the shoes I want, and if *you* were my mommy I would run away."

"Those are the worst shoes I ever saw in all my life," Laurie told her.

"They're beautiful," said Jannie. "All my girls have shoes just like them."

I had added the package with the shoes to my other portage.

"Let's have *lunch*," Laurie said.

I looked at the clock with the faint unconscious hope common to all mothers that time will somehow have passed magically away and the next time you look it will be bedtime. It was ten minutes to twelve; a good eight hours to go before the nightly miracle, but a legitimate time for lunch.

"Well, children," I said, smiling sweetly and falsely around the table in the restaurant, "well, now we're going to remember our company manners, aren't we?"

Jannie looked bright and alert, and said sweetly, "Can we have two desserts?"

"Perhaps, dears," I said with that same sweet smile, "if we eat allllll our lunch."

Waitresses always take a very long time when you are waiting at a restaurant table with children. I would prefer not to believe that this is due entirely to the general appearance and deportment of my children at the table. At any rate, we had been sitting—me with my hands neatly folded, Laurie with his elbows on the table, and Jannie sliding down in her chair so that her chin rested comfortably on the edge of the table—waiting, I say, for perhaps ten minutes, while waitresses scurried busily past, serving the tables on either side of us, bringing extra pats of butter, stopping to chat merrily, hovering solicitously over customers who could not make up their minds.

"When is she going to *come?*" Laurie demanded.

"I want my lunch," Jannie amplified. She reached out and gave a sharp slap against one of Laurie's elbows, so that his head crashed down and his chin cracked on the table. "Keep your elbows off the table," she said admonishingly.

"Now, children," I said in my gentle voice, scowling fiercely at Jannie, "now, children, remember we intended to use our very best manners."

"Well, *she*—" Laurie began righteously.

"He had his elbows on the table," Jannie said. "Mommy dearest, Laurie was putting his old elbows on the table, Mommy dear."

"*Listen,*" Laurie said, "*she* went and—"

"Darlings," I said, my voice more sugary, if possible, than

before, "let us remember that *other* people are trying to eat *their* lunches, too, and we—"

"What?" Laurie said to Jannie, who was whispering earnestly in his direction.

"Nothing," Jannie said, looking attentively at me. "We *are* being good children, Mommy dearest. We *are* letting other people eat their lunch."

"That's right, dear," I said to her, "*my* children are such good—"

"Why are you talking funny like that?" Laurie asked me, interested, just as the waitress showed up beside us. "You sound like a cat."

He and Jannie both began to laugh loudly. "She sounds like a cat," Jannie told the waitress.

"You wanna order?" the waitress said to me.

"I want spaghetti," Jannie said immediately.

"*I* want spaghetti," Laurie said.

"Let me see." I consulted the menu. "Omelette?" I said to Laurie. And, to Jannie, "Vegetable plate?"

"No," Jannie said, "spaghetti."

"No spaghetti today," the waitress said. She sighed deeply, fussing with her hair. "Ony what's onna menu," she said.

"Chicken salad?" I said. "Liver?"

"Liver," Laurie said, and made a noisy gesture of distaste. "Liver-biver-shiver-tiver-wiver-niver—"

"Liver-liver-liver," said Jannie.

"Children," I said, recollecting myself in time, so that

it came out gentle. "We must *not* take up all this time deciding."

"I decided," Laurie said. "Spaghetti."

Jannie switched sides abruptly. "Vegetable plate," she said. "Mommy dear."

"Justa minute," the waitress said, and departed.

Two unpleasant-looking women wearing flowered hats got up ostentatiously from the next table and moved to a table across the room. "Look here," I said, my voice just loud enough to carry across our own table, "one more word out of either of you and *you—*" eyeing Laurie "—will find yourself being spanked right here in public where everyone will laugh at you and *you—*" eyeing Jannie "—will find yourself being spanked somewhere in private where *no* one can hear you. And right now Jannie is going to have a vegetable plate for lunch and Laurie is going to have a chicken salad and I am going to have spaghetti— I mean, a club sandwich. Now does anyone have anything to say?"

They stared at me numbly. Laurie scowled, and showed his teeth, and was quiet. Jannie's face moved, the corners of her mouth turned down, her great blue eyes filled with tears, and she took a deep breath. "Just one howl out of you," I said sweetly, "and all your girls get shut outdoors tonight." She closed her mouth, and blinked.

Laurie made a move as though to reach for his gun. "That man can still take your picture, you know," I said. He put both hands back on the table.

"Ha, ha," Jannie said bitterly to me, "*you*'ve only got one head."

"Put your foot in here," Laurie told me, extending his water glass.

The waitress reappeared. "Kids made up their minds?" she said.

"Vegetable plate," said Jannie meekly.

"Chicken salad," Laurie said politely. "And two cups of coffee, please."

"Two glasses of milk," I told her. "And I will have a club sandwich."

"And Linda will have spaghetti," Jannie said, "and Marilyn will have spaghetti, and Susan will have spaghetti . . ."

"Jannie," I said sharply.

"And Margaret," Jannie whispered, "Margaret has to have the vegetable plate."

If I gave up any idea of my dark suit, all we still had to do was manage the escalator going down and get ourselves into a bus and out again at home. I sighed. "I wonder how Daddy and Sally are getting along," I said.

It was at that moment that the waitress approached our table with the plate of soup and the seven little Ellenoys backed her into those spurs.

We are all of us, in our family, very fond of puzzles. I do double-crostics and read mystery stories, my husband does baseball box scores and figures out batting averages, and says he knows the odds against drawing a fourth ace, Laurie is addicted to the kind of puzzle which begins "There are fifty-four items in this picture beginning with the letter C," Jannie does children's jigsaws, and Sally can put together an intricate little arrangement of rings and bars which has had the rest of us stopped for two months. We are none of us, however, capable of solving the puzzles we work up for ourselves in the oddly diffuse patterns of our several lives, and along with such family brain-teasers as "Why is there a pair of rollerskates in Mommy's desk?" and "What is *really* in the back of Laurie's closet?" and "Why doesn't Daddy wear the nice shirts Jannie picked out for Father's Day?" we are all of us still wondering nervously about what might be called the Great Grippe Mystery. As a matter of fact, I should be extremely grateful if anyone could solve it for us, because we are certainly very short of blankets, and it is annoying not to have *any* kind of an answer. Here, in rough outline, is our puzzle:

Our house is, as I have said, large, and the second floor has four bedrooms and a bathroom, all opening out onto a long narrow hall which we have made even narrower by lining it with bookcases so that every inch of hall which is not doorway is books. As is the case with most houses, both the front door and the back door are downstairs on the first floor. The front bedroom, which is my husband's and mine, is the largest and lightest, and has a double bed.

The room next down the hall belongs to the girls, and contains a crib and a single, short bed. Laurie's room, across the hall, has a double-decker bed and he sleeps on the top half. The guest room, at the end of the hall, has a double bed. The double bed in our room is made up with white sheets and cases, the baby's crib has pink linen, and Jannie's bed has yellow. Laurie's bed has green linen, and the guest room has blue. The bottom half of Laurie's bed is never made up, unless company is going to use it immediately, because the dog traditionally spends a large part of his time there and regards it as his bed. There is no bed table on the distaff side of the double bed in our room. One side of the bed in the guest room is pushed against the wall. No one can fit into the baby's crib except the baby; the ladder to the top half of Laurie's double-decker is very shaky and stands in a corner of the room; the children reach the top half of the bed by climbing up over the footboard. All three of the children are accustomed to having a glass of apple juice, to which they are addicted, by their bedsides at night. Laurie uses a green glass, Jannie uses a red glass, Sally uses one of those little flowered cheese glasses, and my husband uses an aluminum tumbler because he has broken so many ordinary glasses trying to find them in the dark.

I do not take cough drops or cough medicine in any form.

The baby customarily sleeps with half a dozen cloth books, an armless doll, and a small cardboard suitcase which holds the remnants of half a dozen decks of cards. Jannie is very partial to a pink baby blanket, which has shrunk from many washings. The girls' room is very warm, the guest room moderately so; our room is chilly, and Laurie's room is quite cold. We are all of us, including the dog, notoriously easy and heavy sleepers; my husband never eats coffee cake.

My husband caught the grippe first, on a Friday, and snarled and shivered and complained until I prevailed upon him to go to bed. By Friday night both Laurie and Sally were feverish, and on Saturday Jannie and I began to cough and sniffle. In our family we take ill in different manners; my husband is extremely annoyed at the whole procedure and is convinced that his being sick is somebody's fault, Laurie tends to become a little light-headed and strew handkerchiefs around his room, Jannie coughs and coughs and coughs, Sally turns bright red, and I suffer in stoical silence, so long as everyone knows clearly that I am sick. We are each of us privately convinced that our own ailment is far more severe than anyone else's. At any rate, on Saturday night I put all the children into their beds, gave each of them half an aspirin and the usual fruit juice, covered them warmly, and then settled my husband down for the night with his tumbler of water and his cigarettes and matches and ashtray; he had decided to sleep in the guest room because it was warmer. At about ten o'clock I checked to see that all the children were covered and asleep and that Toby was in his place on the bottom half of the double-decker. I then took two sleeping pills and went to sleep in my own bed in my own room. Because my husband was in the guest room I slept on his side of the bed, next to the bed table. I put my cigarettes and matches on the end table next to the ashtray, along with a small glass of brandy, which I find more efficacious than cough medicine.

I woke up some time later to find Jannie standing beside the bed. "Can't sleep," she said. "Want to come in *your* bed."

"Come along," I said. "Bring your own pillow."

She went and got her pillow and her small pink blanket and her glass of fruit juice, which she put on the floor next to the bed, since she had got the side without any end table. She put her pillow down, rolled herself in her pink blanket, and fell asleep. I went back to sleep, but sometime later Sally came in, asking sleepily, "Where's Jannie?"

"She's here," I said. "Are you coming in bed with us."

"Yes," said Sally.

"Go and get your pillow, then," I said.

She returned with her pillow, her books, her doll, her suitcase, and her fruit juice, which she put on the floor next to Jannie's. Then she crowded in comfortably next to Jannie and fell asleep. Eventually the pressure of the two of them began to force me uneasily toward the edge of the bed, so I rolled out wearily, took my pillow and my small glass of brandy and my cigarettes and matches and my ashtray and went into the guest room, where my husband was asleep. I pushed at him and he snarled, but he finally moved over to the side next to the wall, and I put my cigarettes and matches and my brandy and my ashtray on the end table next to *his* cigarettes and matches and ashtray and tumbler of water and put my pillow on the bed and fell asleep. Shortly after this he woke me and asked me to let him get out of the bed, since it was too hot in that room to sleep and he was going back to his own bed. He took his pillow and his cigarettes and matches and his ashtray and his aluminum glass of water and went padding off down the hall. In a few minutes Laurie came into the guest room where I had just fallen asleep again; he was carrying his pillow and his glass of fruit juice. "Too cold in my room," he said, and I moved out of the way and let him get into the bed on the side next to the wall. After a few minutes the dog came in, whining nervously, and came up onto the bed and curled himself up around Laurie and I had to get out or be smothered. I gathered together what of my possessions I could, and made my way into my own room, where my husband was asleep with Jannie on one side and the baby on the other. Jannie woke up when I came in and said, "Own bed," so I helped her carry her pillow and her fruit juice and her pink blanket back to her own bed.

The minute Jannie got out of our bed the baby rolled over and turned sideways, so there was no room for me. I could not get into the crib and I could not climb into the top half of the double-decker, so since the dog was in the guest room I went and took the blanket off the crib and got into the bottom half of the double-decker, setting my brandy and my cigarettes and matches and my ashtray on the floor next to the bed. Shortly after that Jannie, who apparently felt left out, came in with her pillow and her pink blanket and her fruit juice and got up into the top half of the double-decker, leaving her fruit juice on the floor next to my brandy.

At about six in the morning the dog wanted to get out, or else he wanted his bed back, because he came and stood next to me and howled. I got up and went downstairs, sneezing, and let him out, and then decided that since it had been so cold anyway in the bottom half of the double-decker I might as well stay downstairs and heat up some coffee and have that much warmth, at least. While I was waiting for the coffee to heat Jannie came to the top of the stairs and asked if I would bring *her* something hot, and I heard Laurie stirring in the guest room, so I heated some milk and put it into a jug and decided that while I was at it I might just as well give everybody something hot so I set out enough cups for everyone and brought out a coffee cake and put it on the tray and added some onion rolls for my husband, who does not eat coffee cake. When I brought the tray upstairs Laurie and Jannie were both in the guest room, giggling, so I set the tray down in there and heard Sally talking from our room in the front. I went to get her and she was sitting up in the bed talking to her father, who was only very slightly awake. "Play card?"

she was asking brightly, and she opened her suitcase and dealt him, onto the pillow next to his nose, four diamonds to the ace jack and the seven of clubs.

I asked my husband if he would like some coffee, and he said it was terribly cold. I suggested that he come down into the guest room, where it was warmer. He and the baby followed me down to the guest room, and my husband and Laurie got into the bed and the rest of us sat on the foot of the bed and I poured the coffee and the hot milk and gave the children coffee cake and my husband the onion rolls. Jannie decided to take her milk and coffee cake back into her own bed, and since she had mislaid her pillow she took one from the guest room bed. Sally of course followed her, going first back into our room to pick up *her* pillow. My husband fell asleep again while I was pouring his coffee, and Laurie set his hot milk precariously on the headboard of the bed and asked me to get his pillow from wherever it was, so I went into the double-decker and got him the pillow from the top, which turned out to be Jannie's, and her pink blanket was with it. I took my coffee cake and my coffee into my own bed and had just settled down when Laurie came in to say cloudily that Daddy had kicked him out of bed and could he stay in here. I said of course and he said he would get a pillow and he came back in a minute with the one from the bottom half of the double-decker which was mine. He went to sleep right away, and then the baby came in to get her books and her suitcase and decided to stay with her milk and her coffee cake, so I left and went into the guest room and made my husband move over and sat *there* and had my coffee. Meanwhile Jannie had moved into the top half of the double-decker, looking for her pillow, and had taken instead the pillow from Sally's bed and my glass of brandy and had settled down there to listen to Laurie's radio. I went downstairs to let the dog in and he came upstairs and got into his bed on the bottom half of the double-decker, and while I was gone my husband had moved back over onto the accessible side of the guest room bed so I went into Jannie's bed, which is rather too short, and I brought a pillow from the guest room, and my coffee.

At about nine o'clock the Sunday papers came and I went down to get them, and at about nine-thirty everyone woke up. My husband had moved back into his own bed when Laurie and Sally vacated it for their own beds, Laurie driving Jannie into the guest room when he took back the top half of the double-decker, and my husband woke up at nine-thirty and found himself wrapped in Jannie's pink blanket, sleeping on Laurie's green pillow and with a piece of coffee cake and Sally's fruit juice glass, not to mention the four diamonds to the ace jack and the seven of clubs. Laurie, in the top half of the double-decker, had my glass of brandy and my cigarettes and matches and the baby's pink pillow. The dog had my white pillow and my ashtray. Jannie in the guest room had one white pillow and one blue pillow and two glasses of fruit juice and my husband's cigarettes and matches and ashtray and

Laurie's hot milk, besides her own hot milk and coffee cake and her father's onion rolls. The baby in her crib had her father's aluminum tumbler of water and her suitcase and books and doll and a blue pillow from the guest room, but no blanket.

The puzzle is, of course, what became of the blanket from Sally's bed? I took it off her crib and put it on the bottom half of the double-decker, but the dog did not have it when he woke up, and neither did any of the other beds. It was a blue-patterned patchwork quilt, and has not been seen since, and I would most particularly like to know where it got to. As I say, we are very short of blankets.

WITH COLDER WEATHER setting in, and school once more in sight, I took out the somewhat worn pair of red overalls which had had "Laurie" embroidered on them and crossed out, and "Jannie" embroidered underneath; I now crossed out the "Jannie" and embroidered "Sally" on them. They were a little thin in the seat, and the bottoms of the legs were frayed, but the sentiment was there. Sally also inherited hundreds of pullover shirts and thousands of unmatched socks. Laurie got a leather jacket, Jannie took to carrying a pocketbook, Ninki's third litter of kittens turned out to include one without a tail, and the family of a friend of Jannie's eagerly seized upon this one as a particularly delightful pet. Jannie entered a kind of private kindergarten, which consisted entirely of little girls and which met mornings in the home of a retired grade-school teacher; Jannie began to skip instead of walk and giggled unendurably with her friends. By the end of the first two weeks of school the mother of Jannie's friend called up indignantly to tell me that the kitten had suddenly begun to grow a tail, had grown half a tail and stopped, and that they now had a kitten with a half-tail, which they did not regard as a particularly delightful pet, and she strongly implied that we had deliberately misled them into believing that they were getting a kitten which would be permanently without a tail.

Sally at this time gave up any notion of being a co-operative member of a family, named herself "Tiger" and settled down to an unceasing, and seemingly endless, war against clothes, toothbrushes, all green vegetables, and bed. Her main weapon was chewing gum, which she stole out of Laurie's pockets and with which she could perform miracles of construction on her own hair, books, and, once, her father's typewriter.

I estimated that since we had moved into this house I had used up more than five hundred packages of chocolate pudding. A new school bus was proposed, to be put into service the next school year; the younger Harvey boy, who had been in high school when we moved into town, was to be the driver. Most reluctantly, with a great deal of hesitation and judicious packing and unpacking, and some vast confusion with white shirts, my husband made ready for a major trip to New York.

It was a solemn parting at the station; our two older children stood close to us, and Sally sat, rocking, on a luggage cart. Laurie had said "Where's the *train?*" four times, and Sally had indicated seven times that she planned to accompany her father. My husband had said perhaps eleven times that he was sure everything would be all right while he was gone, and I cannot remember how many times I must have said that he was not to worry about *us;* we would be fine. The train was fifteen minutes late, which gave us all time to repeat ourselves, and to make various other completely reasonable remarks like "Boy, I bet *you* wouldn't stand on those tracks when the train comes," (Laurie, to Jannie) and "Are you sure you packed those warm socks?" (me, to my husband) and "Suppose the train doesn't *ever* come?" (Jannie, to her father.)

"Old Mother Hubbid went to the cubbid," Sally said loudly and insistently.

"Boy," Laurie said to his father, "I sure wish that *train* would come. Let's go home," he said to me abruptly, "*he* can get on a train by hisself."

There was a general nervous stirring among the people on the platform; I had begun a stern remark to Laurie about how we had come here to say goodbye to Daddy, after all, but everyone began to say "Here it comes, here it comes," and Sally bounced up and down, shouting, and Jannie and Laurie both moved forward so that I had to grab quickly for the backs of their jackets. "Well," my husband said to me.

"Goodbye, goodbye," I said. My husband, running, turned and waved. The children all waved back enthusiastically and called "Goodbye, goodbye," and I hung on to the backs of their jackets. Sternly repressing a pang of honest envy, I watched the train move off and my husband waving at the window. "Well, children," I said at last, "home we go."

"Has Daddy gone?" Sally asked.

"All gone," Laurie said.

I shepherded them into the car, prevented Sally from climbing right on out the window on the other side, and began to pull on my gloves. "Old Mother Hubbid," Sally said, "went—"

"Hubbid, hubbid, hubbid," Laurie said. "What's so special about Mother Hubbid?"

"*I* was talking," Sally said with dignity. "Old—"

"Can't you ever talk about anything else in the *world?*"

"Can we have a popsicle?" Jannie asked, hanging over the back seat behind my head, "because Daddy's gone away, can we have a popsicle or a piece of bubble gum or a lollipop or a frozen custard or a popsicle? Because Daddy's gone away?"

"We're going directly home for dinner," I said. "Chocolate pudding for dessert."

"No chocolate pudding for *Dad*," Laurie said mournfully.

In honor of Daddy's departure we also had hot dogs and baked beans; I fed the children first and then, fighting down as unworthy the thought of my husband dining, no doubt, on roast beef and caviar in that haunt of iniquity and high living, the railroad dining car, I had my dinner on a tray, eating my hot dog absent-mindedly and reading a mystery story. The house was very quiet after the children were asleep, and I remembered suddenly, without at all wanting to, that our nearest neighbors had gone to Florida for the winter. I went to bed early, taking along my mystery story and the cat, and fell asleep with the light on. Several times during the night I awoke nervously, because the cat was restless, and although it was uncomfortable sleeping with the light on, I was reluctant to turn it off; there was a distinct ominous creaking in the hall just outside my door and I was growing increasingly positive that I smelled smoke. At any rate, I woke up in the morning cross and uncooperative, to find that it was seven-thirty instead of seven (had that ominous creaking been the alarm I had forgotten to set?) and that what looked and sounded like rain outside the window was, actually, rain. I leaped out of bed, slammed the window shut, turned off the light, opened the door and yelled, "Isn't anybody *up?*" There was a swift, answering disturbance, as of several children hastily dropping coloring books and crayons, and moving purposefully toward school clothes. My teeth not brushed (first things first, I kept telling myself), I hurried to the kitchen, set water on to boil for oatmeal, filled the fruit juice glasses, and—first things first—plugged in the coffee pot. By the time Jannie reached the kitchen I had the bowls and spoons out; I gave her a quick appraising glance and said, "Take off that necklace. Those are your best shoes and it's raining. Put on a sweater instead of that blouse. Brush your teeth." And, beyond her to Sally, "Shoes on wrong feet. And I put out a pair of decent overalls for you last night, not a sunsuit. And you've got to wear socks." I put back my head and shouted, "Laurie!"

After a minute he called back "I'm getting dressed."

"Sally," I said, "go and wake your brother."

"It's cold," Jannie said. She shivered elaborately. "It's *terribly* cold."

"If you had on a sweater instead of a silk blouse—" I said. "Sally, wake your *brother.*"

"I'm *cold*," Sally said.

"Awake," Laurie said, appearing in the kitchen doorway in his pajamas. "Hey, it's cold."

It began to occur to me that it *was* cold; I had been moving so fast up to now that I had not noticed the faint undefinable chill on everything I touched—the spoons, the cereal box, the backs of the chairs. I looked at Laurie, and Laurie looked at me, and then he said, nodding, "Yup. I sure bet it is."

I went into the living room, Laurie following me, Jannie following him, and Sally padding on behind, murmuring, "To get her poor doggie something to eat." The thermostat in the living room was set at seventy-two, the thermo-meter below it read sixty-one. I looked at Laurie again and he nodded reassuringly. Gingerly I turned the thermo-state up to seventy-five, to eighty, and, not breathing, we all listened. There was no answering roar from the cellar; the furnace was off.

I am not of a mechanical turn of mind. I am wholeheart-edly afraid of fuses and motorcycles and floor plugs and lightning rods and electric drills and large animals and most particularly of furnaces. Laboriously, over the space of years of married life, my husband has taught me to use such hazardous appliances as a toaster and an electric coffee pot, but no one is ever going to get me to go down cellar and fool around with a furnace. I had a fairly clear notion that the best way to get the house warm again was to march firmly to a little door in the monster's side and press the third little button from the left; my husband and the furnace man, working together, had once shown this to me, their voices rising shrilly as they explained it over and over; *no* furnace, my husband had said, touching his fore-head with the tips of his fingers, has ever exploded because some woman pressed the third little button from the left, *no* furnace. "Lady," the furnace man had said, twisting his hands together, "suppose some day you *got* to start the furnace, and no one's around, say, and you *got* to start it—"

Rising to heights of heroism far beyond my usual abil-ities, I strode responsibly to the cellar door, the children crowding along behind me. "The furnace seems to be off," I said to Laurie. "I'll just run down and start it up again."

"Yeah," Laurie said. "You go right on down." He regarded me without optimism.

I set my hand on the cellar doorknob. "But something might be broken," I said. (Was it the *third* little button from the left? The second? The right?) "I don't want to turn it on if it's broken," I said to Laurie. "I wouldn't like to do it any damage."

"It might be out of gas," Jannie suggested.

I turned to her gratefully. "That's right," I said. "Now I think of it, it would be very dangerous to turn it on if there's no oil. It grinds the parts together," I told Laurie, who nodded gravely. "I better call the man," I said.

Anyway, we were quite late. *Very* late, as a matter of fact; it was eight-thirty before I had gotten all the shoes tied, all the oatmeal consumed, the hair combed, the teeth brushed, the lunch boxes filled, the homework collected, the jackets on, the rubbers located, and had sneaked in a cup of coffee for myself. I lined the children out into the car, checking like an electric eye for handkerchiefs and contraband, and succeeded in rooting out and confiscating a small plastic telephone and two pieces of bubble gum from Sally and a large ring set with a glittering ruby from Jannie. I shut the car door behind them, raced around to the other side to catch Sally going out the opposite window, counted again to make sure I had three of them, and sat down in the driver's seat with a little sigh.

"If you got *up* earlier," Jannie said critically, "we wouldn't have to hurry so."

I opened my mouth to answer, reflected in time that the poor dears were at present fatherless, and said with great moderation, "Well, at least we're in plenty of time *now*." I pressed the starter.

Jannie giggled. "In Laurie's school he sits with the girls because he's so *pretty*."

"*Hey*, now, you—"

"Children," I said, "do be still." I pressed the starter. "After all," I said, with a light little laugh, "Jannie only teases Laurie because she knows he minds it; suppose *you* try keeping your temper, Laurie, and see how quickly she—" I pressed the starter.

"Old Mother *Hubbid*," Sally swept into the silence, "*she* went to the cubbid to get her dog something to eat, and when *she* started to get breakfast *she* had oatmeal." She began to laugh wildly. "Oatmeal," she repeated helplessly, "oatmeal."

I pressed the starter and pulled out the choke.

"Won't the star cart?" Jannie asked. Laurie began to shriek with laughter and after a bewildered minute Jannie joined in. "Old Mother *Hubbid*—" Sally began.

I pressed the starter and pulled out the choke and began to bang both hands on the steering wheel.

"Why don't you get out and crank it?" Laurie asked, howling.

"Why don't you get yourself a horse or something?" Jannie asked.

"Old Mother—"

"Just flooded it," I said, my voice level and restrained and even faintly amused. "Silly old car," I said affectionately, and gave a vicious kick at the clutch.

"Hey," Laurie said, suddenly no longer entertained, "we gonna be *late?*"

"Certainly not. Just tell the teacher that the car—"

"I told her that the *last* time," Laurie said. His voice became panicky. "And she said," he went on, "if I'm not in my sneakers by quarter of nine they'll get a substitute at left tackle and—"

"*Why* won't it start?" Jannie asked insistently. "What's the matter with the car?"

Fatherless or not, I raised my voice. "Never *mind,*" I said. I have been patient with my car through many of its moods, and there is little that we do not know about each other by now, the car and I. It knows perfectly, for instance, that I am made extremely nervous by a kind of low moaning sound it makes when it is unhappy, and I know clearly that if it has come into my car's obscure mind not to start, no siren's tricks of mine can make it. "Sell the filthy thing for fifty cents," I said nastily, and climbed out and went into the house, mumbling to myself, and dialed our village taxi.

"Again?" Mr. Williams said when I told him. "You figure it's the battery again?"

"The children," I said, "have just seven minutes to get to school."

"Well, they won't make it," he said. "Time I get up there and back again. But I figure it ain't going to shock the teachers none, them being late again." He giggled, and I hung up.

I saw Laurie and Jannie off to school in the taxi, stowing away lunch boxes and books, and cautioning Jannie firmly against getting out at the graded school instead of her kindergarten; I asked Mr. Williams to pick Jannie up at twelve and Laurie at three, and said I would pay him later, it being nearly nine o'clock by now. Then—first things first—I came back into the house and shut Sally into her room with her blocks and took up the telephone; since my teeth were chattering I called first of all the number of K. B. Anderson, Plumbing and Heating, and got Mrs. Anderson, who answered the phone mornings in the office. I told her who I was, and all about how our furnace had gone out, and asked could Mr. Anderson please come right over?

"Well," she said, "not *this* morning. He won't be back till dinner-time and then this afternoon he's got to put in a heater over to Sawyer's. Tomorrow, maybe."

"But we have no heat and the children—"

"Maybe not even tomorrow, though, now I think of it," she went on. "On account of that plumber's convention up to Waterville tonight. And you know what *they* are."

I agreed with haste that I did indeed know what they

were, and said anxiously that it was getting colder here, and the children—

"Whyn't you try young Dick Sampson over on Bridge Street?" she asked. "*He* used to do some plumbing afore he was married."

"Sampson?"

"No, it's not Bridge Street at all. I don't know what made me think it *was*. He *used* to be on Bridge Street, but then he took over that television repair service."

"So he won't be going to the plumber's convention?" I asked politely.

"Not *him*," she said with satisfaction. "He married one of the Wiley girls, *that's* why I thought first of Bridge Street. Mildred, I'd say it was."

"But the furnace—"

"East Main," she said. "Knew it would come to me. Or you might even try to get ahold of Bill England. There's one might know what to do, or any of the Hope boys."

"Thanks very much," I said. As I hung up, staring hopelessly at the names I had jotted down (I knew the Hope boys, and I would as soon have frozen to death) it occurred to me that among all the friends I had in town I might locate one with a husband who was not afraid to go down into our cellar and look at our furnace. Nancy, I thought; she and Cliff had once come over and helped us put down a rug. I dialed Nancy and she answered and I asked her how she was and she asked me how *I* was and I told her about my husband's being out of town and she told me about the new chairs they were getting for the porch and I said how I had meant to call her and she said it had been so long since we got together and I said we must have a bridge game sometime next week and she said she would call me and I said I'd get in touch with her and I was just about to hang up when I remembered and said oh, look, there was something I meant to ask her. So I told her the furnace was off and I didn't know how to start it and she said why didn't I call Anderson?

"There's a plumber's convention," I said.

"Again? But when William dropped the hairbrush down the drain and I called Anderson, Mrs. Anderson said there was a plumber's convention *then*. And that was only about six weeks ago because my mother—"

"But do you think that Cliff—?"

"He'd love to," she assured me. "I'll send him over just as soon as he gets home. He'll be *glad* to do it."

We decided we would certainly get in touch with one another very soon, and hung up. I called Eddie at the garage and asked him to come and get my car again, and he sighed and said did I think it was still going to be the fan belt this time? I washed the breakfast dishes and made the beds, and it occurred to me that when Eddie came for the car I might ask *him* to go down cellar and start the furnace, him being a mechanic and all, but when he finally did come for the car, I was on the phone; Nancy had called back to say she was sorry, it wasn't a plumber's convention, it was an oil burner convention, and she had done Mr. Anderson an injustice. So we agreed that we would have a bridge game real soon, and by that time Eddie had disappeared with my car. At lunchtime the taxi brought Jannie home from school and I recalled with abrupt clarity that I had meant to stop on my way that morning and pick up a loaf of bread. I gave Jannie and Sally crackers and peanut butter for lunch, and while they were murmuring sadly in the kitchen I went to the phone and called my friend Carol. She asked how I was and I asked how she was and she told me about the bad cold her boy had been having and I told her about my husband's being out of town and she said we must get together some evening soon. I said I would call her, and meanwhile would she mind picking up a loaf of bread for me when she went down to the store? Because something had gone wrong with my car. She said sympathetically that you certainly needed a car out on our road, didn't you, and did I mind being alone in our big house at night? I said no, oh, no, I was never nervous, and could she also get me a can of tunafish? I felt urgently that there was something I had forgotten, but had no time to stop and think because she was saying was there anything else? It was no trouble at all. So I told her that would be plenty, thanks, and it was so nice of her, and we must surely get together some time real soon.

I put Sally to bed for her nap, settled Jannie with puzzles and books to rest in Laurie's room, made myself some crackers and peanut butter, and sat down again with my mystery story. About two o'clock the small persistent nagging which had stayed with me since I spoke to Carol suddenly resolved itself when I discovered that the motive for the murder in my book had been a large inheritance. Money, I thought. Hadn't my husband given me a check to cash this morning?

The check was in my pocketbook, along with three quarters and a penny. Although Carol would hardly press me for the price of a loaf of bread and a can of tunafish, today was Tuesday and the laundryman was due. The check was surely too large for him to cash, but if I let the laundry bill go for a week, there was Mr. Williams to be paid for the taxis. If I told Mr. Williams I would pay him tomorrow, I could pay Carol for the loaf of bread and the can of tunafish. But tomorrow was Wednesday and that meant that before school Laurie and Jannie would each need thirty-five cents for milk money and my mind stopped dully before the problem of dividing three quarters into two thirty-five-centses. I was debating shelving the whole matter and going back to bed when there was a knock at the back door, and when I opened it, there was Mr. Anderson. "Missus said I should come right over," he explained. "Said you had no heat for the kids."

"The furnace is off," I said, to clarify the situation. "It's down cellar." Mr. Anderson—perhaps because of his pressing social obligations—operates always on a strictly cash basis; there is a rumor about him, implicitly believed by me, that if he is not paid immediately he goes right back downstairs and breaks the furnace again. "I hope you can fix it," I said weakly as Mr. Anderson disappeared down the cellar stairs, conversing cheerily as he went; by the time he had begun a sort of rhythmic banging on the boiler I was in Laurie's room, my back carefully turned to Jannie, examining his wallet, which contained eleven cents—not even enough to solve the milk money problem. I had been hoping for the five dollars his grandparents had sent him for a football, and would have kicked myself when I remembered that I had personally driven him into town so he could spend it on model cars. His bank, however, was on the dresser.

"What you doing?" Jannie asked from the bed. She put down a piece of puzzle to watch me.

"Looking for something," I said truthfully.

"Oh," Jannie said. "Is it there?"

"Yep," I said.

By the time Mr. Anderson came stamping back upstairs I was sitting cheerfully at the dining room table, running my fingers richly through a heap of nickels and dimes. "Just needed starting up, is all," Mr. Anderson said, frowning dubiously at the ornamental cow which is Laurie's bank and at the table knife I had been using to pry my way into it; "Could of done it yourself."

I laughed lightly, as befits a lady who would rather rob a bank than touch a furnace, and said, "And what do I owe you, Mr. Anderson?"

"Dollar'll do it," he said, and watched wide-eyed while

I carefully counted out a dollar in nickels and dimes and swept it off the table and poured it into his hand. "*There* you are," I said. "I hope you don't mind change."

"Well, thanks," Mr. Anderson said. He closed his big hand around the money and carried it that way to the back door, and I followed him, talking with animation about how glad I was that there had been nothing really *wrong* with the furnace, and didn't it look like it might stop raining, after all. Mr. Anderson got into his truck, jingling, and drove off down the driveway without looking back, and I went back to my heap of money and began to set it out in piles of nickels and dimes, humming to myself. I could hardly leave the bank entirely empty, in case Laurie picked it up and expected it to rattle, so I reluctantly returned half a dozen nickels to it. That, it turned out, left me enough to pay the laundryman, but for the garbage man, whom I had completely forgotten, I had to resort to Jannie, who was quite poor, and, with Sally's meagre collection of pennies, left me with forty-three cents in pennies and my original three quarters. Carol came with my loaf of bread and my can of tunafish and resolutely declined to take the pennies, because if she took them home she would only have to put them in *her* penny bank. I had to let the taxi go without paying Mr. Williams, since by that time I had put all the banks carefully back in place and I felt that it might look suspicious to Laurie if I tried paying the taxi fare in pennies. While I was making the creamed tunafish for supper Cliff came to fix the furnace, and I told him that Mr. Anderson had already come, but would he mind getting the top off this jar of mayonnaise? He hit it with a table knife and held it under hot water and tried it in the door jamb and I said I would make a vinegar dressing instead and he said oh, yes, Nancy thought I might like to come over for some bridge tonight; they could get a fourth.

I was about to accept with pleasure when I recalled that our baby-sitter's toll has gone up to forty cents an hour, and since I *had* to have milk money I could afford to play only forty-eight cents worth of bridge, or barely one rubber. So I said, smiling bravely, that I thought I had better stay at home with my fatherless children. Eddie brought my car back about seven; "Carburetor," he said briefly, wiping the steering wheel with a greasy sleeve before getting out. "All set now."

My husband called that night and asked how was everything going, and I said well, the car had broken down and the furnace had gone out and I had run out of money and no one could get the top off the mayonnaise. He asked had he better come right home? and I said of course not, everything was fine *now*, except for the mayonnaise. He was just back from having dinner with friends, he said, and was on his way to a poker game.

I went to bed about ten and lay awake for two hours listening to a funny noise going on somewhere in the cellar or the attic or maybe it was only someone prowling around outside. When I woke up the next morning the sun was out and the children were laughing in the kitchen and I lay in bed for a minute thinking of how a day full of troubles and annoyances, like yesterday, always brought a fine day like today, and I must be sure to remember this in future. Cheerfully I made cream of wheat for breakfast, filled the lunchboxes, brushed the hair, tied the shoes, gathered the books, and got everyone shepherded into the car by twenty after eight. "Well, well," I said, "we're in plenty of time *this* morning."

"Laurie sits with the girls, Laurie sits with the girrrrrrls."

"Now you *listen—*"

"Old Mother *Hubbid—*"

"Children," I said, a smile in my voice, "let's not be cross with one another on such a beautiful day. Let's all be *happy*, and *glad* the *sun* is out. Let's everyone *smile.*"

I pressed the starter.

"Cubbid."

I pressed the starter again.

THE INDEFINABLE SENSE of harvest entered the house, of apples to be stored away, of Christmas in the perceptible future. A fever of activity seized me, and I painted the girls' bookcase yellow. The lawn furniture came indoors and I began wondering if the snowsuits could go another winter. One day I brought Jannie home a little silk scarf, blue and pink check, and she accepted it with pleasure, remarking that she would surely, surely wear it to school the next day. She wore it tied fashionably around her neck, in a trim bow, and I pointed it out to her father, who said it looked very nice indeed. The next day she had threaded her little scarf casually through the top button-hole of her jacket; the day after that she tied it loosely around her hair in back. Wondering, I went off and got myself a little purple scarf. I spent fifteen minutes trying to tie it loosely around my hair in back and it made me look like a chorus girl dressed as a rabbit. I gave my purple scarf to Jannie, and she tied it to her pink and blue one, and wore the two together as a belt around the top of her skirt, from which she had removed the shoulder-straps. The next day she had one tied around her wrist and the other neatly folded on her dresser. Timidly I offered her two more, one gold and one green, and the next day Sally came to breakfast with her hair tied into a topknot with the green one; Jannie was wearing the gold one in *her* hair. I pointed this out to her father, and he said it looked very nice indeed. Emboldened, I came to Jannie with a little white scarf I had bought and asked her to tie up my hair for me and she brought a chair and a hairbrush and worked over me for quite a while, fussing and murmuring and clucking her tongue. Finally she got down and came around and looked at me from the front and sighed and said "Well, go show Daddy." I went and showed Daddy and he looked at me for a long minute and then looked at Jannie, and Jannie shrugged and my husband said to me,

"Whatever happened to that nice blue dress you used to wear? The one I liked?"

I gave the little white scarf to Jannie and went off sullenly and spent the rest of the day mothproofing bathing suits.

Laurie came home from school at about that time with a frightful little ditty which began "Salami was a dancer who danced before the king, and every time she danced she didn't wear a thing . . ." Jannie learned it immediately and they chanted it in chorus. Sally laboriously learned to sing "Jingle Bells."

Two days before his eighth birthday, Laurie rode his bike around a bend, directly into the path of a car. I can remember with extraordinary clarity that one of the people in the crowd which gathered handed me a lighted cigarette, I can remember saying reasonably that we all ought not to be standing in the middle of the road like this, I can remember the high step up into the ambulance. When they told us at the hospital, late that night, that everything was going to be all right, we came home and I finished drying the breakfast dishes. Laurie woke up in the hospital the next morning, with no memory of anything that had happened since breakfast two days before, and he was so upset by the thought that he had ridden in an ambulance and not known about it that the ambulance had to be engaged again to bring him home two weeks later, with the sirens screaming and an extremely proud

Jannie sitting beside him and traffic separating on either side.

We put him, of course, into our bedroom; my mother always used to put sick children into the "big" bed, and I have still that half-remembered feeling that it is one of the signs of being *really* sick, sick enough to stay home from school. My mother, however, never had to cope with anything more complex than my brother's broken arm: I had under my wavering care this active patient with concussion, a broken hand, and various patched-up cuts and bruises; who was not, under doctor's orders, to excite himself, to move his arm; who was not, most particularly, to raise his head or try to turn over; and who was not, it was clearly evident, going to pay any attention to anything the doctor said.

"Now I'm home I can have whatever I want," Laurie announced immediately I arrived in the room with the tray of orange juice, plain toast, and chicken soup which my mother before me believed was the proper basic treatment for an invalid; he cast a disapproving eye at the tray, and said, "Doc said I could have *real* food."

"The most important thing," I told him, "is for you to keep yourself quiet, and warm, and not excited. That dog, for instance."

Toby buried his huge head under the pillow and tried to pretend that he was invisible. "What dog?" said Laurie.

"And," I went on with great firmness, patting Toby absently on the shoulder, "you are absolutely not to lift your head and you are absolutely not to move without help and if you do—"

"I got to go back to the hospital," Laurie said. He wiggled comfortably into the hollow under Toby's chin. "It wasn't so bad there," he said. "*Food* was good, anyway."

"Jannie and Sally are not allowed in this room. No visitors at all for at least a week."

Shax moved softly into the doorway, looked at me and then speculatively at Laurie, and then walked sedately across the room and went up onto the bed, where he settled down without haste next to Laurie's feet, purring. Laurie grinned at me. "Jannie's already *been* here," he said. "She was telling me one of her stories while you were downstairs fixing that junk on the tray, and Sally brought me her teddy bear."

I sighed.

"It's under the covers somewhere," Laurie said. "Doc said you would tell me all about it, all about what happened."

"We won't think about it."

"Doc said I was hit by a car."

"So you were."

"I don't remember." Laurie was accusing. "Seems as though I'd remember *some*thing about it."

"I think it's just as well," I said. "Better to remember pleasant things than sad ones."

"What's so sad about *this?*"

"Keep your head down." I settled back in the armchair and took up my book. "You go to sleep; I'll sit right here."

Laurie closed his eyes obediently, but Toby wriggled and Laurie laughed. "Listen," he said, "tell me about it."

"There's nothing you don't already know," I said. "It's all over, after all."

"Was there a lot of blood?"

"Laurie, surely—"

"*Was* there?"

"There was some," I said reluctantly.

"On the road?"

"Yes. Keep your head down."

"Gee," Laurie said luxuriously. "And the cops—did the cops come? Doc said the cops called him."

"Officer Harrison was there, and he took charge of everything. It was Sunday and he was home cutting his lawn and he came right over when he heard—when it happened."

"When he heard the crash," Laurie said. "Gee, what a noise it must of made."

"Keep your *head* down."

"How many cops?"

"Officer Harrison, and Mr. Lanza, and two or three others I didn't know. I called the State police station and thanked them a few days ago. They were very happy to hear that you were so much better."

"Doc said you fainted."

"I did *not*." I sat up indignantly.

"Did Daddy faint?"

"Certainly not."

"Did Jannie faint?"

"I sent Jannie and Sally down to the Olsons'," I said. "They don't know very much about it."

"I won't tell them," Laurie said reassuringly. "What about my bike—is it all right?"

"Well," I said, "no, it isn't. As a matter of fact, it's broken."

"I *bet* it is," said Laurie, with relish. "Boy, did that bike ever get smacked—I bet it's in a million pieces."

"Keep your head down."

"Hey, what about my clothes?" Laurie said, remembering. "I woke up in the hospital and I had on a night-gown; what about my clothes?"

"Since you're feeling so well," I said, remembering, "I might as well point out that even though I was quite worried about you, I was positively ashamed when they undressed you at the hospital. I distinctly remember telling you to put on clean clothes that morning, and whatever may be said for your shirt, your underwear—"

"They undressed me at the hospital? Who?"

"The nurse. And when I saw that underwear—"

"The *nurse? She* undressed me?"

"Keep your head *down.*"

"Oh, brother," said Laurie. He thought, while Toby, his head on the pillow, breathed heavily and happily, and

Shax stirred, lifted his head, and curled up more comfortably. "Where are my clothes now?" Laurie asked finally.

"Your shoes are put neatly—*neatly*—under the chair in your room. That underwear has been sent to the laundry, and your socks and blue jeans, too." I hesitated. "Your shirt was thrown out," I said.

"Why?" Laurie demanded. "*Why* was my shirt thrown out?"

"It was torn," I said.

"Torn? You mean it was covered with blood or something?"

"No," I said. "It was torn. Cut."

"Cut?"

"Keep your head down. They cut it off you at the hospital."

"They did?" Laurie said, his eyes shining. "They had to *cut* it off?"

"Well, they *preferred* to."

"Where is it?"

"I told you, it was thrown out. They gave me your clothes at the hospital and told me the shirt was thrown out."

Laurie asked accusingly, "You didn't keep that shirt? All covered with blood and you didn't *keep* it?"

"Why should I keep it?"

"Which one was it? The green checked one?"

"That was the one you took off in the morning. You put on the new shirt with the baseball picture."

"*That* one? My new one?"

"There are plenty of others," I said, making a mental note about never going near those baseball shirts again. "How about you go to sleep now?"

"That good baseball shirt? And you went and threw it out?"

"You couldn't have worn it again."

"Who wants to *wear* it?" said Laurie. "What else happened?"

"Well," I said, "Brooklyn lost the pennant that same afternoon."

"I heard the Series in the hospital," Laurie said. "What a robbery."

"Would you like to go to sleep now?"

"I bet Dad was nearly crazy," Laurie said.

"Not at all," I said, "he was—"

"Losing the last day like that. Gee," Laurie said, squeezing down between Toby and Shax, "it's not bad being home."

A month later, with satisfaction only secondary to Laurie's, I took him back to school to pick up his books so he could try to catch up on his work. "Remember," I told him in the car before we went into the school, "thank the teacher and the kids for the nice basket they sent you."

"Yeah," Laurie said. He had chosen ten in the morning as the ideal moment to present himself at school.

"And don't forget to thank the teacher for her flowers."

"Yeah."

"And tell her I'll help you at home with arithmetic."

"Come *on*," Laurie said.

We entered the classroom in triumph; Laurie threw open the door and stood for a moment in the doorway before advancing with a swagger Cyrano might have envied. "I'm back," he said into the quiet of the spelling lesson.

"Thank you *so* much for the flowers," I told the teacher. "Laurie appreciated them *so* much."

Laurie sat on one of the front desks, holding his hand with the traction splint prominently displayed. All the third-grade girls gathered around him, and the boys sat on the floor and on nearby desks. "—And I guess there were five hundred people there," he was saying, "they came tearing in from all over. And the street—you oughta seen the street—*covered* with blood—"

"I'll go over his arithmetic with him," I told the teacher.

"He was doing splendidly," she said absently, her eyes on Laurie.

"—And my good shirt, they had to *cut* it off me, ten doctors, and there was so much blood on it they had to throw it away because it was all cut to pieces and bloody. And I went in an ambulance with the sireens and boy! did *we* travel. Boy!"

"And will he need to go over his reading?"

"Excuse me," said Laurie's teacher. Unwillingly, she moved closer to the spellbinder, her hand still reassuringly on my arm. "And my mother fainted," he was saying, "and my *father* . . ."

THREE

SOMETIMES, IN MY capacity as mother, I find myself sitting open-mouthed and terrified before my own children, little individual creatures moving solidly along in their own paths and yet in some mysterious manner vividly reminiscent of a past which my husband and I know we have never communicated to them; I remember the little shock of familiarity I felt when I first saw Jannie skip down the front walk, and the sense of lost years slipping past, unrealized, when Laurie came home chanting "O U T spells out, and out you go, down to the bottom of the deep blue sea with a dirty dishrag turned inside *out*," although there was a heated family discussion about the second line of "Ibbitty, Bibbitty, Sibbitty, Sab," because Laurie believed that it went "Ibbitty, bibbitty, conoso," and *I* said it was "conothco," and my husband said it was "Ibbitty, bibbitty, canarsie," and it reminded me of the little idiocy which went "Laurie bumbaurie

tiliaurie gosaurie," although my husband said that *that* one
ended "gotaurie." Sally discovered in herself the ability to
chant that most basic and most jeering of childhood tunes,
the "*da*, da, da-*da*, da," or "*I* know a *se*cret," melody;
Laurie began collecting pictures of baseball players, which
came enclosed in packages of bubble gum; in my day
they used to be in packages of licorice. The candy cigarette turned up, and the chocolate apple; they no longer
give away baseball bats with pairs of new shoes, but Bus-
ter Brown still grins with his dog from the soles. A whole
section of forgotten past came back, for instance, one
evening when Laurie remarked joyfully that a house near
the school had a ghost in it and none of the kids from
school would walk past it, although one intrepid adven-
turer named Oliver maintained that he had been inside and
had of course seen the ghost, and "Boy," Laurie said with
reminiscent pleasure, "was *he* scared!"

My husband and I looked at one another; in my case
it was a house on the next block—the one next to the
vacant lot—and the boy who said he had been inside was
named Andy Young (how is it that I have not forgotten
Andy Young in all these years?) and my husband remembered that there was a shack at the back of the school
yard which had a ghost in it and that one Louie Fair
had been inside. In all cases the punchline of the story
was precisely, "Boy, was *he* scared!" My husband and I
found ourselves repeating the same amused platitudes
about boys who went into haunted houses that our parents

had used to us, Laurie retorted that *every*one knew this house was haunted and he bet *we* wouldn't go inside, and there was a familiar split-second hesitation before my husband and I answered, in chorus, that *certainly* we would go inside, if it were not that the house belonged to someone else who would presumably resent our entering without permission. Laurie said Boy, he bet a ghost was sure a scarey thing to see, and his father offered to compose a document demonstrating that our house was haunted if Laurie would take copies of this document and distribute them, like handbills, around the neighborhood. Laurie agreed with delight, and the conversation closed, in traditional style, with the flat statement that Laurie was not to go into the haunted house under any circumstances since it was a) someone else's property and b) if abandoned, probably dangerous, with broken glass and falling beams. Point c) was not mentioned, but I personally have always believed in ghosts; I taught Laurie later a small charm against evil spirits, disguising it as a nursery rhyme. The handbill * was duly composed and Laurie set out with it, although along the way he fell in with evil spirits against whom his charm was powerless and played two innings of softball; when his father asked him later about the handbill he said that Mrs. Wright, down the road, had read it and thought it was very clever and asked Laurie if he had written it himself. Mrs. Collins had not had time to read it right then but said she would send

* See Appendix.

over a plate of cookies later. By the time school started again in the fall, gang warfare had taken over the fourth grade and the ghost was allowed to languish in his haunted house, untroubled again by Oliver, although I daresay that when someday Laurie's son remarks that a friend of *his* has explored a haunted house, Oliver's name will come, freely and with nostalgia, to Laurie's mind.

The opening of school that fall found Sally, scorning the overalls which now read ~~LAURIE JANNIE~~ SALLY, preparing to enter upon nursery school. Jannie's girls had all retired abruptly to a ranch in Texas, from which they very rarely wrote illegible letters to their mother, but Sally now had a house of her own, located approximately and damply in the middle of the river near *our* house; we all heard a great deal about this retreat of Sally's, in which a number of small children Sally's age lived in utter happiness upon lollipops and corn on the cob. Sally visited there, she explained, at night after the rest of us were asleep, and when she was particularly angry with any of us she shouted furiously, "*You* can't come to *my* house!"

Sally had at this time entered with complete abandon into a form-fitting fairyland; I saw her sometimes as wandering perpetually in a misty odd world, where familiar shapes merged and changed as she passed and occasionally a brother or a sister or a parent, stepping from behind a tree, might briefly interrupt her journey; with the exception of Jannie, who slept in the same room and had no refuge from Sally's bedroom stories, I spent more time with Sally than with anyone else, and began to find that a large part of my daily activity was accompanied by Sally's tuneful and unceasing conversation; part song, part story, part uncomplimentary editorial comment. Around the house, my head deep in a pillowcase or the oven, my eyes focussed on that supernatural neatness which the housewife sees somehow shadowing her familiar furniture, it was largely possible to disregard, or not-quite-hear, Sally, but in the car I was entirely what I believe is called a captive audience. We traveled far afield that fall, Sally and I, up and down familiar and unfamiliar roads, going perhaps after pumpkins, or taking a side road because for a minute it looked unusually yellow to Sally, or just going the longest way around because it took us over a covered bridge crossing Sally's river and people living nearby owned a baby goat. "In my river," Sally remarked once, chillingly, "we sleep in wet beds, and we hear our mothers calling us,"—giving me a sudden terrifying picture of my own face, leaning over the water, wavering, and my voice far away and echoing; "The water is probably *extremely* cold," I told her, and shivered. "In the river," Sally said, "no one ever comes except *us*." We drove upon occasion, Sally and I, up and down Murphy's Hill, which was every bit as steep going up as it was going down and led only to a kind of plateau neatly edged with trees; in the fall these trees presented an appearance sufficiently startling to make a trip up (and of course down) Murphy's Hill a rewarding experience even beyond its roller coaster aspects; the vines on the trunks of these trees turned red early, and the trees stayed green late, and a row of straight, youthful green trees with bright red trunks was a sight I have never seen *except* at the top of Murphy's Hill.

Sally habitually rode standing on her head in the back seat, and gave every sign of regarding me as perhaps an additional fixture to the car, a sort of extension of the steering wheel; her conversation included me casually, and my comments became a sort of counterpoint to which she attended when it was necessary, perhaps, to find a rhyme, or perfect a rhythm; we found ourselves one day on a back road, turning a corner suddenly into a herd of cows.

"Do you know who I am?" Sally was singing, on her head in the back seat, "DO YOU KNOW WHO I AM?"

The cows were wandering vaguely—very much, I suppose, in the manner of cows unsupervised and not in the least pleased about it; they crowded the road and moved in all directions at once. "I'm a rat and you're a fish," Sally sang, "and now you know who I am."

"Do turn yourself rightside up," I said. "The road is covered with cows and I can't see out the back window."

There was nothing to do, of course, but stop the car and wait until some avenue opened itself through the cows. I am earnestly afraid of all large animals; I closed the car windows tight and cringed in my seat, entirely convinced that a cow was going to try to climb onto, or into, the car. "Look at all the cows," I said to Sally with a sort of wild gaiety; I did not, after all, want to communicate to a small child my fears, which might possibly be unfounded; "I guess you never saw *this* many cows before."

"*These* are not cows," Sally said. "*These* are giants."

"See how they stop and look at us," I remarked airily, moving over into the center of the front seat. "I suppose *they* wonder what *we* are." I grinned back convulsively at a bovine face next to the window. "Nice cow," I said.

"Lots and lots and *lots* of giants, and when *I* see giants I know their mothers are coming to eat me."

This corresponded so nearly to my own apprehensions that, wildly disregarding the probable suicidal result of frightening a herd of cows into a stampede, I slammed my hand down onto the horn and my foot onto the gas pedal. The cows backed away and turned, lumbering against one another, and finally determined unanimously on one direction, which was down the road ahead of us; running, so that with Sally calling encouragement from a rear window and me leaning on the horn, we found ourselves in the odd position of chasing a herd of cows swiftly down a country road. "Run, giants, run," Sally shouted out the window. I made a broad screaming turn onto a side road and pulled up, panting and listening to the thunder of hooves as the cows made off into the distance. "Golly," I said.

"Giants are very nice sometimes," Sally remarked, turning herself upside down, "and sometimes giants are not very nice and sometimes giants are very nice and sometimes giants are—"

It was the day of Sally's fingers, I think, when we went to get the apples. There was a farm not far away where they sold an honest frost-bitten apple and had a speckled hen in a cage, and Sally and I made it, that fall, one of our regular stopping-off places; Sally was always given an apple to eat, and I always admired the speckled hen, and we came home with the car full of apples and their rich scent; on this day Sally had amused herself by counting the fingers on her left hand, which came out six, and the fingers in her glove, which came out five, and she was deeply involved in the problem of accommodating her fingers into the glove, which had unreasonably fit perfectly until now; the road was narrow and winding, and I was humming to myself and watching the way the sun came through the colored trees. We moved without any recognition of danger onto a scene of fire; I realized as we came around a corner that there had been a vague sense of activity and noise ahead, but as I slowed down the wild approach of the fire engine sounded behind me and I had no choice but to pull my car quickly over into the ditch as the engine rushed by. So there we sat, Sally and I, in the car, unable to turn and go back the way we had come, surely unable to go forward, and—I, at least—most unwilling to stay where we were. "Is it a giant?" Sally asked uncertainly, coming over into the front seat to look out, "is it a giant, or what?"

"It's a fire," I said. "That farmhouse is burning."

"Why?" Sally asked.

I thought fleetingly that perhaps this would be a good time to warn Sally against playing with matches, but my moment had passed; "It looks like a giant to *me*," she said. "Are we going to stay here?"

"Until the road ahead is clear," I said. "We've got to wait till those other cars get out of the way, because we can't turn around."

"Then I will have another apple," Sally said. She returned to the back seat, found an apple, and stood herself up on her head. "I am going to sing an apple song," she said.

We had to stay there for over an hour; it was quite a fire. Had the farmer whose home was burning been of a philosophical turn—which I am fairly sure he was not—and believed that he was due for at least one fire during his lifetime and was having it now, he might have taken great consolation in the way this one came off; his livestock, I learned from brief bulletins from the firemen, was safe, his children securely at school, his wife and farmhands unharmed, his insurance invulnerable, and as we arrived they had been carrying out his television set. The sound country policy of letting the burning house go and trying to save the buildings nearby was being put into practice; the fire hose stretched nicely to Sally's river, and although the house and barn, which were close to one another and both hopelessly lost, flamed ominously, the firemen were successfully soaking down the other outbuildings and the one or two neighboring houses. There was not even a wind.

"I'm a sweetie," Sally sang, "I'm a honey, I'm a poppacorn, I'm a potato chip, all my days for you."

My principal feeling, beyond the primitive terror of the fire itself, was of embarrassment. I was deeply concerned lest these people assume that we, my daughter and I, had come curiously to watch their fire. I wanted very much to catch hold of one of the firemen and explain that we were here entirely by accident, like the fire itself; we had been passing by, I would tell him, on our way home from buying apples, and had been caught by chance on this road; we did not ordinarily race fire engines to fires, I would go on, but in this case, what with the narrow road . . .

"Aren't they through *yet?*" Sally demanded over my shoulder.

"Almost," I said. "The fire engine is getting ready to leave."

"We shouldn't of stayed *this* long," Sally said.

I pulled out of the ditch, and waved cheerily to the farmer's wife as we went by. We reached home to find the rest of our family waiting restlessly for dinner.

"We got apples," I said to my husband, "and we saw—"

"*Giants.*" Sally swung wildly on her father's arm, "*Giants.*" She nodded.

"Giants?" my husband asked me, staring.

"There was a big giant party and they were cooking marshmallows," Sally said. She caught Jannie in a long ominous look. "*Giant* marshmallows." Her voice dropped to a compelling whisper. "And the giants were all stamping around and the *mother* giant sat there and watched them, and the mother giant said 'Wait till those other cars get out of the way and then we can go home.' And I had ninety-seven apples. And we came over the river and the mother giant went in and got drowned dead." There was a short, respectful silence.

Finally Laurie inquired of his father, "Who was Aristides the Just?"

"Friend of your mother's," my husband said absently. "Apple pie?" he said hopefully to me.

"I got to do a report," Laurie said.

"Y'know something?" Jannie asked me. She glanced around at her younger sister and then went on in a low voice, "I don't believe it when Sally tells about giants. Do you?"

"Certainly not," I said. "She's just making it up." And recognized clearly that there was no ring of conviction whatever in my voice. "My goodness," I said heartily, "who's afraid of *giants?*"

During that fall the conflict of individual cultures in our family became explicit, and uncontrollable. My husband and I, a little frayed after a number of years spent—it seems—almost entirely in the society of small children, had managed to build up little sets of foibles which we were reluctant to sacrifice. Laurie had developed opinions which could only be called decided. Sally had not so far seen any reason for doubting that anything could be achieved if you just made enough noise about it. Jannie, who had never in her life doubted anything she said herself although no parental pronouncements sounded to her entirely impartial or, no matter how emphatic, reasonable, entered first grade that fall and came into contact with the public school system.

Now, I have nothing against the public school system as it is presently organized, once you allow the humor of its basic assumption about how it is possible to teach things to children, and my experiences with Laurie have convinced me that the schools are well enough, and my children are well enough, and it is only any chance combination of these two which is apt to become explosive. Laurie succeeded in fighting his way to the fourth grade without showing any noticeable signs of contact with education, but Jannie brought up against the school an impact which must have been felt in the very bedrock of learning, and which certainly put a crack in the family hearthstone.

I had been warned that when a little girl goes to school she prefers to wear dresses and pigtails, but Jannie thought she would rather wear shorts the first day, and an old baseball hat of Laurie's. I struggled out of bed on the morning which was to see Jannie off to school for the first time and combed my hair and dressed myself with the idea of appearing before teachers and other mothers, escorting my daughter, but Jannie told me at breakfast, "If I am going to go to school at *all*, I think I would prefer to go by myself."

After five busy years I no longer attempted to argue with Jannie before breakfast; I nodded and slipped my shoes off under the breakfast table. "You don't mind my coming to the door to wave goodbye to you, I suppose?" I asked, and Jannie, considering, said, "If you don't cry or something."

"Do I have to take *her* to school?" Laurie demanded. "On the bus and all?"

Laurie regarded the new school bus as his personal and exclusive conveyance. "She's got to go to school," I said. "They don't let children grow up and not go to school."

Laurie, regarding his sister, laughed bitterly, and Jannie said, "I believe I'll sit in the other end of the bus from Laurie. I don't care for unpolite boys."

"Do I have to hold her hand?" Laurie asked.

"Certainly you do not," Jannie said. "I prefer to go by myself, thank you. If I am going to school at *all*, that is."

The notion that she might, upon consideration, decide not to go to school at all, was enough for me. "Will you be careful?" I asked.

"Once," Jannie remarked exclusively to Sally, "I had a friend named Susan, and Susan went to the horse racing and she betted on a horse named Susan, and the horse fell through the side of the track and all the horses went to see if he was all right and he had broken the gate and all the men got away and the horses couldn't catch them to bring them back."

"Ah," said Sally intelligently. "*You* can't come to *my* house."

I had no trouble not crying when Jannie left; after all these years during which I have seen one child or another go off to one place or another and managed to control myself except during major crises like Cub Scout award meetings and nursery school Dancing Days—after all these years my goodbye kiss and my wave from the front window no longer exhibit more than the mildest apprehension. Jannie climbed stoutly into the school bus, her brother behind her pretending unsuccessfully that she was just some girl who happened to get on at the same stop he did, and I saw Jannie's head move down the bus to a seat at the end. "Sister's gone to school," I said to Sally.

"Ah," said Sally. "And will she come home again?"

Laurie reported, when he came home at three o'clock, that although he looked for her, and waited at the bus, and even, with some faint vestige of fraternal feeling, asked a couple kids if they had seen his sister, Jannie had not got on the bus, and at four o'clock I was driving back and forth between our house and the school for the sixth time when I saw Jannie wandering and singing along the side of the road. I stopped the car next to her and leaped out, babbling, and she took my hand amiably and said, "I think school will be all right for me, after all."

"Where have you *been?*" I said.

"I followed my teacher home," Jannie said. "I wanted to see where she lived."

At the end of her second week in first grade Jannie remarked one evening at the dinner table, "Mrs. Skinner says paper napkins are vulgar." Mrs. Skinner is the first grade teacher, and it had already, by then, begun to get through to the rest of us that Mrs. Skinner's opinions, relayed through Jannie, were inclined to be vehement, positive, and perhaps even a shade on the critical side. "Mrs. Skinner," Jannie went on, eyeing her brother, "says little boys are made of snails."

"Who's little?" Laurie demanded, stung. "Seems to me—"

"I *beg* your humble pardon," said Jannie—"I beg your humble pardon" is another Skinnerism—"I beg your *humble* pardon, but Mrs. Skinner says that boys any size are made of snails and little girls like Sally and me—"

"Sally and I," said Laurie.

"I *beg* your humble pardon. —like Sally and me are dainty and sweet."

"Huh," said Laurie eloquently.

"And now I think of it, what's so vulgar about paper napkins?" I wanted to know.

"Mrs. Skinner," Jannie said gently, "doesn't care if you *use* paper napkins. Mrs. Skinner will let you use paper napkins if you *want* to. But then you're just *vulgar*, is all."

"Some people," Laurie remarked, addressing his plate,

"Some people just think they know everything, I really do believe. Some people just think they know *every*thing."

"Jannie and me are dainty and sweet, *are*n't we, Jannie?" Sally gestured with her fork, scattering green peas generously onto the table. "And Laurie is full of snails."

"Children, be quiet," my husband said firmly. "Mother and I want to talk." He addressed me through a profound silence. "Did you sew the button on my shirt?" he enquired.

"Water with the meal," Jannie murmured, "is unsanitary."

We had been exposed to Mrs. Skinner from about the third day of school, when Jannie came home with a mimeographed sheet of paper containing her instructions for conduct in the first grade; she was not, I noted from the paper, to come to school with dirty fingernails, broken shoelaces, or odorous lunches. She was to wear dresses or skirts. ("Mrs. Skinner says girls wearing pants are vulgar.") Her hair was to be cut short or braided, her socks matching, and no pins were to be in evidence. ("How about a dental plate for that missing front tooth?" I asked impolitely, and Jannie smiled at me with sweet tolerance.) She was not to wear jewelry (vulgar) or earmuffs. If she intended to visit anyone after school, or to sniffle moderately (immoderate or obtrusive sniffling was not countenanced) or to require a container of milk with her lunch, she was to bring a note. If her shoes needed soling, or she squinted at the blackboard, or created a disturbance during Songtime, Mrs. Skinner would send a note back. No parent was, under any circumstances whatsoever, for any reason up to and including absolute national emergency, to visit the classroom at any time except—Mrs. Skinner's unwilling bow to the school authorities and their tyranny—during Parent's Visiting Week. Children were not encouraged to discuss their home life at school.

"Mrs. Skinner says," Jannie remarked as her father read the mimeographed notice for the third apoplectic time, "that men who smoke are vulgar, especially cigars."

It did not take us very long to find out that Mrs. Skinner thought that raised voices, dining in restaurants, and playing cards were all vulgar. Jannie took to keeping care of her own socks and she bathed every night, and once a week, while we were out carousing at our regular bridge game, she washed her hair inefficiently. "A girl," she told me, "who does not keep herself clean is unwomanly."

"Talking about being clean is vulgar," I told her nastily.

"Clean talk," said Jannie, "is womanly."

"I beg your *humble* pardon," I said.

"Granted," said Jannie.

"This is unbearable," I said to my husband, after Jannie had set out her clean dress for tomorrow with her clean socks, and had cleaned her fingernails and gone to bed, "this is positively vulgar—I mean unbearable."

"What's so vulgar about keeping your hands in your pockets, is what *I* want to know?" my husband said unhappily, looking up from a book catalogue. "I *have* to put my hands in my pockets *some*times; I keep my cigarettes and my wallet and my handkerchief—"

"Smoking is unsanitary anyway," I said.

"Cats give you colds," Jannie remarked the next afternoon when she came home from school; she dropped her jacket into the center of the hall floor and made an ostentatious large circle around poor old Shax, who raised his head and stared at her with honest surprise. "Cats give you colds and dogs give you mange."

"Now, *look*, young lady," I said sternly, "you go right out and pick up your jacket and apologize to Shax. You haven't had a cold since—"

"I *beg* your humble pardon. Mrs. Skinner says cats give you colds."

"Cats do *not*—"

"It's vulgar to contradict."

During a fairly stormy dinner, during which Laurie fled the table in a blind fury, shouting, "What the *hell* do I have to be womanly *for?*" Jannie succeeded in eliminating string beans (unsanitary), coffee (unhealthy), and the clearing of the table by the lady of the house (vulgar). She told her father while I was bringing in the dessert and setting a tray to take upstairs to Laurie that we must really get a housekeeper.

"Who is going to pay for this housekeeper?" her father asked, the way he always asks me.

"Speaking of money is vulgar," Jannie said.

Sally, who demonstrated the far-reaching arm of Mrs.

Skinner by preserving an awed silence when her sister spoke, and by even making some abortive attempts to keep herself clean, said now, "*I'm* dainty, aren't I? Can I have more dessert?"

" 'May,' dear," Jannie said. "*We* say '*May* I have more dessert.' " She implied pointedly by her tone that her father and mother habitually and vulgarly used 'can,' as we do. "Dear Mother," she went on—"Dear Mother" is, I hardly need point out, Mrs. Skinner's presumable manner of addressing *her* mother—"I need two buttons sewed on my jacket before tomorrow. Mrs. Skinner says that if you thread the needle for me I can do them as well as *you* do."

"You may tell Mrs. Skinner," I said tensely, "that I have quite enough to do with the dinner dishes and drawing your—" I hesitated, deleting a vulgar word "—bath, without sitting down to teach you to sew. You may tell Mrs. Skinner that if she is so—" I deleted again "—womanly *she* can teach you to sew. And furthermore—"

"A lady who does not know how to sew nicely is—"

My husband and I flipped a coin—secretly, because money is vulgar and gambling is unwomanly and our expressed opinions were, to say the least, unsanitary—to decide which of us would stop by during Parent's Visiting Week and beard Mrs. Skinner. My husband lost, but I had to promise to stand right outside the door while he was talking to Mrs. Skinner and rush in if he were cornered.

The morning his father was to attend school Jannie looked

him over carefully. "I told you a million times that standing with your hands in your pockets is *vulgar*," she said. "And even though you're made of snails you don't have to—"

"Show it," my husband said miserably. "I suppose it's this tie."

"The tie's all *right*," Jannie said without conviction, and sighed. "I wish you'd sort of give up Parent's Day this month," she said. "I'm going to have a real spell of faintness waiting for you in the car."

I stood outside the door of the first grade room, with a clear view of the health chart on the front blackboard and the row of trim geraniums on the window sill, and I heard Mrs. Skinner saying clearly, in a voice which carried beautifully across the empty desks and out into the hall, but in a voice also not raised and not in the least, I am sorry to say, vulgar, "Your little Joanne is a charming child, charming. So refined." She lowered her voice slightly. "*You* know, sir, that there are children in every class, and from every walk of life, mind you, who are coarse. Who are even unclean."

"Vulgar, I suppose," my husband said.

"Precisely." I could almost hear Mrs. Skinner glowing with satisfaction. "Vulgar, precisely the word I was hesitating to use. But little Joanne . . ." her voice died off tenderly.

"How about your own children?" my husband asked.

"They are many of them unbelievably charming, of

course," Mrs. Skinner said, "but of course from every walk of life . . ."

"No," my husband said, "your *own* children. Children you've—well—*had* yourself."

"I regret to say," Mrs. Skinner said with a soft wistfulness, "that we have not been blessed—"

"Not having children is unwomanly," my husband said, "in a woman."

"True, true," Mrs. Skinner said, and sighed again. "My spells of faintness," she said; "my unfortunate weak limbs . . . but," she added brightly, "you did not want to hear about *my* troubles, sir. We were speaking of your little Joanne—such a charming child."

"However," my husband said relentlessly, "I presume that had you been blessed with little charmers of your own they would have caught colds from cats?"

"I beg your pardon?"

"I beg your *humble* pardon," my husband said. "Is Jannie doing all right in her school work?"

"She is excellent in cleanliness—I don't believe I ever saw a child so conscientious about her nails; her imaginative qualities are unusually good, and so is her general gracefulness. Her singing voice, however . . ."

"How about spelling? Arithmetic?"

"I beg your *humble* pardon?"

"Granted," said my husband.

I tiptoed away at this point, and joined Jannie in the car. While she fidgeted nervously I smoked a cigarette with abandon, dropping ashes on the car seat. After about half an hour my husband came out of the school building; he had his hands in his pockets and he was whistling. "Well?" I asked him as he got into the car, "what happened?"

"Were you all *right?*" Jannie said urgently, "did you *do* anything?"

He untied his tie and draped it over the mirror, took a cigar out of his pocket and put it rakishly into the side of his mouth, and then he turned and grinned at us.

"Curiosity," he said, "is unwomanly."

The dinner table is, in our house, always the family village green, with the big salt and pepper shakers and the plastic table mats silent if appalled witnesses to the intricate weavings of our several dining personalities: Jannie's place is always set left-handed, my husband and I use oversized coffee cups, and Sally requires at least three paper napkins; the dinner, which is cooked by me, tends to be largely upon Sally's level and liberally adorned with chili sauce by Laurie. That night at dinner, Jannie was silent and oppressed. When Laurie pointed out virtuously that she had not touched her dinner, she barely raised her eyes. When Sally observed that Jannie was an impulent girl she did not turn her head, when her father offered her the band from his cigar she gazed sadly upon the ceiling.

"Jannie is invited to Helen's birthday party on Saturday," I informed the table brightly.

"How about I read you ten chapters in your Oz book?" Laurie asked.

"Jannie can be the new mother," Sally said largely, "and Mommy and I will just be the babies and Laurie is the queen and Daddy is a herd of rabbits."

"You may put an ice cube down my back," my husband said earnestly to Jannie.

"Thank you," Jannie said wanly. "I don't feel much like being happy now, thank you."

"Perhaps if I were to lend you my lapel watch?" I suggested.

"I could even read you *twelve* chapters—"

"*You* can come to *my* house."

"*I* think," Laurie observed critically, "if anyone should *ask* me, *I* think she's getting *spots*."

TWO WEEKS LATER, when Jannie was well over the measles and we were only waiting for Laurie and Sally to catch it, I ventured timidly—again at the dinner table—to point out that her nails were dirty.

"What of it?" demanded Jannie, rendered reckless by two lovely weeks of illness. "You think *I* care?"

"What's your name?" Sally asked her.

"Puddentane," Jannie said.

"Where do you live?"

"Down the lane," said Jannie.

"You must keep your nails clean," I said gently, "even if—"

"What's your name?" Sally asked Laurie.

"Laurence," said Laurie.

"Pudd*tane*," Sally said. "When I ask you 'What's your name?' you must say 'Puddentane.' Now what's your name?"

"Laurence."

"Puddentane," Sally shouted, "you bad bad webbis."

"*You* bad bad webbis."

"I am *not* a webbis, *I* said puddentane; I *always* say puddentane. What's *your* name?" she said plaintively to her father.

"Puddentane," he said diplomatically.

"Where do you live?"

"Did you call the health officer?" my husband said to me.

"You bad bad webbis," Sally said reproachfully to Laurie.

"Can I please leave my potato and my meat and my beans?" Jannie asked me. "I don't feel really well *yet*, you know, and I'll eat my bread and butter."

"Eat three mouthfuls of everything," I said. "If they're going to catch it," I told my husband, "there's nothing *we* can do."

"Penicillin?" he said vaguely.

"*That's* no good against measles," Laurie said.

"If I had been addressing you, young man," his father began, "I can assure you that I would have—"

"I couldn't overhelp hearing," Laurie said meekly.

"What's your name?"

"What it comes down to," I said, "is that they might as well have it now as—" I broke off abruptly with a squawk as Sally poked me vigorously with her fork.

"I said 'What's your name?' " Sally reminded me.

"She's too young to have a fork," my husband said. "Little girls should be seen and not heard," he told Sally.

"You bad bad webbis," Sally said gratuitously to her brother.

"If Sally came down with a high fever," my husband said dreamily, "and Laurie came down with a high fever and—"

"Why don't we get a new outside?" Sally asked. "This morning, it was raining and raining." She thought. "And there was a lion on the front porch," she said.

"Really?" said Jannie. "Really, was there a lion on the front porch?"

"Cernly," Sally said.

Laurie put down his fork and turned to his father. "What is long and hard and wears shoes?" he asked. "Bet you a dime you can't guess it."

His father said tentatively, "A horse?"

Laurie guffawed. "Make it twenty cents," he said.

"Surely there was a lion on the front porch," Sally said

to Jannie, "and I saw him and he was walking around very softerly and he ate all the cats and part of the fence."

Jannie addressed me. "*I* was sick in bed, you know," she said. "Was there *really* a lion out there?"

"A horseshoe stake?" my husband said desperately.

"That," Laurie said with relish, "will be twenty cents."

"But a horseshoe stake is long and hard and it wears—" my husband said. "Look, don't the shoes go *around* it?"

"A sidewalk," Laurie said. "It *wears* shoes, see? Now, for another dime, what goes under the water, over the water, and doesn't get wet?"

"I left my rubbers somewhere," my husband said to me.

"You must ask *me* what's my name," Sally said to Laurie.

"What's your name?"

"Tiger," Sally said. "You snick," she told him.

Laurie said triumphantly to his father, who was scowling doggedly at his empty dessert dish, "An old woman crossing a bridge with a pail of water on her head, and counting yesterday and the money you lost to me on the checkers game that's two-seventy-five, and counting my allowance tomorrow that makes two-eighty-five, and the dime you bet me you could eat your bread and butter without using your hands."

"And when you dropped the book and the feather down the stairs," Jannie said.

"Galileo," Laurie told her approvingly, "I forgot. You had a dollar," he said to his father, "that the heavy object and the light object would . . ." he hesitated, looking at me.

"Fall at the same rate of speed," I said helpfully. "It looked like a sure thing."

"Damn it," my husband said, goaded, "I can show you in the book—"

"And twelve cents," Laurie went on inexorably, "for swatting twelve hundred flies."

"*That* wasn't twelve hundred flies," my husband said, "Mother counted them."

"You *gave* them to me to count," I said, "but—"

"*I* can count to twelve hundred," Jannie said. "One, two, three, four, five, six, seven . . ."

"Showing off," I said vengefully, "is vulgar."

"What?" Jannie said.

"Where do you live?"

"Down the lane," said my husband sadly.

"Four ninety-seven," said Laurie, who had been figuring silently.

"Mother will give it to you," my husband said.

DIABOLICALLY, BOTH SALLY and Laurie refused to catch measles after I had gone out and purchased a new thermometer and a large bottle of calamine lotion. My husband and I agreed that it was time that Laurie's natural curiosity about things which did not belong to him should be channelized into a healthy pattern, and that he should be encouraged to give up spending nickels for packs of gum and begin, instead, a coin collection. I did not, at that time—in fact, it seemed like a good idea—perceive any of the parallels which have occurred to me since; the similarity, for instance, between coin collecting and a grasping curiosity about things which do not belong to you, the unfortunate similarity between coins and money; I remember agreeing with my husband that coins were preferable as a collection to, say, stamps, because they wouldn't blow away, or match folders because coins, at least, had some intrinsic value. I remember even saying laughingly that if anything were to be collected, for heaven's sake it might as well be *money*.

My husband and Laurie began on a small scale. I went to the bank and got a roll of nickels and a roll of dimes and a roll of pennies, and they spent an evening examining mint marks and dates and relative condition, and I sat peacefully over my book smiling at them occasionally and thinking how good it was that they should be interested together in such a grown-up fashion. They sent for some little books, named dime books and penny books and nickel books, and each book had a series of little holes large enough for the proper coins, and all coin collectors have to do is find the right coin for the right little hole and put it in. After a while my husband was going to the bank himself with a briefcase. He would get all the money we had changed into coins and then he and Laurie would take all the coins they needed for their books and give me the rest, and I would go out and pay for my groceries in the nickels and dimes which were not needed for the books.

I have never objected to money, as such. But after a while it became necessary to get a huge metal box to keep the coins in, and every mail began to bring heavy little packages of coins from Ruritania and Atlantis and it was suddenly abruptly clear to Jannie and Sally and me that their father and Laurie were planning to get hold of all the money in the world and put it away in their metal box, and a consequent strong bitterness began to show itself around the house. I began to make pointed comments about the last time I had seen a five-dollar bill, and I repeated several times at dinner what the grocer had said to me about people holding up a line at the counter because they had to count out seventeen dollars and thirty-six cents in dimes and nickels and pennies. Jannie took to sleeping with her penny bank under her pillow, and Sally, with a pretty wit, fell to bringing her father small stones and pieces of glass and play money which she embezzled at nursery school. I spent a bag of silver to buy my husband a Piece of Eight for a Christmas present, and had trouble hiding it, since Christmas was still quite a while off, until I thought of keeping it in my pocketbook. Even Sally learned to say "numismatist"; Laurie learned the Greek alphabet from Greek coins and one day turned in his spelling homework done entirely in Greek letters, confounding his schoolmates and thoroughly annoying his teacher.

One Saturday morning an intensely awaited package of coins arrived, and I had to pay thirty-one cents duty charges on it; while I was irritably counting out the money for the postman, Sally took the mail into the study where Laurie and his father were rearranging their classifications, and when I came stamping into the study shouting "Don't we pay enough for this money without—" I found Laurie and his father sitting one on either side of the coffee table, Laurie rocking back and forth and moaning, and his father holding his head in his hands and saying "Oh, no," over and over, and Jannie and Sally regarding them with unwilling sympathy.

"Something wrong?" I asked brightly.

"Something wrong?" Jannie repeated.

"Wrong?" Sally asked.

"Yes," said my husband.

"Look at these darned old *coins*," Laurie said, almost in tears. We looked at the heap of coins on the table, Jannie and Sally and I.

"They're *mixed*," Laurie said.

"Well, my goodness," I told him, "it certainly wouldn't be much fun *collecting* coins if all you did was just put them in the little books and put them in the cabinet. My goodness, half the *fun* in collecting coins—"

My husband raised his head and looked at me. "Listen," he said wanly, "what we ordered was two lots of coins from the same place. One of them was a lot of a hundred and fifty assorted coins of the world."

"Splendid," I said. "I suppose they cost—"

"The other," my husband said, raising his voice, "was a lot of a hundred assorted *counterfeit* coins of the world. And the boxes," he said, "the boxes . . ." He put his head back in his hands.

"They broke," Laurie said. "We got two hundred and fifty coins. Assorted. Mixed."

"Splendid," I said again. "Then all you have to do is sort the counterfeit coins into *one* pile and the *real* coins into *another*—"

"Yeah," Laurie said. "Daddy doesn't feel very well."

This did not seem like the time to enforce my rightful claims to thirty-one cents, so I collected the rest of the mail and left the study with the girls. We sat down on the couch in the living room and opened a letter from the electric company and bills from three department stores and an announcement of the annual fund drive of the Boy Scouts and a pamphlet from a toy company. This last caught the attention of the girls, and we opened it to read. It turned out to be one of those maddening documents in which the desire of children to play with toys is explained and justified, and the desire of parents to buy toys for their children is made painless by a sugar-coating of sound educational advice; "The child's natural impulses are harmlessly directed—" I read, under a picture of a hammering set, and, with a block set, "Little fingers learn busily sense of balance . . ." "Ar," I said, through my teeth.

"What does it say?" Jannie asked. "Read it to us."

The center of the pamphlet was occupied by an article entitled "Healthy Children are Happy Children" or else "Happy Children are Healthy Children," and there was a picture of a sweet-faced mother bending earnestly over her child, guiding his little fingers as they learned a busy sense of balance with a set of blocks. "Who's *that?*" Jannie asked, leaning over to see, "who's that lady? What's she doing?"

I consulted the article. "Children are naturally cooperative and reasonable," I read at random.

"What?"

"*That* means that little girls like you and Sally and boys like Laurie *like* to do things right. That you *want* to learn the best and nicest ways to act."

"I *do?*"

"*I* don't," said Sally emphatically.

"That's not reasonal," Jannie said critically. "Like eating with my fingers; I want to eat with my *fingers*."

"I think the people who wrote this would *let* you eat with your fingers," I said. "Constructive something-or-other."

"Hah," said Jannie.

"Only snicks," Sally opined. "Only snicks."

"Children are happier and better adjusted," I read

grimly, "when given responsibility. The feeling of partici-
pating—"

"*I* know," Jannie said. "Pick up your room, set the table,
hang up your jacket, brush your teeth, wash—"

"No good," Sally said. "*Not* washing."

"—your hands, put away your toys, fold your napkin—"

"And it means that when I ask you to run upstairs to
get me a handkerchief you should go cheerfully," I said,
patting her on the head.

"You just read more of that," Jannie said. "I don't think
it's sensal at all, except about eating with my fingers."

"Parents should never show anger before the child," I
read. "Parents should never show anger before the child.
Parents—"

"Hah," Jannie said again.

"Run in the study, dear," I said. "Ask Dad how he's
coming with his coins."

"Not *me*," Sally said. "Not *me*."

"But *you*—" Jannie said.

"I do *not*," I said. "I never show anger at all, except
that you and your sister and your brother can be far and
away the most irritating, the most infuriating, the most
maddening—"

"Snicks."

"Snicks," I said. I took a deep breath. "Anyway," I
went on, "it says here that Sixes *enjoy* helping around the
house."

"What's a Six?" Jannie scowled. "Am *I* a Six?"

"You're a *snicks*," Sally said, leaning forward to look around me at her sister, "an old snicks."

"And Sally is a Three and Laurie is a Nine."

"Then are you a Thirty-Four?"

"Thirty-Two."

"I will tell Laurie he is a Nine," Sally said, sliding in one movement off the couch and landing walking. Jannie and I watched her open the study door. "You are both snicks," she announced.

"—Thaler," my husband's voice said. "See if there ever *was* such a country as Thaler." He sounded a little shrill. Sally closed the door. "*I* told them," she said, coming back and climbing onto the couch.

"Mother is of course," I read, "interested in her *own* activities, such as Parent-Teachers meetings, cooking for the Girl Scouts, sewing costumes for—" I stopped. "Now what?" I inquired vaguely.

"Brownies," Jannie said. "You promised you would make brownies for the school party."

"I must have been crazy," I said. I leaned back comfortably. "My *own* activities, it says here," I said. "Taking a nap, for instance."

Jannie laughed shortly. "That is the silliest thing I ever did hear," she said. "What does it ever say in there about mommies sleeping?"

"It says I should be relaxed." I ran my finger hopefully down the lines. "It says naturally Mother is not going to handicap her children by teaching them insecure patterns

[204]

of behavior; what would we think, for instance, of a mother who believed herself fond of her children, who nevertheless allowed them to see her in a temper? Or who told them obviously untruthful stories, broke promises, or showed malice?"

"You better make those brownies," Jannie said acutely. "What does show mals mean?"

"You remember?" I asked, "when you told Daddy about my running the car into a telephone pole?"

Jannie grinned. "You said I was a tattletale. You said I—"

"Yes," I said. "Well, that was foursquare, honest-to-goodness malice, right off the boat, and according to the lady who wrote this I should never have said it."

"Well, I'm not a—"

"You are *so*. And every time I think of your babbling to Daddy about that telephone pole I want to—"

"*I* didn't," Sally said. "*I* didn't tell Daddy anything. I will tell him now," and I grabbed for her too late as she slid off the couch again and went to the study door. "Go away," her father said, as she opened it.

"Mommy hit a pole," Sally said.

"*Again?*" My husband's voice rose.

"No, no, no, no, no," I said, coming after Sally. "Sally was just chattering."

"Tattletale," Jannie said promptly.

I stepped in front of her and asked gracefully, "How are the new coins coming along?"

Laurie smiled at me weakly. "So far," he said, "we have a hundred and seventy-five counterfeits."

"Oh, splendid," I said. "I thought there were only a hundred to start with. How does it happen that—"

"Will you *please* close that *door?*" my husband said.

The girls skittering ahead of me, I closed the door sharply and went through the living room and into the kitchen, where I brought up sharply before the sink and the breakfast dishes. "Well," I said brightly, "time to get to work."

"Did Daddy show mals?" Jannie asked. "Who was the lady who wrote all those things?"

"A lady who works with children," I said absent-mindedly, wondering at a sound which came from the study as of many coins crashing against the wall, and calculating with another part of my mind whether there was enough chocolate for brownies, or whether I would have to run out and get some, and hearing with still another part of my mind Jannie's wise voice saying, "Not like mommies, then. Ladies work with children, and mommies *play* with them."

"And *you*'re a snick," Sally said.

Dreamily, rinsing glasses, I had wandered on to cheerful reflections on our holiday season, which included, besides Christmas and Thanksgiving, five birthdays and an anniversary, and which seemed to be racing on with its usual neckbreaking speed, although it seemed at the same time that the days would never pass. It seemed, too, increasingly clear that our hopes for a sixth birthday in our family during the holiday season might be optimistic; the suitcase which Jannie and I share was sitting, packed, in the corner of the bedroom, contemplated lovingly by me the last thing at night and the first thing in the morning—although, as it turned out, what I was contemplating lovingly this time was a suitcase containing Jannie's yellow sundress and a jigsaw puzzle, with which she had secretly replaced my blue satin bedjacket and a dozen mystery stories and a rough draft of an informative letter beginning "Dear . . . Well, we have a new son/ daughter, and so this makes two pair/three of a kind . . ." Since I did not find out, as it happened, that Jannie had repacked the suitcase until I reached the hospital, my fond regard was not in any way tarnished, although secret fears about last-minute Christmas shopping had touched the back of my mind. The same old baby clothes, much the worse for Sally's vigorous infancy, were in the bottom dresser drawer, and there was half a can of Dextro-Maltose 1 in the kitchen cabinet. "It's the home stretch again," my doctor told me affably, apparently relying upon some medical doctrine about any metaphor suiting—by now—the mother of four, "out of the trenches by Christmas." He used to laugh every time he said this.

Oddly enough, the children were able to continue their theoretically normal lives. Laurie pursued his project, for which he vaguely believed he would have a silver arrow from the Cub Scouts, of writing down all the numbers in sequence until he reached infinity; he was at this time well up into the millions, with infinity nowhere in sight. Sally was comfortably settled in nursery school, from which she brought home daily bulletins about a Mr. Grassable (who had as friends Mr. Dirtable and Mr. Sandable) and a gentleman named David who brought gum with him every morning. Jannie followed her own social life, which was only nominally affected by our family holiday season, and which required a good deal of backing and filling on my part. I became reconciled to the last-minute race to town to pick up a book or a toy or a paint set for Jannie to take to a party; invitations arrived by mail and by phone, and it was at last necessary to invest in three extra pair of white socks, to take care of Jannie's social obligations. The afternoon of Rita's party we climbed into the car, Jannie and I, at three o'clock, thanking heaven that Sally had chosen to sleep until now, and making a final check before we started. Jannie was wearing her green party dress, which she had of course chosen herself; it had a tiny white collar and rows of smocking. She had on the official white socks and her school shoes neatly shined, by me. Her best coat still fit her—although it had begun to look like Sally in another month or so—and she was wearing her green beret. She was carrying a small package with a carefully chosen doll inside; the package was wrapped in green tissue paper and the card enclosed was signed, typically, "ennaoJ." There were green bows on her pigtails, and she was wearing, as a special favor, her coral necklace. She looked very grown-up, and unbelievably pretty.

"Have you got a handkerchief?" I asked her before I started the car, and she nodded gravely, deeply aware of her green bows.

"I brought my invitation," she said. "In case we forgot the time or something."

"I only wish I knew more about the people," I said, looking at the invitation with hope, as though its pattern of pink balloons and bright lettering might somehow indicate what sort of person had paid a dime for six of them at the five and ten; "I feel a little bit worried, letting you go off to a strange house."

"I got an *invitation*," Jannie said.

I sighed, and started the car. "She sounded all *right*," I said, "the little girl's mother, I mean. When I called her to get directions to the house, she sounded all right. Richmond Road," I said, "and turn left at the private school."

"I say 'Thank you very much, Mrs. Arden,' when I'm ready to go home."

"Did you say you had a handkerchief?" We turned onto Richmond Road and Jannie settled back and folded her hands in her lap, no longer the everyday Jannie who rode with me, in her blue snow suit, to the grocery and the post office and the bakery, but a dressed-up lady in a white collar and a green beret; "Is Rita a polite little girl?" I asked with great casualness.

"She's all right," Jannie said. "From school."

I have always remembered a birthday party I went to where all the children were older, and strangers, and I sat in a corner all afternoon determined not to cry. "Do you know who else will be there?"

"Pals of mine," Jannie said, exasperated. "From *school*."

"I suppose it's all right," I said.

"Well, now that I'm all dressed and everything," Jannie said.

I peered through the window. "Left at the private school," I said. "We watch for Overlea Drive and turn right. Then there's a sign saying Arden halfway up the hill. She said we couldn't miss it."

"Tell Sally I'll bring her some candy," Jannie said as we made a hesitant left turn around the private school, "and I'll bring Laurie some cake. And don't plan on any supper for *me* tonight—I'll be too full from the party. And the invitation says the party is over at five, so you come and get me maybe about five-thirty. That," she explained, "will give me time to pick up candy and stuff that people have forgotten about, so I can bring it to Sally."

"Have you got a handkerchief? Overlea Drive."

"And I say," Jannie went on, her tone sharpening, "I say 'Thank you, Mrs. Arden,' when I'm ready to come home. And I *have* got a handkerchief."

"Sign saying Arden," I said, "sign saying Arden."

"I've never been here before, you know," Jannie said. "Rita doesn't take the school bus."

"I'm surprised, living so far away from the school," I said. "Sign saying Arden, Private Road."

I turned the car and had to shift into second. "The chauffeur brings her," Jannie said. "I wonder if that's Rita's house way up there?"

It was the only house in sight. We were driving past terraced lawns, rich with ornamental trees and graveled walks; I saw a sundial and what may have been a swimming pool. Above us, on the top of the hill, the house looked like someone's dream of a country club, with picture windows and fieldstone and gabled roofs. "Is that where *we*'re going?" I asked, turning to look at Jannie.

"Seven chimneys," she said. "Rita always *said* she lived in a big house."

We turned onto a circled driveway which took us past a garage holding, I thought, three foreign cars, and came around to the front door. We stopped abruptly because the car parked by the front door was so soft and low and shiny that the irresistable thought of bumping it and perhaps putting a scratch on its fender (that *was* a fender?) made my teeth chatter. One of a pair of matched gray poodles rose lazily from the wide front steps and looked down at us. "Jannie," I said, "look, honey, I've only got on my blue jeans and my old jacket. And my loafers. I'll just wait here and you run on up and ring the door bell. I'll just wait here and see that you get in all right."

Jannie turned and stared at me. "Why don't you come

up to the door?" she said. "You're my mother, aren't you?"

"Yes," I said doubtfully, and climbed out after her. She ran up the steps, nodded cheerfully at the poodles when they approached her, and rang the bell; I followed gingerly, edging up the steps and moving aside briskly when one of the poodles came too close. I had a sudden rich picture of the years ahead, with me hanging around in the shrubbery trying to catch a glimpse of my beautifully-gowned daughter waltzing in the ballroom, and then the door was opened by a maid in a yellow uniform, and behind her clustered a group of little girls in party dresses pink, blue, and white.

"Hi, kids," said Jannie.

"It's *Joanne*," said a little girl in blue, who was apparently the hostess, "*now* we can start the party."

"And *this*," said Jannie grandly, "is *my* mother."

The little girl in blue curtsied, I almost curtsied back, and Jannie said, as they turned to go inside, "*We* live in a bigger house than *this*," and then called back to me, "Don't forget to tell Sally what I'm bringing her," as the door closed.

When I came back to get Jannie at five-fifteen, which I thought a neat compromise on time between the invitation and Jannie's obviously superior planning, I had put on a skirt and a pair of decent shoes. When I rang the doorbell the maid asked me inside, and I waited for barely a minute, listening to the sound of small girls' voices screaming happily from somewhere within, before a woman in gray taffeta and what were probably real emeralds—I would have believed anything by then—came to me, holding out both her hands to take mine.

"So *you*'re Joanne's mother," she said. "*Won't* you come in and have a drink?"

AT ABOUT FOUR o'clock on a Thursday afternoon the express man delivered a huge cardboard box containing a vast collection of curtains and drapes, found in an attic and sent along by my mother, in the hopes that I could use some and make the rest into slip covers or bedspreads or dusting cloths. I took the curtains out and left the big box in the front hall, meaning to take it out and leave it for the trash man when I came downstairs to make dinner. At about four-ten Laurie came out of his room, where he had been painting, and wandered into the bedroom where I was sorting the curtains out on the bed.

"What's the big box downstairs?"

"Some things came in it," I said.

"Presents?"

"No, these curtains."

"Who wants *curtains?*"

At about four-thirteen Sally woke up from her nap, and went down the stairs head first, on her stomach, bumping from step to step and calling me. When she finally found me in the bedroom, after calling me through all the rooms in the house, she asked immediately, "Is it for me?"

"Is what for you?"

"The present. Downstairs, in the hall."

"No," I said, "it was for me. These curtains."

"Can I have them?"

"No."

"*You* can't come to *my* house."

At four-thirty precisely Jannie arrived home, trotted up the front walk, opened the door, and fell over the box in the hall. "Who put this here for me to trip over?" she asked indignantly.

"Mommy's junk came in it," Laurie said. I was by now in the study, inquiring if my husband would like a cocktail before dinner. He said no, he was working on an article about a woman with second sight, and he wanted to keep his own head clear. I went into the kitchen and halfheartedly began to take potatoes out of the bag. Jannie came into the kitchen and asked if she and Laurie and Sally might play with the big box in the hall, and I said yes, if they were quiet, because Daddy was working.

Nearly ten minutes later, after a good deal of giggling and screaming and two trips outside the study by my husband, once to the hallway to say to the children that if they could not keep quiet their mother would send them all to their rooms and once to the kitchen door to say to me that he could not work on the woman with second sight so long as those children were making so much noise,

Laurie suddenly appeared in the kitchen and said delightedly, "Another present came, a real *birthday* present."

Wearily, having been half-expecting it, I put down the paring knife and followed Laurie through the study into the hall. My husband looked up as we passed and said, "This is a study, not a thoroughfare."

In the hall was the same big box, full of something which giggled and kicked around considerably. Laurie and Jannie watched pleasurably while I carefully opened the box, and when Sally popped out everyone screamed with surprise and hilarity. "I don't want *this* present," I said agreeably, "Tell the mailman to take it back." Everyone laughed again, and I went back to the kitchen.

Two minutes later Laurie reappeared in the kitchen. "*Another* present came," he announced.

Since I could not think of any good reason for persisting pig-headedly in my dinner preparations, I put down the paring knife and followed him through the study into the hall. "This is a study, not a thoroughfare," my husband said as we went through.

In the hall Sally and Laurie stood tensely while I opened the box and found Jannie. "I don't want *this* present at all," I said. "Tell the mailman to take this one along with the other." Everyone laughed.

I went back into the kitchen and in another minute Jannie and Sally came in to me. "Another present," Jannie said, and Sally added, "It's got *Laurie* in it *now*."

"This is a study, not a thoroughfare," my husband said as we all went past.

I opened the box, found Laurie, everyone laughed, and I said, "I don't want *this* present, either; tell the mailman to take them all back."

I went back into the kitchen and took up the paring knife again, feeling mildly complacent over my participation in the children's harmless games. There was a short, murmurous moment in the hall, and then the study door from the hall opened and my husband said, "This is a study, not a thoroughfare." Then a great deal of whispering went on in the study, and finally my husband said, "All right, but just once." After that there was much suppressed giggling from the hall.

I was opening the oven door when Laurie, Jannie, and Sally came into the kitchen. "*Another—*" Laurie began, and then, "What's *that?*"

"I read about it in a magazine," I said shyly. "It's got tunafish and whipped cream and potatoes and chopped olives and black bean soup and sweet pickles and all sorts of good things."

"I don't like it," said Sally at once.

"Well," Laurie said compromisingly, "what's for dessert?"

"Canned peaches," I said. "You see, I spent all afternoon with those curtains and—"

"Tunafish?" said Jannie. "Please may I have some without tunafish?"

"I believe I'll make myself a peanut butter sandwich while I'm waiting," Laurie said.

"Girls, you can start setting the table," I said. "Jannie, cups and glasses. Sally, table mats and silver."

"*I* want to do glasses," Sally said at once.

"Don't forget the salt and pepper. Casserole, bread, salad, peaches." I scowled indecisively at the oven door. "What would happen," I asked Jannie, "if I put in tomato sauce?"

"It would be even worse," Jannie said cheerfully.

"Clean towels," I said. "I'll be right down; Laurie, you wash your hands before you touch that bread."

I went out of the kitchen and through the study and through the hall and up the stairs, found the clean towels and brought them down again. "Supper in about five minutes," I said as I went through the study; "Supper in about five minutes," I said as I went past the dining room, "Supper in about five minutes," I said as I came into the kitchen. "Laurie, start telling Dad supper is ready."

Laurie went into the study and came back. "Not there," he said.

"He probably went to wash," Jannie said.

"Salt and pepper," I said, surveying the table. Jannie had set everything left-handed, as usual.

"*I* washed," Sally said, coming out of the bathroom. I glanced beyond her to the clean towel I had just hung on the rack, and sighed. "Laurie and Jannie, wash," I said. "Dad ought to be down in a minute."

"Seems like there was something I meant to tell you," Laurie said, taking his place at the table with his peanut butter sandwich.

"You call those hands clean?"

"I said I didn't *like* this," Jannie said, looking into her plate.

"Seems like it was something about Dad," Laurie said.

NINKI HAD FOUR black and white kittens on December fifth. Their eyes opened, they began to tumble delightfully together on the kitchen floor, and Ninki, svelte and lively, got back to her mouse-hunting. I continued to come downstairs each morning step by step, holding on to the bannister. The morning the first snow fell I came into the kitchen where Jannie and Sally were eating oatmeal at the yellow table, and Elsie, a nice girl whom I had hired to stay with us until the first of the year, was cheerfully spreading mustard on Laurie's lunch sandwiches.

"Good morning," Elsie said brightly. "Still with us, I see?"

"Yeah," I said. "Coffee?"

"Good morning, Mommy dear," said Jannie, in the sweet voice which means she has decided to hold out on her oatmeal until ten minutes to nine, and Sally echoed, "Good morning, Mommy dear, dear morning, good Mommy."

"Uh," I said.

"Thought I heard the car go out last night," Elsie said conversationally, "but then I thought you'd surely wake me if you were going."

"I surely would," I said.

"And how do you feel? Well?"

"I surely do," I said. I took my coffee into the dining room and settled down with the morning paper. A woman in New York had had twins in a taxi. A woman in Ohio had just had her seventeenth child. A twelve-year-old girl in Mexico had given birth to a thirteen-pound boy. The lead article on the woman's page was about how to adjust the older child to the new baby. I finally found an account of an axe murder on page seventeen, and held my coffee cup up to my face to see if the steam might revive me.

"Laurie," Elsie said at the back stairs, "ten minutes after eight."

"I'm *coming*," Laurie said. "Mommy still here?"

"She surely is," Elsie said gaily. "Brush your teeth."

I turned to the sports page.

Jannie's voice rose clearly from the kitchen. "When we get our baby brother," she asked, "will he have his breakfast out here with us?"

"Oatmeal?" Sally added.

"He'll be very tiny," Elsie told them, "and at first he'll spend all his time in the crib and he'll have all his meals from a bottle."

"And I'm going to give him a bath," Jannie said.

"And I'm going to give him some of my oatmeal," Sally said.

"Let's ask Mommy when he's coming," Jannie said.

"Never you mind," Elsie said hastily "Finish that oatmeal."

Laurie came crashing downstairs and I heard my husband's feet hit the floor beside the bed. "Good morning, Mommy," Laurie called from the kitchen. "I was sure you'd be gone *today*."

"Yeah."

Laurie brought his tray in and set it on the table; he began to spoon sugar thoughtfully onto his oatmeal. "You know," he said, "you don't suppose you won't go at all, do you?"

"I've thought of it," I said.

Laurie began to laugh uproariously. "All those baby clothes," he said.

"That's enough sugar," I said. "Read the paper or something."

Laurie took the sports section and propped it up against the coffee pot. "By the way," he said suddenly, looking up from the paper, "the teacher asked me yesterday again what about my baby brother. She's going to sing 'Happy Birthday to You' when it comes."

"Tell her I've gone to Mexico," I said.

My husband came downstairs at that moment, glanced

at me with some surprise, and said, "Good morning, good morning."

"Good morning, Dad," Laurie said. "Mommy's still here."

"Good morning," my husband said in the kitchen to Elsie and the girls, and I could hear Elsie telling him that she had surely thought we would wake her if we left during the night.

My husband brought his tray in and set it down on the table.

"Coins from Hong-Kong should be here today," Laurie told him.

"Ought to write that fellow," my husband said vaguely.

"How do you figure about Mommy?" Laurie asked.

My husband looked searchingly at me. "Damned if *I* know," he said.

I lifted my head from the steam of my coffee. "Look," I said bitterly, "I could go stay in a hotel somewhere and write you when it's all over."

"How do you feel?" my husband asked.

"Bah," I said distinctly.

"So long as you don't have any *children* today," Laurie said. "You got to pick me up at Cub Scouts at five."

"Tomorrow?"

"No," said my husband. "Tomorrow is the Numismatic Society and I didn't go the last time because I had a cold and I didn't go the time before because your mother was here and I'd hate to miss it *again* for a trifle."

"And Sunday of course your aunt and uncle are coming," I told my husband. "How about Monday?"

Elsie put her head around the corner of the kitchen door. "Monday morning I take my driving test," she said, "so don't go before Monday afternoon. I can drive you. And then of course on Tuesday Jannie goes to Kathy's party."

"Wednesday?"

"I *was* planning to visit my sister," Elsie said. "You remember you said it would be all right, you said you would probably be back from the hospital by then and—"

"Is Thursday fairly clear for everybody?" I asked, my voice rising.

"Well, *Friday*," Laurie said, worried, "Friday is Cub Scouts again."

"Have the baby on my birthday," Jannie called from the kitchen.

Jannie's birthday was ten months and some days off. "I'll try to make it," I said.

Laurie laughed. "Mr. Feeley says if the baby's born before Tuesday he'll give you ten percent of his winnings."

"What winnings?" I asked.

Laurie glanced, dismayed, at his father, and his father said elaborately, rising from his chair, "Want to take another look at those Roman coins, son?"

"*What* winnings?" I said insistently.

"Nothing to worry about," my husband said. "Just

something we were . . ." He thought. "Making for the baby," he finished finally.

"A book," Laurie added helpfully.

His father glanced at him with respect. "That's right," he said, "a baby book."

They headed for the study. "It *couldn't* be before Tuesday," my husband was saying to Laurie, as one continuing a private discussion, "the law of probability . . ."

"Ross told me in school yesterday he wants a dime on Christmas Day," Laurie said.

"Tell him we'll give him thirty to one," my husband said.

From the study I could hear my husband saying that Ross's money was as good as gone, and Laurie remarked that he thought he could count the teacher in for maybe even a quarter.

"I wouldn't like to see any more money go on Tuesday," my husband remarked absently, "you can't count on *her* to figure the odds, you know."

"Just like her to pick a day with no money in it," Laurie confirmed. "Is this Nero, Dad?"

"It's the button from my jacket," my husband said. "I meant to ask Jannie to sew it on."

I lighted another cigarette and poured hot coffee into my cup; it did not seem worthwhile doing anything else. "Ten minutes of nine," Elsie remarked in the kitchen.

With a great shout Sally slid off her chair and Jannie

followed. "Come back here and finish this oatmeal," Elsie said as they raced for the front door.

"Bye, Dad," Laurie said. He went through the kitchen to get his lunch box, and stopped in the dining room on his way to the front door. "See you at five?" he asked me.

"Oh, surely, surely," I said.

I followed them to the front door and waved as they got into the school bus; Sally sat at the front window to watch for the station wagon which would take her to nursery school. The mail had come, and I got Sally to pick it up off the floor for me and then went with it into the study.

"All bills today," I said maliciously to my husband.

"Again?" he said. "It seems like it was only—"

"Pay them in Roman coins," I said. I sat down in the straight chair I had brought into the study especially; the upholstered chairs are difficult to get out of without a struggle. "Pay them with your eleven Siamese gambling house tokens," I said.

My husband glanced at me apprehensively. "How do you feel?"

"Pay them in counterfeit Scottish merks," I said. "I feel fine."

My husband touched the stack of mail with one finger, timidly. "One of us," he said, "has got to go to the bank and see Mr. Andrews."

"Not me," I said.

"Of course not," my husband said soothingly. "You

can go in tomorrow morning," he added, "if you're still here."

OUR LOCAL BANK is an informal and neighborly spot, lavish with its hard-covered checkbooks, always ready to look up the value of the Swiss franc, eager to advise on investments or make wills. Its atmosphere is substantially less hushed and reverent than, say, a good movie theatre, with a loud-speaker system which plays soft music for depositors, an air-cooling device which clears the air of the acrid scent of ten-dollar bills, richly upholstered benches for nervous mortgagees; it is a bank dedicated to every friendly pursuit except the swift transference of money. I have had occasion, over the past few years, to deal frequently with the bank's Mr. Andrews, a man of chilling questions and a very cynical view of me, over some minor monies which have passed reluctantly from Mr. Andrews' hands into our bank account, and rapidly from there into the hands of various milkmen, doctors, department stores, and sundry poker cronies of my husband's. Mr. Andrews likes to believe that he is giving me this money as a favor. "We are always glad to lend funds," he is apt to say, with a dim smile, "after all, that's what a bank is *for*, isn't it?" Since Mr. Andrews so obviously believes that that is the main thing that a bank is *not* for, my answer to this is usually a gay laugh and a quick question about how ninety days is six months, isn't it? Mr. Andrews is also fond of saying things like, "Well, *we* have our obligations to meet, too, you realize," and "If we were to accommodate *every-one* who asks us . . ."

Mr. Andrews never says "money," just like that, the way the rest of us do so often; he refers to it reverently as "Credit" or "Funds" or "Equity." I have fallen into the habit of taking one or more of my children with me when I drop in to speak to Mr. Andrews about equity or funds or credit, in the unexpressed hope that their soft pathetic eyes might touch Mr. Andrews' heart, although I know by now that their soft pathetic little eyes might as easily open the door to the vault; the only time, I think, that I have ever seen Mr. Andrews really taken aback was when Laurie, when he had just commenced coin-collecting, asked if he might look over the bank's small change for V nickels.

At any rate, shortly before Christmas, then—and Christmas is of course always a time of great monetary discomfort around our house—I came timidly to Mr. Andrews' bank, at the back of my mind the thought that the children's presents had at least been bought and duly hidden, although not paid for, and holding by one hand my daughter Jannie, in a blue snow suit, and holding by the other hand my daughter Sally, in a red snow suit. The girls had their hair brushed and their boots on the right feet, and if I could raise the cash from Mr. Andrews they were each going to have an ice cream cone. We came into the bank, where the loudspeaker system was playing "Joy to the World," and found that the center paddock, where they usually foreclose mortgages, had been given over to a tall and gracious Christmas tree; because of the holiday season, they were foreclosing their mortgages in a sort of little recess behind the tellers. I sat the girls down on a velvet-covered bench directly in front of the Christmas tree, and told them to stay right where they were and Mommy would be back in a minute and then we would all go and get our ice cream cones. They sat down obediently, and I made my way over to Mr. Andrews' secretary.

"Good morning," I said to her.

"Good morning," she said. "Merry Christmas."

"Oh," I said. "Merry Christmas."

She nodded brightly and turned back to the papers on her desk. I twined my fingers around the ornamental ironwork of the railing, and said, "I wonder if I might perhaps be able to see Mr. Andrews?"

"Mr. Andrews? And what did you want to see him about?"

"Well," I said, coming a little closer, "it was to have been about our loan."

"Your loan?" she said, in that peculiarly penetrating tone all bank employees use when there is a question of money going the unnatural, or reverse-English direction. "You wanted to pay back your loan?"

"I hoped," I said, "that perhaps I could speak to Mr. Andrews."

"Isn't that sweet?" she said unexpectedly.

After a minute I realized that she was staring past me to where my girls were sitting, and I turned and saw without belief that Santa Claus, complete with sack of toys, had come out from behind the Christmas tree and was leaning over the railing and beckoning my daughters to him.

"I didn't know the bank had a Santa Claus," I said.

"Every year," she said. "At Christmas, you know."

Jannie and Sally slid off the bench and trotted over to Santa Claus; I could hear Sally's delighted, "Hello, Santa Claus!" and see Jannie's half-embarrassed smile; people all over the bank were turning to look and to beam and to smile at one another and murmur appreciatively. Because I have known Jannie and Sally for rather a long time, I untwined my fingers from the ironwork and made across the bank for their bench, reaching them just as Santa Claus opened the little gate in the railing and ushered them inside. He sat down under the warm lights of the Christmas tree and took Jannie onto one knee and Sally onto the other.

"Well, well, well," he said, and laughed hugely. "And have you been a *good* girl?" he asked Jannie.

Jannie nodded, her mouth open, and Sally said, "I've been *very* good."

"And do you brush your teeth?"

"Twice," said Sally, and Jannie said, "*I* brush *my* teeth every morning and every night and every morning."

"Well, well, well," Santa Claus said, nodding his head appreciatively. "So you've been good little girls, have you?"

"I've been very *very* good," Sally said insistently.

Santa Claus thought. "And have you washed your faces?" was what he finally achieved.

"I wash *my* face," said Sally, and Jannie, inspired, said, "I wash my face and my hands and my arms and my ears and my neck and—"

"Well, that's just *fine*," Santa Claus said, and again he laughed merrily, caroming Jannie and Sally off his round little belly. "Fine, fine," he said, "and now," he said to Jannie, "what is old Santa going to bring you for Christmas?"

"A doll?" Jannie said tentatively, "are you going to bring me a doll?"

"I most certainly *am* going to bring you a doll," said Santa Claus. "I'm going to bring you the prettiest doll you ever *saw*, because you've been such a *good* girl."

"And a wagon?" Jannie said, "and doll dishes and a little stove?"

"That's *just* what I'm going to bring you," Santa Claus said. "I'm going to bring good little girls *every*thing they ask for."

The fatuous smile I had been wearing on my face began to slip a little; there was a handsome doll dressed in blue waiting for Jannie in the guest room closet, and a hand-

[229]

some doll dressed in pink waiting for Sally; I began trying to signal surreptitiously to Santa Claus.

"And me," Sally said, "and me, and *me*, I want a bicycle."

I shook my head most violently at Santa Claus, smiling nervously. "That's right," Santa Claus said, "for good little girls, I bring bicycles."

"You're *really* going to bring me a bicycle?" Sally asked incredulously, "*and* a doll *and* a wagon?"

"I most certainly am," Santa Claus told her.

Sally gazed raptly at Jannie. "He's going to bring my bicycle after all," she said.

"*I* want a bicycle too," Jannie said.

"Alllllll right," said Santa Claus. "But have you been a *good* girl?" he asked Jannie anxiously.

"I've been so good," Jannie told him with ardor, "you just don't *know*, I've been so good."

"I've been good," Sally said. "I want blocks, too. And a doll carriage for my doll, and a bicycle."

"And our brother wants a microscope," Jannie told Santa Claus, "and he's been a very good boy. And a little table and chairs, I want."

"Santa Claus," I said, "*excuse* me, Santa Claus. . . ."

"Aren't they darling?" a woman said behind me.

"And candy, and oranges, and nuts," Santa Claus was going on blissfully, "and all sorts of good things in your stockings, and candy canes—"

"I forgot, I want a party dress."

"But you must be *good* little girls, and do just what your mommy and daddy tell you to, and never *never* forget to brush your teeth."

I went with haste back to Mr. Andrews' secretary. "I've *got* to see Mr. Andrews," I told her, "I've got to see him *fast*."

"You'll have to wait," she said, looking fondly over to where my daughters were receiving a final pat on the head from Santa Claus.

The loudspeaker system was playing "O Come, All Ye Faithful," I was thinking wildly: bicycle, microscope, bicycle, table and chairs, doll dishes, and my daughters came running across the floor to me. "Look," Sally was shrieking, "look at what Santa Claus gave to us."

"Santa Claus was here," Jannie confirmed, "he came right into the bank where we were and he gave us each a present, look, a little bag of chocolate money."

"Oh, fine, fine, fine," I said madly.

"And I *am* going to have my bicycle, Santa said he was *too* bringing it."

"—and me a bicycle too, and doll carriages and dishes and—"

"—and in our stockings."

"Mr. Andrews will see you now," said the secretary.

I sat my daughters down again and made my entrance into Mr. Andrews' office. His nose still retained a trace of jovial redness, but the jolly old elf's eye was the familiar agate, and the faint echo of jingle bells around him sounded more like the clinking of half dollars.

"Well," said Santa Claus, selecting my loan slip from the stack on his desk, "and what brings *you* here again so soon?'

IT WAS A beautiful morning, cold and clear and full of color, and the taxi driver was just finishing a story about how his wife's mother had come to visit them and canned all the peaches his wife had been planning to put into their freezer. "Just wasted the whole lot of them," he said, and pulled up in front of the house with a flourish.

"There are the children on the porch," I said.

"Beginning to seem like Christmas," my husband said to the taxi driver as I got out, and the taxi driver said, "Snow before morning."

Jannie's hair had obviously not been combed since I left, and as I went up the front walk I was resolving to make her tell immediately where she had hidden the hairbrush. She was wearing her dearest summer sundress, and she was barefoot. Laurie needed a haircut, and he had on his old sneakers, one of which no longer laces, but fastens with a safety pin; I had made a particular point of throwing those sneakers into the garbage can before I left. Sally had chocolate all over her face and *she* was wearing Laurie's fur hat. All three of them were leaning over the porch rail, still and expectant.

I tried to catch hold of all three of them at once, but they evaded me skillfully and ran at their father. "Did you bring it?" Jannie demanded, "did you bring it, did you bring it, did you bring it?"

"Is *that* it you're carrying?" Laurie demanded sternly, "that *little* thing?"

"Did you *bring* it?" Jannie insisted.

"Come indoors and I'll show you," their father said.

They followed him into the living room, and stood in a solemn row by the couch. "Now don't touch," their father said, and they nodded all together. They watched while he carefully set the bundle down on the couch and unwrapped it.

Then, into the stunned silence which followed, Sally finally said, "What is it?"

"It's a baby," said their father, with an edge of nervousness to his voice, "it's a baby boy and its name is Barry."

"What's a baby?" Sally asked me.

"It's pretty small," Laurie said doubtfully. "Is that the best you could get?"

"I tried to get another, a bigger one," I said with irritation, "but the doctor said this was the only one left."

"My goodness," said Jannie, "what are we going to do with *that*? Anyway," she said, "*you*'re back."

Suddenly she and Sally were both climbing onto my lap at once, and Laurie came closer and allowed me to kiss him swiftly on the cheek; I discovered that I could reach around all three of them, something I had not been able to do for some time.

"Well," Laurie said, anxious to terminate this sentimental scene, "so now we've got this baby. Do you think it will grow?" he asked his father.

"It's got very small feet," Jannie said. "I really believe they're *too* small."

"Well, if you don't like it we can *always* take it back," said their father.

"Oh, we like it all right, I guess," Laurie said comfortingly. "It's only that I guess we figured on something a little bigger."

"What *is* it?" asked Sally, unconvinced. She put out a tentative finger and touched one toe. "Is this its foot?"

"Please start calling it 'him,' " I said.

"Him?" said Sally. "Him?"

"Hi, Barry," said Laurie, leaning down to look directly into one open blue eye, "hi, Barry, hi, Barry, hi, Barry."

"Hi, Barry," said Jannie.

"Hi, Barry," said Sally. "Is this your foot?"

"I suppose it'll cry a lot?" Laurie asked his father, man to man.

His father shrugged. "Not much else it *can* do," he pointed out.

"I remember Jannie cried all the time," Laurie went on.

"I did not," Jannie said. "*You* were the one cried all the time."

"Did you get it at the hospital?" Sally asked. She moved Barry's foot up and down and he curled his toes.

"Yes," I said.

"Why didn't you take me?" Sally asked.

"I took you the last time," I said.

"What did you say its name was?" Sally asked.

"Barry," I said.

"Barry?"

"Barry."

"Where did you get it?"

"Well," Laurie said. He sighed and stretched. "Better take a look at those Greek tetradrachms," he said.

"Right," said his father, rising.

"Jannie, you go find that hairbrush," I said.

Laurie, on his way out of the room, stopped next to me and hesitated, obviously trying to think of something congratulatory to say. "I guess it *will* be nice for you, though," he said at last. "Something to keep you busy now *we*'re all grown up."

APPENDIX: HANDBILL

SOME POLTERGEIST INCIDENTS IN THE RESIDENCE OF S.E.H., ESQUIRE

With a Moſt Intereſting Diſcuſſion of the Probable Reſults of ſuch Diſturbances in the Dwelling of a Gentleman.

Mr. H. depoſing, That, Having lived upon this houſe for more than ſeven years together, he has until recent months ſeen no evidence of ſupernatural poſſeſſion, Until, within the months juſt paſt, when his houſe has become ſeemingly a meeting-place, or neſt, for demonic ſpirits;

That, for the ſpace of more than three nights together, his family has been diſturbed by the ſounds of a great running, or ſtamping, which, going on above half an Hour at a time, has cauſed the greateſt Apprehenſion among them;

That his Wife, a Female of nervous diſpoſition and eaſily excited, almoſt into Frenzies by Supernatural Manifeſtations, has at ſeveral ſeparate times been troubled by the Night Mares, as of a Perſonage whiſpering into her Ear ſecrets of Horror;

That, having as was her cuſtom the daily ſpoons in her hand and ſetting them one by one into the Beauſet, ſhe has had at different times one fpoon or another taken forcibly from her hand and on one ocafion this fpoon was afterward hurled, or thrown, violently at her Head;

That, fince thefe manifeftations, a cabinet door belonging to a Televifion fet, will neither ftay clofed nor fuffer itfelf to be latched, although four feparate Carpenters endeavored to perfuade it fhut with their Hammars and a Mr. Feeley, a gentleman, being newly come into the houfe, did ftrike it moft violently with his foot;

That Mifter H.'s fon, a child of fome eight or ten years, doth fo conftruct nightly with his leffon-books a Barrier, or Wall, againft the doorway of his nurfery, in order, as he fays, to *keep out the goblins*, and he doth, befides this, fay that he hath feen feveral times a Wolf, or other large black animal, upon the Roof outfide his Window;

That at night recently, this Manifeftation did take up a Knife, or Dirque, which Mifter H. doth always keep by him left footpads come upon him fuddenly and unawares, and dafh'd it fo wildly againft the wall that it like to have broke into a thoufand pieces;

That for the fpace of fome feven nights running, there hath been in this houfe the found of drums, of laughing, of ftomping, and crafhing of objects, not to be accounted for even by the feveral children of Mifter H., and more, perhaps faith Mr. H., than could even be performed by his children without guefts or other children in company;

Thefe things, attefted to by Mr. H. and his family, have been feen and witneffed by many other perfons who have vifited Mr. H.'s houfe to obferve them, and by the aforeſaid Feeley, gentleman, and all ſuch perſons agree that the houſe is poſſeſſed by a Poltergeiſt, or Evil Spirit, which has in its Intent the moſt Malicious Amuſement at the expenſe of thoſe dwellers in the Houſe;

That Mister H.'s Landlord, a man of ſome means, refuſes either to have the houſe Exorciſed or to allow Miſter H. to Looſe his Leaſe, and that therefore Miſter H.'s only Recourſe, as he ſays, is to open his Houſe to Viſitors at a Penny a View, ſince, as he ſays, it is already become ſo full of Company at beſt that he may as well Charge.

Raising demons

Some of the material in this book appeared in *Woman's Day* magazine under the titles "The Sneaker Crisis," "Worldly Goods," "The Clothespin Dolls" and "Lucky to Get Away," and is reprinted by permission, and a section known as "An International Incident" was first printed in *The New Yorker* magazine.

For Louis Scher

I conjure and command you, O Demons, all and so many as ye are, to accept this Book with good grace, so that whensoever we may read it, the same being approved and recognized as in proper form and valid, you shall be constrained to appear in comely human form when you are called, accordingly as the reader shall judge. In no circumstances shall you make any attempt upon the body, soul, or spirit of the reader, nor inflict any harm on those who may accompany him, either by mutterings, tempests, noise, scandals, nor yet by lesion or by hindrance in the execution of the commands of this Book. I conjure you to appear immediately when the conjuration is made, to execute without dallying all that is written and enumerated in its proper place in the said Book.

Conjuration from the Grimoire of Honorius

ONE

I DO NOT NOW have the slightest understanding of the
events which got us out of one big white house which
we rented into another, bigger white house which we own,
at least in part. That is, I know we moved, and I think I
know why, and I know we spent three pleasant months in
a friend's summer home, and I am pretty sure we got most
of our own furniture back. What really puzzles me, I suppose, is how a series of events like that gets itself started.
One day I went to clean out the hall closet and the next
thing I knew we were trying to decide whether to have all
four phones put on one line, or leave them all different
numbers and list ourselves four times in the phone book.
We decided wrong, by the way. What with the phone
starting to ring for Laurie at eight in the morning and for
Jannie about noon and for Sally in the early afternoon and
every now and then—a high, uncomfortable voice, stam-
mering and usually hanging up unexpectedly—for Barry,
we know now that we should have left the four phones
separate. We should have listed three of them for the children and kept the fourth one private, giving out the number

to the two or three people who either have no children of their own or are still optimistic enough to try to telephone their friends.

We had rented the big white house for nine years. Sally had been born while we lived there, and so had Barry, and the kitchen needed repainting. The stairs and the walls and the positions of the light switches and the crack in the glass of the front door had all become affectionate and familiar to us. Laurie knew the bike routes to everywhere in town from the house, Jannie could cross the street to play with a friend, Sally had slept in Jannie's old carriage on the front porch, where Barry now slept, the shadows of the pillars moving slowly across the plaid carriage robe. All the millions of things we possessed as a family were inside the house, but, inexorably, there came one shocking moment when we discovered that the house was full.

I went, one spring morning, to clean out one of those downstairs half-closets, which begin as very practical affairs, meant to be the resting place for wet boots and umbrellas, and end up as containers for ice skates and then hockey sticks and then tennis rackets and then, by the most logical of extensions, baseball gloves and football helmets and basketballs and riding boots and jackets left behind by visiting children. I had picked up a big cardboard carton at the grocery, and into it I put the baseball gloves and the football helmets and the riding boots and the tennis rackets and the basketball. I put the carton at the foot of the back stairs, so I would remember to take it up the next time I went, and I put clean newspaper on the floor of the closet and went and got all the wet boots from the corner of the kitchen and the spot inside the front door and the back seat of the car, and I lined the boots up in the closet and derived an enormous satisfaction from closing the closet door tight for the first time in months.

Later when I went upstairs I took the carton with me. There was no room for it in the bedroom shared by my two daughters. There was no room for it in the bedroom of my older son, and certainly no room for it in the tiny room where the baby lived. There was no room for it in the attic where we kept sleds and garden rakes. There was no room for it in the attic where we kept trunks and boxes of things I meant to give away someday. I knew there was no room for it in the garage because I had tried a day or so before to put the snow tires in there and had finally to put them in the cellar, consequently there was no room in the cellar because I had barely been able to squeeze in the snow tires. I was not going to leave a carton of football helmets and a basketball in the bedroom which my husband and I shared, particularly since there were already sixteen cartons of books in the corner next to my closet, and I could not leave it in the upstairs hall because there were nine more cartons of books lined up along that wall. Anyway I knew if I left a carton of baseball gloves and football helmets and a basketball right out in the front hall it would only be a day or so before I had to gather them all up again from the living room and the kitchen, and I would probably have to put them all back into the hall closet and then the door would not close again.

With a certain feeling of bewilderment, and a strong sense of the inevitability of fate, I took the carton back downstairs and put everything directly back into the hall closet, and of course the door would not close. I could not find anywhere to put the empty carton, so I took it outside and left it for the garbage man.

A day or so later I decided to put away the winter clothes in moth balls, but the closet I have always used for winter storage was full of boxes holding the baby's clothes and gifts people had sent him, because there was no closet in the small room where we put the baby. It occurred to me that I could put the winter clothes away in a trunk in the far attic, but when I finally got the attic door open I discovered that the trunk was full; my husband had cleaned his filing cabinet and when there was no place to put the papers and correspondence and clippings which were too important to be thrown away but not of any immediate usefulness, like our old college yearbook and the copy of our marriage license, he had carried them up in the laundry basket and put them all away in the trunk in the far attic. I thought that I might buy a cardboard closet to put the clothes away in, but there would be no place to put a new closet, since both the attics were full, unless I put a closet in the baby's room and moved the baby's things out of the moth closet and then put the winter clothes in the old moth closet, but then there would be no place to put the baby, because there was only just room enough in his little room for his crib, and I had to take him in on the girls' bed to dress him.

We had three more attics, but one of them was full of old lumber and bricks left over from the various additions that had been built onto the house, and one of them was full of bats, and the last could only be reached by climbing through a trapdoor in the ceiling of the next-to-the-last attic and even if I could get past the bats and through the lumber and bricks I did not think I could keep taking the baby up and down through a trapdoor.

That night at dinner my husband remarked that he

wished he could get to his place at the dining room table without having to squeeze so past the buffet; either he was putting on weight, he pointed out, or I had moved the table. I said that now we had the baby's high chair in the dining room because there was no place to put it in the kitchen I could not possibly have the dining room table any farther away from the buffet because if there were any less space around the kitchen doorway I would not be able to get in and out at all, and no one would get any dinner. My husband said why not give all the children their dinners around the kitchen table, thus making considerably less congestion and confusion in the dining room at dinnertime, and I had to explain that if I put chairs for all the children around the kitchen table at dinnertime I would have to go around through the study to get from the stove to the sink, and Laurie added indignantly that that was a fine thing, that was, to expect him and the girls to eat in the kitchen and let the baby eat in the dining room.

After dinner Laurie had a friend in to watch television, so my husband and I had to sit in the study. Jannie came in to read in the study because the boys asked her please kindly to let them alone while they were seeing the western movie; Sally was asleep upstairs with the lights out so Jannie could not read in bed, and the light in the dining room was not good enough to read by. With three of us in the study someone had to sit in a straight chair, so I thought I might as well get some mending done and let Jannie have the comfortable chair with the reading light. When I went to get my sewing basket I found that it was full of walnuts the children had brought home. They had not been able to find any place to put the walnuts until we decided what to do with them, so they had put them in my sewing basket, which was already pretty full of socks. Later, when I went upstairs to look at the baby I perceived, seeing almost for the first clear time, that both sides of the staircase were lined with things—books, sweaters, dolls, boxes of crayons —which had been put there temporarily and then left because there was no place else to leave them. I came downstairs and went into the study and stood in front of my husband until he put down his book and looked at me.

"We have too much stuff," I told him. "Dolls and hockey sticks and winter clothes and walnuts."

"I thought there seemed to be more around than usual," he said.

"There is no more room in this house," I said. "We cannot fit in one more thing. Not one."

Jannie lifted her head. "Ninki is going to have kittens again," she said.

"Well, she can't have them here," I said. "There isn't an inch—"

"Last time she had them in the green living room chair."

"When I went by a few minutes ago there were four or five jackets and a pile of library books on that chair," I said.

"Start asking people now if they want kittens," my husband said. He picked up his book again. "Return the library books," he added, with the air of a man settling a petty domestic problem.

"We have got to get a bigger house," I said.

"Don't be silly," my husband said, reading. "There *is* no bigger house."

"A new house?" said Jannie. "Can I have a room of my own?"

When I went down to the grocery the next morning the grocer said he heard we were thinking of moving. We'd been in the old Fielding house quite a while now, he said; perhaps now we were aiming to buy? He *had* heard, just by accident, that Mrs. Wilbur wanted to sell that big place on upper Main Street. It would be good for us to be living on upper Main Street, because then the kids could walk to school, not to mention being right in the school district so Sally could get into the kindergarten. While I was out with the car, he said, I ought to go on up Main Street and take a look at the big house from the outside. "You'll know it by the gateposts," the grocer said.

When I went into the post office the postman said he heard we were thinking of moving. While we were about it, he suggested, we ought to think of getting a house closer in to town. Then we could get our mail in a postbox in the post office instead of having to wait for Mr. Mortimer to come round with the rural delivery, because now that Mr. Mortimer was getting on, and particularly since the day Mr. Mortimer's car skidded and went into the ditch, which they hadn't been able to get parts for it because it was so old, well, the postman said, it must be something of a trial to us not to be getting our mail till three, four o'clock in the afternoon. Did I know that Millie Wilbur was thinking of putting that big house on the market? The one upstreet, with the gateposts? Wouldn't hurt the price of eggs to have a look at it.

Mr. Cunningham in the gas station said he heard we were thinking of moving, and that big white house with the gateposts would be a good buy if you knocked some off Millie Wilbur's price.

Feeling that I was in the grip of something stronger than

I was, I drove slowly on up Main Street. The house with the gateposts was unmistakable, particularly since the left-hand gatepost leaned at a sharp angle inward toward the driveway. I saw maple trees, and a wide lawn, and a barn almost as big as the house. I could almost see our children running on the lawn, swinging from the trees, playing in the barn. I did not notice the sagging front steps or the flaking paint.

When I came up the hill toward our own house it looked small and overstuffed. I carried the groceries in and put them on the kitchen table and then went into the study to speak to my husband.

"I understand we're thinking of moving," I said.

"We are not," he said.

"Millie Wilbur's putting the big old house with the gateposts on the market."

"We are not interested. You may tell Millie Wilbur."

"Must be twenty rooms in that house. And a barn. Trees. Two gateposts."

"I'm sure whoever buys it will have plenty of space. Now I am working," said my husband.

The phone rang, and when I answered it, it was a lady who introduced herself as a Mrs. Ferrier. She understood we were thinking of moving. I said we were not and she said oh, that was fine, because her husband had just been transferred to our town and they had been getting pretty desperate about a house. I said we were not moving and she said they were ready to take just about *any*thing, and when could she come and look around our house? Because, she said, they were living at present with her cousin, all three children, and they were getting so desperate they really didn't care what they got, so long as it was a roof over their heads. I said it was our roof and we planned to keep it over our own heads, and she said would it be all right to drop around tomorrow? I said no, and she said about three, then, and thank you and goodbye.

I still had the extraordinary feeling of inevitability, which I began to identify as the same feeling as I get when I try to stop my car on an icy hill. Before I could get back to the kitchen the phone rang three more times. The first was a local real estate agent, who had heard that I had been looking at the big old house with the gateposts. He was sure I was going to like the inside of the house even better than the outside. The second call was from Mr. Gore down at the bank, who thought that before we went any further on this deal we ought to understand the principles of the mortgage; he said he would be up to see my husband that evening. The third call was from Mr. Fielding, our land-lord, who understood that we were thinking of moving.

I avoided going into the study, because I knew that my husband would ask me who had been on the phone. I went into the kitchen to open my groceries and get out the veg-etable soup for lunch, and I decided that I had better make a potato pudding for dinner, since then my husband would be agreeably full of potato pudding by the time Mr. Gore came from the bank.

When Jannie came home from school that afternoon she said that her teacher had put it into the class news that Jannie's mommy and daddy were going to get a new house and Jannie would walk to school instead of taking the bus. A girl named Carole lived just past the big white house with the gateposts, and Carole passed the big white house every day on her way to school and Carole said it was a very nice house except the people living there were mean and wouldn't give candy on Hallowe'en. Laurie came home late, because he rode his bike to school and on his way home had detoured to have a look at the new house. He reported that it looked pretty good and he had met a very nice lady standing on the side porch and she had asked him lots and lots of questions. He repeated this to his father at dinner, although I made strenuous attempts to interrupt, and his father looked up from the potato pudding to say what kind of questions, for heaven's sake? Laurie said oh, like how much furniture we had, and when we planned to move and things like that, and Laurie added that he had told the lady lots of furniture, and pretty soon. My husband took another piece of potato pudding and remarked mildly to me that I should caution the children against this kind of silly talk with strangers, because that was the way rumors got started, and rumors were harder to stop than they were to start.

Although I told my husband afterward that I believed it was only a coincidence, Mr. Gore from the bank and the real estate agent arrived together. I showed them into the study, closed the door, sent Jannie to read in our bedroom, turned the television set down very low, and went out to wash the dinner dishes.

That, so far as I can recollect, is the first stage of how we happened to start to buy a big white house with two gateposts. After about an hour my husband came out of the study to get the cigar humidor, and a little later he came to the study door and asked if I would get out some more ice. I decided that I might perhaps look officious if I went barging into the study while the men were talking, so I stayed thoughtfully in the kitchen, and finally cleaned all the pantry shelves, thinking of Mrs. Ferrier coming tomorrow. When I heard the front door close, I waited a few minutes and then went timidly into the study.

"Company gone?" I asked, through the smoke.

"Yep," said my husband.

"Any news?" I said.

"Why, I don't know," said my husband. "Were you expecting news?"

I counted to ten. "I thought you might have been talking about the house," I said.

"What house?" my husband said.

"I thought," I said carefully, "that Mr. Gore, and the real estate agent—"

"Bill," my husband said. "Fine fellow."

"I thought you might have been discussing our possible purchase of the house now owned by Mrs. Millie Wilbur. It is a big white house, about halfway up Main Street past the railroad station. It has two gateposts, the left-hand one slightly askew."

"Askew," said my husband appreciatively. He thought. "Wrong side of the tracks," he pointed out. "Didn't tell me *that*."

"It's the right side of the tracks, actually," I said. "I mean, all the big nice old houses are on out there. We're on the wrong side of the tracks *now*, really."

"Depends which side you're *not* on," said my husband acutely. "Well." He nodded and took up his book.

"But what about the house?"

"What house?"

"I am going to bed," I said.

"By the way," he remarked, as I opened the study door. "One more thing about that house. Seventeen people living there."

"What?"

"Seventeen," he said firmly. "Four apartments. One downstairs front, one upstairs front, one downstairs back, one upstairs back, one downstairs front, one upstairs—"

I closed my mouth. "You mean," I said after a minute, "there are four separate apartments in that house? Four kitchens? Four bathrooms? Four—"

"One upstairs back, one upstairs front, one downstairs—"

"Four telephones?"

"One downstairs up."

When I went to see the house with the real estate agent the next morning I learned more about it. There were three acres of land, on which we might someday put a swimming pool, or a tennis court, or a miniature golf course, or a garden. The barn was two stories high, suitable for a summer theater or any number of square dancers. The house had been divided up into four apartments about six years back, and could be un-divided by the removal of beaverboard partitions. (It occurred subsequently to both my husband and myself that what we should have done was put all four of our children, and their possessions, into one apartment and leave the partitions in, but by then it was too late.) There was no wall to go with the gateposts. There were four separate entrances to the house, and the agent assured me that there were indeed four separate kitchens, four separate bathrooms, four separate telephones, and garage space in the barn for four cars.

The agent had keys to two of the apartments, and we went gingerly into the downstairs front, tapping at the beaverboard behind which lurked the downstairs back, and marveling at the wallpaper, which had green funeral urns and laurel leaves. We went outside and out the entrance to the downstairs front and around the corner and in the entrance to the downstairs back, where a little dog yapped at us so persistently that we took only the most perfunctory glance at the rooms. The wallpaper there was of purple rhododendrons with many leaves. We went out again and around another corner of the house to the stairway which led up to the upstairs back apartment. We could not get in, but by craning our necks could get a glimpse of the wallpaper, which seemed to be orange and black birds. Then we went around another corner of the house and came to the entrance to the upstairs front, which was actually the main front door of the house, although we could not get in, and could only guess at the wallpaper; I subsequently discovered that it was a multicolored geometric pattern.

We were just getting into the agent's car to go home when the lady who lived in the downstairs front came home and invited us in again. She had been packing, she said. She had been after her husband for six months to move to Schenectady where her sister lived, and news that the house might be sold had been enough to give him a final push. I asked her if she had done her own decorating —the wallpaper, for instance—and she said certainly not, and one of the big reasons in favor of moving was that the wallpaper was beginning to get on her nerves, not to mention the downstairs back, because, although she had never been one for gossip, since once people started telling tales about their neighbors you never knew where you were, she knew for a fact that the downstairs back were behind on their rent since last fall and the upstairs back never got along with anyone and she wouldn't be a bit surprised to hear that they were separating the way she yelled at him.

The upstairs front were very nice people and she had never heard a word against them from anybody, although she must say if anything would help this blessed wallpaper drive her out it was that radio going going going all day long. Also they were most ungracious about the clothesline and she wouldn't put it past them to have cut it the day her wash fell down.

We backed out, nodding, and got into the agent's car again. I looked back at the house as we drove off and it seemed enormous; next to the barn was what looked very much like a berry patch.

When Mrs. Ferrier stepped inside our front door at one minute before three that afternoon it was perfectly clear to me without hesitation that we were not going to become fast friends. She stood just inside the door, looking around. She looked at the hall closet, half closed, at the flotsam and jetsam lining the stairs on both sides, and at the wallpaper in the hall, which was the cabbage rose design we had chosen with Mr. Fielding nine years before. She closed her eyes for a minute and then, with me following, went on into the living room, where the library books still sat on the green chair and someone had left a jacket on the television set. "Nice large room, if it was fixed up," Mrs. Ferrier said. In the dining room she tapped the table thoughtfully, perhaps looking for termites, and pulled back a curtain to see if the room overlooked the road, glancing briefly at the dust on the windowsill. In the study she nodded to my husband, turned completely around once, and then remarked that we seemed to be making no practical use of the space in our house. "This room would be *much* larger," she said, "if you took out all those books."

Mrs. Ferrier thought the master bedroom should have

faced west, and she barely put her head inside the smaller bedrooms. "They would be much larger," I told her, "if we took out the beds."

Mrs. Ferrier fixed me with her cold eye. "If you took out the beds where would you sleep?" she wanted to know, and I followed her meekly downstairs.

"Well," she said, at the front door again. "How soon can you be out?"

"Good heavens," I said, "I haven't any idea of—"

"It shouldn't take you more than two or three weeks to pack. Most of this stuff I suppose you'll be throwing away; be sure to get a man to carry it off; I don't want it all piled around back or something. I'll stop in someday next week to measure for the curtains. That little bedroom at the head of the stairs will have to be enlarged. Say it takes you a month to get out—I'll have the carpenters here on the first of May."

"I hardly think—"

She smiled at me, which did not make me like her any better. "I thought someone had told you," she said. "I was a Fielding before I married. I told the family that it was a pity to have the old family house falling apart in the hands of strangers; we owe it to the town, after all, to have Fieldings living here. So we are coming home again." She sighed nostalgically, and I unclenched my fingers from the stair rail and said as quietly as I could that I was sure the villagers would be dancing in the streets when they heard that the Fieldings were coming home again. "Goodbye," I added firmly, opening the front door. "I'll see you in a day or so, then," Mrs. Ferrier said, and of course I did not push her down the front steps.

We bought the big white house, at last, by merely signing our names on a piece of paper. Mr. Gore and Mr. Andrews down at the bank arranged the financial transference with an almost invisible maneuver of figures on a card. When my husband asked if we could borrow our money right back again and use the house as security, everybody laughed.

I stopped in at the grocery that afternoon to tell the grocer that we had bought the big white house with the gateposts and he told me a story about a fellow he knew who had rented for twenty years, saving money, until at the end of twenty years he had twenty thousand dollars in the bank, and he bought an old house planning to make it over and now, six months later, he was five thousand dollars in debt. I asked him if he had met Mrs. Ferrier and he said she had been in the store a couple times. "She takes after the Birminghams," he said, "from East Hoosick when old Delmar Fielding married the youngest Birmingham girl and the Fieldings first got into real money." I said I wished the Birminghams had stayed in East Hoosick, and he said a lot of other people had wished the same thing ever since the oldest Birmingham girl had got herself into the Prohibition party and went around making speeches.

He gave me a dozen cartons and I went home and began halfheartedly putting things into them. I took all the overshoes and skates and football helmets out of the hall closet and put them into a carton and put the carton in the hall by the front door. I took all the things off the stairs and put them into another carton, which I stacked in the hall next to the first carton. I was wondering what to put in the third carton when I was interrupted by Jannie to say that Ninki had just had her kittens on one of the comfortable chairs in the study and that my husband was sitting in the other comfortable chair and wanted to know what to do. I sent Jannie back to say that he should go right on reading and I put a clean dustcloth in the bottom of the third carton and went to get Ninki and her kittens, but I was interrupted again by the real estate agent on the phone. Could we move ourselves and family into the downstairs front apartment in the big white house, he wanted to know. Because although the downstairs front was vacating, the people in the upstairs back and the upstairs front were insisting upon at least two months' notice before they moved, and the downstairs back, who had been notified that back rent was to be paid in full, was refusing to move at all. Even if we planned to take out the partitions and change the wallpaper after we were moved in, there would still be a delay of at least two months before we could claim anything except the downstairs front. I had barely hung up the phone when Mrs. Ferrier called to say that now we had actually bought another house she was speeding things up a little because her cousin was getting pretty pointed about having all of them around all the time, so she was arranging to have the carpenters and painters arrive on the twentieth of April and would we please have the house clear by then.

Ninki's kittens were all black except one, who had four white feet. I went to the back porch to leave the carton of kittens and then came back into the study and told my husband that right after supper I was going to go to bed and read a mystery story and if the phone rang again he could answer it. When I heard Mr. Mortimer's car sideswipe our mailbox I got up without enthusiasm and went out to pick up the mail. There were three bills and a letter from my mother saying that a dear old friend of hers was going to

Europe that summer and had not had a chance to rent her summer house. Would we be interested in borrowing the house? It was completely furnished, in a pleasant mountain town seventy miles from where we lived, and had a new washing machine, a dishwasher, an electric mixer, and a deep freeze.

We had never owned a new washing machine, a dishwasher, an electric mixer, or a deep freeze. I read the letter over once to myself, twice aloud to my husband, and again at the dinner table. I sent a telegram to my mother that night, and the next morning I looked in the phone book under "Storage and Transfer" and got in touch with a Mr. Cobb, who listened sympathetically to our problem, and said that he believed that he was just the fellow to settle everything for us. He came to our house that afternoon, and walked with me from room to room; he made little jokes about "folks who never know what they've got until they come to put it away," and, "bet you people have spent a long time gathering up these things," and, "funny how most people don't understand about cubic feet; you take the average man, he knows how long a foot is, and usually he knows what a *square* foot is, from buying carpets and so on, but most people just don't understand the idea of cubic feet." This was so true of me that I could only nod and say it was a shame, the ignorance of the general public. Mr. Cobb was a very considerate person; when he had finished his tour—during which it was brought home to me just how much stuff we had in the garage and the attics and how the children had accumulated swings and slides and sleds outdoors—he sat down in the study with my husband and me and talked the whole situation over with us.

Money, it turned out, was the basic problem in putting furniture in storage, and the next most basic problem was the cubic foot. The concept of the cubic foot was intimately discussed, Mr. Cobb having passed over money swiftly and compassionately, and Mr. Cobb told my husband about how the average man knew about feet and square feet but not cubic feet. Mr. Cobb then remarked that we had a great many things to store, didn't we, and my husband and I said oh, not so much, considering it in terms of *cubic* feet; most of our stuff, we pointed out, was flat, like books. Mr. Cobb smiled slightly and said well, you take ten thousand books, which is what we estimated we had, and you pile them on top of one another, well, that mounted into cubic feet. I said shrewdly that if you took rugs and laid them flat, that was almost *no* cubic feet, and Mr. Cobb said well, it was a funny thing about rugs. Rugs, he said sadly, could not be stored unless they were freshly cleaned and rolled, which made them, he said, spreading his hands in a wide gesture, into cubic feet again. Almost all of Mr. Cobb's function—aside from lighting cigarettes for me, and pausing respectfully when my husband spoke—seemed to consist of taking objects which actually existed in almost square feet, and translating them into cubic feet—rugs had to be rolled, books had to be boxed, pictures had to be put into packing cases. He also suggested helpfully that we stuff as much stuff into other stuff as we could. He then made his last clear translation— nice flat money into cubic feet of space—by suggesting gently that payment was of course in advance, and departed.

We had to do it, at last. You cannot transport four children with clothes and toys and five cats and a dog and a baby carriage and a coin collection and two typewriters and a picnic hamper in one car and still have much room left for furniture. Our borrowed house had all the beds and dishes and chairs and tables that we needed, and in much better shape than those we left behind, and since we only expected to stay until mid-August, to be back and moved in before it was time to get ready for school, we fondly supposed that we would not need heavy coats or electric trains or hot-water bottles, although, as it turned out, the first month we were in the borrowed house it rained every day.

I managed almost immediately to dispose of the dishwasher, by permitting it to chew up and eat one of the imported wineglasses, leaving only the stem, and then I managed to upset the coffeepot into the washing machine, and I was still picking dried coffee grounds out of the childrens' shirts when Mr. Cobb's warehouse receipt, accompanied by bill (payable in *advance*, Mr. Cobb's letter pointed out nudgingly) arrived in the mail, and my husband, apoplectic, strode furiously into the kitchen. "What in the *name* of heaven," he demanded, "is a pedestal burlapped? And why did we want to *store* it?"

I thought. "It's the cats' scratching post, I think," I said. "We could hardly bring it with us, you know."

"Do you realize," said my husband, waving the papers under my nose, "that we also stored one empty crate? Three pieces of canvas? One metal cakebox?"

"I meant to send that cakebox back to your Aunt Sadie," I said. "You remember she sent us that chocolate—"

"Stack six wastebaskets," my husband said. "Snow shovel."

It turned out that what we could not identify the children largely could; we had no trouble with such items as 295: Radio TV cabinet, or the series of eight items labeled 68: Rug, 69: Rug, 70: Rug, and so on. Item 17: Large Green Chest S & M Soiled—S & M turned out to mean Scratched and Marred—was the Pennsylvania Dutch chest which had been given to us as a wedding present by friends in the antique business, and what was Scratching and Marring and Soiling to Mr. Cobb and his goblins was to us a fine antique finish. Nothing of ours, actually, was to Mr. Cobb in precisely tiptop condition; his abbreviations for Bad Order (B.O.), Scratched and Marred, Moth-Eaten (M.E.), Soiled, Rusted, Worn, Torn, Loose, Chipped, and Dented, were listed after almost every item. Double Bed Mattress Burnt brought back vivid memories of the morning I fell back asleep with a cigarette in my hand, Mexican Chair Broken reminded us of the time my husband tried to reach the top of the closet shelf. Tricycle B.O. spoke for itself, although it had been the little girl next door who had put her foot through the spokes.

It was in the odd items, however, that we found ourselves glancing secretly at one another, wondering what furtive hiding places had been invaded, what hidden lairs of junk were now exposed. The Coal Grate, for instance (R. though it was), which none of us could remember; had Mr. Cobb stored in our name some priceless piece of metalwork belonging to old Mr. Fielding, or had he boldly wrested it from the furnace in some mistaken zeal, or had we, indeed, at some past time gone hand in hand and bought our first coal grate, hoping eventually to build a full fireplace around it? The Folding Mirror for Dressing Table S & M, I remembered; it had come off a dressing table which my mother-in-law had sent us with a load of other furniture when she moved from a house into an apartment; the dressing table had long been disintegrated and thrown away, and the mirror had lain in an attic corner for years. In cubic feet it must have been priceless to Mr. Cobb. Round Green Table Iron Base B.O. mystified us all, but Laurie saved us over Occasional Chair Without Cushion Joints Weak; that, he pointed out after much thought, was the chair which had been in a corner of the cellar near the workbench, which he and his father had been using as a sawhorse, thus almost certainly weakening the cushion joints.

We owned an old metal phonograph horn, we discovered, and a mysterious item identified as Trunk M.T.B. B.O.; we finally narrowed this down (Marred, Broken, Bad Order) to the extra T., and considering that this was the trunk into which my husband had unloaded his filing cabinet, we came at last to assume that the T. stood for Trivia, or Too-heavy.

Gradually, during the long summer days, our list became as intimate a part of our daily life as the washing machine grumbling to itself in the kitchen, or the deep freeze doggedly making popsicles downstairs. "Small Round Table S & M," I would cry gaily to Laurie, and he would be allowed one minute before answering, "Girls' room, corner near the window." "147, Fire Lighter," my husband would come back, and if no one could guess it (far corner of the cellar, leaning against the wall) another penny went into the pot for Mr. Cobb. D. R. Table puzzled us, until we realized that it was not a table Dented and Rusted, but our old dining room table; Bundle Metal Discs B.O. were not a little sack of Greek coins my husband had somehow overlooked, but the metal records for our old-fashioned music box, although how Mr. Cobb was able to estimate that they were in B.O. is beyond me. Mr. Cobb made three cents on items 166, 167, and 168, listed individually as Ador. Arm Chair B.O., Ador. Arm Chair Arm Off B.O., and Ador. Arm Chair B.O., since we could all clearly remember armchairs with the arms off, but none that might reasonably have impressed the hard-bitten Mr. Cobb as Adorable. Items 154, 155, 156, and 157 infuriated my husband. "Bundle 4 Bed Slats," he said helplessly. "Bundle 5 Bed Slats, Bundle 4 Bed Slats, Bundle 3 Bed Slats—you simply can't *trust* those people; *we* could have made one Bundle 17 Bed Slats and saved just that much money."

"Consider for a minute," I begged him, "consider item 285, one half Round Side Table—now we *must* have saved money *there.*"

"Red Boot Black Box," my husband murmured.

"My red boots?" asked Sally.

"My black box?" asked Jannie.

"My red box for blacking boots?" asked Laurie.

"Boxing boots?" I asked. "Blacking gloves?"

"It's dented," my husband said, consulting the list. "Probably another Bundle Bed Slats they were ashamed to put down."

One of Mr. Cobb's favorite dodges was a confusing little shortcut known as CU, or Contents Unknown. Small Victrola, CU. Packing Case, CU. Carpet Sweeper with Handle, CU. Carton CU, Carton CU, Carton CU, Flat Carton CU. (The Flat Carton Contents Unknown earned Mr. Cobb another penny.) Kitchen Range CU. (The remains of our Thanksgiving turkey, I believe.) Electric Baseball Game CU. Moreover, after items 68 through 74 ("Rug, Rug,

Rug, Rug, Rug, Rug, Rug") it was satisfying to learn that we had tamed one—item 191, Domestic Rug.

By far the most absorbing sequence turned out to be 133 through 137—Red Parasol, Sword, Sword, Sword, Small Flag. These probably came from the same costume department as 19: Spear and 20: Horsewhip, and we began to think nostalgically of how, as a family, we could have held Mrs. Ferrier at bay, armed with our swords and our spears and our horsewhips and our red parasol, and waving one another on with our Small Flag. At any rate, we were all happy to reflect that the Black Hat Box (204) and the Floor Mop (382) were beyond harm, as was the Pair Auto Tires Worn (158) and, of course, the Odd Drawer from Table (370). Besides, there was nothing so particularly odd about the drawer, it was the *table* that was so odd, appearing and disappearing the way it did.

Whenever I tried to picture the items on Mr. Cobb's list, think concretely of, say, the ashtrays and metronomes and bed tables and kitchen chairs, they fell automatically into place, as they had stood for so many years. I think that during the long days of that summer—and after the first month of rain it was hot all the time—I slowly forgot that our house was not waiting for us, and came to believe that we would go home to the familiar place; my only concession to the idea of a new house was to set my mental picture of our old house in the new location on upper Main Street, and sketch in a barn in back, and the gateposts in front. We received a sharp letter from Mrs. Ferrier accusing us, in so many words, of stealing the garage doors. I threw the letter away because of course we had not stolen the garage doors. I had smashed one of them slightly trying to get the car out one day, and we had taken it off the hinges, but it was right there leaning against the side of the house if Mrs. Ferrier had only used her eyes.

The weather was hot, we went swimming, and the children, even Barry, were brown and lively. Our neighbors were almost all summer folk like ourselves, and agreeable, informal people; the children picked up acquaintances after their own fashions. Because our next-door neighbor, a Mrs. Simpkins, dropped over on our first morning and pointed out most pressingly that it was so nice for her young ones to have what she insisted upon calling "gentle, *refined* kiddies" right next door, I felt that it was incumbent upon me to make immediate overtures of friendship, and I invited the Simpkins children over, sight unseen, for supper. We cooked hamburgers out in the back yard, with Mrs. Simpkins beaming down at us from her kitchen window, but after supper the Simpkins boy settled down to play house with his sister and Jannie. Laurie, refusing ungraciously to be Daddy, spent the evening indoors staring disconsolately out at the lake. "Golly," he said perhaps thirteen times, "golly, I sure wish there was something to *do* around this joint, boy."

When, the next morning, an invitation was delivered to Laurie and Jannie, asking them to take their evening hamburgers in the Simpkins back yard, Laurie refused pointblank, and only the threat of no swimming for one whole week persuaded him to go. He came home immediately after supper, and spent the evening indoors by the front window. "Golly," he said, "if only there was something to *do* around here."

On the third morning Laurie was still at breakfast when the Simpkins boy came down his back steps, his book of pressed flowers under his arm, and made purposefully for our house. Laurie raced out the front door, leaving me to cover his retreat by holding the Simpkins boy at the back door. I asked how Mrs. Simpkins was, and whether the collecting and pressing of wild flowers was not too arduous a hobby for the hot summer days. I said I was sorry, but Laurie had just stepped out and I did not know where he was or when he would be back. I said that when he did come back I would most assuredly tell him that the little Simpkins boy was looking for him and wanted to know whether he would like to pack a picnic lunch and go on a nature walk. After fifteen minutes I closed the back door on the little Simpkins boy with a strong feeling of sympathy for Laurie.

Laurie did not come home until long after the rest of us had finished lunch. When he came in he was in a hurry. He had a long scratch on his cheek, his shirt was ripped, and his nose had clearly been bleeding. He said no, he had not been fighting. He had met some fellows. One of them was named George. He had *not* been fighting. George had a catcher's mitt and another one of the fellows had a bat and George knew where he could borrow a ball. There had been no fighting, and Laurie could not imagine why I should think there *had* been. He and George and the other fellows were getting up a game on the ball field down by the lake, and he promised not to fight any more.

After two or three more fruitless attempts to interest Laurie in wild flowers the Simpkins boy gave up, and became a regular participant in the doll games his sister and Jannie played, with Sally tagging along. Laurie and George and George's friends, who traveled in a pack like wild dogs, spent their long days at the ball field or at the riding stables or in the lake, displacing a hundred times their own weight in water. My husband and I told one another that the children had never seemed happier or healthier. My husband set up a horseshoe-pitching court at one end of our back yard, and in the cool evenings he and Laurie went out to pitch horseshoes while the girls and I sat on the grass and watched them and Barry slept, smiling, on the cool screened porch. After Laurie had won every game every night for four nights in a row my husband decided that he was going to teach me to pitch horseshoes, but it turned out to be almost impossible for me to learn, because the only way I could lift the horseshoes enough to throw was by using both hands. After the evening when I, throwing two-handed, put a horseshoe through the canvas back of one of our lawn chairs, my husband set up a badminton court, which was much more successful. For some reason Laurie could never learn to play badminton at all, and Jannie and I, who both liked the game, never were skillful enough to beat anybody except each other. My husband and I played a lot of badminton as the summer wore on. I refused, as I have been doing every summer since I can remember, to allow anyone to try to teach me to swim, and Sally and I made sand castles while Laurie tried to learn racing dives off the dam and Jannie learned from her father how to do the dead man's float. After weeks of effort Laurie succeeded in teaching Sally a kind of rudimentary dog paddle. Several times the three older children and their father rented a boat and went off on picnic trips; I was always left behind as a punishment for not learning to swim, since, as Laurie explained severely, he and his father would have enough trouble with Jannie and Sally if the boat tipped over without having to save *me*, too.

While they were gone on their boat trips Barry and I lay out in the sun and took long, lovely naps.

Until mid-July, the possibility of entering actively into any demanding situation, much less the practical policies of the State Department of the United States, had not been anything we had considered extensively; although, as a family, we had always been reasonably dutiful citizens. We hung out a flag on Decoration Day, observed the Fourth of July with noisy cheer, paid our taxes with reluctance but on time, sent children to school with an eye to the truant officer, crossed the street with the green light, did not use the mails to defraud—we were sensible, citizenly folk, but not obtrusive. Our active participation in the operations of the government had been confined, not to put too fine a point on it, to voting. This complacent footing was inevitably blasted, abruptly, out from under us, and the slight Japanese accent which Sally retained from the experience lasted for several months.

It was on a pleasant Sunday afternoon, when I was sitting reading a mystery story on our own front porch. Through the still air I could hear the distant enraged shouts of nine-year-old boys discussing reasonably the accuracy of a batted ball; Sally and Jannie, shiny from their morning swim, were playing in the sandbox; Barry had awakened, cheerful, from his nap and was singing to himself in the playpen, watching the sunlight, and holding aloft one small foot. My husband was around on the side porch, slowly relaxing into that heavy-eyed state which hits him about the seventh inning of the baseball broadcast, and which slips imperceptibly into a nap before dinner. I had just showered and changed into a clean skirt and blouse, and was in the process of deciding that it was really too hot to fry the chicken for dinner, and I would make instead some nice cool salad (tunafish?) when Laurie shot down the road on the bike we had borrowed for the summer, and came to a shrieking halt half an inch from the porch steps. "Got to get ready," he said gaspingly, vaulting the porch rail. "Hurry."

"Laurie, it's just too *hot* to race around like that. You'll have sunstroke or something; *nothing* is important enough to—"

"Company," Laurie said. "People coming over. Here."

I rose abruptly. "Company?"

"Got to *hurry*, they'll be here in a minute." Laurie started through the door and I followed after him, saying, "Wait, who—"

"Got to talking to them. Ball field. Said they'd be right over, we got to *hurry*." He turned to the stairs. "Better put on a clean shirt," he said.

If Laurie intended, uncoerced, to put on a clean shirt, immediate and violent action of some kind was called for from me. I moved swiftly to the window which opened onto the side porch, said, "Company," and heard my husband groan. I then passed through the house to the back door, from which I shouted, "Jannie, Sally," and was rewarded by a distant answering voice. "Clean shirt," I said thoughtfully, and went up the stairs two at a time and into the girls' room where I found two nearly clean dresses, skidded into the boys' room where Laurie was buttoning his best Hawaiian print shirt, snatched a sunsuit for Barry, called downstairs, "Porch chairs," and stopped long enough to run a comb through my hair. "Who *are* these people?" I shouted to Laurie, and he shouted back from his room, "Visiting America. One's named Yashamoto, I *think*."

Remotely I recalled rumors I had heard of a group of foreign students visiting our town for a brief vacation and orientation course in this country before going on to study in various colleges and universities all over the country. "How many are there?" I shouted across to Laurie, but he had gone downstairs. Serve them coffee, I thought frantically, or perhaps something typically American—hot dogs? No, no, not in the middle of a hot afternoon. Iced coffee; iced coffee, and there was a box of doughnuts in the breadbox if the children hadn't gotten to it; cookies? I wish I had some ice cream, I thought; can't serve company popsicles from the deep freeze, and I took the three bottom steps in one leap. I was plugging in the electric coffeepot when Jannie and Sally came through the back door; I threw their dresses at them and said, "Company, wash your faces." They disappeared, murmuring, and I moved swiftly in to Barry, who was amused at the idea of wearing the sunsuit, since it was the first article of formal attire he had seen since summer's start. I tied Sally's sash, took a swipe at each head with the hairbrush, heard voices outside, emptied an ashtray on my way to the door, ducked my mystery out of sight, and opened the door. "Good afternoon," I said, only slightly out of breath.

There were six of them. "Good afternoon," said a gentleman in a red, white, and blue striped tie, who was, it turned out, the spokesman. "My name has been Horogai Yashamoto. Thank you very much for invitation to your home."

"We are delighted that you have come," I said, trapped without thinking into a kind of stilted formality. "Will you come in?"

I held the door open and they filed solemnly in past me,

and then lined up inside. Each of them was wearing an identification button, and as Mr. Yashamoto introduced them one by one I kept trying to look sideways at the names on the identification buttons, hoping that they would forgive mispronunciation. The two Japanese men were Mr. Yashamoto and Mr. Masamitsu, there were three people from Argentina, Mr. and Mrs. Fernandez and Mr. Lopez, and a tall gentleman with a black beard, who was from Ceylon and whose name I never learned, because I got it first as Babar and no amount of correction, after that, could make me change it. "How do you do," I kept saying, "how do you do."

For one hideous minute we all stood just inside the front door, smiling eagerly at one another and all obviously try-ing helplessly to find some civil, neat, appropriate comment for the situation; then, blessedly, the side porch door opened and my husband, inadequately briefed by Laurie, came in with his mouth open. "Good afternoon," Mr. Yashamoto said, with his little bow, "thank you very much for invi-tation to this home. We are pleased to have met you. We are pleased at seeing family life here."

My husband took a deep breath. "Glad you could come," he said manfully. "Hi," said Laurie, appearing behind him. "Hi, fellas."

Mr. Yashamoto bowed again to Laurie. "Our small friend Lorri," he said, pleased. "We are meeting your parents now."

"And my sisters," Laurie said, waving at Jannie and Sally, who were standing shyly in the kitchen doorway. "This big one's Jannie. The little one's Sally."

Mr. Yashamoto approached formally, and bowed to each

of them. "Jonni," he said. "Salli." "H'lo," said Jannie almost inaudibly, and Sally giggled and crossed her feet.

"*And* my brother Barry," said Laurie.

Mr. Yashamoto, following Laurie's pointing finger, bowed again, to the playpen. "Balli," he said.

"Well," said Laurie, who seemed at the moment to be in entire control of the situation, "let's all siddown, then."

Hesitantly, edging and backing and bowing and countering, they found chairs. I sat briefly until I was positive that our visiting gentlemen were firmly set into position, and then said, "Excuse me," and raced back into the kitchen, where I took down glasses and set them on a tray, got out ice, spread the doughnuts thinly on a plate, and padded the spaces between them with gingersnaps. Give the coffee another five minutes, I thought, sugar and milk, spoons. When I came back into the living room I found our guests sitting, each with hands folded in lap, and all turned intently to Laurie, who was saying, "And the thing is, when you're playing second and there's a man on first, see, you wanna—" Everyone stood up again when I came to the doorway, and I said, "No, no, sit down, please," and finally sat myself, abruptly, onto the telephone table chair so that Mr. Yashamoto and Mr. Masamitsu and Mr. Fernandez and Mr. Lopez and Mr. Babar would also sit down. Hastily, I noted that Mrs. Fernandez was giving Laurie that gaze of hypnotized attention which usually means a state of utter bewilderment, that my husband was eying Mr. Yashamoto in the manner of a monomaniac who intends shortly to enter upon his exclusive field of interest—in this case, of course, coins—and that Jannie and Sally between them had cornered Mr. Fernandez. Laurie gave every impression of being about to describe, in detail, the several innings of his latest game, and Mr. Babar had a small notebook in which he was writing busily, pausing occasionally to glance curiously at the books on the shelves, or the children's bare feet, or the rug, or the table lamps, and then returning to his notebook to write again. I thought of telling him that the house was not ours, and that we claimed almost nothing in it, and then reflected that the furniture was of rather better quality than what we had left in the grasp of Mr. Cobb, so I was quiet.

"Trouble with *most* longball hitters, you got to—" Laurie was continuing purposefully, and I turned to Mr. Lopez, who was on my left, and I smiled at him politely and he smiled back. I strongly suppressed a basic superstition which came unbidden to my mind (if you talk *loud* enough you can *make* them understand) and said, very softly, "And how long have *you* been here, Mr. Lopez?"

He looked surprised, and thought. "Ten minute?" he said at last, tentatively.

"No, no. How long have you been in this country?"

Again he thought. "Juan," he said hesitantly. "Juan Lopez."

I smiled largely, and nodded. "And do you like it?" I asked.

"Oh," he said, pondering. "Very much," he said finally, and we both smiled, and nodded, and repeated "very much," and smiled again.

"This is fine country," Mr. Yashamoto said. "Very eatable food in this country."

"We especially," Mr. Masamitsu said suddenly, "we *especially* enjoy hot dog. And mustard," he added wistfully. "And spaghetti."

"Boy," Laurie said, and sighed. "And relish. And pickles."

"Peeckle?" Mr. Masamitsu turned wonderingly to Laurie. "Peeckle?"

"Peeckle," said Sally, enchanted into speech, "peeckle, peeckle, domineeckle."

"Anyway," Laurie said, loudly overriding his sister, "I suppose you know what *rice* is, I guess? I guess you eat a lot of rice at home, don't you?"

Mr. Masamitsu shuddered delicately. "Indeed no," he said with eagerness, "indeed I do not; me, I eat no rice. Indigestion," he said widely, and everyone smiled, and nodded.

Mr. Babar for a minute raised his head from his notebook, regarded Mr. Masamitsu intently, obviously debated making a note, and then reluctantly refrained; instead he leaned toward Sally and touched her hair gingerly and Sally turned, giggled, and said "Hey!"

"You are most kind," Mr. Yashamoto said suddenly to my husband, "to allow us to come into this country of yours."

It was at this moment that, as I say, the United States government, flags flying, walked into our living room and sat down. I could see my husband's eyes widen and knew that without warning the same realization had come to us both; here we were, unprepared, in a sort of ambassadorial role, forced to stand or fall by our reasonably representative way of life; we spoke simultaneously—was that "Yankee Doodle" sounding in the distance?—"Nice of you to come," my husband said largely, and I said with a great heartiness, "I hope you enjoy it here." Then everyone smiled and nodded again to each other, and I muttered, "Coffee?" and fled to the kitchen.

Jannie and Sally, with great plans for passing cookies, followed me into the kitchen, and I gave Jannie the sugar and milk to carry, and Sally the plate of doughnuts, and came after them with the tray of iced coffee. Each of our guests solemnly accepted a glass of iced coffee and—I believe most of them thought this a ceremonial to be followed precisely—a spoonful of sugar and a little milk, and then, finally, one doughnut. Food, no matter how ceremonial, had its usual gracious effect, and I felt my position as international hostess relax slightly as, glasses and doughnuts in hand, our guests stirred, and rose, and spoke to one another, and moved around.

Mr. Yashamoto at last entered into an animated conversation with my husband about Japanese coins. Laurie and Mr. Masamitsu discussed with loving detail the several beauties of the hot biscuit, the hamburger, the corn on the cob. Jannie took Mr. Lopez by the hand and led him off to see Ninki's kittens, Mr. Babar settled down to a painstaking scrutiny of the bookcase, Sally was telling Mr. Fernandez, with dramatic action, the story of the three bears, and I came over to sit beside Mrs. Fernandez on the couch and said, "What a *lovely* skirt." It was flaming red, with heavy gold embroidery around the hem, and I would have given my eyeteeth to have one like it. "Lovely," I said.

"Yes?" she said. "I not espeak English, no."

I thought deeply. "Lovely," I said, touching her skirt, and she watched me and then, touching her skirt, said imitatively, "Lovelee?"

Inspiration came to me. "Wait a minute," I said, holding

up one finger in what I believed might be a universal gesture for patience, and I hurried over to where Barry, in
his playpen, was thoughtfully chewing on his sunsuit strap.
I lifted him, gave him a quick swipe across the bottom to
make sure he was dry, and then brought him back and put
him into Mrs. Fernandez' lap. "Baby," I said triumphantly.

She put her arms around him and hugged him, and Barry,
craning his neck back to see her, regarded her for a minute
with a slight frown, then apparently decided that she was
friendly and smiled. I wondered briefly, watching him, if
Barry's warm smile was not precisely the smile, friendly
but bewildered, which we had all been using toward one
another as a substitute for communication, and I looked
upon my younger son with fond pride.

"Bébé?" said Mrs. Fernandez. She held out her finger
and Barry grasped it and they both smiled again; she looked
at me and we both nodded and laughed. Barry reached up
and took hold of one of her gold earrings and she spoke to
him rapidly in Spanish, and Barry smiled, and she and I
looked at one another, and laughed. It was a masterpiece
of communication.

"Balli?" she said to me.

"Barry."

"Ah," she said. "Barri." She spoke to him again, and he
answered her in *his* language, which was surely as com-
prehensible to her as mine, and he showed her his four
teeth and got her earring in his hand to play with. We
were getting along famously; we were all beaming at one
another once again when a voice spoke suddenly behind
me. "Do you eat?"

Startled, I turned; it was Mr. Babar, squatting beside my

chair. "Do you eat—" he thought, pencil in hand "—breffist food?" he finished finally.

Blinking, I said, "Well, of course, we send for space goggles from the cartons, and compasses and things, but I personally—"

"The little Balli—what eats he?"

"Cereal," I said meekly. "Strained baby food." Mr. Babar frowned, shaking his head, and Mrs. Fernandez and Barry stared, uncomprehending, from one to the other of us. I sighed and stood up, giving them both my universal sign for patience, and went into the kitchen and came back with an unopened box of Barry's cereal and a jar of strained squash. I handed them to Mr. Babar and he scowled at them, making notes in his book. "Most very interesting," he said, and reluctantly gave them back.

I felt like an idiot, but I said, "Would you like to keep them? I have plenty more."

"Keep them? Take them with?"

"If you want to." I gestured foolishly, but Mr. Babar said with pleasure, "Thank you very much; this is of the utmost great value," and hastily, as though afraid I might after all insist upon taking back my cereal and my strained squash, he hastened to his briefcase and stored them away. Then, coming back to where I was sitting, he asked, pencil poised, "Shampoo?"

I nearly did international relations an irreparable harm by giggling. After a minute, however, I said, sober-faced, "I wash my hair with it. So do my daughters."

"Ah." He wrote. Then he touched the sleeve of my blouse with the tip of the pencil. "How much?" he asked.

I stirred uneasily, and glanced around to see if my husband was listening, but he was showing Mr. Yashamoto our Japanese netsuke, a lovely little ivory carving which had been my birthday present. "This," I heard Mr. Yashamoto say incredulously, "is *Japanese?*"

"Eleven-ninety-eight," I said very softly to Mr. Babar, "but if you don't mind—"

"Eleven *dollar?*"

"It's nylon," I said, "but please don't tell—"

He beamed. "Ah," he said. "*Nylon.*" And he made another note.

Mrs. Fernandez was singing softly to Barry, who lay back against her arm making small quiet noises, and Jannie and Mr. Lopez came back into the room and I heard Mr. Lopez saying, "People from different countries seem different, my Jonni, but cats—never. Cats are always much alike."

"Except," said Jannie intelligently, "that some of them are black and some of them are white and some of them are gray and some of them are striped."

"True, true," said Mr. Lopez, and Mr. Babar, apologetically, touched me on the arm to attract my attention. "Television?" he asked anxiously.

Suddenly, in the middle of a sentence, Mr. Yashamoto glanced at his watch and rose. "One hour," he announced, and our guests stood, all together. Mr. Yashamoto came across the room and bowed quickly to me. "Thank you very much for visit to your home," he said. "You have been most instructive."

I leaned down to take Barry from Mrs. Fernandez and she hugged him and handed him to me. Between the two of us we managed to pry her earring out of his hand. "An opportunity not to miss," Mr. Babar said to me, and then, unexpectedly, "I will not reveal cost of clothing." I could have sworn he winked at me.

Mr. Lopez shook hands with Jannie, and Mr. Fernandez removed Sally from *his* lap. "How about a game tomorrow?" Laurie said to Mr. Masamitsu, and Mr. Masamitsu bowed. "Swell," he said precisely, "idea."

"I do hope you'll come again," I said generally. "We have enjoyed your visit so much." I turned to Mrs. Fernandez and said, "It has been a real pleasure." "Bébé," she said, touching Barry's head. "Barri."

"Come any time," my husband said roundly to Mr. Yashamoto, "show you some more of those Japanese coins."

They were all moving gradually toward the front door, and then, when they reached it, passed through it in single file, as they had entered, and lined up again on the front lawn.

"Thank you once more very much," Mr. Yashamoto said, and my husband and I both said, "Do come again," and Laurie called out, "Be seeing you, fellas," and Jannie and Sally called, " 'Bye, 'bye, 'bye."

They wandered off down the country road, our guests, conversing among themselves, and pausing once for a minute while Mr. Babar turned and took a long look at the outside of our house. Then he wrote quickly in his notebook, and they went slowly on.

August came upon us soon thereafter, and Laurie began saying "school" in a dreary voice, and giving us monologues which usually began, "Why'd they ever invent *school*, anyway, if they'd *only—*" My husband and I asked one another what had become of the summer, and at the dinner table we wondered constantly that the weeks had seemed so short. Laurie reported that Mr. Yashamoto had turned into a pretty fair shortstop, and then, sadly, that they had all gone. Mr. Yashamoto had promised to write to Laurie, and had left behind a snapshot, taken by Mr. Masamitsu, of himself and Laurie standing together grinning, with the lake behind them and a baseball bat in front of them, and Laurie put the picture up on his bedroom wall. Mrs. Simpkins stopped over one morning to say that her boy had settled down to studying his arithmetic against the approach of school, and they had seen so little of Laurie they wondered if he was studying, too. I said that Laurie had been teaching his sister Sally to dog-paddle.

With the departure of Mr. Yashamoto and Mr. Masamitsu the baseball season suffered a perceptible slump, and Laurie had been moping, sad and listless, his occupation gone, until he fortunately recollected the existence of the riding stables. As a matter of fact, it had seemed to me at first that Mrs. Simpkins' inquiry after Laurie was ironic, since I thought it unlikely that anyone living only next door could be in any doubt about Laurie's current interest. The first sign of Laurie's presence was always the panting arrival of our big dog Toby, then came the crash of Laurie's bike hitting the ground, and then, vividly, sometimes from as far away as ten or fifteen feet, the inescapable air of horse.

From a stable sage named Jerry, Laurie had managed to pick up such valuable items of information as the probable hands high of horses, what a cinch is, and certain aphoristic opinions which seemed to me more suitable for a men's smoker than a family living room. His father, whose interest in horses was confined to their shoes, was required, as the only other man around the house, to listen to unending detail about a black and white bay—or it may have been a bay and white black, or black and bay, or even spotty, as Sally suggested—whose name was Popeye and who was supposed by the bloods around the stable to be exceedingly dangerous. Sally and Jannie and I believed implicitly that Popeye had eaten a former stableboy and perhaps even another horse, and it became a custom with me to glance quickly at Laurie when he came home to see if there were any marks of horse's teeth on him.

We planned to leave our borrowed house earlier than most of our neighbors were planning to leave their summer houses, because we thought to give ourselves two good weeks to get moved before school. As a result, the last days of our summer vacation were filled with farewell parties. We had been out playing bridge on Saturday night and because it was our last Saturday night had been persuaded to stay for one rubber over our quota (and would have won it, too, if my husband had led back a spade that time); when we got home we were both a little irritable (and so was the baby-sitter, coming sleepily out to the car with her coat thrown over her shoulders) and entirely because of my husband's forgetfulness I neglected to set the alarm. As a result I woke up on our last Sunday morning with one of those guilty starts, and found myself staring unbelievingly at an alarm clock which had slid secretly past eight o'clock and somehow gotten itself around to half-past ten.

Now, I do not believe that my children will pack up their little clothes and their small treasures in colored bandanas and set off, trudging sadly down the road out into the cold world—I do not *really* believe that my children will run away from home if Mommy is not up in time to give them breakfast, but this morning the house was suspiciously quiet, and when I cried out "Laurie?" and then "Jannie? Sally?" there was not even an echo to answer me. My husband stirred uneasily and I snarled at him, rolling out of bed and racing into the girls' room, saying "Jannie? Sally?" in a voice which became more urgent as I perceived that they were not there, but that they had most certainly *been* there for some space of time after arising; the toys were out of the bookcase and a fort of some kind had been built with dresser drawers in one corner of the room; Jannie's box of very small glass beads had been broken open and the beads scattered around thoughtfully near to the door so that, barefoot, I managed to step on several thousand.

As a last heartbreaking touch—a tender gesture for Mommy, no doubt, and probably performed just before the final exit into the world—both beds had been made, crookedly and with the sheets hanging, but still made, with the spreads put on. In Laurie's room, *The Boy's Book of Baseball Stories* lay open on the bed, and Barry, who after nearly nine vivid months of life had developed a kind of patient cynicism about his family, was lying in his crib talking to himself and playing agreeably with Laurie's hairbrush. I absent-mindedly picked up Laurie's pajamas, which were sprawled on the floor, and looked into them vaguely, saying "Laurie?" Since his dirty socks and dirty shirt and bathing trunks and riding boots were on the floor I could see no reason for hanging up his pajamas, and dropped them back onto the floor and said to Barry, "Where is Brother?" He stared at me, and then smiled.

Followed by Barry's sudden wail, I went padding from step to step downstairs and into the kitchen, where I was suddenly made aware of my optimistic conclusion the night before that I would leave the dinner dishes and do them in the morning. "Laurie?" I said. "Jannie? Sally?" There were three cereal bowls on the table, two empty and one half empty, and, glancing at the cereal boxes where they sat high on the shelf, I reflected briefly on the magical capacities of children who are hungry and relieved of the pressing assistance of adults. I decided that I could not go out hunting for my children until I had clothes on, and went back upstairs to dress. I had brushed my teeth and combed my hair and was looking for a clean handkerchief when I heard the clear sweet voice of my long-lost daughter Sally. "Mommy?" she was saying in the kitchen, "Mommy has gone to Fornicalia to live. Where my grandma lives, grandma. Would you please like some breakfast?"

Concluding, and rightly, that she was talking to the milkman, who needed urgently to be told that he must leave three quarts of milk instead of five, and a dozen eggs, I went to the head of the stairs and shouted, "Sally? Tell him to leave eggs and three quarts. Then stay exactly where you are until I come down."

I slammed the dresser drawer shut, hoping it would wake my husband, slid into my shoes, and raced downstairs to find Sally, who has a kind of literal mind, frozen halfway between the door and the table. "Can I move now?" she asked, as I came to a stop, "move?" There were five quarts of milk on the table, and three dozen eggs. "Sally," I said helplessly, "where have you been?"

Sally, who was then almost four years old, has always been very pretty. Any time I am prepared to spend an hour or so working on her, she is very lovely indeed, although her general appearance is of a child barely kept in a state of minimum human cleanliness by the most stubborn determination. Her hair was not cut short until she was six, so that summer it was still long and curly; since this particular morning she had been on her own for several hours she was recognizable largely by the voice and by the horrible doll she was carrying. She had chosen to put on a sunsuit, which would have been perfectly reasonable if she had not put it on backward; her hair was not able entirely to conceal the condition of her face, and from where I stood it looked very much as though she had gotten a lollipop from somewhere, because there was a lollipop stick wound in one curl. "Where have you been?" I asked again.

"Out," she said inconclusively. "I been visiting, visiting." Her odd jangling manner of speech had never annoyed me more, and I said sharply, "Visiting where?"

She waved. "Around," she said.

"Where is Jannie? Laurie?"

"Laurie is on his bike. Jannie got eaten by a bear, eaten."

This was so close to my guilty expectations that I went nervously to the kitchen door and looked out; there were no bears but at least part of Sally's general appearance was explained by the impressive line of mudpies on the back step. Following a reasonable train of thought, I asked, "Did you have breakfast?"

"I had it at Amy's house, Amy's."

Amy's mother was one of the sweetest people I had met that summer. Her children were always spotless, and they were fed at correct times in an immaculate kitchen. I had never heard Amy's mother raise her voice to her children and she always seemed to have time to make her own clothes. "You *would* go to Amy's," I said.

"Well, I told Amy's mother that I did not have any

breakfast, breakfast, because my mommy did not wake up and give it to me, mommy. And Amy's mother said I was a poor baby, baby, and she gave me cereal and fruit, cereal, and she said there, dear, and she gave me chocolate milk and I *did* remember to say thank you, remember."

I made a mental note to stop over later and tell Amy's mother laughingly that Sally had certainly fooled us, hadn't she, because I was right here making breakfast and Sally had just run out and I had spent *hours* looking for her and . . . "I told Amy's mother you were gone away to Fornicalia," Sally said, seating herself at the table before her half-finished bowl of cereal. "Laurie got me this cereal but he put on too much milk and I went to Amy's."

She seemed satisfied that she had given me a reasonable account of her morning, and I said "California" absently as I began to clear dishes out of the sink and stack them. "Hickory Dockery Dick," Sally said musically. "Why did they come home wagging their tails behind them, tails?"

By half-past eleven I had coffee making and had located Jannie (breakfast at Laura's house, scrambled eggs and orange juice and toast because Jannie's mother was still asleep because Jannie's mother had not come home until way, way late last night) and had had word of Laurie, who called to say that he was at the stables helping water the horses and would be back in a little while for lunch. "I see you finally got up," he remarked over the phone. "Yeah," I said.

I had fed Barry and put him in his playpen, and was feeling a little bit less like the delinquent mother whose children are found begging in the streets. Sally told me a long story about an elephant she and Amy had encountered, which asked them civilly the way to the zoo, zoo, and gave them each a piece of bubble gum, a delicacy ordinarily forbidden Sally, but I had to let her keep it because it was a present from an elephant. By the time my husband came stomping downstairs I was sitting at the kitchen table drinking coffee and smiling maternally at Sally; I gave my husband another smile of patient, tolerant understanding, and asked him sweetly if he would care for coffee? He nodded, and sat down at the table, but he jumped when I lifted the frying pan. "Eggs?" I asked him, and he shook his head no.

"Dockery Hickory Dick," Sally said. "Later will you take us swimming, Daddy, swimming?"

"Of course he will, dear," I said largely, and my husband turned his head and looked at me for a minute.

"Daddy would *like*—" I was going on maliciously when the back door opened gently and Jannie said, "Can I change to a dress?"

"Good morning, dear," I said.

"Good morning. Can I? My white sundress? You didn't wake up this morning, did you?"

"Jan, later Daddy will take us swimming, Daddy."

"Can I change to my bathing suit?" Jannie switched smoothly. "Can I change to my blue bathing suit?" She was wearing a pair of shorts and a blouse which she dearly loved but which was so small for her that she could only button the top button, and it left a two-inch gap over the top of her shorts. "So I'll be all ready when we go swimming?"

"Can *I* wear a dress, dress? *Can* I?"

"No," I said. "Later. No."

"Can I anyway go barefoot?"

"Can I, barefoot?"

"You're already barefoot," I said, puzzled.

"But you weren't awake so we could ask, so I thought," Jannie said judiciously, "that I had better ask *now*."

"You may go barefoot," I said.

"Thank you," Jannie said. "May I change to my bathing suit?"

"*I* had breakfast at Amy's," Sally said. "Ha-ha."

"Ha-ha," Jannie said. "*I* had breakfast at Laura's."

"Horrible," my husband said. "Way to bring up children," he explained to his coffee cup.

"And Daddy will get you each an ice-cream cone," I said to Jannie and Sally.

Sally nodded approvingly. "But furstaneta finish my cereal," she said. "Furstaneta" translates precisely as "First I need to," and it precedes most of Sally's important actions; in this case, tipping her bowl of cereal onto the floor.

"Bring up children," my husband said.

There was a scratching at the back screen and Toby put his head in and looked around at us. Almost immediately there was the crash of Laurie's bike hitting the ground outside. "Daddy will take you swimming, too," Sally told Laurie, as he came through the door.

"Not me, kiddie," Laurie said blandly, relieving Jannie of the piece of bread she was covering with mayonnaise as he went past, and leaving her gazing astonished from the jar of mayonnaise to her empty hand. "Me, I'm on Popeye this aft."

"Don't come any closer till I finish my coffee," his father said.

"Buddy's gone lame," Laurie told his father.

"If his shoes are too tight tell him I'll take them," my husband said.

"Horses don't get lame from tight shoes, bud," Laurie said. "How about some food?" he asked me.

Slinging one leg over the seat of his chair, he pulled the jar of mayonnaise toward him. "Jerry says," he told Jannie, "that kid sisters are only good to have if they're sixteen years old and have no big brothers."

"Laurie," I said, "that is hardly the way—"

"To address your ever-loving family," Laurie said. "Jerry says," he went on, "you got to have families, because otherwise where would you borrow money?"

"Good lord," my husband said, just as Jannie put in suddenly, "Mommy, where am I?"

"Sitting at the kitchen table," I said. "Why?"

"I just all of a sudden couldn't remember how I got here," Jannie said, looking around at all our startled faces. "I don't remember *any*thing."

My husband and I stared at each other. "Jannie," he said, "tell us what happened."

"I fell, I *believe*," Jannie said. "I believe I fell."

"Where did you hit yourself?" I asked.

"Down on the woodpile," Sally said. "Jannie fell off the woodpile, Jannie."

"Did you?" I asked. "When?"

"I don't remember," Jannie said, pleased.

"Your own name?" Laurie asked with interest. "Because it's Jannie."

"How old are you?" Sally asked.

Jannie giggled. "Now I don't even remember *that*," she said.

"What were you playing on the woodpile?" I asked.

Jannie took a deep breath. "Well," she said, "I was playing on the woodpile with Laura and Laura's brother Johnnie and we were playing pirate ship and Laura was the captain and Johnnie was the first mate and I was the shrew—"

"Crew."

"Shrew. And I was the shrew, and I said I was going to dive overboard looking for fish and Laura said that was no way to catch fish you had to use a spear and *Johnnie* said—"

"And then you fell?"

"Not *yet*. And Johnnie said I was supposed to dive overboard to be dead, see, because I was a captured maiden and so I said I would only pretend to dive overboard because even if you were captured maidens you *couldn't* go jumping off the woodpile. Could you?" she appealed to Laurie.

"Depends," Laurie said judiciously. "I know that ole horse Buddy—"

"Anyway," Jannie said, "Laura said I had to jump and Johnnie said he would if I would and so then I fell."

"But you can't remember anything about it?"

"Well," Jannie said doubtfully, "I *do* remember a little bit about playing on the woodpile. But now I think I *have* forgotten my name."

"It's Jannie," Laurie said.

I glanced, frowning, at my husband, and he shook his head and shrugged. "It was all on television, all," Sally said suddenly. "We saw it at Amy's house, Uncle Bob's program, Amy's, and the little cow that laughs all the time, cow, he fell and hit his head and then he couldn't remember all about Uncle Bob and the trip to the moon, moon."

"It was *not*," Jannie said, "it wasn't, it wasn't."

"And we all said we couldn't remember," Sally said. "Can we go swimming now, swimming?"

"Now," Jannie said reproachfully, "now I can't even remember your name."

"It's Sally," Laurie said.

"Shall I put a cold cloth on your head?" I asked solicitously.

"Perhaps I better go lie down for a minute," Jannie said, her voice noticeably weaker. "I'll just leave my bread and mayonnaise."

"Suppose," I said, "you go lie down for a minute and take your bread and mayonnaise with you, since you seem to have made four slices of bread and mayonnaise and I do not see that you have eaten more than half of one."

"But I don't feel—"

"If you are too ill to have your nice bread and mayonnaise, then you are too ill to go swimming."

Jannie sighed, and thought, and sighed again. "This is not very fair," she pointed out. "Swimming might be very good for my poor head."

"Say, kid," Laurie said to me, "how about some sandwiches to take down to the stable?"

"Make them yourself," I said, reaching for the coffeepot.

"No woman knows how to cook, anyway," Laurie said. "Jerry says," he told his father, "that the worst thing about having a wife is she does the cooking." His father nodded bleakly.

"If any big-mouthed brother of a horse cares to take over the cooking in *this* house—" I began indignantly.

"But if I eat *all* my bread and mayonnaise, then I will be—"

Laurie guffawed. "If I'm a brother of a horse then what's Jannie?" he demanded, and then, without waiting for the indignant answer Jannie was opening her mouth to deliver, he remarked, "Here comes Amy, simple."

"Amy?" said Sally, just as I was saying, "Simple is not a polite name for—" and my husband was saying, "Any young man as fresh as—" and Jannie was saying, "Horses don't have sisters, they have—" "Amy?" Sally said. "May I please have two cookies, two, one for Amy and one for me, cookies?"

"You may, you may," I said hastily. "Provided you eat them outdoors." If Sally's refrain conversation is difficult to bear, Amy's repetitive conversation is worse; where Sally repeats the vital word, Amy repeats the whole sentence; Sally is the only one in our family who can talk to Amy at all. "May I please play with Sally?" Amy was saying through the back door screen, "is Sally here so she can play with me?"

Sally slid off her chair and made for the cookie jar. "Amy," she shouted, "Daddy is going to take us swimming, swimming, and ask your mommy if you can come, your mommy."

"My mommy," said Amy solemnly, opening the screen door and joining Sally at the cookie jar, "doesn't let me go swimming right now, because I have a cold. I have a cold, so my mommy doesn't want me to go swimming, because I have a cold. I have a cold," she told me, "so my mommy won't let me go swimming."

"Because she has a cold," Laurie said helpfully. "See, she has a cold and so—"

"Laurie," I said feverishly. "Sally and Amy, please take those cookies out*doors*."

"Anyway," Jannie said with finality, "then that makes

Sally a horse, too, because if Laurie is the brother of a horse, then Sally—"

"If you ask your mommy can we each have two cookies," Amy began, preceding Sally out the screen door, "then maybe if your mommy says we can have two cookies—"

Delicately Laurie shut the door behind them, and remarked consideringly to his father, "You know, you take that Riff. Now there's a nag can jump and run and about everything, and then there's Raff, and he's Riff's own twin brother and you think that horse can jump?" The phone rang.

"It's probably a horse for Laurie," Jannie said, inspired.

"I'll get it," my husband said, abandoning Laurie in midsentence.

"I'll just change into my bathing suit right now," Jannie said, taking advantage of my preoccupation with the ringing of the phone to leave two slices of bread and mayonnaise behind the toaster. "See you later, kid," Laurie said, patting me on the head.

"Well, well, well," my husband was saying over the phone. "Isn't this a *surprise*." He turned and grinned evilly at me. "But you've *got* to come on over," he said, "we'd never forgive you if you didn't stop in. And plan to stay on for dinner," he said, looking away from my dropped jaw. "Pot luck, of course."

Two days before we were to leave, we got a letter from the real estate agent at home, saying that all four apartments in our new house were empty, the downstairs back having loaded their clothes and their television set in a pickup truck in the middle of the night and made off without further reference to the back rent. The agent said that a checkup on the downstairs back apartment indicated that they had been systematically removing furniture and household goods for some time; perhaps ever since they were first informed of the sale of the house. Nothing was left in the downstairs back apartment, not even the lightbulbs or the curtain rods, and the agent was of the opinion that they would have taken the glass out of the windows if it had not been broken already. My husband thought that we should keep the downstairs back apartment intact, repair the windows, and rent it out again. I thought that if we rented the apartment again, we should make out a lease since, although we had not had a lease with Mr. Fielding for nine years, I was still rankling over the arrogant terms in our old lease for our apartment in New York, and I thought that we could give the people who compose leases a lesson in generosity and broad-mindedness. It turned out, however, that the only truly unjust clause which rankled with me was the one prohibiting tenants from keeping mockingbirds, and it seemed pointless to plan to rent our downstairs back apartment with a lease urging the tenants to keep mockingbirds, so we thought we would not rent the apartment.

We wrote to Mr. Cobb and asked him to give us back our furniture on August twentieth. We thought that it would take us about three hours to drive home, so we told Mr. Cobb to expect us around noon. Because there was no place we could reasonably hope would take in six of us, with dog and cats, overnight, we planned to spend our first night at home in our new house. "We will be camping out," I told the children. "We will all pitch in and help together," my husband said, "and not expect Mother to cook a real dinner or anything that first night."

It had been impractical, in terms of simple cubic feet, to let Mr. Cobb store our books, after all, and we had at last agreed with a friend of a friend that if he let us leave our books in his empty warehouse we would arrange to have them moved whenever he needed the space for something else. Early in August he had written asking if we could move the books, and we said he could put them in our new house, the downstairs front of which was then empty, and we would of course pay for the trucking and unloading. I do not think that either my husband or I remembered this clearly; we knew, of course, that there were two hundred cartons of books, but we still thought of the books as lined neatly on bookshelves, even though we had packed them ourselves. Because of the mounting expenses connected with our moving, we decided that we would not plan to have the house painted or the wallpaper removed for a while yet, my husband pointing out that the way things were piling up we would be lucky if the children could get a shoe each to wear to school.

I had already discovered that during the short space of the summer we had accumulated so much more property that it was not going to fit in the car going home, so I had borrowed cartons from the grocer in our summer town and packed them with whatever I could fit in, and mailed them off home, where the postman, thinking that we would have enough to worry about in our moving without coming down to the post office to pick up packages, had taken them up one evening on his way home and dropped them off on the front porch of our new house. As a result we were able to fit into the car very nicely going home, with the dog, the cats, the children, the typewriters, the coin collection, the baby carriage, and the picnic hamper, although our departure, full of sad goodbyes, was a little marred by the discovery that I had put the car keys in an old pocketbook which was in a carton now on the front porch of our new house, and we had to un-pack the glove compartment of the car to get the spare car keys and in order to unpack the glove compartment we had to clear the front seat of the car because we were crammed in so tight.

When we got home it was later than we had expected, around two o'clock, and our new house was waiting for us, eager, expectant, and empty, with the cartons on the front porch. The front door was unlocked and so, we discovered, were all the other doors. There was a great tangle of door keys in the kitchen sink of the downstairs front, but none of them fit any of the doors in the house. Inside, divided among the several rooms of the downstairs front, were our two hundred cartons of books, spread ju-diciously so that their combined weight would not go through the floor. The phone in the downstairs front had been disconnected, and Laurie went around and in the downstairs back and reported, shouting through the kitchen wall, that that phone had been disconnected, too. Then he went out and up to the upstairs back, where *that* phone had been disconnected, and around and up to the upstairs front, and of course that phone had been disconnected, too. Barry was still in the car, in his car bed, and so were the coin collection, the typewriters, the picnic hamper, and the box with Ninki and her five kittens. I got into the car and drove down to the railroad station where there was a pay phone. I looked up the number of the E. J. Cobb Storage and Transfer Company, and when I got Mr. Cobb on the phone I said well, here we were, and was our furniture on the way over?

Mr. Cobb was quiet for a minute, and then he gave a little silly laugh. "Look," he said, "I certainly do hope that you're not going to be sore at me or anything."

"Why on earth should I be sore at you or anything?" I asked. "I only called to find out about the furniture."

Mr. Cobb laughed the silly little laugh again. "I know how you ladies all like to have things arranged just so," he said. "My wife—"

"*My* furniture."

"Well," said Mr. Cobb. "'See, the men got the small truck all loaded for you. All ready. That truck could roll right now."

There was a long silence. Finally Mr. Cobb started all over again. "I know how you ladies like to have everything just so," he said. "I just hope you're not going to be sore at me."

"I think after all I *am* going to be sore at you," I said.

"Mostly," Mr. Cobb said in an aggrieved tone, "mostly, people are always rushing you and telling you to be sure and certainly get their furniture right there and ready to roll at exactly a certain time. And then mostly those same people don't even bother to be there or anything. *Mostly*, you can figure if you deliver the furniture on the day they say, why, there won't even be anyone there to sign for it. That's just the way it goes," he finished brightly.

"I suppose it is," I said. "Now, about our furniture. Right now we don't even have a place to sit down, so if you could—"

"I could send over a bench or something," Mr. Cobb said.

The operator cut in, to say that my three minutes were up, and I could hear Mr. Cobb's phone hang up emphatically. I had to go to the ticket agent to get change, and when I came back I had to look up the number of the E. J. Cobb Storage and Transfer Company again, and this time the phone was answered by a female voice. I told her who I was and asked for Mr. Cobb.

"I'm sorry," she said. "Mr. Cobb is out of town."

"He was there just a minute ago."

She turned away from the phone and spoke to someone. "—had to hurry—" a voice said indistinctly in the background. "I'm sorry," she said into the phone again. "Mr. Cobb has just left for Philadelphia. He was in a great rush to catch his train. What?" she said off the phone. "Oh. He probably won't be back before Thursday," she said to me.

"I see," I said. "Well, I don't really want Mr. Cobb in any case. I want my furniture."

"I'm sorry," she said. "If it's furniture you want, you will have to speak to the foreman."

"Then let me speak to the foreman," I said.

"Just a minute," she said, "I'll see if he's in. Freddie," she called, off the phone, "you know that load of goods was supposed to be put on yesterday and Ed forgot? You got enough on to go? Well, *you* come and talk to her, then."

There was another silence, and then a man's voice on the phone. "Yeah?" he said.

"What about my furniture? It was supposed to be delivered at noon today."

"You the lady with the goods supposed to go out today?"

"Yes," I said. "I am."

"Well, that goods is not loaded yet." He thought. "We ain't got it on the trucks," he explained.

"Why not?" It was getting warm in the telephone booth, and I opened the door.

"Because we didn't load it on yet. Ed says to tell you he's sorry and he hopes you ain't sore."

"Your three minutes are up," said the operator, and the foreman said "boyoboy," and hung up.

I had one more nickel and before I looked up the number of the E. J. Cobb Storage and Transfer Company I took a deep breath and planned roughly what I was going to say so I would not have to waste any of my three minutes. When I rang the number again Mr. Cobb answered. "Hello?" he said. "Cobb Storage."

"All right, now," I began, and Mr. Cobb gasped.

"This is the Cobb Storage Company," he said in a different, high voice. "Did you want something?"

"Yes," I said. "And if you are Mr. Cobb you had better get onto that train you are in such a hurry to catch, and I am warning you right now that Philadelphia is not half far enough and Thursday is not half long enough because in approximately four minutes I am going to arrive at the E. J. Cobb Storage and Transfer Company with a crowbar and when I get there I am going to come into the E. J. Cobb Storage and Transfer Company warehouse with my crowbar and when I come in I am going to start swinging that crowbar right and left smashing whatever is closest, and if whatever is closest turns out to be Freddie that is going to be all right although I would rather it were Mr. Cobb or his secretary. And," I went on, raising my voice, "now I think of it I am going to bring Mr. Tillotson the policeman and my lawyer with me and I am going to have you arrested for stealing even if you are not Mr. Cobb at all. And after I have you arrested for stealing I am going to call our insurance company over at the bank and tell them that every stick of furniture we own has been stolen with malice aforethought by Mr. Cobb of the E. J. Cobb Storage and Transfer Company and we want to collect all our insurance on it so we can buy more to replace what Mr. Cobb has stolen, and left us without even anything to sit on. And then I am going to send you the bill for hotel accommodations for our family of six from now until we get furniture for our house, and our dog will have to board at the kennel and so will our six cats, and then I think I am going to bring suit against Mr. Cobb for extreme mental anguish brought about by his stealing all our furniture so we came home to an empty house with nothing to sit down on." I stopped for breath.

"I am extremely sorry that you are taking this attitude," Mr. Cobb said.

That is a phrase which has always annoyed me. I raised my voice a little higher, and the ticket agent, who had been craning his neck around the corner of the ticket booth, ducked back down inside.

"Now look," I said, "I am not going to be insulted by some trifling little insignificant worm of a storage and transfer man who scratches and mars and steals people's furniture and I should think that you could regard yourself as pretty lucky because I have not really lost my temper yet, but I am going to if you keep talking about attitudes because what attitude can people take when they have no place to sit down? And if you think for one minute that you can retire to Philadelphia with the profits from stealing our furniture you are very much mistaken, because the next person you will deal with will be my husband and *he* is not a poor defenseless woman."

"If you would try to be calm," Mr. Cobb said.

"And I am not going to be insulted on top of everything else and if you think you can talk that way to a lady you had better think again because I am right now going out to tell everyone I know in town that the E. J. Cobb Storage and Transfer Company not only steals furniture entrusted to them for storage and breaks and smashes everything but they also yell curses and obscenity at people just trying to get their furniture back and by the time I finish with you you will regard yourself as extremely fortunate if they let you out of jail long enough to fire Freddie, because I personally am going to—"

"Your three minutes are up," said the operator.

I still had a good deal I wanted to tell Mr. Cobb, but when I went to get more nickels the ticket agent peered out at me from the back of the ticket booth, and shook his head no. I got back into the car and drove to our new house, where I found that my husband and the children were sitting on cartons of books and eating potato chips. My husband said that they were trying to decide what to name Jannie's new room and Laurie's new room, since Jannie and Laurie were going to share the upstairs back apartment, and each of them would thus have a small bedroom and a larger room for other activities and there was quite a problem in thinking of names for these larger rooms. Laurie thought he would like to call his room Laurie's Laboratory, because since it had formerly been a kitchen he could keep the sink in and do chemistry there and maybe set up a darkroom to develop pictures and we could get him a microscope. Jannie wanted to call hers a

Study so she could study there, but my husband said that *he* had a study, and two studies would be confusing, and he suggested that she put her books in there and call it Jannie's Library. I said she could call it her salon, and Laurie said a salon was not a nice name for a room where a little girl kept her books, but she could call it Jannie's Joint. Sally said why not put her bed in there, bed, and then she could call it her bedroom? Or, Laurie thought, she could call it her Giggle Room, because that was all she ever did, anyway.

Jannie, who had been for the past ten days engaged in running one joke into the ground, said smartly that Laurie's room, then, should be called Laurie's Stable, and he could keep a horse in there, and besides, it always looked like a stable. She was going on to elaborate this last point when a moving truck stopped in front of the house and began a complicated maneuver to enable it to back across the rhododendron bush beside the front steps. We all went to the front door and a man got down from the truck. From his voice and general air of graceful self-possession I strongly suspected that it might be Freddie. He removed his hat respectfully and remarked that he hoped he had gotten the right house. My husband said never mind about the right house; if that was furniture in that truck we would take it. Freddie said that Ed hoped we weren't going to be sore at him, because they had certainly meant to deliver our furniture today and had even gotten this small truck loaded, so Ed decided that they should bring over what they had, just so's we could have some furniture in the house tonight, and they would bring over the rest tomorrow, absolutely, on Ed's personal word of honor, or the next day at the very latest.

We explained that due to certain obstructive difficulties in our house it was going to be necessary to take some of the furniture to the upstairs front apartment and some around to the back entrance and up the back stairs to the upstairs back apartment, and that the furniture in the downstairs front was going to have to be very carefully spaced so that the weight of the furniture and books would not go through the floor. Freddie said he understood perfectly. The first thing that came off the truck was my husband's workbench, which the men carried out back to the barn. Then came Laurie's bicycle and Jannie's and Sally's tricycles, which the children offered with pleasure to ride out to the barn. I stood on the front porch with Barry in his carriage, to tell the men where to put things, and my husband stayed inside, to do as much arranging as he could, and to see that nothing went through the floor. They unloaded our glass-topped coffee table, and I checked to make sure that Mr. Cobb had not smashed the glass top, and then told them to take it into the living room downstairs front, and then they unpacked the old music box, which has always gone in the dining room, and inside, my husband, already arranging, moved the music box to the corner where the buffet was going to go, because the music box has always been on top of the buffet.

Things were going so smoothly that I decided to drive down to the grocery and get some beer, because it was an almighty hot day, and while I was gone the men unloaded the ping-pong table, which went in the barn, and Laurie's desk, which went into the upstairs back, and the cushions from the living room couch, which my husband arranged where the couch was going to be. The movers and my husband and I drank beer, and the children drank grape soda, and Barry had a bottle of orange juice, and then the movers unloaded the hall table and two bridge tables and my husband's desk and Jannie's puppet theater and our two laundry hampers. After the laundry hampers, which I recalled were full of clothes, came four barrels of dishes, and the guest room bed tables, and the odd dressing table mirror, which my husband arranged temporarily in the upstairs hall. The number of things in the moving truck seemed endless. I checked the piano bench, and the carton which held the waffle iron and the electric broiler and the dog's dish. There was a carton of piano music, and a barrel of toys, and then Sally's toy box and Jannie's toy box and Barry's bathinette. Sally and Jannie retired to Sally's new room to unpack the barrel of toys, the rugs arrived, were stacked in the front hall, and my husband put our big silver fruit dish in the middle of the dining room floor where the dining room table was going to be. Finally, from the very back of the truck, came the picnic table and benches, and the outdoor barbecue. The men then brought in an odd leg from something, had another can of beer, thanked us, were thanked, and departed with the truck, cutting across the front lawn.

In our new living room, then, we had perhaps sixty cartons of books, the piano bench, the coffee table, and the carton of piano music. In the dining room were the music box, another forty cartons of books, and the silver fruit dish. In the kitchen were four barrels of dishes, and a carton with the waffle iron, the electric broiler, and the dog's dish. Upstairs in Sally's room were her toy box and a barrel of toys, unpacked. The guest room had two bed tables. In what was going to be the new study was the odd leg off something and my husband's coin collection, which he had brought in out of the car, and another fifty cartons of books. In the front room where we planned to put the television set were another fifty cartons of books and the picnic hamper. In my husband's and my bedroom was a carton, sent by me from our summer home, which held half a dozen wet bathing suits wrapped in aluminum foil, three plastic sandpails, Sally's blue sunbonnet, and Laurie's collection of shells. It was half-past six.

I heated Barry's baby food and his bottle in the hot water from the kitchen sink, fed him sitting on the piano bench with a carton labeled Miscellaneous Non-Fiction for a tray, cleaned him as well as I could, and changed him into his pajamas. I opened a can of dog food and fed Toby on a newspaper on the kitchen floor, and Ninki in the top of an old mayonnaise jar I found in the pantry. Then we shut all the animals inside the new house, got the rest of us, including Barry's carriage, back into the car, and drove to our local inn. Everyone had a hot bath, and the inn was serving its special pecan cinnamon honey pie for dessert that night. The children fell asleep early after their tiring day, and my husband and I played bridge with a nice couple in the lounge.

The rest of our furniture arrived at half-past six the next morning. The men had already carried in a great deal of it by the time we got to our new house. Freddie told us confidently that he had figured out where everything went, and some of his arrangements were so tasteful and judicious that we left them: the big dining room buffet in the television room, for instance, and the lawn chair in the pantry, which turned out to be a very practical arrangement, because later on when we got a washing machine we had to put it in the pantry and while I was doing the wash

I could sit down. We had to leave the buffet in the television room because the men had brought it in through the front window and Freddie said he was pretty sure they couldn't get it out again and anyway there was more room in there than there was in the dining room, with the table and all them cartons of books.

One of the things the men left in the front hall was the carton of football helmets, ice skates, and tennis rackets. With a feeling of pure triumph I dragged the carton over to our new hall closet, and unpacked it. I put in the ice skates and the basketball and the hockey sticks and the overshoes and then I got up off the floor and tried to close the closet door. After a minute or two I repacked all the things in the carton and called Laurie and told him to take it out to the barn. He said in a worried voice that the first floor of the barn was nearly full and if I wanted to put my car in there we were going to have to start putting things up on the second floor of the barn. I called to my husband, who was down cellar checking the furnace, and he said that what with the junk the previous people had left down there, and our own collection of cellar odds and ends, there wasn't going to be room down there for much more. When the next carton of odds and ends came in I waited until no one was looking and then carried it secretly around the house and put it in the downstairs back apartment.

Just before lunchtime the men got the refrigerator installed and working, and for some reason that comfortable old clatter made the house seem more familiar than anything else. I said I would go right down to the grocery for meat and milk and eggs and butter, and on the way I gave in to a kind of irresistible nostalgia and turned the car onto the old side road and out the three miles to take a look at our old house. When I came around the corner I stopped the car and stared; it was like meeting an old friend who has dyed her hair and taken to wearing tight velvet pants and mascara. The house was painted bright yellow, and at first I could not understand why it looked so odd, and yet so ordinary and like every other house we had passed driving home the day before. Then I realized: Mrs. Ferrier had removed the four white pillars.

TWO

BEFORE WE HAD been in our new house six weeks, the back apartment was full of things, and the crooked gatepost had become a topic on which we were all morbidly sensitive. When we bought the house, my husband and I both assumed, upon the candid statement of the real estate agent, that the only thing defective on the property was the left-hand gatepost leaning off at a rakish angle. The roof, the furnace, the wiring, the plumbing, the foundations—all of these, we believed innocently, were new, newly repaired, or so solid that not even an earthquake could shake them. "But," the real estate agent told first me, and then my husband, and then both of us together, "I'd be a pretty poor businessman if I tried to tell you that gatepost is *straight*." We were forced to agree: that gatepost was emphatically crooked, and the real estate salesman was not a pretty poor businessman at all. The gateposts were massive stone affairs, although there was no wall to go with them; they stood at the end of a driveway which, while nicely dry during the summer months when we looked at the house, was not the splendid sweeping affair the gateposts seemed to imply. Nevertheless, my husband and I told one another with shy pride that the gateposts gave our meager three acres something of the air of an estate, except that of course the left-hand gatepost was a little crooked. When we talked it over afterward, though —the real estate agent reeling back to his office, the papers in his hands, and no doubt giggling incredulously to himself all the way—we decided that all we had to do was put up maybe a fence, and get the gatepost straightened, of course, and put in some kind of a lawn, and maybe a couple of more bushes on the side of the house where the wall had kind of fallen in—anyway, we thought, standing by the gatepost and regarding our land, it was not going to take much to get the old place looking like a mansion again.

We have no local firm of gatepost-straighteners, but every deadpan wit within the county limits had a stab at us. The man who came to repair the roof thought that we ought to get someone to hitch a team to the gatepost and pull it straight. The man who came to repair the furnace suggested that we dig out under the post on the uninclined side, and let the post settle down even-like. The electrician took a few minutes off from ripping out the dining room ceiling to say that what we had to do was dig out the roots of the tree under the gatepost. The plumber thought no; we better get a man to move the gatepost over two, three feet. I finally developed a kind of answer for use around the grocery and the post office, about how I'd taken a lot of trouble pushing that gatepost as crooked as it was, and any time I wanted it straight I would go on out and push it back again. My husband took to saying around the barbershop that it wasn't that that gatepost was crooked, it was that the other one was too straight. Laurie solemnly assured the kids in fifth grade that it was only specific gravity kept the gatepost up at all. Among ourselves we tended to avoid the subject, and after a while I got so I could drive the car between the gateposts without ducking sharply to the right. During one severe late-summer storm we all stood anxiously at the front windows, wondering if the gatepost would go down, but it stood staunch; what did go down was a tree across the street, smashing part of the front porch of a man who had asked Sally why *she* didn't take the gatepost apart and build it up again straight.

I still had to drive Sally to nursery school, and after a while the two older children took to waiting and riding along. Our new house was only two blocks from their school, but, as Jannie explained, it got very very very tiresome walking past the same houses every time. We had been in our new house for over six months, through our family holiday season, which begins early in October with Laurie's birthday, then continues through Sally's birthday on Hallowe'en, and Jannie's birthday a week later and then Barry's birthday and Thanksgiving, and finally the long home stretch into Christmas. On Laurie's birthday we were still unpacking books, I remember, and his friends dined in the shadow of the half-filled bookcases in the dining room. By Sally's birthday the men had come to sand the pine floors, and all the downstairs furniture was piled in the dining room and all the other floors were freshly varnished, so Sally had a birthday party in the kitchen, with crepe-paper barricades across the doors to prevent her guests from straying onto the fresh varnish, and balloons and lollipops hanging from the ceiling. By Jannie's birthday we could use the dining room again, but the upholsterers had taken all the good dining room chairs to freshen the tapestry backs, so Jannie's friends had a picnic dinner sitting on the glittering varnished floor. Barry was too little to have a birthday party, which was just as well, because that was when they were repairing the plumbing in the bathroom downstairs, and they had taken out the bathtub and put it in the study where my husband fell into it one night when he could not sleep and went downstairs to get a book. Since Thanksgiving came on Barry's birthday that year, the men took the day off and went away and left the bathtub in the study from Wednesday afternoon until Monday morning. It was the most practical wastebasket we ever had in the study, but they came on Monday and put it back. Barry got a blue teddy bear for his birthday, and he named it Dikidiki.

The new house had a very good spot to put the Christmas tree, in the bay window of the living room, and from far down past the railroad tracks, coming home through the snow, we could see the lights of our Christmas tree shining from our house. There was a good sledding place for Jannie and Sally down behind the barn, although Laurie went up to the hill with the other boys. That Christmas we got a movie camera and a projector and screen, and I took movies of Barry in a pink snowsuit being tumbled off a sled pulled by Laurie in a brown jacket and a blue hat and Jannie in navy blue with a red scarf and Sally in green, with pompons on her hat. I took pictures of our house and our trees and our barn. In the long winter evenings we sat in the dark living room and my husband, running the projector with Laurie's help, showed us the pictures of Barry tumbling off the sled and Laurie in brown throwing a snowball at Sally in green with pompons on her hat, and Jannie standing proudly beside a monumental snowman, and the bare branches and snow-touched roof and the barn somehow at an angle because I had trouble holding the camera with gloves on. The children enjoyed looking at the pictures of themselves, and got very restless when they had to watch pictures of the house and barn.

We drove past the old house now and then, and I observed with contempt that Mrs. Ferrier had tried to compensate for the naked look of the porch by putting some kind of a grayish scratchy bush on either side of the steps. When the winter was over they might blossom into great colorful things, but I did not, somehow, envy Mrs. Ferrier with her yellow pillarless house and her scratchy bushes; she did not even have a crooked gatepost.

Along about the beginning of February, when the days of winter seem endless and no amount of wistful recollecting can bring back any air of summer, I caught one of those colds which last for two days in the children and two weeks with me. I got to feeling that I could not bear the sight of the colored cereal bowls for one more morning, could not empty one more ashtray, could not brush one more head or bake one more potato or let out one more dog or pick up one more jacket. I snarled at the bright faces regarding me at the breakfast table and I was strongly tempted to kick the legs out from under the chair on which my older son was teetering backward. I could not think of anything to serve for dinner which was not dull, or tasteless, or unusually full of bones. There was never any news in the morning paper. The mail was slim and almost entirely composed of letters beginning "We are sure that through some oversight you must have neglected . . ."

This state of mind is not practical in a household which

continues to move relentlessly on from breakfast to mail to school to bath to bed to breakfast, no matter how *I* feel. My only conscious positive wish was for the doctor to drop in—casually, perhaps, coming to pick up an old syringe he had left lying around—glance at me suddenly and exclaim, dropping his bag and turning pale, "Good lord— look at you! Why, you should be in the hospital," and, turning angrily to my husband, "Are you crazy? Can't you see that your wife is desperately ill?" I took my temperature twice a day, and limped carrying in the dinner dishes.

One morning the cleaner returned my gray suit with a button missing and I cut my finger slicing rye bread for toast for my husband and the children had been late for school. There was a letter in the mail from an old friend of mine who was driving through our town on her way to visit another old friend, and if I could take a couple of days off and go along we could all three spend a *marvelous* weekend comparing pictures of our children and talking about the time Marjorie cut her hair.

I read this letter to my husband, holding my bandaged finger well in sight. "It would have been nice to have gone," I said wistfully, and sighed. "Oh, well," I said. "Here's another bill from the telephone company."

"I don't want to know about it," my husband said, regarding the beverage I had served him for coffee. "You go along on that trip, do you good." He hesitated, and then said stoutly, "I'll take care of the children."

"Fine," I said, before he had quite finished speaking, "then if you think I should, I *will* go. Do me good to get away for a while," I told him. "You won't have any trouble, not if I'm only gone two days."

"I am perfectly capable of running this house," he said. "*Perfectly* capable. You just leave a list of things the baby eats, and so on. And who to call if someone gets sick."

"I usually call the doctor," I said, and went hastily to write to both my friends and sew the button on my gray suit and wash out a couple of blouses and generally compose myself to leave in two days' time. My husband can turn on the stove and answer the telephone, but it seemed to me that it might help if I arranged to have the children largely out of his way; the baby, of course, had to stay at home, but I called my friend Kay and asked if our Sally could spend Saturday afternoon playing at her house, and perhaps stay for dinner. I explained that I was leaving Saturday noon for a short visit with a friend and returning Sunday night, and she said golly, what a lucky break for me, and since my husband would be a bachelor Saturday night how about he came to their house for dinner? I said that he had to stay home with the baby, and she said well, anyway, Sally could stay overnight with them. I said wonderful, I would do the same for her sometime.

Then I called my friend Helen and asked if Jannie could visit her Jennifer on Saturday afternoon, because I was going out of town for two days and she said gee, she wished *she* could get away for a day or so, and sure, they'd love to have Jannie for the afternoon and supper, and overnight, too, if I liked, and why didn't my husband come over for supper, too, since he would be all alone? I said he had to stay at home with the baby, and she said then they'd expect Jannie sometime on Saturday.

Then I called my friend Peg and said could Laurie come over to her house Saturday afternoon because I would be away, and she said some people got all the breaks, someday *she* was going to go away for a weekend, and her William would be delighted to have our Laurie around on Saturday and if he felt like it he could stay overnight, and why didn't my husband drop over and take pot luck with them for dinner? So I said my husband had to stay at home with the baby, but we'd take a rain check on it, and I'd send Laurie along after lunch on Saturday.

The next morning, the day before I was to leave, Sally brought home from nursery school an almost undecipherable piece of paper which translated (I called the child's mother and checked it, finally) as: "My birthday party is on Sunday at three o'clock and Sally can come. This is from Pat." I called Kay and she said yes, her Ellen was invited, too, so why didn't Sally plan to stay at their house Sunday night instead, and she would pick them up after the party and see that they got to nursery school Monday morning. That way, she added, she would be able to take Ellen into town to get shoes on Saturday afternoon, as she had originally thought of doing. However, she said, if it would be more convenient for me to have things the way we first planned it . . . I said no, no, it would probably be just as simple for my husband to have Sally out of the way on Sunday, and I would try to arrange to send Sally to play with the twins on Saturday. So I called my friend Dorothy and asked if my Sally could spend Saturday afternoon with her twins and she said gladly, how lucky I was to be able to get away, would my husband like to come for dinner and I said he had to stay with the baby and she said she would give Sally supper and bring her home afterward.

When the children came home from school Friday afternoon Laurie was very much excited over an invitation he had received to go to the movies with his friend Oliver on

Saturday night, and when I said that he had been invited to stay overnight with William he groaned and said but he *had* to go to the movies, he had *told* Oliver he would, he would go to William's some other time. So I called Peg and she said that was all right with her, send Laurie along on Sunday afternoon and she would take the boys skating and bring Laurie home after dinner, since Sunday was a school night. As I hung up the phone rang again and it was Helen, to say that some old friends of theirs had just phoned that they were coming for the weekend so there wouldn't be room for Jannie overnight; could she give the child supper and send her home? And if she came over Sunday afternoon she could go skating with them and she and Jennifer could make fudge or something. I said of course, how nice of them to take Jannie when they had company and all, and Jannie was extremely pleased.

Friday night I ironed a blouse and washed my hair and did my nails, and Saturday morning I took Jannie to her dancing school and made a casserole of scalloped potatoes and sausage. While I was busy in the kitchen Laurie ran out the front door, calling over his shoulder to say that he was going down to Rob's, and he telephoned later to say that he was staying for lunch. My husband was working in the study, and Barry was in his playpen; Sally hung around me in the kitchen, getting in my way.

I cooked the casserole and then put it in the refrigerator; since I was being picked up at eleven-thirty the best arrangement for the children's lunch seemed to be cheese and jelly and peanut butter and a loaf of bread set out on the kitchen table. I went to get Jannie at dancing school and when I came back my husband came out of the study and asked me if I had noted down where the children were

expected to be so he could keep track of them, and anything else I thought he ought to know. I had fifteen minutes
or so before I needed to dress, so I went to my desk and
took up a pencil.

SATURDAY, I wrote, and then thought. A simple
chronological outline seemed best suited to my husband's
particular requirements, so I drew a line under SATUR-
DAY and continued: Give Barry chopped vegetable soup
and a bottle of plain milk, warmed, for lunch; Sally will
have lunch at home (peanut butter, etc., on kitchen table);
Laurie lunch at Rob's, Jannie at home. Milk in refrigerator.
Sally to play with twins one o'clock, for dinner, home by
bedtime. Jannie at Jennifer's, including dinner, home by
bedtime, Laurie riding lesson three o'clock, home for dinner, movie evening with Oliver. Barry in playpen 3-5,
supper casserole to go in oven 5:30, oven 375 degrees.
Barry rice and liver soup and peaches for supper, bottle
bedtime. Feed cats, dog. Laurie knows where dogfood is.
Laurie right to bed after movie, Sally, Jannie jellybeans at
bedtime. SUNDAY: Sally home till 3:30, then Pat's party
(do not forget birthday present, wrapped, on desk). Sally
wear shoes to party, pink party dress (white socks in top
left dresser drawer, if none there, blue will do). Comb
hair. Bath if possible. Check neck. Laurie at William's,
after lunch, ICE SKATES, William's for supper, home
bedtime; school night, check homework, early bed. Jannie
at Jennifer's, Sunday afternoon, supper, fudge, ICE
SKATES, SWEATER. Home bedtime, school night,
check homework, jellybeans. Barry Sunday breakfast
cereal, bottle, lunch applesauce, cats milk Sunday morning, milk in refrigerator, did you leave casserole in oven
Saturday night? Barry Sunday noon chopped vegetable

soup, bottle, nap outdoors if weather clement, Barry Sunday supper chopped vegetable and bacon soup, bottle, pudding, feed cats and dog. Do not wait up for me. Cube steaks in refrigerator if you care to cook them, otherwise leftover casserole; jar in refrigerator labeled Mayonnaise is extra coffee to heat up. Bread in breadbox. Leave note for milkman Saturday night DOZEN EGGS, LB. BUTTER, COTTAGE CHEESE. Cover all children 10:30 Saturday night. SALLY PAJAMAS TO ELLEN'S, TOOTHBRUSH. Salad. Do not let Jannie forget extra sweater going to Jennifer's, scarf. Check Sally Sunday morning for sniffle. Add note milkman ½ PT. SOUR CREAM. Thirty-five cents in change on top of refrigerator in case Laurie needs money for movies. Six jellybeans is plenty.

We had a moderately pleasant weekend, although it snowed all the time and I lost another button off my gray suit and everyone seemed to have aged noticeably. My friend dropped me off in front of the house about nine on Sunday evening, and I was glad to get back, seeing the house lighted up and even the upstairs rooms bright, although the children should have been in bed. The dog met me at the door, wagging his tail, and there was an ominous thud as some cat leaped hurriedly off the kitchen table.

"Hello?" I called, setting down my suitcase. "Where is everyone?"

The only answer was the gentle stirring of a paper on the coffee table, and I went over and picked it up.

SUNDAY, it said. Barry and/or dog ate all directions. Have taken all children incl. Barry to hamburger stand for dinner, movies. Barry fond of movies, went yesterday too, also fr.fr. potatoes. Don't wait up for us. Casserole on kitchen table, cats not fed. Milkman left two dozen eggs. Jannie says six jellybeans is not plenty. Leave front door unlocked. Jar in refrigerator labeled Mayonnaise was mayonnaise.

Nothing is stable in this world. As soon as Barry was old enough to be regarded as a recognizable human being, with ideas and opinions, it became necessary for the other children to change him around. Since he was now too big to fit into a doll carriage, Jannie amused herself by dressing him in costume jewelry and ribbons. Sally sat on the floor next to the playpen and sang to him because, she said, it made him dance. Barry was clearly too formal a name, and we took to calling him B. B was too short, however, and he became Mr. B, then Mr. Beetle, and finally Mr. Beekman. He stayed Mr. Beekman until he was almost ready for nursery school, and then came around full circle, moving back to Mr. B, then B, and, at last, to Barry again. At one point he developed a disconcerting habit of answering no matter *who* was being called. Thus, dancing, and decked in ribbons, Beekman walked instead of creeping, and learned to drink from a cup.

With the coming of our first spring in our new house it was overnight astonishingly clear that our trees and grass and bushes and flowers were real. They all showed a first pale green just like all the other trees and grass and bushes and flowers up and down the street, and I went out and took movies so we could all sit in the dark living room and see that our trees had surely turned green at the tips of the branches. The snow turned into mud, particularly in our driveway. My husband added up the winter's fuel bills and said it would be cheaper to take the barn apart and burn it stick by stick, then start on the furniture. I got up one bright Sunday morning and saw the sun and the blue sky and could not bear the thought of just driving casually down the street to the news shop to get the Sunday papers. I told the children that because it was such a particularly springlike morning I was going to get the papers by driving out the back road and out along the river road and then up the other way to the news shop, and home, and they could come with me if they liked. They got into the car, solemnly discussing the possibilities of the weather's getting enough into Mommy's head to provoke a popsicle all around. I did not expect to get out of the car, since Laurie could run into the news shop and get the papers, so I was wearing an old coat, warm and comfortable in spite of the way it looked, high, sheepskin-lined leather boots, and a red and white scarf tied over my hair, which I had combed only haphazardly, since it has always been very awkward for me to comb my hair properly until I have had my morning coffee. My husband was still asleep, and I left the coffee making in the electric coffeepot, and bacon in the pan ready to fry when I got back.

The sun was rich and the air was fresh, and I drove down the river road contentedly, deeply appreciative of the warmth of the sunlight after an all-night rain, my car splashing richly through the deep puddles. The road was extremely muddy and quite slippery, and I was glad that I had not, after all, had the snow tires taken off when it began to look like spring. I was thinking with some complacency, as a matter of fact, of how my husband had told me to get the snow tires taken off and I had forgotten. On the front seat beside me Mr. Beekman stood straight and alert in his car-chair, scanning the road ahead for possible cookies; now and then he turned to me and inquired, "Daddy?" In the back seat the three other children held converse among themselves, with raised voices and various pushings. Jannie, on the assumption that it was a matter of grave universal interest, gave us the names of the cowboys in her Red Rider gang at school; Laurie kept one hand caressingly on the barrel of the BB gun his grandfather had sent him over my urgent disapproval; he rattled BB's in his pocket and commented unceasingly upon the availability of passing objects as targets; Sally stood on her head on the back seat, singing. "Daddy?" Mr. Beekman asked insistently.

"Sunshine," I said, and sighed with satisfaction.

"Won't get many crows *today*," Laurie opined drearily. He has never yet, to my knowledge or his, shot a crow with his BB gun. "Too wet underfoot."

"If *I* was space cadet," Jannie said, "you know what *I*'d do? I'd take an asteroid on, like, Friday night, and then when it started to rain on Saturday again—"

"Thursday, you'd have to," Laurie said. "Never do it on *time* on Friday, light years and all."

"Cookie?" Mr. Beekman suggested.

I breathed deeply and happily, blew the car horn twice as I came to the bad right turn, shifted into second, pulled the wheel around, and turned the corner into the path of a car coming, fast, the other way.

I was annoyed, because I was startled, and I put my foot down on the brake and simultaneously and instinctively shoved my right elbow into Mr. Beekman's stomach to keep him from pitching forward from his car-chair.

"Woomph," said Mr. Beekman, and I pressed harder on the brake because my car was not stopping or even slowing down. I was suddenly acutely aware of the flimsy wooden bridge which was all that separated my car from the drop to the river on the right; I said "Floor" loudly, and hoped the children would understand; I tried to pull over to the left onto a broad lawn on that side of the road, and my car still would neither stop nor turn. I saw briefly that the driver of the other car was leaning far back in his seat, as though he too had his feet pressed down flat on the floor, and I braced myself against the back of the seat and put one foot on top of the other on the brake pedal, as though some kind of force might prevail upon the car to stop.

It was perfectly clear that the two cars were going to hit, skidding into each other, and I told myself firmly, there is plenty of time to stop, plenty of time. From a great distance I could hear the children's voices raised in what seemed to be enthusiastic cheering. The only question in my mind was perhaps a little academic: I was wondering how hard we were going to come together, and I was impatient at the ponderous independent movement of my car; if it was going to go off and smack into another car I wanted to get it over with. During the interminable moment between my putting my foot on the brake and the crash, I even had time to comprehend that none of us would be hurt, and then the long familiar nose of my car, intent upon destruction, swung itself with a shattering impact into the other car. Fantastic, I thought, sitting there for the first silent second, and that coffee cooking away at home.

"Cookie?" said Mr. Beekman into the silence.

"You all right?" I took my elbow out of Mr. Beekman's stomach. "Children, are you all right?"

"Sure," said Laurie. "Say, that was a *good* one." He sounded pleased.

"*I* got on the floor," Sally said, "and I found a penny."

"We all got on the floor, except Laurie peeked," Jannie said.

"Can I keep it?" Sally asked. "The penny?"

"Boy," Laurie said with relish, "was *Mom* ever scared. You hurt or something?" he asked me.

"I'm not hurt," I said. "I was *not* scared." I felt very calm, sitting there comfortably, and then I realized that we were all talking with excited speed, that the echoes of the crash were still sounding along the country road, and that the doors of the other car were slamming open; the other driver stumbled out, his legs shaking and his face white, and he yelled at me, "What you think you're *doing*?"

Deliberately I unclenched my left hand from the wheel and opened the door and climbed out; it was not until this moment that it had occurred to me that we were extraordinarily lucky that I, at least, had been going slowly, and it was at that moment only the thought of my innocent little children in the car which prevented me from speaking my mind fully. "What," I said, snarling, "do you think *you* are doing? Coming around a turn like that at that speed on a slippery road and we could all have been killed?" My voice began to quaver suddenly, and I stopped and counted ten. "At that speed," I said, through my teeth.

"You insured?" he asked.

"Certainly I'm insured. Coming around a curve like—"

"Mom," Laurie said from the back window, "can we get out?"

"No," I said, not turning. "Now listen here," I began to the other driver, and then the woman who was standing by his car, who had gotten out when he had and was standing there rubbing her forehead, took a step forward and said, "Nearly killed *me*." "Now listen here," I said again, and Laurie leaned out the back window and said, "Mom, can we get *out*? You all right?"

"The steering wheel hit me in the stomach," I said, realizing then why I was standing as though I had just been kicked by a horse. I straightened up with an effort and said, "Now listen here—"

"I wonder what Daddy is going to say," Jannie remarked brightly.

"Ooh," I said, and doubled up again.

"*You*'re hurt?" the other woman said, and laughed shortly. "What about *me*?" She rubbed her forehead and brought her hand down and looked at it hopefully for blood. "You insured?" she asked.

"Oh, shut up," I said.

"*My* little boy got hurt," she said. "He's still in the car, hurt too bad to move."

"*What*?" Hastily, I made my way past her, thinking that she must surely be stunned or shocked, and got over to their car, where the man was leaning in through the front door, arguing. It was so slippery that I had to hold on to the fenders of the cars to keep on my feet.

"Come on *out*," the man was saying. "No one's going to hurt you." Finally he reached in and pulled out a small boy about six years old. "You all right?" he asked the boy.

"Sure," the little boy said.

"He is *not* all right," the woman said, pushing past me to grab the little boy. "He is *not* all right," she insisted, her voice rising, "he's covered with blood."

"Good lord," I said helplessly.

"Where you hurt?" The woman began to run her hands frantically along the little boy, feeling the outside of his snowsuit. "You hurt in the head, like me?"

"No," the little boy said, "I feel fine." He smiled at me, and I smiled back nervously.

"There's blood on his *hand*," the woman announced loudly. "Look, blood all over his hand." She held up his hand and the man and I leaned forward and saw a small scratch and a little blood. The man wiped the blood off with his handkerchief and looked deeply at the scratch. "You hadn't ought to do that," the woman told him. "Leave it for them to see."

"I did it before, anyway," the little boy said. "I did it over to Grandma's house, on the door."

"It's awful," the woman said hastily. She put her hand to her head. "I feel faint," she said.

"I should think so," I told her sweetly, "traveling at that rate of speed. We're supposed to call the state troopers," I said to the man. "We can't move either of these cars, and no one can get past us along this road, and anyway an accident has got to be reported. Will you call them," I said, "or shall I?"

He looked at his wife for a minute, and then said, "I'll do it."

I watched with irritation as he looked again at his wife, and then moved off toward the nearest house. "Mom," Laurie called, "can we get out *now*?"

"Just be patient," I said. "Sing or something."

Jannie struck up halfheartedly with "The Old Chisholm Trail," and the woman said, "Are you insured?"

I opened my mouth and then shut it again, reminding myself of the explicit instructions on my insurance papers, instructions about not discussing an accident with any but properly constituted authorities. I turned instead to look at the damage to my car. "Junior's hurt bad," the woman said as I walked away. The road was covered with bright fragments of chromium grillwork and broken glass, my fenders were crumpled unrecognizably, the front license plate leaned drunkenly sideways, bent almost double. "Oh, brother," I said, thinking of my husband peacefully asleep at home. The other car gave a momentary impression of deep embarrassment, as though it were hoping to tiptoe way when no one was looking; it leaned backward, somehow, and it was not until I looked at it clearly now that I saw that what I had assumed from a brief glance earlier was wholesale destruction was actually the car's natural condition; the lopsided body and buckled doors were rusty, the back window had been broken long before this morning, and there were grounds for deep suspicion in the clothesline which held one door shut. "Got to keep an eye on you," the woman said suddenly, from just in back of me, "see you don't tamper with the evidence."

"I was thinking of lifting my car off the road and hiding it under a bush," I said, regarding Junior, who was climbing over the front of my car, kicking off loose pieces of grillwork.

"Wouldn't put it past you," the woman said, "ramming us like that. You better start looking for trouble, lady, because Junior's hurt bad and I hit my head on the windshield and I think I got a concussion." She rubbed her head vigorously.

"Uh-huh," I said, and made my way back to my own car and got into it and sat down.

"Mom," Jannie said, "when we going home?"

"In a few minutes," I said. "We have to wait until the police get here. The man's gone in to call them."

"Boy," Laurie said longingly, "I could sure get a good shot at that kid from here."

I sighed, and nodded. I saw the man coming back and I rolled down the window and called to him, "Did you get the troopers?" He did not answer me, but addressed his wife. "I got ahold of Carmen," he said, and she said, "Okay." Then the man turned to me and said, "Don't worry, lady," and looked again at his wife.

"Sergeant Smith of Homicide," Laurie said. "Gotta sew this case up good, Inspector."

"Crime," Jannie pointed out conclusively, "does not pay."

"Right as always, Watson," Laurie said. "Jeeps, looka the hot rod."

I blinked; this was surely not the state police? Then the man, who was still standing near my car with his wife, said, "Carmen," and I was reassured. Carmen's car was perhaps slightly older than the one which had hit me, but it seemed resolutely to be hiding its age; Carmen's car was painted in glorious reds and whites, striped and gaudy; it looked like a chorus girl dressed as an automobile. "In my day," I said irrepressibly, "they used to write things on them, like 'Going my way?' and 'This way out' and—"

"What?" Laurie said. "Write on *cars?*"

The driver of this amateur circus wagon, who was, presumably, Carmen, got himself out of it somehow, and came to stand next to the woman and man on the road. He glanced briefly at me, and then at my car, and reached out to touch the hood tenderly. "Sure did a job on *this*," he said. "Sure did," said the other man.

Carmen glanced thoughtfully at the other car, at the woman, who immediately rubbed her forehead, and then at Junior bouncing on what was left of my front bumper. "Anybody hurt?" he asked.

"Junior's all cut up," the woman said.

"That so?" Carmen turned toward Junior. "Where you hurt, kid?" he asked, and silently the little boy held up his hand for inspection. "Yeah," said Carmen. He shook his head. "Sure did a job on that car," he said.

"I know him," Laurie said suddenly. "Mom, I—"

"Shh," I said.

"But Rob and me've seen him *hundreds* of times, and—"

"Here are the troopers at last," I said thankfully. "*Now* we can get home soon." The troopers' car was black and smooth and very official; its license read "State Police" and the men inside wore the wide hats and faintly gallant uniforms which I had seen before and admired secretly; I was a little shocked to see how *very* state-trooperish they seemed, but when they stopped their car and got out and came striding toward us, I opened the door of my car with a feeling which Laurie, in a whisper, expressed to perfection.

"*Jeepers*," Laurie said.

"You suppose they ever caught a cattle rustler?" Jannie wanted to know.

"Daddy!" Mr. Beekman said with satisfaction.

The two troopers, who looked almost exactly alike and

acted with almost identical motions, glanced at the other driver. "You the man called?" one of them asked, and the other driver nodded. Then both the troopers moved to look at the two cars and the debris in the road. One of them took out a notebook and pencil, and the other asked the questions; they glanced briefly at me, standing next to my car. By this time, anxious to co-operate fully with the law, I was holding in my hand my driver's license, my car registration, my insurance card, my gas credit card, and the receipt for a registered letter to a coin dealer which I had sent off several days before for my husband. "Anyone hurt?" the trooper asked.

"My little boy," the other driver said swiftly, "he cut himself bad. My wife got a bad crack on her forehead, maybe a concussion. No one in the other car got even scratched."

"Medical attention?"

"My cousin here, he's waiting to get them to a doctor. They wanted to stay, make sure everything was legal, first."

"That's right," said the woman. "Junior's all covered with blood, but we didn't want *her* getting away with anything."

"Hey," I said. I turned to the nearer of the troopers. "Look," I began, hesitating because I was concentrating on not raising my voice, on sounding as reasonable as possible, "listen," I said.

The other driver cut in smoothly. "Y'see, officer," he said, "we were coming home from church, my wife and me and the baby, and coming along the road here like we do every day, and this lady here, and I'm not saying she was out of her senses with drink or anything, but she come along over this road maybe fifty, sixty miles an hour, and—"

"I did not," I said flatly. "He—"

"Well, now," Carmen began, "I don't want to make any trouble for the lady, and I suppose what I say favoring my own cousin won't count for much, anyway, but she's got to admit she was on the wrong side of the road. I noticed her around here a lot, that big car, and maybe she doesn't always care about what happens to other people." He looked blandly at the trooper. "I guess that's what she's got insurance *for*," he suggested.

"But he wasn't even *here*," I said wildly.

Carmen and his cousin smiled understandingly at one another, and Carmen shrugged and said, "Not that I want to counterdict a lady, but *she* knows I saw what happened, and I guess I ought to kind of point out to her that it won't do no good to *lie* about it. I was right behind Verge here, following him down the road. From church," he added faithfully.

The trooper looked at me. "Well?" he asked coldly.

"Teaching her little children to tell lies," Carmen said sadly to his cousin, and they both nodded.

I stood there literally helpless with fury. I do not remember that I have ever been so angry in my life. Everything I tried to say ended in a gasp, and I gestured violently; perhaps the trooper thought I was reaching for a shoulder holster, because he took a step backward, and then Laurie spoke cheerfully from beside me. "Mommy's mad," he said, "so *I'll* say what happened. Recognize that guy, sheriff?" He spoke over his shoulder to Jannie, nodding at Carmen at the same time.

[91]

"Sure do, cowboy," Jannie said. "Toughest hombre in—"

"I'm the Black Knight of the Forest," Laurie said graciously to the troopers, "and my squire and me recognized this fellow because we see him a lot, him and the guy he calls his cousin here, because they go up and down these back roads all the time, stealing horses."

"Rustling cattle," said the Black Squire.

"And one day we were playing in that old hot rod the guy has, and it's got a false bottom and the bottom's full of drug traffic."

"Admirable, Watson," said the Black Squire approvingly. "Cattle rustlers and addicts, *they* are. And the reason they waited till my mother came along here was they are planning to blow up the old bridge."

"With stolen dynamite," Laurie finished. He looked at me brightly and smiled; apparently the defense had rested its case.

"Old Cap'n Hook," Sally shouted then from the back window of my car, "where's your crokkerdile, old Cap'n Hook?"

The troopers were regarding Laurie with sober attention, and I had the sudden first suspicion that they had not given entire belief to Carmen and Verge. "Officer," I began calmly, "shall I try to describe what happened?"

"Yeah," Carmen said loudly, "let s hear *her* tell it." He looked at Verge and they laughed.

"Ramming into people," the woman said. She rubbed her forehead and said "I ought to get to a doctor."

"Hey, listen." Junior spoke up suddenly. "Hey, listen, you guys. *Hoppy*'s after these two, both."

"Good work, kid," Laurie nodded approvingly. "Our spy in the confederate camp," he told the troopers.

"Oh?" Jannie twisted her face into a ferocious scowl. "Who let out Murphy's bull?" she asked sternly, and Junior retired behind his mother. "I ain't hurt," he said distinctly.

"*And* they're moonshiners," Laurie said.

"Hey," said Carmen, grieved. He glared at Laurie. "Watch out who you're calling names, bud," he said.

"Children," I said, "get back in the car at once. My little boy," I told the trooper, "is very excited. Naturally, the question right now is not the . . . ah . . . occupation of these gentlemen." I smiled kindly on Carmen. "I was coming slowly along the road," I said, "and when I got to this bad turn I slowed down, shifted into second, and blew the horn. As I came around the turn I saw this other car coming *quite* fast, and both cars skidded, and hit. *Then*," I went on, "this gentleman went into that house over there and called his cousin and told him to come over."

"Ask that guy does he have a license to drive," Laurie said, putting his head out of the car window, "I *know* that hot rod, just *ask* him. Ask him about how his kid got kept after school for throwing stink bombs, *ask* him."

"Cattle rustlers!"

"Where's your crokkerdile?"

"Well." The trooper shook his head. "Let's get this thing straight," he said. "This moonshiner was coming slowly along the road on his way home from church. Church?"

"Yeah," said Verge without conviction.

"And this lady was coming around the turn at a speed of—"

"About fifteen miles an hour," I said sharply.

"Gangsters!"

The trooper looked at Verge. "I guess so," Verge said miserably.

"Train robbers!"

"And the driver of the third car, the hot rod, was—"

"About two, three miles back," Carmen said hastily.

"And the lady was driving recklessly?" the trooper asked, his pencil poised delicately above his notebook.

Verge swallowed, looked at Carmen, and then down at the ground. "I guess we won't prefer charges," Carmen said generously. "Give the lady a break on the whole thing, officer," he said.

"Say, Lieutenant." Laurie was out of the car again. "Like to have a look at my BB gun?" he asked.

Half an hour later I stopped my car, battered and limping, in my own driveway, with the bacon in the pan in the house ready to fry and the coffee by now probably boiled dry, and my husband peacefully asleep. For a minute we all sat in the car, breathing deeply, and then I asked shyly, "Laurie, was any of that true?"

"Any of what?"

"About the moonshiners and the dynamite and the false bottom on that car?"

"What about it?"

"Is it true? Did you really find a false bottom in that car?"

"We're not *allowed* to play in somebody else's car," Laurie said, shocked. "What would Dad say? Hey," he added suddenly, "I'm going to tell Dad right now."

"*I'm* going to tell Daddy," Jannie said. They struggled, pushing, out of the car, and raced for the house, with Sally following and shrieking, "Daddy, Daddy, Mommy hit another car and smashed it all up and the police came and I found a penny and Mommy—"

"Maybe I'll just stay out here," I said to Mr. Beekman, and he nodded.

"Cookie," he said sympathetically.

Verge's wife telephoned me about a week later and told me with enormous satisfaction that she had not had a concussion after all, but a deviated septum, and she had the doctor's word to prove it, and they were going to sue me for plenty for her deviated septum and Junior's many injuries. I think Verge forgot about it, though, because there was an item in the paper a few days after that saying that Verge had miraculously escaped injury when his car went through a guard rail along a back road and rolled down the hill into the river. Sole witness to the accident was his cousin Carmen, who had been driving along behind him. They were going to bring suit against the township for criminal neglect.

The children were changing in the new house. They belonged in the town now. Laurie could go over to the gym in the evenings to see the basketball games, and Jannie walked to the library after school. I took movies of Sally riding her tricycle up and down the back walk, and of Barry being pulled in a wagon and walking unsteadily across the porch. The gatepost continued crooked. When the sap was definitely running that spring we thought we would tap our maple trees, and my husband consulted the Encyclopaedia of Social Sciences for directions, while I drove down to the grocery to get mason jars. Laurie drilled holes in four maples, just as the encyclopaedia said to, and we hung the jars on pegs under the holes. I set up a washtub on the back of the stove. Some friends from New York called to ask if we were free for the weekend because they thought they might drive up and we said we were sorry but we were sugaring off, and could they make it the weekend after? Laurie and his father kept emptying the jars full of sap into the washtub on the back of the stove, and we kept it boiling day and night. After nearly five days we had boiled down about a pint and a half of syrup, and we put it into tiny medicine bottles, about enough for one pancake each, and sent it to all our friends, with a label saying it came from our own sugarbush. We estimated that what with the electricity and the repairs to the stove and the mason jars and the pots and the laundry bill and the wallpaper in the dining room peeling off from the steam our maple syrup had cost us about seventy-five dollars a gallon. I took movies of Laurie tapping the maple trees. Someone told us later that you were supposed to strain the sap before you boiled it.

I went down one morning to get the mail, and there was a magazine from the Junior Natural History Society for Laurie, a letter from my mother, six bills which I passed on unopened to my husband, and a birthday card for me. I opened it, looked at it, thought for a minute, and then leaned around to look at my husband past the coffeepot. "When is my birthday?" I asked him.

"Good heavens," he said, staring.

"For the past eleven years, I believe," I said icily, "I have had to remind you regularly once a year that my birthday is on . . ." I hesitated. "Oh," I said. I held out the card. "Then why do I get a birthday card today?"

He looked at it with a kind of relieved smile. "Mistake, probably," he said. "Someone must have made a mistake.

They thought," he explained more fully, "that today was your birthday. You're sure it's not?" he asked anxiously.

"I could telephone my mother," I said, "or look up my birth certificate. And I've written it down for you a hundred times."

"Then why," he asked, putting his finger on the vital point, "send you a birthday card? You suppose someone thought it *was* your birthday?"

"That must be it," I said.

He took the card away from me and scowled at it. "Signed L or F or maybe even J," he said. "Nothing but an initial. Wouldn't you think people—"

I took the card back again. "F," I said. "I'm sure it's F. And the envelope is certainly addressed to me, right name, right address."

"Then someone must have made a mistake," he said with finality.

"But who?"

My husband was opening the bills. "Now *here's* a *real* mistake for you," he said, nodding. "The dress shop. Thirty-seven—"

I took my birthday card and tiptoed away.

Although our life pursues a fairly even tenor, generally, it is very easy to upset our family equilibrium, and a minor unsolved mystery is surely a splendid way to do it. When my husband left the breakfast table he came into the kitchen where I was gathering myself together to defrost the refrigerator and said, "Any ideas?"

"No," I said, "unless a kind of hash . . ."

"About that card, I mean," he said. "Any idea who sent it?"

"Someone whose name begins with L or F," I said. "Linda? Laura? Florence? Laurence?"

Laurie's name is Laurence, but he sends people birthday cards only under the most extreme persuasion, and only if I buy them first and then sit him down and hand him the pen to sign and address them, and, besides, he always signs them "Laurie," with a flourish underneath, and "Anyway," I said, finishing my train of thought aloud, "he would have given it to me to mail."

"And why send a card to you? He never did before."

"And Sally and Barry can't write, and if Jannie wanted to give me a birthday card she'd just *give* it to me, and besides Sally only believes in birthday cards if she gets invited to the parties and Barry—"

"Must be some kind of a mistake," my husband said heartily, and went on into the study, still carrying the bill from the dress shop.

About half an hour later I stopped by the study and said, "You know, I've been thinking. About that birthday card—"

"Mistake, probably," my husband said absently. He was putting a new ribbon into his typewriter, and had involved himself deeply.

"But I don't recognize the handwriting. It looks like a child's, almost. Look at the envelope."

"I *can't* look at the envelope," my husband said. "I need another hand as it is."

"Well," I said, "either by a child or maybe someone writing left-handed. As though they were trying to disguise their handwriting, you know. Almost illiterate."

"Well, ask Laurie," my husband said. "He's the only illiterate child *I* know." He thought. "Except for the rest of your children, of course," he finished generously.

I went and asked Laurie and Laurie said no, he had never seen the birthday card before. "Why?" he asked. "Your birthday or something?"

"My birthday is a hundred and forty-three days off and I want a plain silver necklace to go with my new black dress," I said. "I was just curious about why someone sent me a birthday card."

Jannie had never seen the card before, but thought it might have been meant for her. "I haven't had as many birthdays as *you* have," she pointed out, "so people are more liable to make a mistake on *mine*."

Sally was not expecting any birthday cards, either, but added shrewdly that although her birthday was quite a while off, there would be no harm in her taking the card and keeping it until it *was* her birthday. "Then they wouldn't have to send me another," she explained.

Old Beekman did not recognize the card, but seemed to think that he would like to have it anyway. He offered me half a lollipop and a broken airplane in exchange, and was loudly indignant when I rejected what he must have regarded as a supremely fair offer.

"Cookie?" he suggested tearfully. "Candy, cookie?"

"Well," I said, returning to my husband in the study, "about all I can think of now is to call everyone I know and ask *them*. Even though it seems kind of silly to send someone a birthday card and disguise your *hand*writing. I mean, why bother to send it at all?"

My husband, who was typing "Now is the time for all good men to come to the aid of their country" over and over again, looked up briefly and said, "Also, they used a two-cent stamp. Didn't notice *that*, did you?"

I took up the envelope and looked at it again. "Most people only use two-cent stamps around Christmastime," I said. "For Christmas cards, you know. Sometimes you come across them in a desk drawer or something but *most* people—"

"No," my husband agreed. "You won't often find anyone who remembers to use a two-cent stamp the rest of the year."

"Looks kind of . . . well . . . cheap, doesn't it?" I said. "Sending me a birthday card and then going out to get a two-cent stamp to mail it with. Imagine!"

"Might just as well not have gone to any trouble about it at all," my husband said.

"Naturally," I said reasonably, "it's nice of them to want to send me a birthday card and of course I appreciate the thought and all, but it *does* seem that if you're going to disguise your handwriting and go buy a two-cent stamp you're a very strange sort of person, is all."

"What's another penny, anyway?" my husband asked. "The way things cost these days, a three-cent stamp is *nothing*. They probably just had the two-cent stamp left over from Christmas."

"Imagine!" I said again. "Keeping an old two-cent stamp from a Christmas card. I wouldn't be surprised if they *steamed* it off."

"Fine lot of friends *you*'ve got," my husband said indignantly. "Probably an old leftover birthday card too. See if another name's been erased."

"*I* wouldn't be surprised," I said. "Naturally, I don't expect a gift from every casual acquaintance, naturally, but

I *do* like to think that if anyone is going to send me a card, well, after all, I get enough birthday cards so's I don't have to take any old—"

The phone rang, and I went to answer it. It was my husband's Aunt Lydia, and after I had asked how she was and how Uncle George was, and she had asked after me and my husband and the children I said how nice it was of her to call, because we hadn't heard from her in so long, and she said oh, she just thought she'd call, and she was surprised that *we* hadn't called *her*, and I said, well, I had been meaning to. Then she said well, she really wouldn't have called at all, actually, only she was going out for the day and of course today *was* her birthday and she thought we might have been planning to call *her* and she wanted us to know she wouldn't be there, because of course she usually expected to hear from us on her birthday, even if it was nothing but a card. "But I *sent* . . ." I said, and was suddenly silent.

She was saying oh, really, because then wasn't it funny that it hadn't arrived, because really she wouldn't have bothered to call at all except she was going out for the day and it being her birthday of course . . . I handed the phone silently to my husband and went and looked at my birthday card. "Happy birthday, Aunt Lydia," my husband said into the phone, and I stood there looking at the card and wondering at the way my handwriting had deteriorated since college.

My husband said goodbye to Aunt Lydia and hung up and came back into the study. "Funny thing," he said, going toward his desk, "here Aunt Lydia didn't get a card on her birthday, and you got a birthday card but it wasn't your birthday. Funny."

"Yeah," I said.

"I thought I'd write that place a letter about their bill," my husband went on, "tell them they can't get away with *that* kind of thing."

"Some days," I said, dropping my birthday card into the wastebasket, "*every*thing just seems to go wrong, doesn't it?"

Laurie and I entered that spring into a most complex and subtle series of strategies. I would sigh deeply and wistfully at the dinner table, staring mournfully into space and refusing dessert, and when my husband asked me what was wrong Laurie would move in with a direct frontal attack. Or Laurie would come home from school with his face artistically smeared with mud and the look of a cowed and fearful wild creature; he would fling himself drearily into a study chair and when his father asked what on earth he had been fighting about *now*, I would cry indignantly that it wasn't fair to blame the poor child for something he couldn't help, he was the laughingstock of the neighborhood and it was our fault. Jannie came in with us after a while; she would sit on her father's lap and say, "Poor poor Mommy," and, "*Why*, Daddy?" in a particularly piercing nasal tone. After about a month—four days short, actually, of the time Laurie and I had originally figured it would take—my husband gave in. Laurie and Jannie and I chose a brown and cream station wagon, with gold and cream inside, and we gave the man the old car with its nose smashed in and one headlight hanging crooked, and when my husband went for a ride in the new station wagon he said that of course since we were in debt for the rest of our lives anyway with the house payments we might as well buy a car too and go bankrupt in style and didn't I think the gold oil gauge and speedometer were perhaps a little gaudy?

I took a movie of the decrepit old car being driven away and the glittering new car standing in the driveway. I went out and bought a new car-chair for Beekman, one that had a small steering wheel and gear-shift lever attached; when I put Beekman into his new car-chair he turned the steering wheel and said "Beep beep?" experimentally, and we all laughed and told him he was a brave smart boy. By the end of a week I was no longer fumbling wildly for the brake pedal in the new car, and Beekman was manipulating his steering wheel and gearshift with such wild abandon and skillful maneuvering as to earn himself the title of Mad-Dog Beekman; I could not, at any time of the day or night, attempt to sneak the car out of the driveway without attracting Beekman's attention, and he would hurl himself wildly at the doors and windows, calling out to wait a minute, he would be right there, and subsiding at last into hysterical terrors at my trying to drive without him.

For my part, I found it extremely difficult to drive with dual controls, trying to ease around a tight corner with Beekman beside me shifting rapidly from high to reverse to second, swinging his wheel around sharply and yelling "Beep beep." I used to try letting the car roll backward out of the driveway without starting the motor, but Beekman's room was in the front and as soon as I got as far as the gateposts he would apparently catch some reflection of light and I would see his small infuriated face pressed against the window and hear the crash as Dikidiki hit the wall, and after a minute my husband or Laurie or Jannie or Sally would open the front door and call that I was to wait, they were just putting on Beekman's jacket.

Usually, whenever Beekman drove, Sally wanted to come too. And whenever Sally came, Jannie thought she had better come along. And when Beekman and Sally and Jannie came, Laurie figured that we might just stop in at a movie or some such, and if we did he wanted to be along. As a result, whenever I went shopping in the new car, everyone came except my husband, who could not, for a long time, look at the new car without telling me how we were going bankrupt in style. One Saturday morning I almost got off without Beekman, who was learning from Sally how to cut out paper dolls, but before I was out of the driveway they were calling to me to wait a minute, and by the time I finally turned the car and headed off toward the big supermarkets I had all four of them with me, Sally accompanied by her dolls Susan and David and Patpuss, all dressed entirely in cleansing tissue, and carrying—although I did not know it when she got into the car —a pocketbook containing four pennies and a shilling stolen from her father's coin collection.

I suppose I should have known that all was not going to go well when I found a parking space on Main Street on Saturday at noon, with seventeen minutes paid for on the parking meter. Finding a parking space at all was so exceptional an occurrence that I wisely determined to disregard the fact that the car on my left—an out-of-state car, by the way, from some state where land is not so jealously parceled out as it is here in Vermont—was straddling the line. I eased my car in with only the faintest grazing sound, although it was immediately plain that if we were going to get out of our car at all, we were going to have to do it by sliding out the doors on the right-hand side.

"Jeepers," Laurie remarked, gazing from his window at the car next to us, "cut it a little close, didn't you?"

"It was Beekman," I said nervously. "He kept pulling to the left."

"Jeepers," Laurie said to Beekman, "you want to watch where you're going, kid."

"Dewey, dewey," said Beekman, this being a combination word he used for a series of connected ideas, roughly translatable as: Observe my latest achievement, far surpassing all my previous works in this line, a great and personal triumph representing perhaps the most intelligent progress ever accomplished by a child of my years. "Dewey," said Beekman pleasurably.

We made a pretty family group as we got out and set forth to do the marketing; after a preliminary skirmish by Laurie and me we got the back of the station wagon open, and removed and set up Beekman's collapsible stroller, and when I wiggled Beekman into it and managed to get one of his legs on either side of the center axle, he sat nobly, bowing to right and left. Laurie and Jannie spoke to one another for a minute about who was to push the stroller and then, with a certain strong pressure from me, put one hand each on the handle and pushed that way. Sally walked directly in front of the stroller, so that it bumped the backs of her ankles at each step, at which she said "Hey." Laurie and Jannie said "Look *out*," and Beekman said "Dewey."

I myself walked a step or two behind, holding anxiously to my pocketbook and trying to decide about dinner on Tuesday. In my pocketbook I had three single dollar bills and twenty-six cents in change, and a check for fifty dollars, wrung from my husband that morning by a series of agile arguments and a tearful description of his children lying at his feet faint from malnutrition.

I took Beekman into the first supermarket in his stroller, against the rules, and so I felt that it was only right to show my confidence in the store by cashing my check there as we left. I remember that it was the one moment of the day when the manager steps out for a cup of coffee and one of the clerks, whom I remember as fairly small and with lightish hair, cashed my check for me, counting out the fifty dollars in ten-dollar bills.

"Better count it yourself," he said, showing me the money, and I spread out the ten-dollar bills, peering at them through the leaves of the artichokes which were an unjustifiable extravagance except that Jannie and I were fond of them, and said, "Okay, okay," and stuffed four of them into my pocketbook, where I already had the three single bills and twenty-six cents in change.

I got in line at the check-out counter, with Beekman in his stroller and Jannie and Sally and Laurie crowding around me, and I gave the clerk the ten-dollar bill to pay for the artichokes and the canned shrimp and the box of cookies which Beekman turned out to have selected from a shelf as we went by. At that point I discovered that artichokes, which only a few weeks ago cost twenty cents, if not eighteen or even seventeen, had gone up now to thirty-five cents. I protested violently, holding up the line behind me, and the manager, returning unwanted from his coffee break, most unreasonably supported the girl at the counter. I threatened darkly not to buy his artichokes at all, but to go to the other market where I knew, and the manager knew that I knew, the artichokes were never quite as fresh.

The manager, a tactless man to be in a position of such responsibility, said that that was all right with him. I said that I would not take the artichokes, and the manager said all right, no one was going to make me buy them. I said that when I was a little girl in California artichokes twice as big and twice as green as these were two for a nickel, and the manager suggested that I go back to California for my artichokes, then. Finally, when the children grew restless and the people behind me in the line began asking one another why on earth she didn't take her money and get out instead of keeping people standing here waiting, I let go of my ten-dollar bill and took my change and my bag of groceries and made my way out, grumbling.

I then went to the other supermarket to get the things that I always buy there, this time with a strong feeling of satisfaction at having shown the artichoke-manager that I was not to be trifled with. In this second supermarket I spent (although I did not subsequently find it necessary for my husband to know the exact amount) twenty dollars and twenty-six cents, which I paid with the precise change.

We then discovered that the electric company was closed. The shade was drawn and the door locked and we stood pathetically outside with our noses pressed to the glass. "Well," I said, rapping sharply, "what a way to run a business! Why, you'd think they'd *want* people to come and buy things. My goodness, you'd think—"

Jannie looked through the crack between the shade and the doorframe. "Is it closed?" she asked. "Because there's someone *in* there."

Beekman giggled, and Laurie, who was generally faintly embarrassed by having the rest of us follow him around, retreated half a dozen paces down the sidewalk and stood with his back to us, whistling and apparently scanning the street for casual acquaintances. Sally crouched beside Jannie and helped look through the crack. "Let us in," she howled, "let us in, let us in."

I rattled the door handle irritably.

"Let us innnnn," Sally shouted, and Beekman giggled wildly.

"Here someone comes," Jannie said. The door opened a little bit and Jannie and Sally, pushing, opened it wider and shoved themselves in. "Come *on*," Jannie said urgingly to me but I hesitated, because the girl who opened the door was making feeble brushing motions at Jannie and Sally and saying that they were closed, that she had only come to tell us that they were closed.

"Dewey," Beekman explained, and Laurie sighed, took a brief glance around to see if anyone he knew was watching, and stepped over to us. "Look," he said to the girl, "tomorrow's Father's Day. We got to get him a electric razor. On the bill."

"—taking *inventory*," the girl said. "There's no one here."

"But we *got* to," Jannie said, "on the bill because there wasn't any money in our banks at all, because Mommy—"

"So," I put in hastily, since Jannie was apparently prepared to enlarge indefinitely upon this purely personal subject, "we thought if we made the down payment we could put the rest on the bill."

The girl hesitated, looking from one to another of our eager faces, and then Sally said softly, "Poor Daddy's Father's Day," and the girl smiled sympathetically and said, "All right. I'm not supposed to, you know, because we're closed. But I'll put it on the books like a regular sale and they'll all think someone else did it and I guess it'll be all right."

"It would be really terribly nice," I said gratefully.

"Only you've got to promise not to say *I* did it," the girl said.

"I won't say a word," I promised.

"Silent as the grave," Laurie confirmed.

"I promise," Sally said.

"I promise," Jannie said.

"Dewey," Beekman said.

It was a perfectly simple transaction. The girl entered the sale of the razor on the books, payments to go on our electric bill. (Perhaps my husband would not even notice and anyway he could hardly *say* anything, it being his Father's Day present.) I gave the girl one of my ten-dollar bills to make the down payment, which was four-fifty. When she went to the petty cash box to get me my change, I said, "You know, this is really very kind of you." Sally was asking Laurie which could win more fights, a giant or an airplane, and Jannie was amusing herself by humming softly and opening and shutting the doors of the sample refrigerators lined up against the wall. The girl said, "Glad I was able to do it." Then I suddenly glanced around and said, "Beekman?"

The stroller sat, empty, in the middle of the electric store. "Beekman?" I shouted. *"Beekman!"*

"Beekmen?" the girl asked, pausing with her hands full of bills, "what are beekmen?"

"Beekman!" said Jannie, running to the door.

"Beekman!" said Sally, going to look behind the counter.

"Dewey, dewey?" said Beekman from very far away.

"Beekman!" said Laurie, getting down to look under

the stroller. "I don't really believe," he said thoughtfully, "that Dad would even like that razor if we went and lost Beekman."

"He's got to be here somewhere," I said.

"Dewey, dewey?" said Beekman remotely.

The salesgirl put down her two handfuls of money and went and opened the oven door of a sample stove. "Dewey," said Beekman, pleased.

"Is this what you were looking for?" the girl asked.

"Those are nice big ovens," I said, interested. "The one I've got now won't hold anything larger than an eighteen-pound turkey."

"Some of these models have two ovens," the girl said. "I can't show them to you *now*, but if you'd come back some other time . . ."

"I will," I said. I gathered Beekman up and went and put him into the stroller and fastened the strap tight and put the package with the electric razor on top of him to help hold him down. "This is really most kind of you," I said ineffectually. "I'll certainly be back for another look at those stoves."

The girl, who still smiled agreeably but was beginning to look, I thought, faintly regretful, said, "Nothing at all, really."

I said, "Well, we promise not to say a word, don't we, children?" and the children all promised again.

I took the change the girl held out and put it into my pocketbook and said, "Well, thanks, too, for finding Beekman," and the girl went over and opened the door for us and said, "Glad to do it." We wheeled the stroller out, all saying "Thank you," and the door closed firmly behind us.

Now, I am not going to pretend that when she handed

me my change I counted it. I was thinking about that stove, and whether I could convince my husband that now there were so many in our family an eighteen-pound turkey was not big enough, and I was wondering how Beekman had gotten out of his stroller and I was noticing at the same time that that red jacket was really getting too small for Sally. And I am not going to maintain that when that impertinent girl told me artichokes had gone up to thirty-five cents, although they were surely no more than twenty-three or twenty-four cents not a week before—I won't say that I stood at the counter with people pushing behind me and the manager arguing and checked over the change *she* gave me. And it is, I think, not unreasonable that when the clerk cashed my check I merely glanced briefly at the fan of bills. My husband's subsequent contention—that I could only count up to five when we were married and have not learned anything since—is unjustified and easily disproven any time I want to go to so much trouble. All I know is that when I then sat down in the car with Beekman shifting gears aimlessly beside me I counted the money in my pocketbook and I had thirty-three dollars and twelve cents.

"Laurie," I said, "what's six times thirty-five?"

Laurie thought, mumbled, and finally said, "It's two hundred and ten."

"And add two hundred and fifteen?"

Laurie growled and mumbled further. "That makes four hundred and twenty-five."

"And twenty-nine cents for Beekman's cookies?"

"Hey," Laurie said, overtaxed.

"It doesn't matter anyway," I said. "It just *can't* come out right. I couldn't end up with thirty-three dollars, could I?"

"Why?" Laurie said.

"Somebody has given me ten dollars too much," I said.

"What for?" Jannie asked.

"Either the man who cashed my check or the girl with the artichokes or the razor lady. Not the second supermarket," I said, thinking, "because I gave them the exact change. A ten-dollar bill stuck to a single, probably."

"Nice of them," Laurie said.

"Yeah," I said, pleased. "Now I can—"

"We talk about that kind of thing in Cub Scouts," Laurie said. "Suppose somebody gives you too much money for change—what do you do?"

"Oh," I said. I sighed. "Well," I said, "I guess I'd better go back to the electric store. Maybe when Beekman got lost she got the change mixed up."

"Or maybe even you had more to start with?" Jannie suggested.

"No," I said, "because when I went and asked Daddy for money he said he didn't have any and I looked then and I said how do you expect me to buy groceries for this family with three dollars and twenty-six cents and I counted it carefully *then* because Dad wanted to know was that all I had left from the money he gave me yesterday. And Dad said—"

"But the razor lady won't let you in," Sally said.

"Sure," I said. "If I tell her—"

"I just bet she won't, though," Sally said.

"And you can't wait till they figure it out and find out they gave you too much," Laurie said, "because she wasn't supposed to anyway and if she did give you too much she wouldn't tell anyway and you promised you wouldn't.

And if she didn't give you too much and you go in next time they're open and ask, then you'd be telling anyway."

"And we all promised," Sally pointed out.

"And if she didn't give you too much and she gets in trouble anyway, boy, will *she* be mad," Jannie said.

But I went back to the electric store and knocked on the door and called and shook the handle and even tried to see in through the glass of the windows but no one inside would come. It seemed impractical to me to put the ten-dollar bill into an envelope and slide it under the door without an explanation, particularly since I was not at all sure I got it there and I certainly did not want to call public attention to my problem by endeavoring to shout an explanation through the door in hopes of her hearing me from inside. So I turned away reluctantly and started off for the other end of Main Street to the artichoke supermarket. The children watched me from the car, waving enthusiastically as I passed.

I came into the supermarket and found the manager in his cubbyhole. I gave him a friendly smile. "Look," I said, "I wanted to see you just to ask—"

"Lady," he said, "there is just absolutely *nothing* I can do. There hasn't *been* any change in prices. I mean, just the normal seasonal change. You can't really think I—"

"It's not that, it's—"

"The principle of the thing. I *know*." The manager sighed. "Listen," he said, "all you dames get mad because of prices and what do you do? You blame me. But what do you think *my* wife—"

"But I don't *care* about your wife, I only want to tell you—"

"Look," he said. "You want to return the artichokes?

[113]

You go return the artichokes, and I'll tell the girl to give you your money back. Not a general policy, remember," he said, shaking his finger at me warningly. "Don't think you can come in any old time and bring back artichokes, coffee, bread, anything, you don't like the price."

"Thank you very much," I said. I nodded at him politely and left. So now I've got this ten dollars, I was thinking miserably, plodding back to the car.

My children were all leaning out of the car windows in an interested fashion and a policeman was talking to Sally. "Do you want your nice mommy to be arrested?" he asked hotly.

Laurie and Jannie laughed and even Beekman smiled. "Yup," said Sally.

"Look, honey," the policeman said in a persuasive kind of voice, "you just give me one penny now and when your Mommy comes back she'll give *you* a penny. Won't she, son?"

"Sure," Laurie said. "I bet Mom will give you *two* pennies, Sal."

"Three," said Jannie.

Sally deliberated. Finally she said, "You're a nice man and my little baby Patpuss says you can have her shilling."

"What?" said the policeman.

"If you promise not to ask little girls for money ever again," said Sally primly.

"Look, Sal," said Laurie in haste, "*anyway*, what're you going to do with your penny?"

"Bubble gum," said Sally.

"I bet you if Mommy gets arrested you're not going to get any *bubble* gum with that penny," Laurie said darkly.

"It's my penny," Sally said, "and he can't have it." She retreated, murmuring, to the farthest corner of the car.

"Please, little girl," the policeman said coaxingly.

"Shilling," said Sally with finality, "or nothing."

"But I can't put a shilling in a parking meter," the policeman said.

"Here, officer," I said, stepping forward generously. "See? I'm putting a penny in the parking meter and now the little girl's nice mommy won't be arrested."

The policeman sighed and wiped his forehead. "Thanks, lady," he said. "You know, I hate giving tickets for these things and that little girl, she's got a penny."

"Really?" I said. I turned and scowled dreadfully at Sally.

"Thank you, lady," Laurie said with rare presence of mind.

"Well, dears, you are certainly very welcome," I said through my teeth.

Beekman leaned forward, puzzled, to peer at me through the glass. "Mommy?" he inquired doubtfully.

"Silly baby," said Jannie, laughing lightly. "Our dear mother will be coming along real soon now."

"Well, thanks, lady," the policeman said. He wiped his forehead again and shook his head. "Imagine that poor woman," he said.

"Uh-huh," I said. "Imagine that poor woman."

The policeman went on down the street and the half-dozen people who had stood around on the sidewalk watching went on back to their own business. I went into the doorway of the music store, where I stood earnestly scrutinizing the new records in the window, and after a few minutes I came back and got into my car.

"You give back that ten dollars?" Laurie wanted to know at once. "Whose was it, anyway?"

I backed the car out of the parking space without difficulty, although Beekman was making a resolute left turn. "Well," I began warily, "turns out I couldn't find anyone to give it to. Consequently," I said, "I still have it. No one would take it," I said defensively.

"I suppose we better just ask Dad," Laurie said.

"Well, I meant to bring that up, too," I said. I turned the car into the parking space of the hot-dog stand and stopped. "Suppose," I suggested, beginning to wiggle Beekman out of his car seat, "suppose we just don't bother Dad with it; he always has such a lot on his mind. Anyway, he'd take it. So why don't we all just go in here and I'll—"

"I know," Laurie said, struck with an idea, "let's *give* it to him." He began to giggle. "Tie a ribbon around it," he said, "and give it to him for Father's Day."

"Hey," Jannie said with pleasure, "let's just do that."

"But," I said, "I was going to use it to buy everybody hot dogs and—"

"Boy," Laurie said, "I bet he never got a Father's Day present like that before. Boy!" He wheeled and raced after Sally and Jannie, who were already opening the door of the hot-dog stand; I could see Sally whip around the end of the counter inside and slide up onto a high stool. I took Beekman under my arm and started after them. "Dewey?" said Beekman eagerly.

Father's Day was duly observed; the weather grew warm; the incredible day arrived and school was out for the summer. Sally's nursery school had a little party for the old ones who were graduating into kindergarten the next fall. Jannie was promoted to the third grade. Laurie was promoted to the sixth grade. My husband was invited to teach at the girls' college just outside our town, and accepted, planning to start in the fall when Jannie went into third grade and Laurie into sixth grade and Sally into kindergarten. I began to think with an uneasy sensation which I finally identified as pure stagefright of the mornings next spring, when Barry would begin nursery school and I would be all alone in the house. I made tentative plans for garden work, and thought that with all the free time I was going to have I might get some reading done. I could even take courses at the college if I wanted to, things I had always meant to take when *I* was in college and never gotten around to—endocrinology, for instance, or Advanced French. I could reorganize the linen closet and finally get the ragged towels down at the bottoms of the piles, instead of right on top where they always came out for company. I asked my husband what I should do with the long empty mornings I was going to have next spring, and he said that by that time the floors would need another coat of varnish. I said indignantly that I was certainly not going to stay home varnishing the floors all by myself while he was off teaching in a nice cool college, and he said then why didn't I get some practice cooking? I said I got all the practice cooking I needed, thank you, and went off and mooned over the red and tan jacket Laurie wore when he first went off to nursery school.

Then my mother wrote that Aunt Gertrude was home again, and I really ought to take the children to see her once, before, as my mother said, she "left her cottage for good." It was a matter of a two-hour drive each way, which was a lot for me with children in the car, but I had not seen Aunt Gertrude for many years, and my husband was not correct in assuming that my interest was wholly venal. During the greater part of my married life my Great-Aunt Gertrude was in the hospital; Laurie was only a baby when I heard from my mother that Aunt Gertrude had been found by a neighbor lying at the foot of her back steps with a broken hip, and my mother added in a postscript that Aunt Julie had written *her* that when the old lady woke up in the hospital and found out where she was, and why, the only thing that worried her was what would become of her cats. Finally, the cats were fed and cared for by neighbors, and they bred among themselves as they always had, pure white, and the old ones, unlike Aunt Gertrude, died off, and the new ones grew up. Although the neighbors fed them and tried to take them in, they lived, the young ones as well as the old, around Aunt Gertrude's back door, sheltering under the steps. The neighbors wrote us that it was amazing, the way the kittens grew up to cry at the door which they had never seen opened.

Aunt Gertrude stayed in the hospital for so many years that the original cats, and the generation following, had all died off or wandered away, but there was a splendid group of pure white kittens at the back door when the doctors finally decided that Aunt Gertrude, so old and so lonely for her cats and her roses and the low echoing ceilings of her little house, ought to be brought home for what the family gracefully called "the little time left to her." The family brought forward an unmarried cousin to feed the cats and tend the roses and wheel Aunt Gertrude out into the sunlight every morning, and it was generally conceded among the nieces and nephews that all the available family ought to make a point of calling upon Aunt Gertrude at least once before—as my mother so delicately put it—she "said goodbye to us all." There was, moreover, a pressing, but civilly silent, competition among several of the nieces over the mahogany breakfront which Aunt Gertrude had inherited from our common great-great-grandmother, and which Aunt Gertrude used to keep fancy sewing and catfood in. As a matter of fact, after my mother said that about Aunt Gertrude's saying goodbye, she added a postscript about how if Auntie said *one word* about the breakfront I was to *let her know at once,* and she could fly East if necessary.

"Laurie and Jannie and Sally ought to see her once," I told my husband with a kind of wistful smile. "They ought to see her once, before she Leaves the Family Forever."

My husband gave me a long thoughtful look. "You know perfectly well your cousin Barbara is going to get that breakfront," he said.

"In that little apartment of hers?" I laughed bitterly. "I wouldn't put it *past* her, of course, but—"

"Give Aunt Gertrude my love," my husband said, putting his paper up before his face.

"It's so many years since I saw her last," I went on, with a pang of real terror. "She used to *scare* me so." The long road over the hills, the thousands of roses, the homemade fruit cake. . . . I shivered. "Petit point," I said inadequately. "Preserved figs."

When, at last, with the three older children mumbling uneasily in the back of the car, I came over the long road which brought me into the pleasant valley where Aunt Gertrude lived in her small house with her cats and her roses, I found that a dozen unexpected memories came back at me: the dust, and the woods coming down to the back of Aunt Gertrude's cottage with the soft hills behind, and the way the cottage itself always seemed so tall until you came right on to it, because of the high stone steps which led up from the road.

"Children," I said, when we came in sight of the woods, and the roses, and the steps, "children, Aunt Gertrude is very old, you know."

"Is she a witch?" Sally asked, peering through the car window. "Because if she's a witch can she eat little children?"

"I want you to behave quietly," I said, deciding upon a tactful by-pass to Sally's question, "and there is to be no giggling, and no arguing, and no shoving."

"Do I have to kiss her?" Laurie asked.

"I rather think not," I said, remembering suddenly and vividly the soft and wrinkled old cheek which Aunt Gertrude had, so long ago, presented to me. "Just remember that Aunt Gertrude is *very* old."

"Is she a hunderd?" Sally asked.

"I wouldn't be surprised," I said.

"Is she a thousand?"

"Well . . ." I said.

"A *million?*"

Laurie wriggled miserably. "I don't *want* to go," he said.

I stopped the car in front of the high stone steps and turned to look at Laurie. "Look," I said reasonably, "it's only this once."

"But I'm going to *break* something," Laurie said. "In that little house, I'll sit on the wrong thing or I'll step on something or I'll fall *over* or something."

I laughed and told him, "I stepped on a cat once. Aunt Gertrude laughed, but my mother was embarrassed."

"Did you get spanked?" Sally asked with interest. "Is she going to say abracadabra, Aunt Gertrude? Witches always say abracadabra. If she's a million, is that very old?"

We got out of the car, moving slowly, and stood below in the road, looking up at the steep steps and the pink roses above. "I'm scared," Jannie said; she came over and slipped her hand into mine. "Is Aunt Gertrude big?"

"No," I said. "Very small."

"I'm scared," Jannie said simply.

I took a deep breath. "Come along," I said, and we went up the steps, me well in advance, and Sally coming far behind on her hands and feet. I found, with a kind of bewilderment, that I had to bend my head to come onto the porch, although Laurie and Jannie and Sally passed easily under the low archway framed in roses, and I knocked on the door with the conviction that it had been only a day or so since I last saw its glass panel, engraved with a floral design, and chipped in the lower right-hand corner. "Ooh," said Jannie softly as the door opened, and I remembered the rich smells of fruit cake and marmalade and dried rose petals and cinnamon.

It was Cousin Maude who opened the door, and I stood breathless for a minute, the children pressed nervously close to me, while Cousin Maude told me that Aunt Gertrude was as well as might be expected, and, sighing, that Aunt Gertrude seemed as spry as ever, and I reported to Cousin Maude upon the health and prosperity of all the cousins she hadn't seen recently, and she told me about Uncle Frank and the horse, which I had already heard from my mother, expurgated.

"I brought my children to say hello to Aunt Gertrude,"
I explained at last, trying unsuccessfully to step aside from
the clinging creatures at my skirts. "They wanted to meet
her." This was a statement so patently false that even
Cousin Maude forbore to comment. "Hello, darlings," she
said perfunctorily. "I'll see if the old bird's awake," she
said to me.

"I want to go home," Jannie said, very audibly.

"Me, too," Laurie said.

Cousin Maude went to the door of the bedroom and
listened; the cottage had only two rooms, and I remembered clearly that sounds from one room were heard distinctly in the other; when Jannie began again, "I *want*
to—" I took her hand tight and shook my head violently,
and she was unwillingly quiet. Cousin Maude nodded and
beckoned us to the bedroom doorway, and, dragging Jannie and followed without enthusiasm by Laurie and Sally,
I went to the doorway.

"Aunt Gertrude," said Cousin Maude in a loud and
vivacious voice, "here are some *visitors* for you, and isn't
that *lovely?*"

"Oh, *go* away," said a voice from within, and I suddenly
remembered Aunt Gertrude so vividly that it seemed like
my mother pulling me instead of me pulling Jannie.

"Hello, Aunt Gertrude," I said weakly.

She was lying in bed, with pillows propping her up,
and she was wearing a pink satin bedjacket trimmed with
lace. After one look at her I recognized clearly that Aunt
Gertrude had remained the wickedest and liveliest old lady
in the world and was going to stay wicked and lively, very
probably, until she got bored and left her cottage for good.
"How do you feel, Aunt Gertrude?" I asked from the

doorway; it was involuntary. Asking it, I remembered my mother again and realized that she had felt as nervous as I did now, when I was as scared as Jannie.

"Another one?" Aunt Gertrude said, and chuckled. "Come in, dear," she said. "'What's that you've got with you? Children?"

"This," I said, pulling, "is my son Laurie. And my daughters Jannie and Sally."

"H'lo," said Sally, who seemed to be the only one still able to articulate.

Aunt Gertrude waved largely at a long sofa upholstered in apricot satin which stood parallel to her bed. "Sit down," she said, and, wordlessly, my children obeyed. I stood behind them protectively. Beyond us, the roses touched the windowpane and the sky was blue; inside, Aunt Gertrude leaned forward and regarded us with her old eyes open wide. "Now," she said. "Tell me what you learned in school today, my dears." She pointed to Laurie. "You, boy," she said. "What's your name?"

"Laurence," said Laurie in a whisper.

"Named after your Uncle Clifford? Indeed. Good girl." And she nodded approvingly at me. "And what did you learn in school?" she asked again.

"Fractions," said Laurie, paralyzed.

"So did we," said Aunt Gertrude, nodding profoundly. "Loved every minute of it, *I* did. Never got the footwork straight," she said in an aside to me, "but no point letting on. Now, *you*, what's *your* name?"

"Joanne."

"Pretty girl," said Aunt Gertrude. "Your mother ever tell you about the time I danced with the Prince of Wales?" She laughed hugely. "Mercy!" she said.

"Did you?" Jannie asked, "did you honest, with a prince?"

Aunt Gertrude laughed again. "Let's see your hair, child," she said. Jannie came, glancing at me, up to the bed, and Aunt Gertrude touched her hair lingeringly. "Can you sit on it?" she demanded.

Jannie giggled suddenly. "I never tried," she said. She looked over her shoulder and backed up to the sofa and tried to sit down on her hair, and Aunt Gertrude said tolerantly, "Said I was the prettiest girl on the floor, he did. Wasn't true, you know," she said, shaking an admonishing finger at Jannie, "at least three prettier than I was. Never get thinking you're prettier than you are, child."

"Did he wear a sword?" Laurie asked, fascinated. "Aunt Gertrude?"

"Sort of thing one *had* to say," Aunt Gertrude went on, nodding. "I had the prettiest hair, though. *I*," she said sternly to Jannie, "could *sit* on *my* hair, don't forget *that*."

"I'll try," said Jannie obscurely.

"And *you*," Aunt Gertrude said, turning to Sally, "what have *you* to say for yourself, girl?"

Sally thought. "What do you use for teeth?" she asked.

"*Sally!*" I said.

"Good question." Aunt Gertrude leaned back, thinking. "Play much baseball?" she asked Laurie unexpectedly.

Laurie, caught completely off base, faltered and said, "I guess so."

"It was a million-dollar infield," said Aunt Gertrude, and shook her head sadly. "That was before I met Mr. Corcoran, of course," she told me. "My late dear husband."

"Naturally," I said.

"Mr. Corcoran," she told Laurie, "was not an athletic

type of man like yourself. Most refined, of course, but not altogether athletic. A little chess now and then, occasionally a game of bowls, or, on warm evenings, croquet. Sad for one so enthusiastic as I."

"Did he have a sword?" asked Laurie tenaciously.

"No," said Aunt Gertrude, "but he had good sound investments. *There* was a dance for you," she went on dreamily, "and I was in yellow, most daring then, of course; taffeta. Alençon lace. And *very* daring," she added archly to me. "You ask about teeth," she continued. "It was a trip in those days, my dears. I remember we once had a rabbit in the carriage, but of course my mother spoke to the man at once. We never imagined that she was so fanciful."

"—a sword?"

"It's all very long ago," Aunt Gertrude said. She looked at the children. "You wouldn't remember," she said.

"Where is that rabbit now?" Sally asked.

"Fine children," said Aunt Gertrude, nodding sleepily. "Fine children. Married that young man, did you?"

"Nearly thirteen years ago," I said.

Aunt Gertrude nodded again. "I liked that young man," she said. "Nice young fellow. Green striped suit."

"Not *that* one," I said, horrified, "no, no, Aunt Gertrude, not that one. I—"

"Strong resemblance," Aunt Gertrude said, nodding at Laurie. "I always did like that fellow."

"He's a radio announcer somewhere in Ohio now," I said. "I married—"

"Reminded me of your Uncle Clifford," Aunt Gertrude said. She brought her head up suddenly. "When's that fool girl going to put me to sleep?" she demanded.

We tiptoed out, the children and I, and Aunt Gertrude stirred, and smiled, and spoke softly to herself. I told Cousin Maude that Aunt Gertrude was asleep, and the children and I went precariously down the steep stone steps. Halfway down I stopped and said, "We ought to take some roses home with us; Aunt Gertrude always used to tell me."

Solemnly, avoiding thorns, I picked a huge pink rose for each child and one for myself, and we got back into the car. Before I started the car I looked up once at Aunt Gertrude's house and wondered if I would ever come there again; in the mirror I could see the three children sitting quietly on the back seat, holding their roses. We had come out of the valley, and up the long green hill, and could see far behind only the great heap of roses that was Aunt Gertrude's cottage, before Jannie moved slightly, and spoke.

"Someday, *I* think," she said, "that prince is coming back."

"With his sword," said Laurie.

There was another long silence, and then Sally said, "She wasn't a witch at all, and I don't know why Mommy said she *was*, Aunt Gertrude. I *liked* her."

"I'm going to keep my rose forever," Jannie said, and Sally said, "*I'm* going to keep mine, too."

"She's sure pretty lucky," Laurie said.

"Golly," Jannie said, "and the prince coming back, and all."

I was not yet done with nostalgia, as it happened. I wrote my mother about our visit to Aunt Gertrude and she wrote back that in hopes of the breakfront she had gone up into the attic to see if she could dig out some of that old china, and in the course of this exploratory journey she had "turned up a few things you will recognize, ha-ha. I thought you might like to have them, so am sending them on."

Through a series of those coincidences which are sometimes regarded as progress I found that I had pretty much outgrown the contents of the carton which arrived a few days later, and after a quick look at the top layer I ought really to have put it right away in the farthest corner of *our* attic, but without really thinking I picked up one of the autograph albums (how could I have forgotten Violet Manning, who wrote on a purple page, "Oh, my friend, our days will soon end, don't forget, your friend Violet"?) and then of course I started taking out the little china dogs I used to keep on my dresser, and the battered feather fan someone sent me from Honolulu, and the tiny mother-of-pearl opera glasses which showed a tiny picture of Niagara Falls. Then at the bottom of the carton was one of my grandmother's corset boxes which I had not thought of for all these years, and when I saw it, all the agonies of the summer when I was fourteen came back like a cold wave over my head and the opera glasses and the feather fan and Violet Manning all fell into place abruptly and I could only say, "Gosh."

During the long summer when I was fourteen years old, I made, with the collaboration of my friend Dorothy, four hundred and thirty-one clothespin dolls. I know that never before or since have I made so many of anything, or with so much enthusiasm, and I feel increasingly, now, that there is not enough time left in the world to make four hundred and thirty-one things; perhaps some quality of adolescent fervor has disappeared. I know that the summers these days are not so long or so warm as that summer when I was fourteen; perhaps if they would go back to the longer, warmer summers they used to have I would be less apt during the winter to require two martinis before dinner.

I cannot remember *why* Dorothy and I made so many clothespin dolls, any more than I can remember why we used to spend hours at a time sitting on the back porch at our house eating pomegranates and breaking occasionally into wild shrill giggling fits, and I cannot remember the exact day which separated the barren years without clothespin dolls from the days when we thought of nothing else. I do believe that it was probably my mother's suggestion, because she was always asking us if we couldn't find something to *do*, girls, and because I can remember the bright-eyed enthusiasm with which she approached us frequently, suggesting one or another occupation for growing girls, which she had read about in a magazine somewhere—that we should plan a bazaar to sell homemade cookies, for instance, or take long walks to gather sweet grass, or fern, or look for wild strawberries, or that we should learn shorthand. It seems only reasonable to suppose that the clothespin dolls were just another such suggestion, although I cannot understand why the idea held so much more immediate appeal than gathering wild strawberries.

My mother supplied the original materials, although Dorothy and I had to buy subsequent supplies from our allowances after my mother had washed her hands of the whole thing. The next summer we were interested in playing piano duets, Dorothy playing the bass, and my mother very soon came to wash her hands of piano duets. The following summer was the one when I began to write a book of poetry which I planned to illustrate myself and

Dorothy took up the cello; that would have been the summer we were almost sixteen and I still have the first pages of the book of poetry. I have not felt equal to taking it out and reading it over recently, nor have I shown it to my husband, but I recall that the first poem was entitled "On Clouds," and the second was entitled "To a Rose," and that is as far as I care to go in recollections of my book of poetry. Dorothy and I had by then grown a little apart, what with her cello lessons three days a week and me spending a good deal of time sitting among the nasturtiums at the foot of the garden thinking of rhymes; many years ago, when Jannie was a baby, my mother wrote me that she had run into Dorothy's mother on the street and Dorothy was married and had a little boy. I always meant to write her.

That summer when we were fourteen had been an unusually hot summer, even for the warm summers we had then. I remember because our hands were always slightly damp and the paper would stick to our fingers. At first we kept our clothespin-doll supplies in a wicker basket Dorothy's mother gave us, but after a while we needed three huge cartons which were full of crepe paper in various colors. We used to paw through the assorted papers on the rack at the back of the stationery store, looking for the odd pinks and blues of faded crepe paper, and one roll of black paper which had been water-soaked gave us a lovely moiré effect. We had gold and silver paper, and of course the clothespins, which were the old-fashioned, round-headed kind, not the utterly efficient snap clothespins which may have come into general use because Dorothy and I had dressed up most of the round-headed clothespins there were.

Day after day during that hot summer we carried our three great cartons lovingly, and staggering, back and forth from my house to Dorothy's house, to the kitchen at Dorothy's or the dining room at my house. We needed the largest possible table in either house because of the magnitude of our operations, and we always left tiny scraps of paper on the floor. If we wanted to set out our clothespin dolls and compare them or label them or count them, we had to use the long hall at Dorothy's house. The only place we ever found in which to store our clothespin dolls without tangling them or crushing them was in the collection of corset boxes my grandmother had been accumulating for a number of years; these corset boxes were just wide enough to hold a clothespin doll crosswise, and long enough to hold exactly twenty-five clothespin dolls each. My grandmother had saved her corset boxes to hold torn silk stockings, which she dyed and crocheted into rugs, but my mother persuaded her to give up the corset boxes and keep her stockings in the wicker basket instead. When we stopped making clothespin dolls one afternoon, we had seventeen corset boxes full, and one almost full. We stacked the eighteen corset boxes in the corner of the dining room at my house, where we happened to be that afternoon, and they stayed there for quite a while, along with our three cartons of material, because my mother did not dare hope for a long time that we had really stopped making clothespin dolls.

The making of clothespin dolls is based upon the debatable assumption that a round-headed clothespin looks enough like a human figure to wear clothes. Allowing—as I believe my mother was the first to point out—that the top looks like a little head, and the bottom looks like little feet, clothing the middle part requires only an infinity of patience and a good deal of paste. We began, Dorothy and I, with ladies dressed in wide skirts, and we used cotton for hair, making a figure roughly like those on sentimental valentines. To make the skirts it is necessary to gather a length of crepe paper and paste it onto a strip of heavier paper—we used brown wrapping paper—as a sort of belt which will fit neatly around the middle of the clothespin. Crepe paper will stretch efficiently in one direction, so that if the skirt is cut on the correct bias it is possible to flare it out and even put a neat ruffle around the bottom. A particularly advanced type of female clothespin doll had several skirts of different colors, making for a rather bulky waist but a rich display of petticoats; this doll would of course stand up much more gracefully than one wearing, say, a sheathlike evening gown. The bodice was made of a contrasting color, and a short cape was frequently worn. We made bonnets to go over the cotton hair, with a foundation of more brown wrapping paper, a ruffle of crepe paper, and an occasional decorative rose. The result was as authentic as a clothespin doll can presumably be. My mother was vastly pleased with the first half-dozen clothespin dolls, and set one on her dresser.

In the beginning we did not concern ourselves unnecessarily with style or personality, aiming sensibly at getting as many as possible done and onto my mother's dresser, but with practice small refinements crept in and we began to think more of the product; as a matter of fact, we got so we could set up a cotton-haired lady clothespin doll in about three minutes, and we had to think of something to make it harder. Shoes, we discovered, are impossible on the prongs of a clothespin. The feet could be covered with silver or gold paper, but nothing could make a clothespin's feet look as though they had shoes on, not even buckles. Small pieces of colored string made acceptable belts, the lace edging that used to come on candy boxes was splendid for ruffles and lace collars. We tried arms made of tissue paper, but they usually fell right off.

We used homemade flour paste, because we used a good deal of paste and we had to pay for our own supplies. Almost anything could be molded, I recall, from a combination of crepe paper and homemade flour paste. To make a hat for a clothespin doll we started with a piece of brown wrapping paper cut to the correct size, coated it with paste, added a layer of crepe paper, more paste, more paper, and so on until it was thick and workable and could be shaped to the right style. When we had our hats shaped we used to set them on the windowsill where they dried solid in about fifteen minutes, and one of the things that persuaded my mother to wash her hands of clothespin dolls was a row of brown fedoras on the dining room windowsill; once dried, the paste and crepe paper combination was as heavy and hard as rock; if the hat fit the clothespin doll in the first place no power on earth could shift it once it was on.

Dorothy used this method very successfully to make a pail to go with a milkmaid doll, although it took her all one afternoon to shape the pail so it was symmetrical and no clothespin doll ever born could have carried it with a tissue-paper arm. On the milkmaid doll, and several after that, we used brown yarn for hair, either in long braids ending in a bow, or wound around the top of the head on a coronet. Braiding three strands of brown yarn is remarkably easy compared to anchoring an upswept hair-do on the head of a round-headed clothespin.

We started out making men in about the state of mind which I suppose created them in the first place—we had run out of kinds of women, and had to think of something else. The first man, as I remember, was a soldier, bright in regimental pink and blue, with a silver paper sword and a tall hat never seen outside the pages of Grimm. Dorothy and I had created him together, and we both found him so lovely that we set out to make an army, all in different colors, but gave up after only a dozen or so. Boots were much more practical than shoes; it was possible to make a high, swaggering sort of boot out of silver or gold paper, and this led us of course into the free-lance, or D'Artagnan, type of soldier, with a short cape and a rakish hat trimmed with crepe-paper feathers, and even, in one lamentable case, Cavalier curls.

By this time all odds and ends of material had begun to find their way to us, and when my mother decided to take the sequins off her black evening dress, or when my uncle found himself with a half-used roll of tire tape, or when Dorothy's mother gave up the idea of choosing new wallpaper that year, the sequins and the tire tape and the wallpaper sample book came to us. We tried making black boots with the tire tape, but they were sticky.

Use of crayon or paint was regarded as unworthy, and I remember a patient, infuriating afternoon when Dorothy laboriously made a plaid shirt, weaving the plaid herself out of tiny strips of colored paper. I was usually able to make two or three dolls during the time it took Dorothy to make one, but hers always had something like plaid shirts or ruffled skirts where each ruffle was lace-edged, or a tiny bouquet made flower by flower.

The final stage was, I suppose, inevitable; after we had gone through every conceivable fancy-dress creature imaginable, we fell to copying people we knew; it represented the last point of imaginative decay before the deadly advent of the piano duet. We made a small image of my mother in a purple housedress and one of Dorothy's mother in a pink dressing gown, and made my father and hers, but there was nothing to put on the fathers except gray business suits, which were extremely difficult to make, and we had to distinguish between the two fathers by their ties. Dorothy's father had the inevitable plaid tie and I made my father a kind of full cravat with polka dots which he assured me earnestly did not resemble anything he had ever worn or would ever wear or could even, he told me, dream of wearing in his worst nightmares.

The four hundred and thirty-first clothespin doll was, I remember, a lady doll in a wide skirt with cotton hair, and I remember as well Dorothy's putting her scissors down on the dining room table and saying clearly, "I don't want to make clothespin dolls any more."

I think we must have gone directly on from there into piano duets, because I know that although our eighteen corset boxes full of clothespin dolls stayed in the corner of the dining room and then in the hall closet for a long time, the cartons of material got emptied out after a while so we could use the cartons to keep our piano duets in. I also remember that company who used to have to look at four hundred-odd clothespin dolls now had to listen to Dorothy and me playing "The Charge of the Uhlans," and "Selections from the Bohemian Girl," but I cannot remember how long it might have been before my mother decided that eighteen corset boxes full of clothespin dolls were in the way in the hall closet and she told Dorothy and me to please stop playing duets for five minutes and go get rid of those clothespin dolls. She suggested that if we take out the ones we liked best she would be glad to see that the rest were disposed of. Dorothy and I each took one box full of our personal favorites—Dorothy had, by rights, the plaid shirt doll and the milkmaid, and I took several of the soldiers, which I had always fancied, and my best cotton-headed ladies. I put my box of clothespin dolls in my bottom desk drawer, where I afterward kept my book of poetry, and one day my mother drove Dorothy and me and sixteen boxes of clothespin dolls to the Children's Hospital in San Francisco, and waited outside while Dorothy and I took the clothespin dolls and went in. We were both wearing black patent-leather shoes and white socks, and we had to walk across a polished marble floor and I was desperately afraid of slipping and spilling clothespin dolls all over the lobby.

"I hope they don't think we're bringing them your grandmother's corsets," Dorothy whispered to me. We left the boxes at the desk with an unpleasant woman who was too busy to say thank you, and who made no move to open the boxes to see what they were. About a week later we got a printed form from the hospital, addressed to Dorothy and me together, since both our names had been on the boxes; the printed form said thanks for our gift, the children in the wards would appreciate it. On the bottom of the form someone had written, "For Indian beadwork."

I don't suppose, strictly speaking, that after that day clothespin dolls came into my head from one year to the next. When I had to have a place to hide my book of poetry I must have taken the box of clothespin dolls and put them away with the feather fan and the autograph albums and the china dogs. The whole batch of them got sensibly put up into the attic, where they would have stayed in perfect safety, untroubled by any longing of mine for them, if my mother had not gotten to thinking about the old china, which wasn't there anyway, as I could have told her, my brother and I having used it long before that for tea parties in our tree hut.

I was sitting on the living room floor, holding the feather fan and reading through the autograph albums, when I heard the voices of my children outside, on their way home for lunch. I made a frantic effort to scramble all the things back into the carton, but I was too late. "What's *that*?" Laurie said, coming into the living room, and "Let *me* see," Jannie said behind him. Sally came over and sat down on the floor next to me, and possessed herself of the feather fan, which for some reason struck her as irresistibly funny.

"Never *mind*," I said, snatching childishly. "It's *mine*." I was unreasonably angry at Sally for laughing at my feather fan, and then Jannie got hold of the box of clothespin dolls. My mother (at least, I prefer to *think* that it was my mother) had tied a blue ribbon around the box, and before I could stop her Jannie had untied the ribbon and opened the box. "Ooh," she said, and Laurie, peering, said, "Jeeps."

I had forgotten D'Artagnan, I am afraid, and the soldiers in pink and blue, and the cotton hair. I had forgotten the name labels in Dorothy's neatest handwriting; I had forgotten the line of four hundred and thirty-one clothespin dolls going down the long hall at Dorothy's house. I had forgotten the hats and the feathers and the yarn hair and the silver boots. "Looka *this* one," Laurie said. "I found one named Linda," Jannie said. "I want that one with the blue hat," Sally said.

"Hey," Laurie said, "this one's got no name."

I looked over my son's shoulder at the green shirt and at the name label which read only "?" and snatched the doll out of his hand. "You let that alone," I said. I had slept with that clothespin doll under my pillow for several weeks, hoping it might influence my dreams and my future, although I have really no quarrel with my present husband.

"What'd *I* do?" demanded Laurie indignantly. "*I* was only looking at the little doll, *I* didn't—"

Tenderly I set out the clothespin dolls on the floor, stopping to fluff out Linda's skirt and adjust D'Artagnan's feathers. We had builded better than we knew, thanks to our homemade paste. Although some of the hats had come off, not one was dented, not one star had faded from the queen's cloak, not one sword was tarnished nor one buckle askew. The children, enchanted, helped me stand them up. Then, inevitably I drove off, as my mother had so long ago, with all the children in the back of the car. We bought crepe paper and gold paper and silver paper, and the grocer found a box of round-headed clothespins in his cellar. I remembered how to make the paste, even the pinch of salt which makes it stick better.

When we moved to Vermont into a big house, my mother had offered me the old dining room table, which was made of some incredibly solid substance—perhaps paste and crepe paper—that stood up under my brother and me for twenty years, and is surely good for a hundred more; I have every intention of giving it to Jannie when she marries. My father and mother were always telling my brother and me to keep our feet off the heavy pedestal which is the foundation of the table, and now I sit at dinner with my feet resting comfortably and tell my children to keep their feet off the table. It was with a telescoping of time that made me feel faintly ghostlike that I found myself sitting at the same table with a box of clothespins and a dozen packages of crepe paper. My first fear, that in all these years I had forgotten how to make clothespin dolls, turned out to be unjustified; perhaps making clothespin dolls is not a knack which evaporates with time. "See?" I said to the children, "you take a little piece of brown paper to fit around the doll's waist, and you gather the crepe paper, and you make a little bodice. . . ."

"*That*'s not the way," Laurie said. "What you want to do is, you want to take the clothespin and you drill a hole through it and then you put something like, for instance, a pipecleaner through the hole, and then you've got arms, see? And that silver stuff's no good for swords, what you need is *plastic*, and then you really *got* something, boy."

"And those *clothes*, Mommy dear," said Jannie. "*Mine* is going to be a lady in a bathing suit."

"Mine's going to be a Martian," Laurie said. "I need the scissors, Mom. You can make yours in a minute."

Sally rode around and around the dining room table on her tricycle, the feather fan proudly displayed on the front. "I'm a airplane," she sang triumphantly. "I'm a old witch riding a broomstick."

"I think real cloth," Jannie said thoughtfully to her brother.

"Plastic," Laurie said firmly. "Anyway, *paper*'s no good." He looked with interest at his sister's doll, which had on the bottom of a two-piece bathing suit. "What you need *there*," he said with enthusiasm, "is *toes*."

After they had given up I made a doll with cotton hair and a yellow skirt and a blue cape, carrying a parasol, and I took it in to my husband in the study.

"What's that?" he asked.

"It's a clothespin doll," I said. "I made it for you."

"It's very nice," he said. "How did you happen to think of making me a clothespin doll?"

"I just thought you'd like one," I said.

"Thank you," he said, and he put the clothespin doll on the corner of his desk.

I went and picked up the dining room and put all the crepe paper away and washed out the dish with the home-made paste. Later that afternoon my husband, who was clearly very much puzzled, asked me again what had decided me to make him a clothespin doll, although of course he was very pleased to have one, and I said that I used to be quite a hand at making clothespin dolls. "A long time ago," I told him.

THREE

A T ABOUT TEN O'CLOCK on an evening late in February
the entire pattern of our collective lives was violently altered. My husband and I, sitting in the kind of
companionable stupor that sets in when all children are in
bed and presumably asleep, were startled at hearing a sudden astonished "Oh!" from Sally's room. As we half rose,
looking at one another, her voice lifted in the greatest,
most jubilant shout I have ever heard: "I can READ! I
can READ!"

It turned out she could, too. After we had calmed the
other children ("Sally had a bad dream") and put them
back to bed with another piece of candy each, Sally came
down and sat in the living room in her red pajamas and
read to her father and me the first chapter of *Ozma of Oz*,
the book I had been reading *her* before she went, as I
thought, to bed. She explained that every night after I had
turned out the light and gone downstairs, she had been
going over and over the book I had read her, trying to
apply the reading knowledge she picked up in kindergarten, and tonight, without effort, the letters on the page had

fallen together and become readable; she had gone along for a page or more before she realized that she was reading the words. We listened, congratulated her, remarked on how surprised her teacher would be, and asked what she had been using for light, teaching herself to read up there in bed. After some hesitation she admitted that she had found that it was possible to slant the book so it caught light from the hall, where we always left a nightlight burning. My husband, who used to read at night when he was a boy with a flashlight under the covers, said that inadequate light was harmful to the eyes. I, who used to read at night when I was a girl by the street light outside my window, said that little girls who stayed awake reading at night were very apt to be sleepy in school the next day. Sally agreed soberly, as befitted one newly admitted to an esoteric society, and went back upstairs with *Ozma of Oz*. When I went up to cover her later she was asleep with her light on and *Ozma of Oz* open on her stomach.

The most immediate impact of Sally's reading was on Laurie. I went into town and bought Sally a bedlight, and Laurie had to put it up. The small bookcase in her room, which had been adequate for picture books and the Oz books I had been steadily reading my way through, starting with *The Wizard of Oz* with each child, and going right on down the line, so that there are, by now, great swatches I can read with my eyes shut—her bookcase turned out to be far too small for the books she confiscated from the rest of us, and Laurie had to build her a new bookcase. Everyone moved up a notch. Sally's collection of picture books went into Barry's room, where Laurie, who was by now asking and getting twenty-five cents a shelf, built another bookcase to hold the books Barry already had, and the collection he inherited from Sally. Sally took over from Jannie an enormous accumulation of fairy tales, Uncle Wiggly stories, Bobbsey Twins books, and *Barnaby*. Jannie, annoyed at the great gaps in *her* bookcase, went into Laurie's room and selected from the books he had gathered those which she felt were suited to her taste and refinement. Jannie thus came to read *Tom Sawyer* and *Treasure Island* and *Little Men*, the last having fallen into Laurie's hands through an accident; he thought, he said bitterly, from the title that it was a book about *boys*. I was disturbed because there were five copies of *Alice in Wonderland* in the house and no child would read it. Laurie was so indignant over the loss of everything except *Little Men* that I went into the bookshop and got him an omnibus Jules Verne, and his father gave him a book of Sherlock Holmes stories. I could hardly buy Laurie a book without getting books for Jannie and Sally, so, because I preferred to keep my own old copies of each, I brought home *Little Women*, and *The Rootabaga Stories*. Just to square everything nicely, I got a gun that shot corks for Barry, which was a mistake.

As I say, the immediate impact was on Laurie. Still reeling under the combined magic of Jules Verne and six dollars earned from building bookshelves, he invested his money in tools and lumber. He replaced a board in the back steps, for fifty cents, put up a set of shelves in the kitchen for two dollars, explaining that his price went up when things had to be anchored to the wall, and built a record cabinet as a surprise for his father, declining payment but accepting the cost of the lumber and nails. With our permission he opened three charge accounts, one at the lumber yard, one at the big hardware store in town, where they sold tools, and one at a little hardware store around the corner from us, where they sold nails and little metal brackets for anchoring things to walls.

He dismissed almost at once the notion of making a flying machine, but he and his friend Rob made a complicated kind of fort in the field next to the barn, with a padlock on the door and an involuntary window where two boards did not quite come together. The boys kept all kinds of treasures in their fort, but lost interest in it abruptly when they discovered that Sally had been going, eel-like, in and out the window of the fort and that she had returned to me, with great amusement, the package of cigarettes and the package of matches she found inside. I told Laurie with some heat that it was perfectly all right with me if he wanted to smoke and stunt his growth and ruin his wind for baseball and basketball and football and ping-pong; it was a silly habit, I told him, and expensive and useless, and if he wanted to smoke he could buy his own cigarettes and stop taking mine. His father suggested a pipe as more manly, and a day or so later in the five-and-ten I found a particularly revolting-looking corncob pipe, and I picked up a tin of tobacco and brought them home and gave them to Laurie to smoke. That did not make him sick, either, so his father gave him a cigar and when he smoked half of that without ill effects we decided that we were attacking this thing in the wrong way, and we told Laurie that he was absolutely forbidden to smoke under any circumstances, and if he did, he would first of all be heavily fined, and then we would close his charge accounts at the two hardware stores and the lumber yard. I do not for a minute suppose that that had any slightest effect on him, but at any rate Sally never found any more cigarettes, and the fort blew away in a particularly heavy windstorm.

With three reading children in the house, competition over Barry, who could be read to, was very heavy. I still retained my post as bedtime reader—I began again with *The Wizard of Oz*—but Laurie and Jannie and Sally found themselves sometimes all reading aloud from different enticing works, each hoping to lure Barry who moved, basking, from one to another. For a little while Jannie forged ahead through a brilliant imaginative stroke; she refused to read aloud, and offered, instead, to tell stories made up out of her own head. This began the Jefry stories, which were about a little boy named Jefry who had an elephant who was called Peanuts because he ate so many . . . "What?" said Barry. "Cabbages," said Jannie firmly. Jefry had a bear named Dikidiki, just like Barry, and Jefry irked Sally so considerably that she brought out her boy doll Patpuss, renamed him Jefry, announced that he was her little brother, and commenced telling him stories about a little imaginary boy named Barry, who had a bear named Dikidiki just like Jefry. This became the competing Barry series. One evening Laurie came staggering from the Story Hour in the kitchen, and announced to his father that he had just made up a story about a little boy named Dikidiki who had two imaginary bears, Barry and Jefry, and we had to make a rule that stories must be told one at a time, and last no more than two minutes by the kitchen clock.

Barry resigned from the position of Beekman when he entered nursery school, because everyone there called him Barry again. When it was almost time for him to start, I went up to the closet where I had happily stored all the snowsuits in moth balls. I found the snowsuit Laurie had worn our first winter in Vermont and which Jannie had worn later when *she* entered nursery school; I had taken the hood off and Jannie had worn a little blue furry cap. When I checked it for Barry I found that the wrists were really too frayed to be mended, but I decided to keep it anyway because the snowpants were solid enough and the jacket could probably serve in some emergency. Jannie's second snowsuit, which she had gotten when Laurie took to wearing ski pants and a windbreaker, was too large for Barry and was pink besides. I remembered now that Sally had not been able to wear Laurie's first snowsuit three years before because the sleeves of the jacket had been too frayed *then* to be mended, but that I had kept the snowsuit because it would probably be useful in some emergency. Sally's first snowsuit had been inherited from a friend; it was light blue and had a fur collar and cuffs, and I had passed it on when Sally outgrew it and it was now being worn by a little girl named Anne Elizabeth in West Haven. I tried Laurie's first windbreaker on Barry, and the sleeves hung down and the belt went around his knees, so I went downstairs and told my husband that before Barry started nursery school he would have to have a new snowsuit and my husband said that was ridiculous, there must be a dozen snowsuits up in the closet.

Barry's new snowsuit was brown, and the hat had fur ears, and when I looked at him trying it on to show his father and his brother and his sisters, I realized acutely how strange it was going to be now during the long empty mornings. I asked my husband if he was aware of the fact that for eleven years there had always been one youngest child around the house all the time and he said he was only too aware of it and eleven years was longer than they gave you for anything except barratry and mayhem. Somewhere I found a long red feather. I fastened it to Barry's fur-eared hat, and when it broke I got another and put *that* one on, and I got another one later and put it on the cap he wore in the late spring and another on the little straw hat he wore during the summer, so that from the time he was two and a half he always wore a feather, sometimes red, and sometimes white or black or blue, and people who saw him on the street or in stores or the library or the post office or the bank came to recognize him—and, I suppose, me—by the feather, and on the rare occasions when I went shopping without him, people everywhere would say, "Where's the Indian?" or "the feather boy?" or "Robin Hood?"

Barry also achieved a certain kind of family distinction by becoming the one child who did not care for pudding, but preferred eggs. A lot of the enthusiasm went out of my pudding-making when I knew that while the rest of us were eating pudding for dessert I would have to fry an egg for Barry. I have always been fascinated by the contemplation of growth in the children, the development of small quirks and odd little habits as they change into individuals, but I admit that with six of us going different directions it is sometimes very difficult to set up any kind of an over-all pattern and plan from it; food is perhaps the best example of this. The only actual staples in the house were milk and peanut butter. These were the lowest common denominator in the kitchen; nothing else was common to all six, and yet everyone complained constantly about the food. My husband said that it cost too much, Laurie said that there was not enough variety, Jannie said that we did not have mashed potatoes half often enough, Sally just complained that she had to eat it, and Barry thought that there were not enough eggs. I myself thought that making dinner and cleaning up afterward every night was too great an effort to make if all I was going to get was complaints, and anyone who wanted to live on milk and peanut butter from now on was welcome to as far as I was concerned.

Finally, after a good deal of worry I went out and bought a couple of epicure magazines, and leafed through them all one morning looking for something exciting I could serve for dinner, and I found a recipe for a casserole dish based on stuffed cabbage with ground round steak and cashew nuts which I thought I could try. I could not make it the way the recipe said to, however, because, inevitably, it contained ingredients which were distasteful to my family. I decided to leave out the onion in the recipe because Sally would not eat anything so highly flavored as onions. I could not mix the ground round steak with rice because Laurie loathes rice. My husband could not bear tomatoes in any form, Jannie would not touch cabbage, and no one in the family except me cared for sour cream. When I had finished eliminating from the casserole what I had was a hamburger studded with cashew nuts, which was undeniably a novelty, although I am afraid that on the whole my casserole was not a success. Everyone carefully removed the cashew nuts and set them aside, and Laurie asked irritably if we *always* had to have hamburger for dinner.

The day the spring term of the nursery school opened I thought that Barry had a little cold, so I kept him home, but I had to let him go on the second day, and I took him over and told the teachers about his little cold and hung around for about half an hour, because, as I explained to the teachers, Barry had never been away from me before and I thought he might cry. Finally I got tired of standing in the corner and I went over to Barry where he was working at the sandbox and I told him gently that I thought I would go along back home now. Barry said, "Yep," and reached out to remove a small truck from the hand of a little girl. "I'll be going, then," I said. "Yep," Barry said. "I'll see you later," I said. "Yep," Barry said. "Well, good-bye," I said. "What?" said Barry, looking up. "Oh," he said. "'Bye." After a few minutes I tiptoed quietly to the door so he would not notice me and be sad. I waited in the doorway for a minute; he had moved on to the toy trains and when I said again, "Well, goodbye, Barry," he did not hear me. I drove home very slowly because I had plenty of time before I had to pick him up at eleven-thirty and when I got home at last I went and sat in the study and listened to the refrigerator rattling in the kitchen and the furnace grumbling down cellar and the distant ticking of the alarm clock up on my dresser.

On Wednesday morning, and Thursday, and Friday, I sat in the study and did the crossword puzzles in the morning paper, but on Saturday of course there was no nursery school and I nearly went crazy with Barry tagging along behind me everywhere I went, pestering me while I tried to get things done, and I was very glad when Monday morning came around again and he went back to nursery school. Sally told us one day that she had been sent for into the first-grade room to read to the first-graders. Jannie came bursting into the house the day the first tulip came out to shout that she had been chosen for the part of the Fairy Rosabelle in the third-grade musical play, and she would have to sing one song all by herself, and probably dance. A few days later she brought home her music, and I played it on the piano and Jannie practiced it until everyone in the family was infuriated by finding that we were all humming and whistling it; Barry would sing it at breakfast ("I am the Fairy Rosabelle, I bring the spring's first floooooowers") and by lunchtime I would be forcing myself to sing "Clementine" as resolutely as I could in an attempt to drive the Fairy Rosabelle out of my mind. My husband said that several times he had found himself entering a classroom with the odd little dance step which accompanied the Fairy Rosabelle, and that he had been quite embarrassed when one of his students asked him what was the name of the song he kept whistling.

Before the snow was quite off the ground, the single tulip showing brave and bright against the snow and mud near the barn, Laurie was out in his light jacket, oiling his glove and throwing easy pitches to Rob. The girls received from their grandmother a big box containing two jackets of some plastic material, with silly little matching caps. One jacket was pink and one was blue, and Sally perceived at once that in the jackets she and Jannie looked like Easter eggs, and they capered off to school, singing to the tune of the Fairy Rosabelle that they were two little dancing Easter eggs. Consumption of peanut butter went up that spring to three jars a week. Even Easter egg jackets and the Fairy Rosabelle and the first tulip could not compensate, however, for the pestilence which annihilated our cats, leaving us with only one black kitten, named Yain, who had been the oldest and strongest of the group of Ninki-kittens who traveled with us the summer before we moved into our new house. For a long time Yain went around thinking he was the only cat left in the world, and out of desperation he developed a close friendship with our big dog Toby, who was usually afraid of cats. The vet told us that we must either have the house fumigated or wait several months before getting any more cats, and for a long time while I sat in the study mornings doing crossword puzzles Yain would pace restlessly through the house, looking for another cat.

My husband had by then been teaching for several months, and I was slowly becoming aware of a wholly new element in the usual uneasy tenor of our days; I was a faculty wife. A faculty wife is a person who is married to a faculty. She has frequently read at least one good book lately, she has one "nice" black dress to wear to student parties, and she is always just the teensiest bit in the way, particularly in a girls' college such as the one where my husband taught. She is presumed to have pressing and wholly absorbing interests at home, to which, when out, she is always anxious to return and, when at home, reluctant to leave. It is considered probable that ten years or so ago she had a face and a personality of her own, but if she has it still, she is expected to keep it decently to herself. She will ask students questions like "And what did you do during vacation?" and answer in return questions like "How old is your little boy now?" Her little pastimes, conducted in a respectably anonymous and furtive manner, are presumed to include such activities as knitting, hemming dish towels, and perhaps sketching wild flowers or doing water colors of her children.

I was not bitter about being a faculty wife, very much, although it *did* occur to me once or twice that young men who were apt to go on and become college teachers someday ought to be required to show some clearly distinguishable characteristic, or perhaps even wear some large kind of identifying badge, for the protection of innocent young girls who might in that case go on to be the contented wives of furniture repairmen or disc jockeys or even car salesmen. The way it is now, almost any girl is apt to find herself hardening slowly into a faculty wife when all she actually thought she was doing was just getting married.

I put in four good years at college, and managed to pass almost everything, and got my degree and all, and I think it was a little bit unkind of fate to send me back to college the hard way, but of course there *were* things I might have done—or, put it, people I might have married—which would have landed me in worse positions. Bluebeard, anyway.

The three big thorns in the faculty wife's ointment are her husband, her husband's colleagues, and her husband's students. Naturally a husband presents enormous irritations no matter what he is doing, and I think it is unreasonable to regard a teaching husband as necessarily more faulty than, say, a plumbing husband, but there is no question but what the ego of a teaching husband is going to be more vividly developed, particularly if he teaches in a girls' college. For instance, when I accompanied my husband to a student party and we were greeted at the door by a laughing group of students who surrounded him, calling out, "Hello, there," and, "You *did* wear the orange tie, after all," and, "Class was simply *super* this morning," I could figure, as I stood alone in the hall moodily looking for a place to put my coat, that it was going to be proportionately more difficult, once home, to persuade my husband to put up the new shelves in the kitchen. He was going to lie back in his chair, flaunting the orange tie, and tell me to get a boy for things like that.

Well, I suppose husbands are all alike, at least the husbands of my friends were. Before my husband commenced professor many of my friends had been from the group of faculty wives, although they were in general understandably reluctant to wander out of their proper setting, and it was pleasant, now, to meet them as a colleague. We usually made a comfortable little group as we gathered in the corner just to the right of the doorway at student parties. "Hello," we cried gaily to one another, "you here *too*? *How* are the children? Did you get to that perfectly ripping affair last night at that other student house? Are the children well? Is there any news of a raise in faculty salaries? And the children—how are *they*?"

Of course, if one of us ever happened to mention that she was getting a new refrigerator, or that her husband had just had an article published in the *Wiltshire Archeological and Natural History Journal*, or that they were turning in the old car on a new convertible, a certain coolness was apt to arise. Someone might come out with the story of a woman *she* knew who got herself hopelessly tangled in the descending top of *her* convertible and was late for a Trustee Tea, or someone would tell about what happened to some friends of hers with their new refrigerator the night they went out and left it alone for the first time, or we might mention with becoming modesty the articles *our* husbands have had in the *Journal of American Ethnobotany*, or the *Physical Culture Quarterly*. These coolnesses developed easily into open quarrels, with consequent feuds and taking sides and the comparative merits of publication

[152]

in Wiltshire and East Lansing openly discussed, and the husbands bowing distantly in the faculty lounge.

I found, however, that there *were* sizable advantages to our connection with a college community. It was easier to get a piano tuner, for instance, and information, such as how to lay out a basketball court, or how to figure compound interest on a mortgage, was easily obtainable from the reference books in the library. Once, when my husband was out of town and I wanted to start the little wood-burning hot-water heater which was attached to our furnace, I took advantage of living in a seat of learning, and called the chemistry professor and asked him how you started a little wood-burning hot-water heater. He said that he personally lived in a college house which had electricity laid on, but why didn't I try the logic professor, who was accustomed to working out problems and things? The logic professor said that his work was purely theoretical, and the person I really wanted was the natural science man who ought to know how to start fires from camping out looking at ferns and stuff. The natural science man said that everyone knew that forest fires destroyed millions of dollars of animal life every year and if I wanted to start a fire I ought to get hold of the painting teacher who could probably bring over some turpentine and old canvases. The painting teacher said well, he *knew* turpentine was no good, but one of the literature teachers had been at Yaddo once, and *he* ought to know something, after all. The literature professor said that aside from washing himself in steep-down gulfs of liquid fire he managed to keep pretty well away from the stuff. I finally called the college president and he said he had the same sort of gadget in *his* house, and he came down and started it, but it went out.

Unlike faculty wives, students are nice girls who have come to college to get an education. The students I encountered had very little concern with anything outside of getting an education and so could not be expected to waste much time investigating the home lives of their teachers. I never, for instance, met a student who was the least bit interested in my sketches of wild flowers, and their anxiety to know the ages of my children was, to say the least, perfunctory. On the other hand, almost all the students I met were well mannered, civil, and nicely brought up. They were extremely thoughtful, and courteous to the point of chivalry. They were kind to children and to animals. If they slammed a door, it was never knowingly in the face of a stray puppy or a small baby. If they knocked someone down, it was inconceivable that it should be a teacher or another student. If they brought up some date who played professionally for the Green Bay Packers, he would carefully avoid practicing his inside blocking on someone's roommate's mother. I can say, categorically, that I never saw any student, of whatever year, kick a sick cat. They were, as I say, neat, well mannered, and demure. Their clothes were subdued, sometimes so much so as to be invisible. When they gave parties they took pains to invite only the most congenial people, such as their teachers and selected other students. I never, for my own part, found any difficulty in declining an invitation to a student party, if I got one at all, or in leaving, once I was there. I learned to have nothing but admiration for the student's faith in her teachers, and the kind of innocent devotion which was frequently so touching; I am reminded of the student who crept up, one spring dawning, to leave a basket of fresh strawberries upon her teacher's pillow. Or the student who resolutely refused to remove a lilac sweater her teacher had once admired, and became known, by her junior year, as "The Purple Kid," although she dropped out, abruptly, during one Christmas vacation and was only seen once thereafter, in Paris with a retired manufacturer of pinball machines.

Perhaps the only quarrel the faculty wife might have with her husband's students is their spirit of pure scientific inquiry; they were very apt to throw out the baby, as it were, with the bathwater, particularly when baby-sitting. As a matter of fact, I once had a conversation with a student upon this very topic; it was rather late at night, and we were among the dregs of a student party. She was there because she was a hostess and I was there because it was beginning to look as though there were no good way of getting my husband home. I was wearing my "nice" black dress and holding a glass of ginger ale and she was wearing a strapless short evening dress, pink, with gardenias in her hair, and holding and perhaps even drinking a glass of the punch they had been serving at the party, made of equal parts of sweet vermouth, vodka, and cold cocoa. We were sitting on the floor and I had already asked her about her vacation and she had told me she spent six weeks working as a feather duster in a museum, sometimes dusting feathers and sometimes feathering dusters, and that she had found the work very constructive and very useful in influencing her in the eventual choice of her senior program, and I had told her that my little boy was three now. After a short, agonized silence, broken only by the harmonies of six voices doing something from *La Bohème* in another corner of the room, she turned to me and asked, "Listen, when you were young—I mean, before you kind of settled down and all, when you were—well, *younger*, that is—did you ever figure you'd end up like this?" She waved her hand vaguely at the student living room, my "nice" black dress, and my glass of ginger ale. "Like *this*?" she said.

"Certainly," I said. "My only desire was to be a faculty wife. I used to sit at my casement window, half embroidering, half dreaming, and long for Professor Right."

"I suppose," she said, "that you *are* better off than you would have been. Not married at all or anything."

"I was a penniless governess in a big house," I said. "I was ready to take anything that moved."

"And of course you *do* make a nice home for your husband. Someplace to come back to, and everything so neat."

"My spinning lacks finesse," I said. "But I yield to no one on my stone-ground meal."

"And *he*'s lucky, too, of course. So many men who marry young silly women find themselves always going to parties and things for their wives' sake. An older woman—"

"He was only a boy," I said. "How well I remember his eager, youthful charm; 'Lad,' I used to say, fondly touching his wanton curls, 'lad, youth calls to youth, and what *you* need—' "

"He's *still* terribly boyish, don't you think?" She bent a tender glance upon my husband, who was waving a cigar and telling an enthralled group of students an expurgated story of how he graded examination papers. "He's always so full of vitality."

"You should see him at home," I said. "We never have a dull moment *there*, I can tell you. Absolutely nothing but boyish vitality and youthful charm all over the place. He's positively faunlike. Why, I could tell you things—"

"I don't suppose," she said, blushing slightly and studying her fingernails, "that he talks much about us students at home, does he?"

"He babbles about you all the time," I assured her, and rose and went over to the noisy group of which my husband was the center. "Hail, ruddy stripling," I said.

"What?" he said, startled.

"Never mind," I said. "You leaving now or do I have to carry you home?"

I decided that I was going to fewer student parties after I ripped part of the sleeve out of my black dress helping a freshman climb a fence. By the end of the first semester, what I wanted to do most in the world was invite a few of my husband's students over for tea and drop them down the well.

On the other hand, I was in sad trouble at the kindergarten over the practice of magic by my daughter Sally. Almost between one day and the next, it seemed, Sally had somehow picked up both the knack and the inclination for doing magic, and although I felt that magic was no career for a girl, and her father felt that Sally showed hardly enough talent to get ahead in the magic game, Sally told all around the kindergarten that the ban against magic, finally, was entirely our fault. Little children five years old cut me dead in the street. There was a rumor that I was going to be expelled from the Lunchtime Mommies. Sally told around the kindergarten that she was being unfairly condemned, that ever since we moved into the house we all knew that someday something had to be done about the gatepost. And she said that the refrigerator was not completely destroyed, the way her father maintained it was, and that anyway we had agreed to say nothing more about the clock and besides that the old man at the door started it, which was probably true.

It had been a rainy Saturday morning, so I knew that the refrigerator door was going to stick. The old man came to the back door not long before lunchtime, and he came—I knew it the minute I saw him—to chat about the gatepost; after a year in the house I could spot them at five hundred yards. He opened by saying well, so they finally got someone to buy the old house, did they? I leaned my head against the doorframe and said oh, yes, they finally got someone to buy the old house. Well, he said with the light coming into his eye, had we fixed on anything yet about that there gatepost?

I winced. Sally was painting at the kitchen table behind me, and I knew she was eavesdropping. Barry was in a corner of the kitchen at his toy table, disassembling a truck, and clearly not interested at present in the gatepost. The rest of the family was lucky enough to be out of earshot. Laurie and Rob were still building their fort at that time, working from the inside out because of the rain, and I could hear, faintly, the sound of hammering. Jannie was in her room, theoretically cleaning out her dresser drawers, but actually doing some kind of an acrobatic dance in front of her mirror, and singing the Fairy Rosabelle. The distant, unwilling sound of a typewriter from the study made it sound as though my husband was working, although I sometimes believe that he has a device (perhaps a woodpecker?) which taps the typewriter for him while he sleeps on the study couch. It was clearly going to rain all day; far away against the barn I could see the small brave orange dot which was still our only tulip.

"Take them *both* out, that's what *I'd* do," the old man

said at the kitchen door. "Make a nice little fireplace with them stones. Winter, *this* house, you *need* a fireplace."

"Awfully nice of you to stop by," I said, pushing at the door.

"Never did think to see anyone *living* here," he said, nodding profoundly at the broken step which Laurie had promised to fix as soon as they finished the fort. I sneezed, and shivered, and the old man settled himself down on the porch rail and recounted in detail the names, addresses, and contributing neglect attached to the downfall of every gatepost for miles around, then went on to examine the subject of leaning fences, discussed with ardor the striking of trees by lightning, and even digressed slightly to tell me about Morton's chimbley going down brick by brick onto the senior Morton, who was cleaning trout by the rain barrel.

"*Any*one can make things fall *down*," Sally said softly behind me. "It's getting them back *up* again is *hard*."

"Now you take that well Ananias Watkins was figuring to dig," the old man went on relentlessly.

"Yes, indeed," I said with wild finality, "I've got to go and open the refrigerator now."

"There was him and his two boys digging out this rock—"

"Thanks ever so much." I slammed the door and leaned against it.

"That gatepost." Sally shook her head mournfully, and then set down her paintbrush and looked at me. "*Why* can't I?" she asked.

"Because it is a great big gatepost and you are only a little tiny girl and you have made enough trouble with that magic already, what with poor little Jerry Martin afraid to go to bed at night and his mother keeps calling me and calling me to get you to take the spell off again—"

"I won't," Sally said stubbornly. "He called me a name."

"And no amount of teasing is going to talk me into letting you go to work with magic on that great big gatepost because you are only a little—"

"The refrigerator? Can I anyway magic the *refrigerator*?"

"When I want my refrigerator door unstuck I will get hold of a man who can unstick refrigerator doors, or at least your father."

"Suppose I just—"

"No," I said. "No magic, no no no."

Murmuring, Sally gathered together her brushes and her paper, and then her eye fell upon Barry, crooning over his truck. "Peabody," she said to him hopefully, "you want I should turn you back into a rabbit?"

"No, a boy with a truck," Barry said.

"*No* one *ever* lets me do *any*thing," Sally said. She thought, and then slid down from her chair and approached Barry. "Peabody," she said winningly, "my true love?"

"*No*," Barry said. "Play with this *truck*."

"Remember," Sally said, "you always *used* to be a rabbit, and it was only me got you into a baby in the *first* place."

"Oh," said Peabody. Reluctantly, he put down the truck and scrambled along after her. "Peabody," he explained to me as he passed.

"Maybe," Sally said suddenly, "maybe I will get me another rabbit and make another baby. A little girl."

"Under *no* circumstance," I said. "Barry is quite enough."

"A little *girl*?"

"Girl?" Barry insisted.

"Sally," I said firmly. "Not one more word."

"Then can I magic the refrigerator?"

I hesitated, and the day was lost. Sally turned joyfully and hurried into the study, Barry trailing along behind. I could hear Sally telling her father in the study that she and her helper Peabody had some very terrible magic to do for Mommy.

"Very nice," her father said.

"—so I need a lot of paper and pencil for me and two pencils for Peabody my helper because he writes with both hands."

"Magic?" her father said suddenly. "Just a minute now—what about that clock?"

"This is Mommy magic. Peabody my helper and I are going to unstick the refrigerator. Mommy *asked* us to."

"But when the clock—"

"You suppose I can do all this magic all by myself with just Peabody my helper without a *pencil?*"

I heard the sharpening of pencils only dimly; in order to open the refrigerator on a rainy day it was necessary to hold the sink with one hand and brace one foot against the wall, pulling and cursing. I was pounding the refrigerator door with my fists when Sally and Barry returned to stand and watch me from the kitchen doorway.

Sally chuckled. "You pull and pull and *pull*," she said, "and here a little girl like me will open it right open with magic for you." Then, forcefully, she gestured. "Peabody," she said.

Peabody moved forward, pencils alert. "Now," Sally said. "Three times backward, singing with me." She began to march backward around the kitchen table, singing, "Dearest sweetest Sally is the best girl in the world, dearest sweetest Sally, the most magical of all." Her helper followed her, shuffling uneasily and looking over his shoulder. "Magic magic magic," he sang, until he broke off abruptly, said, "My truck!" with vast delight, and made for the toy table.

"It's all right," Sally said hastily. "I can finish without him." I sat down on the kitchen stool and reflected upon rain and refrigerators.

When Jannie appeared in the kitchen doorway I thought for one stunned moment that it was something conjured up by Sally's magic before I recognized the unmistakable earmarks of the Fairy Rosabelle. She was wearing a pink ballet skirt, a quantity of junk jewelry mined from my dresser drawer, and a wreath of artificial roses around her head. She fluttered over to where I sat and bent over me, touching me gently on the head with her wand.

"Why so dreary, lonely mortal?" she inquired. "Is there aught that Rosabelle can offer to brighten thy sad lot?"

"Yes," I said. "You can set the table for lunch."

Rosabelle laughed, a little tinkling laugh. "We fairies sip only the dew from early violets."

"So will the rest of us," I said darkly, "unless we get the refrigerator open."

"Yonder approaches an honest woodcutter," Rosabelle remarked, hovering about six inches over my head. "Mayhap *he* will lend us his stalrit—stal—stal—"

"Stalwart," I said. "Sally, for heaven's sake stop that bellowing."

"I'm through," Sally said with dignity. "It's only the magic writing now." She settled down at the kitchen table and seized her pencil, scowling horribly.

"Hence," Rosabelle said as the back door opened, "hence, noble woodcutter, wouldst aid a damsel in distress?"

Barry leaped up joyfully. "Laurie," he shouted, "see my truck, will you fix it together?"

"Don't get in *my* way, Laurie," Sally said, "because I'm magicking the refrigerator door and *you* might come unstuck."

"Laurie," I said flatly, "go over and open that refrigerator."

"Dig *her*," Laurie said, regarding Jannie. "Who're *you*— the mad fiend from Planet X? When's lunch?" he asked me.

"I'm the Fairy Rosabelle," Jannie said.

"*Cra-zy* mixed-up," Laurie said, with the air of one making an original remark. "Hi, Salamander."

"Don't *call* me *Salamander*, because Mommy wants me to magic—"

"Laurie," I said, "go over and open that refrigerator."

"Real cool," Laurie said. "Real real cool. What's the matter with the refrigerator?"

"You know perfectly well if your father hears you talking like that you will be fined, maybe even fifty cents. The refrigerator door is stuck."

"*That* all?" He laughed shortly. "Poor old lady," he said, and patted me on the head as he went by. He took hold of the handle on the refrigerator door and pulled. "*Crazy*," he said, pulling. "This thing is real gone shut."

"Canst Rosabelle aid thee, honest lad?"

"Hah?" said Laurie. "Oh. Why don't *you* pull *me*?"

Jannie took hold of Laurie's belt and pulled, and Barry screamed, "Game, game," and hastened over to tug on the back of the pink ballet skirt.

"Cadabra!" said Sally, but the door did not open.

"Mixed-up," said Laurie, gasping.

The study door opened and my husband came into the kitchen. "When's lunch?" he asked. "What are you doing that for?"

I let go of the back of Barry's overalls. "We're opening the refrigerator," I said. "Why?"

"Nothing," he said. "I just wondered when was lunch?"

"When I get the refrigerator door open," I said.

"Why?"

"Because the milk is inside. And the butter, and the cold roast beef you said you would like to have for lunch today."

"No," he said. "I mean, why do you open it like that? Letting the children play with it? After all, a refrigerator is a complex machine, not a toy."

"Ooh, that nervous man," Laurie said.

"Laurence," his father said sternly, "one more word in that oleaginous jargon and you will pay a substantial fine."

"Yes, sir," Laurie said.

"Perhaps," my husband said condescendingly to me, "perhaps I have never thought to mention this to you before, but the way to deal with a stubborn piece of machinery is to use your intelligence. I cannot understand why you think you can open this refrigerator door by force. Do not attempt to impose your will upon it, do not bang upon this refrigerator, do not shake it. Losing your temper," he said kindly, "*never* does any good. That is very likely what made it stick in the first place. The thing to do," he said, still in that patient voice, "is to take hold of the handle gently—*gently*, remember—and use the slightest downward pressure. Then—" and he made a dramatic wide gesture of opening the refrigerator door, which came completely off the refrigerator and fell against him, so that he backed up across the kitchen floor, staggering, with the refrigerator door in his arms.

"Dig *that*," Laurie said in admiration.

"*Jeekers*," Sally said, eyes wide. "I went and unstuck the wrong *side*."

"Please put that down somewhere," I told my husband with a good deal of annoyance. "When I let you open the refrigerator door I hardly expected that you would go ripping it off and carrying it around the kitchen like—"

My husband set his back against the wall and put the door gently down onto the floor. He stood looking at it without saying anything and the children gathered gravely around him. "I did mean to unstick the *other* side," Sally said apologetically.

"*Craaaaazy*," Laurie said. "She ripped it right off the hinges."

"Sarah," my husband said at last, controlling his voice, "go to your room. Get a man to fix that," he told me tensely. "Not a five-year-old girl with magic. A refrigerator repairman. Call him on the telephone and tell him to come over and fix that refrigerator. Not a five-year-old girl with magic—a man."

He slammed the study door behind him.

The refrigerator repairman said he would come over right after lunch, and all the time I was getting out the roast beef and slicing tomatoes I could hear sounds of lamentation from Sally's room. Her father permitted her to come down for lunch, and when she came to her chair at the table she stopped to whisper in my ear. "I fixed *him*," she said, with an evil scowl at her father. "I'm going to show *him* about how magic is better. He can just *wait*."

I thought of Jerry Martin afraid to go to bed with a

spell on him and of little Cheryl whose doll's head was on backward now because she had pushed Sally in the snow, and I said apprehensively, "What?"

Sally laughed. *"Don't* worry," she told me ambiguously. "It's really good," she added, seeing me frown. "Just about how Daddy will know magic is better."

Conversation at lunch was monopolized by Laurie, who was planning a party for his birthday which was still seven months off. He wanted to invite twenty-one friends for lunch and a football game on the side lawn. He thought that it would not be any great inconvenience to put up goal posts, and he would get a can of white paint and do the yard lines himself. I thought that it would be much nicer, since we could not be sure yet what the weather was going to be like in October, if he planned on inviting two friends over for supper, and they could go to the movies. Laurie pointed out that if he invited twenty-one friends he would automatically get twenty-one presents, which was, he felt, real crazy. His father fined him fifty cents. Jannie suggested that it would be nice to have a play or at least a pageant honoring Laurie's birthday, and proposed the Fairy Rosabelle because then, she added prudently, she would not have to bother to learn something new. Sally, hugging herself, said that we were all going to have a wonderful surprise and Daddy would be sorry he had talked so mean about her magic. My husband remarked that the practice of magic was going to cost a certain young lady a considerable amount in fines before very long. Sally smiled mysteriously, and said he would be *glad* when he found out about her surprise. "Anyway," she added, *"Jannie* can still tell time on the clock, sort of."

"But Jannie is left-handed anyway," I said. "Besides, we decided not to say anything more about the clock."

"Maybe I could invite the whole class," Laurie said. "All but the girls, of course. We could have a track meet, or a rifle shoot, maybe. Is it all right to build a campfire?" he asked his father. "We'll promise to pick up the lawn afterward."

I said that unless table manners improved generally *no* one needed to think about birthday parties, and lunch continued as usual, except that Sally occasionally giggled to herself, and declined dessert, which was tapioca pudding, on the grounds that she was too excited about her surprise. Jannie was fined ten cents for elbows on the table, and Laurie talked himself out of a dollar and a half. All fines were remitted when my husband remarked absent-mindedly that his pudding was real cool. Barry was fined one jellybean for feeding tapioca pudding to his truck. Sally said my *goodness*, we were going to be so surprised.

The refrigerator man arrived while I was clearing the table, and he had a pair of hinges which luckily fit the door. Barry was allowed to stay up from his nap to watch the man put the door on again. My husband came out into the kitchen to watch, too, and he and the refrigerator man had a long, learned talk about baseball and what was apt to happen in Brooklyn during the coming summer. Laurie entered the conversation and was fined a quarter for saying that he thought Milwaukee would take the pennant.

I happen to like Milwaukee and so, since I did not have a quarter, I thought I would go upstairs and get the laundry put away. I heard my husband and the refrigerator man telling each other goodbye, and the refrigerator man saying we ought to think about a new refrigerator, really, because this one was getting pretty old and shaky and my husband said he was glad I had gone upstairs before the refrigerator man said that. I heard Sally singing "—is the best girl in the world." I went to the top of the stairs and called down for her to stop it, but I could not make her hear me.

I was putting away pajamas in Barry's room, which is in the front of the house, when I heard a crash which I thought at first was the refrigerator door falling off again, and then I realized that it came from outside and sounded irresistibly like the car of the repairman of the refrigerator backing into a stone gatepost. Almost at once, from the front porch, I heard Sally's voice raised in fury. "*Jeekers*," she wailed, "wrong side *again*."

My husband fined himself five dollars for remarks made upon this occasion. The man who came a few days later about the insurance felt that rather than going to the expense of having both gateposts straightened it would be simpler to take them down altogether, before, as he explained, "they fall down on someone's head and *really* cost you money."

No one around town ever remarked upon the fact that our left-hand gatepost leaned at an angle and our right-hand gatepost was now just slightly off its foundations. I got the impression that there was a general feeling that we ourselves had made the ultimate deadpan joke about the crooked gatepost, and further discussion would be superfluous. I was just as pleased to leave it that way.

We tried to enter Sally in dancing school, but she came right home again. She sulked for a week at home, and stormed around the kindergarten like a mad thing. There were high words in the study after dinner, but all pencils were confiscated, and, even though it was agreed that we were not going to say anything more about the clock, my husband made Sally take the spell off Jerry Martin and turn Cheryl's doll's head around again, and fix it so the teacher's umbrella would open right, the way it used to. We got Sally a pair of roller skates, but she gave them to Jannie. She announced at dinner one night that when she grew up she was going to be a mean mean old lady who lived in a forest and people came to her for advice and spells, except, she added, turning to look directly at her father, except wicked trolls.

The refrigerator door went right on sticking, but I discovered that I could open it by pounding violently on the side of the refrigerator with the frying pan. When I did this Sally liked to sit on the kitchen stool and sneer.

Then, after perhaps ten days, it seemed that she was relenting a little. She agreed to say good night to her father, and they were able to get back to work again in the kindergarten. Before I could do more than wonder at the change, she came down with chicken pox, although I do not believe it was deliberate. Laurie and Jannie had both had chicken pox, so, on the assumption that Barry might as well catch it now as later, I let him play freely with Sally, and during the long afternoons he sat on the foot of her bed, coloring, looking at books, and listening to Sally's stories.

We were coming to have, at that time, a distinct feeling around the family that most of our knotty domestic problems were pellucidly clear to Barry, although he tactfully forbore to comment on them. He had taken to chattering a good deal, a kind of cheerful running series of observations, but he spoke almost entirely in his own language, which bore a disconcerting similarity to our own, so that it was possible to be entrapped into listening closely to him, persuaded that he was communicating something of vital, although cheerful, importance. Consequently I was sure that Sally might safely confide in him and I could sometimes hear his small voice reassuring her in lovely long elegant sentences. As a result of this, of course, Sally became almost the only person able to translate Barry, although I believe that her translations were somewhat free, since Barry seemed so often to be saying exactly what Sally wanted him to.

When Sally's spots had begun to fade and she was allowed to come downstairs, interestingly pale and requiring a good many small services, to lie on the living room couch, she was very sweet to all of us. She permitted her father to bring her little phonograph and set it up beside the couch and she accepted, with a wan smile, the small offerings from the rest of us—*Little Women*, from Jannie, and a little carved dog from Laurie, and paste and colored paper from me; illness, in fact, seemed to have taught her the fruitlessness of anger; we did not perceive at once that something had taught her the usefulness of guile. It was not until her convalescence was almost complete that she showed her hand. One morning Laurie and Jannie had gone off to school as usual, and Sally was enjoying the rare freedom of lingering late over her breakfast while her father and I had our second cups of coffee; because of the imminence of chicken pox Barry had been kept home from nursery school, and he was pushing grains of cereal down to the bottom of the bowl with his cereal spoon and giggling helplessly when they popped up again.

"Sally," I said tactfully, "it is most pleasant to have you well again."

Sally gave me an inscrutable smile. "I have enjoyed being sick," she said. "Thank you very much for letting me."

"Not at all," I said. "Barry, eat your cereal."

Barry put down his cereal spoon and regarded me darkly. "You untreat me like a genman," he said. "Once more, Pudge."

"*Barry!*" Sally opened her eyes wide. "Dearest Mommy did *not* untreat you like a gentleman, and you went and said Pudge without making the magic sign and that's *awful*."

Hastily Barry slid off his chair and turned slowly around three times. "There," he said.

"Wait," Sally said. "I did, too." She got down and circled.

I stared, bewildered, and my husband put down the *New York Times*. "Besides," Sally said to Barry, "you promised."

"Can I have a srop?" Barry asked me.

"A srop? What for?"

"Dangerous trees."

"Sally?" I said, appealing.

She smiled and shrugged.

"What is Pudge?" my husband said.

I shook my head, but Sally and Barry both got down off their chairs and circled slowly.

"*You* better watch out," Sally told her father. "Or else make the magic sign."

"Get a srop," Barry advised.

"Or say something else," Sally said. "Call him the Great Wizard. Or the Most Powerful One."

"Great Grizzard," Barry said.

"All right," I said, "but *who*—?"

"Well." Sally leaned back in her chair and took on her storytelling face, eyes wide and looking far away, hands clasped under her chin. "Well," she said, "when I decided to put together the land of Oz and the country of the hobbits and Rootabaga and Mother Goose Land, because they were all scattered all over and I kept forgetting which book I had to take to get to each country—well, anyway, I decided to put them all together. Fairyland, too, of course. So it's all called Gunnywapitat now, and Ozma lives there, and all the hobbits, and the Cowardly Lion and the old woman in the shoe, and Peter Pan, and Oberon and the rest, all there where I can get to them easy. Gunnywapitat. And Pudge helped me."

"Magic sign," my husband put in nervously.

"Thank you." Sally got down and turned around. "So I put the entrance to his country right under his tree. Pudge's tree." She turned around. "And Barry needs a sword to pertect him because all the other trees have evil spirits trying to get into Gunnywapitat, the big tree and under it all the magic world."

"Yggdrasil?" said my husband, startled.

"What?" said Sally. "Anyway, we go to visit and it's always in the middle of the night or else while you're busy or something and if we go in the day we take weapons, because lots of times children go in and they do not ever come out except maybe after—oh, ten years or so. And then they're old and everything has changed and all their friends are gone and their mothers and fathers." She gave her father a brief look. "And down there *every*one does magic," she said.

"So I need a srop," Barry said.

[172]

"And we have parties with lots of candy and cookies. And the entrance is guarded by lagatours and dragatours."

"And policemans."

"Of course," she said, glancing again at her father and then at me, "*you* couldn't go."

"*I* am Trixie Pixie," Barry said smugly. "A lepercorn."

"There is one whole city made of chocolate," Sally said. "Even the houses and the cars and the dogs and cats, all chocolate."

"Can I unfinish? My cereal?"

Sally spent most of the morning drawing me a map of Gunnywapitat, showing the chocolate city (Mishmutat) and the river of wild animals (Cody Wop) and the upside-down section (Gilywimpis) and Pudge's capital city (Gunypostafall); in Gilywimpis, she told me disturbingly, even the birds had wings. In the afternoon the sun was shining and it was so pleasant that I said that she and Barry might play outdoors for a while if they stayed near the house and Sally was careful not to get herself tired, or chilled, or excited. Barry asked to be put into a long-sleeved skirt because they were going to play Gunnywapi-tat, and he made himself a srop out of a twig. For quite a while I was in the kitchen, cleaning the refrigerator and then scrubbing the kitchen floor, which I had not had time to do while Sally was sick, and I heard them playing happily outside. "Lagatours!" Sally shouted once. "Charge!" "Avaunt!" Barry cried, and charged, presumably brandishing his srop.

Later, when I went upstairs to straighten Sally's room and make the bed, because I thought that probably she would not want to stay up for dinner after playing outdoors, I could still hear them distantly for a while, but when I moved on to pick up the crayons from Barry's floor they were out of earshot. I decided to straighten Barry's bookcase, and so I stayed upstairs longer than I had thought to, and when I came down to the kitchen again I went to call them in for fruit juice and cookies, and they were not there. I went outside and looked up and down the driveway, and out across the lawn, calling them, and then went and looked in the barn, calling them, and then behind the barn, still calling, and then I went all around the outside of the house. Anywhere farther than that was out of bounds, as they both knew.

I sat down on the back steps and tried to think. I knew they could not have come to any harm because our big dog Toby was lying comfortably in the sun in the barn doorway and even though Toby has never growled at anyone except the laundry man I was fairly sure that he would do *some*thing if any danger approached, even if it was only to come into the house and try to hide behind me. Toby's presence also argued that they were nearby. I called again and again, and Toby lifted his head and looked at me wonderingly, as though Sally and Barry were right in plain sight and he could not understand the increasing agitation in my voice. I did not like to go in and call my husband at the college; when I saw Laurie come up the street on his bike I got up and went to meet him with as little appearance of concern as I could manage.

"Laurie," I said, "Sally and Barry have wandered away somewhere. I can't find them."

"Pudge's tree, probably," Laurie said. He rode past me and toward the barn door, going swiftly, directly at Toby. Toby yawned and closed his eyes, and Laurie braked the bike an inch from Toby's nose. "You lazy dog," he said. Toby yawned again. "Go look in Pudge's tree," Laurie called back at me.

"Where *is* it?"

He took his bike into the barn, wheeling it carefully past Toby, and reappeared. "I thought *you* knew," he said. "Want a cookie?" he asked Toby, and Toby, alert, rose and followed him toward the back door.

"Laurie," I said, "*listen.*"

"Sure," he said. "Don't you worry. Pudge'll bring them back okay."

Jannie came along a few minutes later, lingering and giggling with her friend Carole; Jannie said that Sally and Barry were almost certainly in Pudge's tree, and Carole added that her little sister Jeanie had often told all of them at their house about Sally's friend Pudge and his magic tree. "Jeanie says that Sally goes there *lots*," Carole said, and Jannie added, "Pudge takes good care of them, it's all right," and they went on into the house to join Laurie and Toby at the cookie jar.

For almost half an hour, only the combined efforts of Laurie and Jannie, and Carole's offers to go home and get Jeanie and ask *her*, prevented me from telephoning my husband at the college, or our local policeman, or at least my mother in California. Then we heard laughter from behind the barn, and Sally and Barry wandered toward us, holding hands and chatting happily.

They refused to say where they had been. I held on to them, and stumbled questions, trying to keep my voice gentle, and Sally shook her head and smiled. "I said I wouldn't tell about it," she explained. "You *can't*, with a magic country, because then they won't let you come back, ever. Were we gone for ten years? Because everyone looks about the same."

"Barry," I said, "where did you go? With Sally?"

"Cookies," he said, grinning. "Many happy cookies, and the flowers on a queen."

"He says he won't tell," Sally said hastily.

The next morning, when I got up after a night spent checking on Sally and Barry every half hour, I found a great tub full of spring flowers on the back porch, tulips and daffodils and pussy willows. There was a note tucked in among the stems, and it read: "Thanks so much for letting the children come; delighted with their little visit. Tell Barry I'll send him a 'flinky' one of these days. Hope you like their flowers. 'Pudge.' "

I showed the note to my husband privately, and we decided that perhaps it was not altogether healthy to let Sally fill her mind with these fancies, and we would say no more about it. However, later, when Barry stopped in the bathroom doorway to watch his father shaving, it seemed a good moment for a diplomatic question, and his father said carelessly, "By the way, when you went to Pudge's yesterday, what was he wearing?"

"Crown," said Barry.

"Was anyone else there?"

"Trixie Pixie?"

"No," said his father. "Where did you go?"

"You are the daddy," said Barry reassuringly, "and I am the Barry, and Sally is the Sally, and Jannie is the Jannie and Laurie is the Laurie and Mommy is the Mommy."

When I married the man who is at present my husband and the father of my children it did not occur to me to specify that his behavior should in no way prevent my buying an evening paper. It is not a usual request to make during such a ceremony, for one thing, and, for another thing, the possibility of my being unable to buy an evening paper if I wanted one seemed, to say the least, remote.

Actually, it was only for about three days that we had to do without the paper. Thanks to a fortunate hurricane which took part of the cornice off the First National Bank most of the affair was quickly forgotten, and since my husband's cigarette lighter broke almost at once, the subject largely died down, to be revived only by the most tactless and humorous of our friends. I wonder sometimes if things could have been handled differently in some way, but of course there is not much use worrying about it now. If, perhaps, I had refused to call Mr. Williams back in Burlington? If I had neglected to answer the phone at all?

Whenever the phone rings I have of course the quick wonderful thought that some remarkable and astonishing surprise is going to happen. ("Lonesome for you in California; plane tickets arriving special delivery. . . ." "Investigation proves you only surviving heir . . .") However, what I always expect is a kind of surprise for *me*, too. When I answered the phone on a bright morning when the sun was really warm and the trees were really green and the air had that authentic scent of flowers, it was a call for my husband, from a man with a pleasant, although unfamiliar, gentlemanly voice. He asked for my husband by calling him "the Professor," which is perhaps a legitimate title for a teacher in a girls' college, but which is a title rarely, if ever, used except by the kind of friend who thinks that sort of thing is terribly funny. At any rate, I held out the phone and remarked that it's for you, Professor, and my husband grudgingly put down a gold *moidore* he was checking for precise weight and went to the phone.

I heard him say "Hello?" and then "What?" and then "*What?*" Then he sighed and said, "All right, all right. And what did you say your name was?"

There was a long silence and then he hung up.

"Yes, dear?" I asked, hovering. ("Paris concern offering all expenses you and family . . .")

"Look," he said. "I want you to pick up that telephone and call a man named John Williams, at the *Gazette*, in Burlington, Vermont. Person to person. Collect."

"Why?"

"Never *mind* why. He just said that if I thought it was a practical joke I could hang up and call him right back and prove he was a real person."

"Why should you have to prove—"

"Never *mind* why," my husband said again. He laughed shortly. "Prominent local educator!" he said.

Eying my husband apprehensively, I took up the phone and put through a call, person to person, collect, to John Williams, Burlington *Gazette*, Vermont. Because Burlington is only a hundred miles from the small Vermont town where we live my call went through smoothly, unlike a call to New York City, for instance, when—because of course New York City is not in Vermont—it is sometimes necessary to spell out everything, beginning with N for Norman, E for Edwin, W for Wilfred, Y for Yolanda, and so on. When I heard the same pleasant unfamiliar voice on the other end of the line, and he agreed that he was indeed John Williams, I said, "Hello, Mr. Williams?"

"Right," he said cheerfully. "Give us the Professor."

I might say that I have rarely seen such an expression on

my husband's face. Delighted, he was, and yet incredulous. He kept saying, "I can't believe it," and, "This *must* be a joke." He and Mr. Williams talked for a long time, and every few minutes my husband would give a little giggle.

When he finally said, "Well, I'll see you on the fifteenth, then," and hung up, there I was, right next to him, curious, and—I had been married for fourteen years—deeply suspicious.

"Well?" I said in a voice used by wives who have been married for fourteen years. "Well?"

"Well," my husband said, putting his shoulders back and pulling in his stomach. "*Well.*"

I followed him into the study and resisted a strong impulse to slap the gold *moidore* right out of his hand. "*Well?*" I said.

My husband looked at me out of the corners of his eyes and opened and shut his mouth several times. "Now I want you to be reasonable," he said at last.

I prepared myself to be reasonable. I sat down quietly in a chair, clenched my fists, and smiled tightly. "It's only," my husband said, "that I have to go to Burlington."

"So?"

"Well," he said hesitantly, "I'm going to Burlington, is all."

"How perfectly splendid," I said. "I know how you've longed to see Burlington."

"*I* don't know why they picked on me," my husband said. "A prominent local educator is what Mr. Williams kept telling me. It certainly isn't anything *I* ever thought of doing. And of course," he finished brightly, "it might *still* be a practical joke."

"You are going to *have* to stop twisting your hands like

that," I said. "And if you give that evil chuckle once more I will gag you with a dish towel."

"I can't help it," my husband said, "I feel like a fool."

"Hah," I said eloquently, and got up and headed for the kitchen and the breakfast dishes. "Look," my husband wailed despairingly. "I *got* to go, I *said* I would, and besides it's *not* what you think."

"I bet it is," I said.

"It is *not*," he said, coming after me. "It's only a kind of contest, sort of. I'm a judge, sort of. And even if I am a judge it doesn't necessarily mean—"

"Yes?" I said, when he stopped abruptly.

"Well," he said.

"If I may presume to ask just one question," I said carefully. "If I am not too presumptuous, if I am not in any way interfering with your private affairs—and please believe that I would not for a moment dream—"

"Look," he said.

"If you are absolutely sure that I can be trusted with your secret mission, may I just possibly ask—what *are* you judging?"

"Girls," he said.

"*What?*"

"They want me to be a judge in the beauty contest to choose Miss Vermont, so she can enter another contest and be Miss America."

I am genuinely sorry for the way I acted then. I have tried to explain to my husband but of course there is really no way of explaining, or at least none that would help the situation any. I am really sorry, though. I was sitting on one of the kitchen chairs with the tears running down my cheeks and my sides aching and my husband standing there looking offended and saying, "Well, I didn't really think it was as funny as all *that*," when the back door slammed open and Laurie trotted in, shedding jacket and hat as he came. He was always the first child home at lunchtime, because he rode his bike to school. Moreover, although not overly endowed with personal dignity, he had a strong and uncompromising estimate of what was proper and fitting, particularly in a parent.

"Where's lunch?" he said. "What's wrong?" He looked from me to his father, and said, "Hey?"

"Laurie," I said feebly, "Daddy is going to judge a beauty contest."

"*Dad*," said Laurie, turning purple.

"Prominent local educator," my husband said defensively.

"Oh, my gosh," Laurie said. "Oh, my gosh, my gosh. Does anyone *know* about it?" he demanded of his father.

"Look," my husband said.

"What about my friends?" Laurie said. "Suppose someone finds out?"

"It's an honor," my husband said. "For heaven's sake, you'd think someone in this house would think it's an *honor*."

"Here come the girls," I said, in a hushed voice. "They will have to be told, I suppose."

"Yeah," Laurie said bitterly, "the whole *world*'s probably going to be told. Oh, my gosh. Yeah," he said to the girls as they came through the door, "get out the old man's bathing suit. He's a crazy, mixed-up daddy."

I went out onto the porch and captured Barry, who had finally been prevailed upon to accept the notion of a nursery school car pool, and rode home three days a week with a neighbor, but then still had to be dragged and pushed and wheedled up the back walk to the lunch table.

"They was muskets in my school this day," Barry told me, as one reporting a grievance, "muskets."

He came through the door and made directly for his father, to whom he announced insistently, "They was muskets in my school this day, muskets."

"Mouses," Sally said softly, "mouses in his school."

"Look, Dad," Laurie said confidentially, "you got to realize that there are fellows in this town would *love* to get a thing like that on me. I can see Ernie Smith now." And he closed his eyes and shuddered.

The only person in the family immediately delighted was, of course, Jannie, who had taken to putting red polish on her toenails secretly, and had gotten three valentines from friends of Laurie's in sixth grade. Jannie perceived that she had all this time been seriously underrating her father, the Beauty Contest Judge, and she asked most ingratiatingly if she might be allowed to sit next to him at lunch.

"Daddy is going to see a lot of girls," Sally told Barry. She turned to me. "Daddy likes to look at girls, doesn't he?"

There was a deep, enduring silence, until at last my husband's eye fell on Jannie. "And what did you learn in school today?" he asked with wild enthusiasm.

"Daddy is a Chinese temple gong," Barry remarked. "Daddy may ride on my steamroller."

"He did not," Sally said, amused. "Daddy is a *nice* man."

"*I'm* going to be in beauty contests when *I* grow up," Jannie said, reaching dreamily for the bread and butter. "I bet I win, too."

"Somebody goofed," Laurie said drearily.

Three days before my husband was to leave for Burlington there was a prominently placed article in our local afternoon paper about the beauty contest. It included a picture of my husband, identified by name and address. Laurie announced that he had a bad cold, a headache, an undefined pain somewhere in the middle of his back, and a blister on his heel, and was, as a result, forced to stay home from school for at least a week. Jannie brought eleven members of the Starlight 4-H Club home to compare her father in real life with his picture in the paper. Many of our female friends telephoned to ask what their chances might be if they decided to enter the beauty contest. Since my husband's students are all girls, there was a certain amount of oblique comment in his classroom, and he was compelled to confess that he found it inexpedient to enter the faculty dining room. The article in the paper said, "Prominent Local Educator to Judge Statewide Beauty Contest."

It turned out that one of .the contestants came from nearby, and she offered to drive my husband up to Burlington. The offer was made through Mr. Williams, and my husband told me reluctantly that Mr. Williams had assured him that there would be no improper influence brought to bear upon him during the ride. I told him how rare a man he was, to be able to preserve an absolutely impartial opinion upon such controversial matters, and went off in a surly mood to the grocery, where I met a friend who said *she* would be *scared* to let *her* husband judge a beauty contest.

"Might as well move out of *this* town," Laurie kept telling his father grimly.

On the morning of the day that he was to leave my husband was not able to eat any breakfast. He sat at the table in his best suit, wearing a tie someone had brought him from Italy, toying with a little piece of waffle, and telling the children over and over that they must behave themselves and be good children and he would bring them all something from Burlington.

"At least you could be considerate enough to leave at *night*, at least," Laurie said. "This way, you go right through the center of town in broad daylight."

My husband stirred nervously. "I was thinking," he said to me. "You know, I don't even know how they judge these things. What standards they use, or anything."

"As a prominent local educator," I said unkindly, "you were probably expected to do your own research."

"It's a real public disgrace," Laurie said.

The children and I crowded unashamedly onto the porch to gape at the possible Miss Vermont when she drove up. She seemed a very nice girl, rather shy, and quite pretty. She had a good-looking car.

Under the enigmatic gaze of his family my husband descended the steps and greeted the maiden and her escort, a formidable-looking creature who was apparently a combination chaperon and attendant, since she kept giving little hitches to her charge's clothes, and adjusted a scarf carefully over the shining golden curls before the two of them got into the car.

"I hope you win," Laurie said grudgingly as they went down the walk. "I bet *she*'s the prettiest girl there," he added with unexpected local patriotism.

"I hope you win, Daddy," Sally said, and Jannie gazed with rapture on the golden curls.

"Going Daddy," said Barry mournfully, and we all came indoors.

During the day there were eleven telephone calls from people wanting to know if he had really gone. Most of them had thought of something funny to say. The afternoon paper had another picture of my husband and a long story about the festivities he would encounter in Burlington. They included an imposing list of guest appearances and a Pageant of Beauty.

Laurie still flatly refused to go to school, and during the afternoon he made the serious tactical error of deciding instead to accompany me to the barbershop to get Barry's hair cut. Several of my husband's colleagues had stopped by to chat with the barber. Luckily, Barry had decided that this was not the day he had selected to have his hair cut, and Laurie and I were too busy holding him down in the chair to hear more than a fraction of what was said.

"How come you didn't go along?" someone asked Laurie, and someone else said, "How do you ever *get* a job like that, anyway?"

"He spent years studying," Laurie said grimly. I was holding both of Barry's ears tight so the barber could get it even across the front. Barry was shouting, "Too early! Too early!" which Sally told me meant that he wanted everyone to be quiet and wait a minute.

"You think he's ever coming back?" the barber asked me humorously.

The grocery was worse. A number of acquaintances of ours were doing their shopping, and both Laurie and I had the clear feeling as we entered that all conversations all over the store had stopped, while everyone turned to look at us. People told Laurie, and told me, and then told us both together, that my, what an odd hobby my husband had, and did we think he was ever coming back, and was he going to make a career of this kind of thing. As a small consolation I got Laurie and Barry each a popsicle, and did a lot of split-second planning to insure that I would not have to shop again for four days.

Although I am not ordinarily nervous when my husband is away from home, I found it extraordinarily difficult to occupy myself that first evening. I put the children to bed and wandered around the house straightening things. I washed out a couple of the girls' dresses and a pair of stockings of mine, and waited for the phone to ring. I did not really suppose that there had been an accident, of course—our possible Miss Vermont looked like a cautious driver—but I finally made a batch of cookies and then sat down with a book, within reaching distance of the phone. By the time my husband called I was almost asleep.

"How are you? How is everything?" I asked, bemused.

"Very nice," he said. "The hotel is nice and we had a nice dinner. She's a very nice girl."

"Fine," I said. "Just fine. I was in the barbershop this afternoon and—"

"Except," he said, "I spilled coffee on my gray pants."

"Wash it out right away," I said. "In the barbershop—"

"She already did," he said. "There's going to be a Pageant of Beauty."

"I know. It was in the paper. Pete said—"

"We judge them in evening gowns and in bathing suits and for compatibility."

"Really?" I said. "I'm so glad you're glad you decided to go."

"What?" he said.

"Nothing," I said. "I got Barry's hair cut."

"Fine," he said. There was a long silence. "How is everybody?" he asked finally.

"Fine," I said.

"I'm very glad to hear it," he assured me. "Well, I have to get up early. There's a breakfast."

"How exciting," I said. "Goodbye."

The children and I had a lovely time the next day. Laurie resolutely declined going to school, and he and I spent the morning making a cheese soufflé for lunch. When the girls came home in the afternoon and Barry got up from his nap all of us sat around the kitchen table and made things out of colored paper. Laurie and I felt strongly that there was no point in going down for the afternoon paper, particularly since the news shop is always crowded around the time the paper comes out, and there would be a lot of people standing around and gossiping. Laurie pointed out, in addition, that the morning paper had already been delivered, and that he personally found a second paper superfluous. I myself felt that I had read all I cared to about the Pageant of Beauty, although I have heard since that the article that evening was little short of overwhelming.

When my husband called that night he was a little bit upset. "It didn't come out," he said immediately, "that coffee stain."

"That's too bad," I said.

"I've got to wear it to the Pageant. But Charmian says no one will notice. All the girls were very nice about it."

I asked with restraint, "Have you found out what standards apply?"

"You know something?" he said. "One of the girls here used to live in Brooklyn."

"Have her put some baking soda on it," I said.

"That's what Sandy suggested. She was the one in the pink dress who gave me a bandage for this scratch on my finger." There was a long silence. "How are the children?" he asked.

"All fine. And you?"

"Say," he said, "there's an interesting fellow here, another judge. Used to judge cattle. Did you know that you can tell a cow's age by the rings on the horns?"

"No," I said. "I didn't."

"Nice fellow. *He* likes Barbara for Intellect."

"A number of people have called you," I said.

"Is there any mail?"

"Yes," I said with malice. "There are a lot of new coins from that place in Chicago."

He sighed. "I wonder if I should give up coins," he said. "Start collecting something else for a while."

The next day was Saturday and the children and I took a long drive out into the country and had hot dogs for lunch at a diner in the next town. We got back late, too late, we agreed, to bother to go down and get the afternoon paper, which was probably sold out anyway. My husband called while the children were having dinner.

"I'm on my way to the Pageant," he said. "That coffee stain doesn't show at all."

"Your father called," I said. "I told him where you were."

"We do the judging tonight," my husband said happily. "I guess I'll be home tomorrow."

"That will be nice."

"Thirty-four and a half inches," my husband said to

someone on the other end of the phone. "You tell her I don't care *what* her mother said."

"Your *father* said—"

"What?" said my husband. "Just a minute. No," he went on to whoever was talking to him, "I'm calling my *wife*."

I closed my mouth tight, so I would be sure not to say another word, and hung up very gently.

I was sound asleep when my husband came home. He arrived at four that morning, wrinkled, scratched, coffee-stained, and irritable. Our local entry had not won, and, disgruntled, had loaded my husband into her car and come home in a huff, dropping him off on the corner with his suitcase. "Woosh?" I said when I opened my eyes and saw him coming into the room.

"Fine, fine, oh fine," he said. "Anything happen while I was gone?"

"Hm? Oh. Nothing, except Laurie is never going to speak to you again and your father says to call him the minute you get home, no matter what time it is."

"You'll have to send this suit to the cleaner's," he said. "Look, I got a cigarette lighter. It says JudgeMissVermontBeautyContest. Look."

I leaped back as he flashed the lighter under my nose. "A memento of your day of glory," I said with a gentle smile.

"That reminds me," he said. "Got to make a note to write that girl Linda. Turns out she's very much interested in coins."

Wearily I sat up and reached for a cigarette. "Well," I said, "who won the beauty contest?"

"Hm?"

"Who won the beauty contest?"

"Oh, I don't know," my husband said vaguely. "Some girl."

The next morning, Sunday, Laurie gathered his courage together and called his friend Rob; either Rob was superlatively tactful or he had a short memory, because Laurie invited him over and they spent the day in Laurie's room playing jazz records. Jannie and Sally and Barry made mudpies in the dirt near the barn, and late in the afternoon Laurie and Rob, emerging from Laurie's room, volunteered to build a sandbox, which pleased the smaller children, although the sandbox, complete, turned out to be ten feet square and to hold, as I subsequently discovered, a staggering amount of sand. My husband was in the study all that day, arranging the coins from the place in Chicago. Although Laurie did not speak to his father, he did not actually *not* speak to him, and passed him the salt at dinner with an air almost friendly.

The next morning everyone went back to school. It was my morning on the nursery school car pool, so about eleven-thirty I left my kitchen by the back door, after checking to see that the stove was turned off, except for the oven on "warm" where the lunch casserole was waiting. The table was set, the bread sliced, the cake ready on a plate, and my decrepit old refrigerator was rattling and grumbling to itself; since the weather had turned warmer, it opened more easily, but it had developed a kind of excited cackle which it turned on every twenty minutes and which made it alarmingly difficult to—say—count spoons in the kitchen, or figure how many baked potatoes, or hear what anyone was saying from the next room. My husband was lunching at the college, the three older children were due home from school at various times up until twelve-fifteen, and everything was ready for my return with Barry. On the corner I encountered Sally, who got out of school early because the kindergarten children were escorted by their teacher past the bad train crossing in the center of Main Street, and who tended to get home around a quarter of twelve, after stopping off at Pudge's tree with Jeanie. I persuaded Sally into the car, stopped briefly at the store to get a carton of cigarettes, collected Barry, tired and sandy-faced, from the nursery school, and reasoned and enticed into the car the two neighboring children who are the other members of the car pool. I dropped the two other children off at their separate front doors, and drove home. I made this identical trip three days a week, keeping to a consistent time and route.

Once in our own driveway, I escorted Sally and Barry from the car up the walk to our back door, opened the door, and we went in. Sally said at once, "If what I smell is lunch I don't want any," and fell to coughing wildly. Barry choked, and I gasped, with tears in my eyes. I have never smelled anything like it before—it was dreadful; sickening, and almost visible in the quiet kitchen. In wild haste I shoved Barry and Sally back out onto the porch, thought of the oven, and, with my hands over my face and my eyes full of tears, dashed across the kitchen and turned the oven off.

The odor seemed less strong near the stove, but I opened the oven anyway and looked in, to make sure nothing was burning inside, although I had never before made a macaroni and ham casserole that turned into poison gas. Sally and Barry peered interestedly through the kitchen window. I soaked my handkerchief at the sink, and covered my face with it; I thought of fire—although heaven only knew what could be burning to smell like that—and hurried through the downstairs rooms, sniffing and looking into corners, but it was clear that the gas existed mainly in the kitchen. The other rooms had a faint trace of that frightful odor, but I could breathe naturally in them, and it was only when I came back into the kitchen that it caught me by the throat again, and I fell to coughing and choking.

The rattling and creaking of the old refrigerator was so much a familiar part of the kitchen that it was a minute before I realized that a good part of my uneasiness was its silence. Then, understanding that the refrigerator was mute, I went to it quickly, opened the door, and got such a lungful of the gas that I reeled wildly over to the back door and out onto the porch. "What's for *lunch*?" Sally asked as, tearful and strangling, I clung to the porch rail.

Since Barry was too little to leave under Sally's dubious supervision on the porch, I thought that the wisest thing was to put both of them back into the car. Barry was considerably disturbed at the notion that he was about to be taken back to nursery school without any lunch or dinner or breakfast the next day, but I told Sally to sing to him, and, as her voice rose quaveringly in the kindergarten health song, I went around the house and in through the front door to the telephone in the hall. I called the refrigerator people and got the repairman on the phone. "My kitchen is full of some terrible gas from the refrigerator," I said.

There was a short, nervous silence, and then the repairman, his voice unsteady, asked, "Anyone in the house?"

"Well, the children are coming home for lunch—"

"*Children?*" said the repairman.

"I took them outside," I said, bewildered.

"Thank heaven," said the repairman.

"Is there something wrong, then?"

"Where's the refrigerator?" he asked.

"In the kitchen," I said.

"Near a door?"

"Well, there's a back door out onto the porch. But is there something—"

"Can we back a truck up there?"

"I guess so. My rosebush—"

"This is no time to worry about *rosebushes*," he said. "We can get a crew together and be over there in about an hour. Meanwhile, don't let anyone go in the house. Better get the children well away. Don't go lighting any matches."

With trembling fingers I put out the cigarette I was smoking.

"Lock the doors till we get there," he was going on.

"But is there something *wrong*? I have lunch all ready, and it's after twelve now, and the children have to be back at school by one, and the table is set—"

"Look," he said, his voice rising, "you still *in the house?*"

"I had to telephone," I said.

"You hang up and you get out of that house as fast as you can go," he said and so, abandoning my kitchen and my casserole and—as my husband pointed out later—his coin collection and the garnet sunburst my grandmother gave me, I fled.

Sally was reciting the Pledge of Allegiance when I got back to the car, and Barry was reading Jannie's library book, which was overdue because I had carried it around in the car for three days, meaning to return it. Sally broke off as I approached to ask what was for lunch. I found a crayon in Barry's jacket pocket and, deciding that desperate measures were to some extent justified, tore the flyleaf out of Jannie's library book and wrote on it a note saying POISON GAS DO NOT ENTER which I put on the back door with a pin from my shoulder strap. Locking the house seemed silly, since all the keys were hanging on a hook next to the refrigerator. Through the kitchen window I could see my pocketbook, where I had set it down on the kitchen table. Everything looked very quiet and peaceful inside, with the bright plates on the blue tablecloth and the villain refrigerator presiding silently. A faint whiff of that appalling odor seeped through the crack of the kitchen door, however, and I hastened down the walk to the car.

Since it was several minutes after twelve, I started off with Barry and Sally, intending to pick up Laurie and Jannie and take everyone to the soda shop for lunch. I found Laurie with no trouble; he was on the corner, fighting furiously with Rob. I blew the car horn and Laurie, disheveled and snarling insults over his shoulder, got into the car. "My *mother's* here," he remarked viciously, rolling down the car window and putting out an evil face, "but you just wait'll later. Can I learn to play the trumpet?" he asked me.

"No," I said.

"But Rob's learning clarinet and Stuart and Willie are learning drums and the music teacher says I got a talent."

"It's too noisy," I said. "Trumpets cost too much and besides the house is full of poison gas."

"I'll practice outside," Laurie said. "In the barn, maybe.

And I can pay you off from my allowance. Besides," he said with deep pleasure, "I got a talent."

"The house is full of poison gas," I said.

"All *right*," Laurie said. "I *told* you I'd practice in the *barn*." He leaned his head again out of the car window and shouted, "You *better* run, you rat—you just wait'll I get back, you rat."

Jannie was not in sight, so I drove on to the school. There was no sign of her there, so I turned around and drove back home, with Laurie and Sally and Barry fidgeting in the back of the car, and watching both sides of the street for Jannie. When I got home I turned around in the driveway and drove back to the school again, and then— Laurie by now threatening to leap bodily out of the car and make his own way, lunchless, back to school before he was hopelessly late—back home again. Then, struck by an idea, I ran up and opened the back door, which still said POISON GAS DO NOT ENTER, and shouted, "Jannie?"

"Yes?" she said, from upstairs. "Where is everybody?"

"You get out of this house at *once*, do you hear me?"

"Why?"

"Come downstairs," I howled, beginning to cough again.

"All right," Jannie said. She came down the back stairs and I snatched up her hat and coat from the kitchen chair and grabbed her by the wrist and hauled her outdoors. "What's the *matter*?" she kept saying.

"Did you see that sign?" I pointed to POISON GAS DO NOT ENTER.

"Sure," she said, "but I had to change to my pink skirt because this morning Kate wore *her* pink skirt and I told her this afternoon I'd wear *my* pink skirt too."

"That sign says do not enter," I said.

"Sure," Jannie said, "but I didn't think you meant *me*."

"Didn't you *smell* anything?"

"No," she said. "Only lunch cooking."

Glancing back through the kitchen window I saw my pocketbook still on the kitchen table.

When I stopped the car in front of the soda shop it was a quarter to one, and our dog Toby, who had been made very nervous by having everyone leave the house when they should have been in having lunch, and then going away and coming back and going away and coming back, had concluded that some general catastrophe had occurred and we were planning to leave him behind to face it alone. He consequently followed the car to the soda shop and refused to be left outside. He was far too big to fit comfortably under those little wire tables they have in soda shops, and ordinarily he would have perceived this, sooner or later, but having been abandoned once had so upset him that he was wholly deaf to threats and orders; every time I led him outside he waited till someone opened the door and then sneaked in again and came and tried to get into my lap, his comfort when the whole world has gone wrong.

The soda shop was, as usual during lunch hour, full of high school students, who regarded all of us, and particularly the dog going in and out, with extreme curiosity, and caused Laurie agonies of embarrassment. "Let's go home," he kept saying to me in an urgent undertone. "I don't *care* what it's like."

All four of the children ordered banana splits for lunch, and I asked for a cup of coffee. Just as the waitress was putting down my coffee, one of the high school students, pushed by another, came crashing down onto our table, knocking the dog off my lap and upsetting Barry, who began to cry.

"That was the *captain* of the *football* team," said Laurie, purple. "Let's go *home*."

I restored Barry, indicating his banana split, and sat down. The dog got onto my lap again. I gave up my coffee, since I could not reach the table anyway. Because my pocketbook was still on the kitchen table I had to borrow a check from the man in the soda shop and make it out and ask him to cash it. I also called my husband at the college and told him he had better come home because the house was full of poison gas.

When I got back to the table Laurie was propped up nervously, half standing and half sitting, talking to the music teacher from the school. "Here's my mother," he said with relief. "Can I learn to play the trumpet?" he asked me.

"No," I said. I sat down and the dog got on my lap. The high school students had begun to wander out, on their way back to school.

"We like to think that all children have an instinctive love of music," the music teacher said to me.

"We can't even get in the *house*," I said. "How could he take trumpet lessons?"

"The trumpet only costs a hundred and twenty-five dollars, and he will enjoy it all his life," the music teacher said. "Lessons and music extra, of course."

"I had to cash a check to pay for these banana splits," I said.

"I will enjoy it all my life," Laurie said hopefully.

"Small weekly payments," said the music teacher.

"—talent," said Laurie.

"The house is full of poison gas," I said.

"I'll practice in the barn," Laurie said.

"The house is full of—"

"He *said* he'd practice in the barn," the music teacher added sharply.

"His father doesn't even know about the *refrigerator* yet," I said. "How can I tell him it's a trumpet too?"

"I'll send you an illustrated brochure," the music teacher said.

"Well, *you* sure weren't very polite to *her*," Laurie said to me as the music teacher went out the door of the soda shop. "All she wants is to develop my talent."

I took the children back to school half an hour late. Barry and Sally and the dog and I came home, to find that the refrigerator people were already there. They had a huge truck and a dolly for carrying the refrigerator, and they backed the truck over the lawn and over my rosebush to the back steps, and they put handkerchiefs over their faces and went in and got the refrigerator with a good deal of grunting and complaining. The dog and Barry and Sally and I stood on the porch watching. I felt a pang, seeing the old refrigerator go—I had had it for thirteen years, after all—but with the back door open I could smell that horrible smell clearly, and the dog put his head into the kitchen once and then went back and climbed in through the car window and sat in the car for the rest of the afternoon. Just as they were wheeling the refrigerator across a bridge of planks and onto the truck my husband arrived in a taxi. "Is everyone all right?" he asked me, and I said yes, everyone except the dog, although I personally did not think my head would clear for several days. My husband put his head inside the kitchen door and breathed deeply and then backed up, coughing. "Golly," he said.

"It's much better now," I told him. "The man opened all the windows and doors and it's clearing out fast."

"What are you going to do with it?" my husband asked the men, who were settling the refrigerator onto the truck.

"Take it down to the dump and throw it in," one of the men said grimly. "This kind of thing is *dangerous*."

"But wait a minute," I said, suddenly realizing that it was my refrigerator going off like this. "What about the milk and the butter and the eggs and the cold chicken? And the fruit juice and the cheese—"

"You wouldn't want *this* food no more, lady," the truck man said. He slapped the side of the refrigerator and laughed. "I wouldn't even want to *show* it to you."

"Oh, dear," I said helplessly. The men got into the truck, and as it started to pull away from the porch the car of the salesman from the refrigerator company turned into the driveway.

Since I had been talking about a new refrigerator for a number of years, I was able, unhesitatingly, to put my finger on the precise one I wanted; I even knew the page in the catalogue where its picture was. They let us go back into the house so my husband could write a check. We kept all the doors and windows open and by the time they delivered the new refrigerator late that afternoon the gas was almost gone. My husband, shaken and pale, was sitting in the study looking at his checkbook. The new refrigerator was glittering and bright, rich with shelves that pulled out and pushed in, and freezing compartments and little plastic boxes for keeping things and racks and bottle holders and vegetable bins and it was absolutely silent. Experimentally, the children and I put a jar of jelly on the top shelf. Finally, I went timidly into the study and explained to my husband that all our food had gone away with the old refrigerator and I was terribly sorry but I was afraid that I needed some money because otherwise there would not be anything for dinner; and I knew he had been dined so well in Burlington.

The refrigerator man had told me to boil all the dishes on the table, and anything else which had been exposed to the gas, and after I had boiled all the dishes I was prepared to take a fairly strong stand on the subject of a dishwasher, since the refrigerator people handled dishwashers too and would give us quite a nice discount if we bought them both at once, and there was, in fact, the exact dishwasher I had been wanting for so long, only a page or two past the refrigerator in the catalogue. I went into the study diffidently and told my husband all this, adding that I was terribly sorry but I was afraid that I needed a dishwasher because my hands were so red and rough from washing all those dishes that I was probably not going to be able to do anything else for a long time, and besides, I told him thoughtfully, it did not become a professional beauty contest judge to have a wife with hands toil-worn from housework.

When the dishwasher was installed the next day I went to work and washed all the dishes I owned; it took six loads. It was nice to have everything so clean and sparkling, but the children and I felt that although the refrigerator and the dishwasher looked nice in the kitchen, and there is nothing really shabby about our nice kitchen range, although it is six years old, the kitchen floor, which was done by a previous owner in dark red and brown linoleum, was disgraceful. It quite took away the charm of the acres of white porcelain in the kitchen. I went into the study and told my husband that the kitchen linoleum was shocking, and suppose some of his new friends should decide to visit him, how would he feel about the shocking kitchen floor? We decided on a nice light green, with red and blue and yellow polka dots, and I got a new tablecloth to match it. Laurie and I decided that during the following winter we would paint all the kitchen woodwork yellow.

What with all the installations and getting the linoleum down it was nearly two weeks before we were back to normal, but one Saturday morning at last I was in my bright kitchen, putting dishes into the dishwasher and wondering why I had not had a dishwasher long ago, when Laurie came unhappily down the back stairs and into the kitchen. "Listen," he said.

"Yes?"

"Dad home?"

"He's gone down to get a haircut. Why?"

"Well, look." Laurie shuffled his feet, ran his fingers through his hair, and sighed. "Look," he said.

"Well?" I said.

"You know the sodium bisulphite Dad gave me to do in my chemistry set?"

"Yes. I mean, I guess so."

"Well." Laurie hesitated. "I lost it," he said.

"That's too bad."

"I put it in a pan with the acid I was using and put it on the radiator there and you remember how cold it was just before we got the new refrigerator because we all said it was too cold for late spring? And the radiator must of gone on? And now I found the little pan but it's *empty*."

I turned around slowly and looked at him. "Laurie," I said, "that sodium what-do-you-call-it and the other stuff mixed together—what would they do?"

"I don't know," Laurie said. "That's what I was going to find out. Why—you know where it is?"

I looked around at my lovely kitchen, with the polka dots on the floor and the new refrigerator glowing, its great shelves heavy with the fancy foods I had never been able to fit into the old one, at my dishwasher and my new tablecloth. "Maybe you'd better just not mention it to Dad just yet," I said.

"You think he might worry?"

"Well, yes," I said. "I think he might." I closed the dishwasher affectionately.

"You think he'd take away my chemistry set?"

"I'm almost certain of it," I said.

"*Then* can I learn to play the trumpet?"

Before the children were able to start counting days till school was out, and before Laurie had learned to play more than a simple scale on the trumpet, and even before my husband's portable radio had gone in for its annual checkup so it could broadcast the Brooklyn games all summer, we found ourselves deeply involved in the Little League. The Little League was new in our town that year. One day all the kids were playing baseball in vacant lots and without any noticeable good sportsmanship, and the next day, almost, we were standing around the grocery and the post office wondering what kind of a manager young Johnny Cole was going to make, and whether the Weaver boy—the one with the strong arm—was going to be twelve this August, or only eleven as his mother said, and Bill Cummings had donated his bulldozer to level off the top of Sugar Hill, where the kids used to go sledding, and we were all sporting stickers on our cars reading "We have contributed" and the fund-raising campaign was over the top in forty-eight hours. There are a thousand people in our town, and it turned out, astonishingly, that about sixty of them were boys of Little League age. Laurie thought he'd try out for pitcher and his friend Billy went out for catcher. Dinnertime all over town got shifted to eight-thirty in the evening, when nightly baseball practice was over. By the time our family had become accustomed to the fact that no single problem in our house could be allowed to interfere in any way with the tempering of Laurie's right arm, the uniforms had been ordered, and four teams had been chosen and named, and Laurie and Billy were together on the Little League Braves. My friend Dot, Billy's mother, was learning to keep a box score. I announced in family assembly that there would be no more oiling of baseball gloves in the kitchen sink.

We lived only a block or so from the baseball field, and it became the amiable custom of the ballplayers to drop in for a snack on their way to the practice sessions. There was to be a double-header on Memorial Day, to open the season. The Braves would play the Giants; the Red Sox would play the Dodgers. After one silent, apoplectic moment my husband agreed, gasping, to come to the ball games and root against the Dodgers. A rumor got around town that the Red Sox were the team to watch, with Butch Weaver's strong arm, and several mothers believed absolutely that the various managers were putting their own sons into all the best positions, although everyone told everyone else that it didn't matter, really, *what* position the boys held so long as they got a chance to play ball, and show they were good sports about it. As a matter of fact, the night before the double-header which was to open the Little League, I distinctly recall that I told Laurie it was only a game. "It's only a game, fella," I said. "Don't *try* to go to sleep; read or something if you're nervous. Would you like an aspirin?"

"I forgot to tell you," Laurie said, yawning. "He's pitching Georgie tomorrow. Not me."

"*What?*" I thought, and then said heartily, "I mean, he's the manager, after all. I know you'll play your best in *any* position."

"I could go to sleep now if you'd just turn out the light," Laurie said patiently. "I'm really quite tired."

I called Dot later, about twelve o'clock, because I was pretty sure she'd still be awake, and of course she was, although Billy had gone right off about nine o'clock. She said she wasn't the least bit nervous, because of course it didn't really matter except for the kids' sake, and she hoped the best team would win. I said that that was just what I had been telling my husband, and she said *her* husband had suggested that perhaps she had better not go to the game at all because if the Braves lost she ought to be home with a hot bath ready for Billy and perhaps a steak dinner or something. I said that even if Laurie wasn't pitching I was sure the Braves would win, and of course I wasn't one of those people who always wanted their own children right out in the center of things all the time but if the Braves lost it would be my opinion that their lineup ought to be revised and Georgie put back into right field where he belonged. She said *she* thought Laurie was a better pitcher, and I suggested that she and her husband and Billy come over for lunch and we could all go to the game to-gether.

I spent all morning taking movies of the Memorial Day parade, particularly the Starlight 4-H Club, because Jannie was marching with them, and I used up almost a whole film magazine on Sally and Barry, standing at the curb, wide-eyed and rapt, waving flags. Laurie missed the parade because he slept until nearly twelve, and then came downstairs and made himself an enormous platter of bacon and eggs and toast, which he took out to the hammock and ate lying down.

"How do you feel?" I asked him, coming out to feel his forehead. "Did you sleep all right? How's your arm?"

"Sure," he said.

We cooked lunch outdoors, and Laurie finished his breakfast in time to eat three hamburgers. Dot had only a cup of coffee, and I took a little salad. Every now and then she would ask Billy if he wanted to lie down for a little while before the game, and I would ask Laurie how he felt. The game was not until two o'clock, so there was time for Jannie and Sally and Barry to roast marshmallows. Laurie and Billy went into the barn to warm up with a game of ping-pong, and Billy's father remarked that the boys certainly took this Little League setup seriously, and my husband said that it was the best thing in the world for the kids. When the boys came out of the barn after playing three games of ping-pong I asked Billy if he was feeling all right and Dot said she thought Laurie ought to lie down for a while before the game. The boys said no, they had to meet the other guys at the school at one-thirty and they were going to get into their uniforms now. I said please to be careful, and Dot said if they needed any help dressing just call down and we would come up, and both boys turned and looked at us curiously for a minute before they went indoors.

"My goodness," I said to Dot, "I hope they're not nervous."

"Well, they take it so seriously," she said.

I sent the younger children in to wash the marshmallow off their faces, and while our husbands settled down to read over the Little League rule book, Dot and I cleared away the paper plates and gave the leftover hamburgers to the dog. Suddenly Dot said, "Oh," in a weak voice and I turned around and Laurie and Billy were coming through the door in their uniforms. "They look so—so—*tall*," Dot said, and I said, "Laurie?" uncertainly. The boys laughed, and looked at each other.

"Pretty neat," Laurie said, looking at Billy.

"Some get-up," Billy said, regarding Laurie.

Both fathers came over and began turning the boys around and around, and Jannie and Sally came out onto the porch and stared worshipfully. Barry, to whom Laurie and his friends have always seemed incredibly tall and efficient, gave them a critical glance and observed that this was truly a baseball.

It turned out that there was a good deal of advice the fathers still needed to give the ballplayers, so they elected to walk over to the school with Billy and Laurie and then on to the ball park, where they would find Dot and me later. We watched them walk down the street; not far away they were joined by another boy in uniform and then a couple more. After that, for about half an hour, there were boys in uniform wandering by twos and threes toward the baseball field and the school, all alike in a kind of unexpected dignity and new tallness, all walking with self-conscious pride. Jannie and Sally stood on the front porch watching, careful to greet by name all the ballplayers going by.

A few minutes before two, Dot and I put the younger children in her car and drove over to the field. Assuming that perhaps seventy-five of the people in our town were actively engaged in the baseball game, there should have been about nine hundred and twenty-five people in the audience, but there seemed to be more than that already; Dot and I both remarked that it was the first town affair we had ever attended where there were more strange faces than familiar ones.

Although the field itself was completely finished, there was only one set of bleachers up, and that was filled, so Dot and I took the car robe and settled ourselves on top of the little hill over the third-base line, where we had a splendid view of the whole field. We talked about how it was at the top of this hill the kids used to start their sleds, coasting right down past third base and on into center field, where the ground flattened out and the sleds would stop. From the little hill we could see the roofs of the houses in the town below, half hidden in the trees, and far on to the hills in the distance. We both remarked that there was still snow on the high mountain.

Barry stayed near us, deeply engaged with a little dump truck. Jannie and Sally accepted twenty-five cents each, and melted into the crowd in the general direction of the refreshment stand. Dot got out her pencil and box score, and I put a new magazine of film in the movie camera. We could see our husbands standing around in back of the Braves' dugout, along with the fathers of all the other

Braves players. They were all in a group, chatting with great humorous informality with the manager and the two coaches of the Braves. The fathers of the boys on the Giant team were down by the Giant dugout, standing around the manager and the coaches of the Giants.

Marian, a friend of Dot's and mine whose boy Artie was first baseman for the Giants, came hurrying past looking for a seat, and we offered her part of our car robe. She sat down, breathless, and said she had mislaid her husband and her younger son, so we showed her where her husband was down by the Giant dugout with the other fathers, and her younger son turned up almost at once to say that Sally had a popsicle and so could he have one, too, and a hot dog and maybe some popcorn?

Suddenly, from far down the block, we could hear the high school band playing "The Stars and Stripes Forever," and coming closer. Everyone stood up to watch and then the band turned the corner and came through the archway with the official Little League insignia and up to the entrance of the field. All the ballplayers were marching behind the band. I thought foolishly of Laurie when he was Barry's age, and something of the sort must have crossed Dot's mind, because she reached out and put her hand on Barry's head. "There's Laurie and Billy," Barry said softly. The boys ran out onto the field and lined up along the base lines, and then I discovered that we were all cheering, with Barry jumping up and down and shouting, "Baseball! Baseball!"

"If you cry I'll tell Laurie," Dot said to me out of the corner of her mouth.

"Same to you," I said, blinking.

The sky was blue and the sun was bright and the boys

stood lined up soberly in their clean new uniforms holding their caps while the band played "The Star-Spangled Banner" and the flag was raised. From Laurie and Billy, who were among the tallest, down to the littlest boys in uniform, there was a straight row of still, expectant faces.

I said, inadequately, "It must be hot out there."

"They're all chewing gum," Dot said.

Then the straight lines broke and the Red Sox, who had red caps, and the Dodgers, who had blue caps, went off into the bleachers and the Giants, who had green caps, went into their dugout, and at last the Braves, who had black caps, trotted out onto the field. It was announced over the public-address system that the Braves were the home team, and when it was announced that Georgie was going to pitch for the Braves I told Marian that I was positively relieved, since Laurie had been so nervous anyway over the game that I was sure pitching would have been a harrowing experience for him, and she said that Artie had been perfectly willing to sit out the game as a substitute, or a pinch hitter, or something, but that his manager had insisted upon putting him at first base because he was so reliable.

"You know," she added with a little laugh, "*I* don't know one position from another, but of course Artie is glad to play anywhere."

"I'm sure he'll do very nicely," I said, trying to put some enthusiasm into my voice.

Laurie was on second base for the Braves, and Billy at first. Marian leaned past me to tell Dot that first base was a *very* responsible position, and Dot said oh, was it? Because of course Billy just wanted to do the best he could for the team, and on the *Braves* it was the *manager* who assigned the positions. Marian smiled in what I thought was a nasty kind of way and said she hoped the best team would win. Dot and I both smiled back and said we hoped so, too.

When the umpire shouted, "Play Ball!" people all over the park began to call out to the players, and I raised my voice slightly and said, "Hurray for the Braves." That encouraged Dot and *she* called out, "Hurray for the Braves," but Marian, of course, had to say, "Hurray for the Giants."

The first Giant batter hit a triple, although, as my husband explained later, it would actually have been an infield fly if the shortstop had been looking and an easy out if he had thrown it anywhere near Billy at first. By the time Billy got the ball back into the infield the batter—Jimmie Hill, who had once borrowed Laurie's bike and brought it back with a flat tire—was on third. I could see Laurie out on second base banging his hands together and he looked so pale I was worried. Marian leaned around me and said to Dot, "That was a nice try Billy made. I don't think even *Artie* could have caught that ball."

"He looks *furious*," Dot said to me. "He just *hates* doing things wrong."

"They're all terribly nervous," I assured her. "They'll settle down as soon as they really get playing." I raised my voice a little. "Hurray for the Braves," I said.

The Giants made six runs in the first inning, and each time a run came in Marian looked sympathetic and told us that really, the boys were being quite good sports about it, weren't they? When Laurie bobbled an easy fly right at second and missed the out, she said to me that Artie had told her that Laurie was really quite a good little ballplayer and I mustn't blame him for an occasional error.

By the time little Jerry Hart finally struck out to retire

the Giants, Dot and I were sitting listening with polite smiles. I had stopped saying "Hurray for the Braves." Marian had told everyone sitting near us that it was her boy who had slid home for the sixth run, and she had explained with great kindness that Dot and I had sons on the other team, one of them the first baseman who missed that long throw and the other one the second baseman who dropped the fly ball. The Giants took the field and Marian pointed out Artie standing on first base slapping his glove and showing off.

Then little Ernie Harrow, who was the Braves' right-fielder and lunched frequently at our house, hit the first pitched ball for a fast grounder which went right through the legs of the Giant center-fielder, and when Ernie came dancing onto second Dot leaned around to remark to Marian that if Artie had been playing closer to first the way Billy did he might have been ready for the throw if the Giant center-fielder had managed to stop the ball. Billy came up and smashed a long fly over the left-fielder's head and I put a hand on Marian's shoulder to hoist myself up. Dot and I stood there howling, "Run run run," Billy came home, and two runs were in. Little Andy placed a surprise bunt down the first-base line, Artie never even saw it, and I leaned over to tell Marian that clearly Artie did not understand all the refinements of playing first base. Then Laurie got a nice hit and slid into second. The Giants took out their pitcher and put in Buddy Williams, whom Laurie once beat up on the way to school. The score was tied with two out and Dot and I were both yelling. Then little Ernie Harrow came up for the second time and hit a home run, right over the fence where they put the sign advertising his father's sand and gravel. We were leading eight to six when the inning ended.

Little League games are six innings, so we had five more innings to go. Dot went down to the refreshment stand to get some hot dogs and soda; she offered very politely to bring something for Marian, but Marian said thank you, no; she would get her own. The second inning tightened up considerably as the boys began to get over their stage fright and play baseball the way they did in the vacant lots. By the middle of the fifth inning the Braves were leading nine to eight, and then in the bottom of the fifth Artie missed a throw at first base and the Braves scored another run. Neither Dot nor I said a single word, but Marian got up in a disagreeable manner, excused herself, and went to sit on the other side of the field.

"Marian looks very poorly these days," I remarked to Dot as we watched her go.

"She's at *least* five years older than *I* am," Dot said.

"More than that," I said. "She's gotten very touchy, don't you think?"

"Poor little Artie," Dot said. "You remember when he used to have temper tantrums in nursery school?"

In the top of the sixth the Braves were winning ten to eight, but then Georgie, who had been pitching accurately and well, began to tire, and he walked the first two batters. The third boy hit a little fly which fell in short center field, and one run came in to make it ten to nine. Then Georgie, who was by now visibly rattled, walked the next batter and filled the bases.

"Three more outs and the Braves can win it," some man in the crowd behind us said. "I don't *think*," and he laughed.

"Oh, *lord*," Dot said, and I stood up and began to wail, "No, no." The manager was gesturing at Laurie and Billy. "No, no," I said to Dot, and Dot said, "He can't do it, don't let him." "It's too much to ask of the children," I said. "What a terrible thing to do to such little kids," Dot said.

"New pitcher," the man in the crowd said. "He better be good," and he laughed.

While Laurie was warming up and Billy was getting into his catcher's equipment, I suddenly heard my husband's voice for the first time. This was the only baseball game my husband had ever attended outside of Ebbetts Field. "Put it in his ear, Laurie," my husband was yelling, "put it in his ear."

Laurie was chewing gum and throwing slowly and carefully. Barry took a minute off from the little truck he was placidly filling with sand and emptying again to ask me if the big boys were still playing baseball. I stood there, feeling Dot's shoulder shaking against mine, and I tried to get my camera open to check the magazine of film but my fingers kept slipping and jumping against the little knob. I said to Dot that I guessed I would just enjoy the game for a while and not take pictures, and she said earnestly that Billy had had a little touch of fever that morning and the manager was taking his life in his hands putting Billy up there in all that catcher's equipment in that hot shade. I wondered if Laurie could see that I was nervous.

"*He* doesn't look very nervous," I said to Dot, but then my voice failed, and I finished, "does he?" in a sort of gasp.

The batter was Jimmie Hill, who had already had three hits that afternoon. Laurie's first pitch hit the dust at Billy's feet and Billy sprawled full length to stop it. The man in the crowd behind us laughed. The boy on third hesitated, unsure whether Billy had the ball; he started for home and then, with his mother just outside the third-base line yelling, "Go back, go back," he retreated to third again.

Laurie's second pitch sent Billy rocking backward and he fell; "Only way he can stop it is fall on it," the man in the crowd said, and laughed.

Dot stiffened, and then she turned around slowly. For a minute she stared and then she said, in the evilest voice I have ever heard her use, "Sir, that catcher is my son."

"I beg your pardon, ma'am, I'm sure," the man said.

"Picking on little boys," Dot said.

The umpire called Laurie's next pitch ball three, although it was clearly a strike, and I was yelling, "You're blind, you're blind." I could hear my husband shouting to throw the bum out.

"Going to see a new pitcher pretty soon," said the man in the crowd, and I clenched my fist, and turned around and said in a voice that made Dot's sound cordial, "Sir, that pitcher is *my* son. If you have any more personal remarks to make about any member of my family—"

"Or mine," Dot added.

"I will immediately call Mr. Tillotson, our local constable, and see personally that you are put out of this ball park. People who go around attacking ladies and innocent children—"

"Strike," the umpire said.

I turned around once more and shook my fist at the man in the crowd, and he announced quietly and with some humility that he hoped both teams would win, and subsided into absolute silence.

Laurie then pitched two more strikes, his nice fast ball, and I thought suddenly of how at lunch he and Billy had been tossing hamburger rolls and Dot and I had made them stop. At about this point, Dot and I abandoned our spot up on the hill and got down against the fence with our faces pressed against the wire. "Come on, Billy boy," Dot was saying over and over, "come on, Billy boy," and I found that I was telling Laurie, "Come on now, only two more outs to go, only two more, come on, Laurie, come on. . . ." I could see my husband now but there was too much noise to hear him; he was pounding his hands against the fence. Dot's husband had *his* hands over his face and his back turned to the ball field. "He can't hit it, Laurie," Dot yelled, "this guy can't hit," which I thought with dismay was not true; the batter was Butch Weaver and he was standing there swinging his bat and sneering. "Laurie, Laurie, Laurie," screeched a small voice; I looked down and it was Sally, bouncing happily beside me. "Can I have another nickel?" she asked. "Laurie, Laurie."

"Strike," the umpire said and I leaned my forehead against the cool wire and said in a voice that suddenly had no power at all, "Just two strikes, Laurie, just two more strikes."

Laurie looked at Billy, shook his head, and looked again. He grinned and when I glanced down at Billy I could see that behind the mask he was grinning too. Laurie pitched, and the batter swung wildly. "Laurie, Laurie," Sally shrieked. "Strike two," the umpire said. Dot and I grabbed at each other's hands and Laurie threw the good fast ball for strike three.

One out to go, and Laurie, Billy, and the shortstop stood together on the mound for a minute. They talked very soberly, but Billy was grinning again as he came back to the plate. Since I was incapable of making any sound, I hung onto the wire and promised myself that if Laurie struck out this last batter I would never never say another word to him about the mess in his room, I would not make him paint the lawn chairs, I would not even mention clipping the hedge. . . . "Ball one," the umpire said, and I found that I had my voice back. "Crook," I yelled, "blind crook."

Laurie pitched, the batter swung, and hit a high foul ball back of the plate; Billy threw off his mask and tottered, staring up. The batter, the boys on the field, and the umpire, waited, and Dot suddenly spoke.

"William," she said imperatively, "*you catch that ball.*"

Then everyone was shouting wildly; I looked at Dot and said, "Golly." Laurie and Billy were slapping and hugging each other, and then the rest of the team came around them and the manager was there. I distinctly saw my husband, who is not a lively man, vault the fence to run into the wild group and slap Laurie on the shoulder with one hand and Billy with the other. The Giants gathered around their manager and gave a cheer for the Braves, and the Braves gathered around *their* manager and gave a cheer for the Giants, and Laurie and Billy came pacing together toward the dugout, past Dot and me. I said, "Laurie?" and Dot said, "Billy?" They stared at us, without recognition for a minute, both of them lost in another world, and then they smiled and Billy said, "Hi, Ma," and Laurie said, "You see the game?"

I realized that my hair was over my eyes and I had broken two fingernails. Dot had a smudge on her nose and had torn a button off her sweater. We helped each other up the hill again and found that Barry was asleep on the car robe. Without speaking any more than was absolutely necessary, Dot and I decided that we could not stay for the second game of the double-header. I carried Barry asleep and Dot brought his dump truck and the car robe and my camera and the box score which she had not kept past the first Giant run, and we headed wearily for the car.

We passed Artie in his green Giant cap and we said it had been a fine game, he had played wonderfully well, and he laughed and said tolerantly, "Can't win 'em all, you know." When we got back to our house I put Barry into his bed while Dot put on the kettle for a nice cup of tea. We washed our faces and took off our shoes, and finally Dot said hesitantly that she certainly hoped that Marian wasn't really offended with us.

"Well, of course she takes this kind of thing terribly hard," I said.

"I was just thinking," Dot said after a minute, "we ought to plan a kind of victory party for the Braves at the end of the season."

"A hot-dog roast, maybe?" I suggested.

"Well," Dot said, "I *did* hear the boys talking one day. They said they were going to take some time this summer and clean out your barn, and set up a record player in there and put in a stock of records and have some dances."

"You mean . . ." I faltered. "With *girls?*"

Dot nodded.

"Oh," I said.

When our husbands came home two hours later we were talking about old high school dances and the time we went out with those boys from Princeton. Our husbands reported that the Red Sox had beaten the Dodgers in the second game and were tied for first place with the Braves. Jannie and Sally came idling home, and finally Laurie and Billy stopped in, briefly, to change their clothes. There was a pickup game down in Murphy's lot, they explained, and they were going to play some baseball.

FOUR

THAT SUMMER WAS one of the hottest we had ever had, and I got sunburned sitting on the hill over third base. The day Laurie pitched a no-hit shut-out I thought I had sunstroke. In the middle of the fifth inning, when people began murmuring in the bleachers, and counting every strike, I went up over the top of the hill and down the other side to where there was a tree and some grass and I sat there; I could not see the ball field, but I could hear the umpire's calls and, then, the excitement rising. I sat in the shade and figured out that there were only seventeen more days before school started. Sally and Jannie were going to need new winter coats; a year from now I would be getting Barry ready for kindergarten. The first winter we were in our new house, when Laurie used to go sledding on this hill, he could stand just about where I was sitting now, and see our back porch, and I used to signal him that it was time to come home by hanging a dish towel over the porch rail; I could not see the back porch now because the trees were still thick. In another few weeks, I thought, the leaves would be coming down again. School, birthdays,

Thanksgiving, Christmas, the long spring days, and then another summer. I could hear cheering from the ball field. The years go by so quickly, I thought, rising; he used to be so small.

The last few days of summer go faster, though, than any other time of year. In honor of Sally's entrance into second grade, and Jannie's triumphant arrival at fifth grade, I sat them down one evening and, with my husband's help and much advice and laughter from Laurie and Barry, cut their hair short. Both girls, enchanted with their light heads, admiring each other, feeling incredulously at the cut ends, began to cry when they saw their own hair which I carefully put away in a package in my dresser. At that time Laurie was wearing his hair long, and cultivated into a careful wave over his forehead, by means of the adhesive assistance of several evil-smelling compounds. "Hello, little girl," Sally said repeatedly to Laurie, and, to Jannie, "Hello, little boy." Barry asked for a set of cowboy holsters for his approaching fourth birthday. Dikidiki, old and shabby but still perceptibly blue, slept now in a small bed made for him by Laurie, with a pillow sewed by Jannie and a coverlet decorated with crayon pictures by Sally. Dikidiki slept almost all the time, day and night, until something troubled Barry, or angered him, and then he would go to his room and get Dikidiki and they would retreat together to the far corner of the guest room and sit behind the window curtain. Sally and Jannie were allowed to buy one book a week each, from their allowances, and Laurie one popular tune arranged for the trumpet.

Toby, who was finding the summers hotter than they used to be when he was a puppy, suffered a good deal, walking back and forth to the ball field after Laurie. In addition to a certain amount of stiffness in his old joints, a malady which my husband and I regarded with ready sympathy after a summer of sitting on the car robe on a grassy hill over the ball field, his fear of thunderstorms, always acute, increased with advancing age. He could sense thunder long before it was audible to the rest of us, and all that summer the first intimation that the ball game might be rained out was Toby, heading home in a black streak.

Yain had been rudely jolted out of his fool's paradise by finding that there was another cat in the world, after all; one day Jannie came home from the ball field with a tiny, frightened black kitten which had been wandering pathetically around the refreshment stand. Could we keep it, she wanted to know, it would be her cat and she would promise to take care of it all by herself and no one else wanted it and it would *die* and if she promised to take care of it could she keep it for her very own? I said that I supposed it would be all right because our quarantine on cats was nearly ended. After a couple of days of heavy cream and fresh meat and raw eggs beaten in milk, and regular brushing with Jannie's doll hairbrush, the little kitten was sleek and shining, and wholly unafraid of Yain, who loathed him. Jannie named the kitten Stardust, but the rest of us called him Gato.

"You see," Laurie explained to Jannie, "Stardust is all right for a name for *people* and stuff, but a cat should have a decent name."

"I used to have a cat named Creampuff," I said defensively.

"I bet you did, too, kid," Laurie said. "And you never learned to ice skate, or to sled."

"I *couldn't*," I said. "There wasn't any *snow*." I thought, staring out the kitchen window reminiscently, "The first snowsuit I ever saw was the one Laurie had when he was a baby. I used to read about snow, and I saw pictures of it, but until I was grown up and came to live in the East I couldn't really imagine what it was like." Looking out at the lawn, I thought of the drifts piling up against the hedge, and the wind whipping past the back door, and the icy sidewalks, and I shivered. "I didn't know when I was well off," I said.

Jannie prompted me, softly. "And you used to live next door to a candy factory. . . ."

"To a man who *owned* a candy factory. Mr. Thompson. And just before Christmas every year he would take my brother and me to visit his candy factory."

"—and he would tell you to eat all you wanted—" Jannie went on.

"And on the first floor," Laurie came in, "were the people making little hard Christmas candies, and ribbon candy, and candy canes, and you and your brother always tried to remember not to take a candy cane because they lasted so long you had to leave out some other things—"

"And on the second floor they were making caramels, with big pots boiling and if you took a caramel you had to keep chewing on it and you missed the fudge—" Jannie said.

"And on the third floor they were making little mints, peppermint and lemon and orange and cinnamon, and if you took a cinnamon one it was so peppery you couldn't taste anything for a long time—" Laurie continued.

"And on the *top* floor," Jannie said, "were the ladies dipping chocolates, and when you got way up there you were so full of candy canes and cinnamon mints and cara-mels you couldn't eat any chocolates."

"But he always gave us a little box to take home with us," I said. "We used to put the little boxes under the Christmas tree. He was very nice, Mr. Thompson."

"Everything was much nicer in the olden days," Jannie said.

Sally said, "Uncle Louis says that when *he* was a little boy they had to chase him to school with a stick."

"They're going to have to chase *me*, boy," Laurie said grimly. "Only two weeks from Tuesday. Golly."

"Uncle Louis said when someone gives you a hamburger it isn't polite to look inside to see if they put a two-inch salute firecracker in, and so Uncle Louis didn't, but Mr. Feeley already had, and Uncle Louis got relish in his hair when it blew up."

"You know what I think?" Laurie said, coming to look out the window with me, "I think next summer maybe I'll get a job, like down at Mike's delivering groceries. I bet I could earn plenty that way, and then someday when I had enough I could get a little sports car. Boy," he said. "Dig me driving a red and white M.G. to school."

By the Saturday before Labor Day a decided atmosphere of cool restraint had taken over our house, because on Thursday my husband had received a letter from an old school friend of his named Sylvia, saying that she and an-other girl were driving through New England on a vaca-tion and would just *adore* stopping by for the weekend to renew old friendships. My husband gave me the letter to read, and I held it very carefully by the edges and said that it was positively touching, the way he kept up with his old friends, and did Sylvia always use pale lavender paper with this kind of rosy ink and what was that I smelled—perfume? My husband said Sylvia was a grand girl. I said I was sure of it. My husband said Sylvia had always been one of the nicest people he knew. I said I hadn't a doubt. My husband said that he was positive that I was going to love Sylvia on sight. I opened my mouth to speak but stopped myself in time.

My husband laughed self-consciously. "I remember," he said, and then his voice trailed off and he laughed again.

"Yes?" I asked politely.

"Nothing," he said.

I set the letter down tenderly in the center of his desk and said well, I guessed I had better get along to the breakfast dishes and he said that reminded him. "Sylvia," he said. "She's always so neat. *You* know. Nail polish, and things like that."

I put my hands in back of me and said yes, I understood.

"I would take it as a personal kindness if things looked a little better than usual this weekend when Sylvia comes. Sort of spruced up—maybe wash the children and stuff. Everything nice." He gestured. "*You* know," he said.

"By all means," I said warmly. "I wouldn't for anything in the world have Sylvia see the house looking the way it usually does. I shall go at once and mend that broken board in the front steps."

"What?" my husband said, but I closed the study door softly behind me, stood in the hall and counted to a thousand. Then I stamped up to the guest room, where I swept the cobwebs off the ceiling as though I were pulling hair and completely wrecked what little nail polish I had opening the side guest room window so I could shake the mop out over the open study window just below. I took the guest room curtains down to wash and the curtain rod fell on my head. I scrubbed the bathroom floor and cleaned out the closet and washed down the hall woodwork and cleaned all the upstairs ashtrays and then I took a shower and came downstairs and made dinner. I was feeling very righteous and forgiving until my husband glanced down at his veal cutlet and asked absently if he had remembered to tell me that his friend Sylvia was a marvelous cook.

On Friday morning I vacuumed all the downstairs rooms and washed down more woodwork and did the kitchen curtains and scrubbed the kitchen floor and polished the copper bottoms on the saucepans and dusted the living room and washed the glass in the front door and cleaned off the top of my desk and carefully put my leaking fountain pen down on my husband's class notes. Then I put furniture polish on the dining room table and the two sideboards and washed the piano keys and cleaned all the downstairs ashtrays. I washed all the clock faces and the television screen. I arranged my husband's collection of canes in the front hall. I swept the front porch and the back porch and went out with a damp cloth and cleaned off the lawn chairs. I called the grocer and ordered two ducklings to roast for Saturday dinner and said I would take two dozen ears of corn if it was fresh picked. Then I took a shower and came downstairs and made dinner and remarked to my husband that we were having roast duckling for dinner on Saturday night and at first he looked pleased, then he said in a worried voice that lots of people didn't care for roast duckling and maybe I'd better make it ribroast or something instead because he didn't want Sylvia to get a wrong impression.

On Saturday morning I woke up with my fists clenched and my teeth grinding and got out of bed telling myself that today I was not going to say an unnecessary word to anybody and I was going to smile all day long and I was going to keep my temper, keep my temper, keep my temper. I sang a careless little French song while I dressed myself and brushed my hair and then I let up the shade with a snap that was sure to wake my husband with a jolt. I stopped singing and nearly went back to bed, because it was raining outside. The last Saturday morning before school started, Labor Day weekend, summer's closing, and it was raining. Laurie was supposed to play baseball that afternoon. Jannie had engaged to walk down to the library with her friend Carole, where the two of them were permitted to check books in and out if their hands were clean. Sally had been invited to visit a neighbor's sandbox. I had thought to put Barry outdoors riding his bike while I finished up the housework. Laurie had his trumpet lesson on Saturday morning and this meant that I would have to drive him and trumpet there and back. For a minute I wondered whether I had left the guest room curtains out on the line, but of course I had.

"—Saturday?" my husband inquired drowsily.

"Saturday," I confirmed, using no unnecessary words. "Rain."

"Sylvia's coming."

I kicked his slippers under the bed and started downstairs. Barry fell in behind me as I passed his doorway; he must have seen that it was raining, because he was carrying Dikidiki. Sally capered out of her room singing her song about Harf, Booney, and Ray, three giants whom I did not ordinarily find tiresome and revolting. Our guests were due about two o'clock. Sally and Barry had been washing paint-brushes in the clean bathroom.

Behind me on the stairs Barry was making plans. "Because today is his *birthday*, Dikidiki Bear, and we will have a party for him, and all the bears and rabbits and dolls and even Skunk will come."

"And Mommy will make Dikidiki Bear a little cake," Sally said joyfully. "And we will wrap little presents and Mommy will make some lemonade to put in the doll dishes and a little cake and we can all have some candy."

Without employing an unnecessary word I plugged in the coffeepot and sent Barry up to wake his brother and Sally up to wake her sister, and I let the dog out and the cats in. I gathered up the dripping morning paper and declined to answer when my husband came downstairs and remarked that it *would* have to rain this weekend. I did not speak when Laurie smashed down the stairs into the kitchen and pointed with a furious finger to the rain running down the kitchen window. I closed my eyes in patient silence when Jannie remarked from upstairs that it always rained, *always*, when she had something planned and this just settled it, that was all. My husband told Sally and Barry about the nice lady who was coming to visit and added that if they behaved quietly and docilely all weekend they would each have a present on Monday morning, and Dikidiki Bear, too. Jannie came downstairs carrying her raincoat and her library books and remarked drearily that this was the kind of thing that always happened to her, *always*. My husband went to the kitchen window and looked out and then turned to me.

"Do you think it will rain all weekend?" he asked.

"Yes," I said.

After breakfast Sally and Barry retired to the playroom to brush and beribbon Dikidiki and his relatives. I drove Laurie to his trumpet lesson and came home and gathered up the breakfast dishes and put them in the dishwasher, trusting that I would get down to sweep the kitchen floor before two o'clock, and trudged upstairs to finish off my housework.

It was the morning to change all the sheets and because I detest changing sheets I wanted to get it done quickly so I could make a lemon pie for dinner and maybe even get a chance to sit down for a few minutes before two o'clock. I gathered up ten clean sheets and six pillowcases and went first into Barry's room, where I removed six teddy bears—cousins of Dikidiki Bear not yet invited to the party—a green rabbit, two hidden lollipops, and a wooden train from the bed, shifted the bed very cautiously in case Yain had been chasing Gato again and Gato was hiding here, and stripped and made the bed, neglecting square corners in favor of speed. Then I took up my armload of linen and made my way into Sally's room, sighed, and removed from her bed a stack of coloring books, a disintegrated box of crayons, two dolls, and an Oz book; under her pillow was a half-finished drawing she was doing on commission for her father. It was called "Two Witches Drinking Tea in a Cave," and it puzzled me for a minute until I realized that the blue-faced witch on the left was a vivid likeness of the dentist's nurse. I put the drawing on her desk, stacked the rest of the stuff on the floor where she would be sure to fall over it, and stripped and made the bed quickly, checking first in case Gato had been chasing Yain and Yain was hiding here, and dispensing with square corners.

When I came into Jannie's room, I perceived at once

that she had been washing her own sweaters again, because her red nylon sweater, still sopping, fell from the top of the door onto my head. There was another wet sweater over the end of the bed and the box of soap flakes which she had bought with her allowance had spilled on the floor. I thought of how efficiently the washing machine did sweaters, and picked up *Little Women*, closed it, and put it back in the bookcase. On Jannie's bed were half a dozen fashion magazines, a box of popcorn left over from the movies, all the clothes she had taken off for the past week, and a little girl's make-up kit. I put the clothes in a heap near the door where *she* would be sure to fall over them, with the box of popcorn plaintively on top, and piled the rest of the things on the bookcase so she could not get to *Little Women* without putting them away. Under the desk I found what seemed to be a letter, addressed in Jannie's handwriting to "Charles J." with a heart drawn in one corner. I put it on top of the make-up kit, took the wet sweaters to hang over the edge of the bathtub, checked for Gato and Yain, and stripped and made the bed, with no square corners.

In order to get into the magpie's nest which Laurie called his bedroom, it was necessary to pass a series of forbidding signs which read "Private" and "Keep out—this means YOU" and "No admision without my permision." Once inside, there was a narrow passageway between the electric train table and the wall, if the closet door was shut. Beyond that, a quick turn past the end of the bookcase, an agile twist around the dresser, and you were in, knee-deep in old handicraft magazines and pictures of baseball players. I knew the way because I came in once a week to change the sheets. It always took a minute to find the bed.

Underneath the bed were half a dozen cartons of odds and ends, an Erector set half built into a parachute jump, and three or four heavy boards with which he was someday going to make either a surfboard or a pool table. Reflecting that after making the bed of a twelve-year-old boy week after week, climbing Everest would seem a laughable anticlimax, I checked for Yain and Gato and made up the bed, standing on a carton of camp souvenirs and reaching with care around the parachute jump. I did not bother with square corners, and it was not possible to put the bedspread on, because it was draped over the window to make a kind of darkroom where Laurie had apparently been developing his own film. Because he had been to a school dance the night before his best pink shirt was over the lampshade and his black string tie was wound around the neck of the china rabbit on his dresser. After feeling around on the floor for a few minutes I found his good gray pants, which I put on a hanger and in the closet. His baseball uniform was hung up on the closet door, in perfect order, brushed and even, next to a picture of Don Newcombe. I lifted a corner of the bedspread over the window to check what I already knew, which was that the rain was still coming down, gray and dismal.

I gathered up all the used sheets and put them in the hamper, checking to make sure that Yain and Gato were not hiding in the hamper first, and got the laundry listed and ready to go. It was time to pick up Laurie and his trumpet, and I still had a lemon pie to make. On the way downstairs I stumbled over Sally's doll dishes, neatly arranged for a party on the bottom step.

It was not possible, in any case, to say an unnecessary word to Laurie on the way home, because he explained ceaselessly and with great rage that if this crummy rain didn't stop there would be no baseball game. "How we going to *play?*" he demanded of me indignantly, "how we going to play baseball in this *rain?*" He flexed his right arm. "It's already stiff," he told me drearily, "that's all I *need*, for heaven's sake." He stamped into the house and up the back stairs. "Who messed up everything in my room?" he howled.

It was a quarter to twelve. I opened the cabinet to get out the peanut butter and Laurie remarked from the kitchen doorway "—never get to play baseball, so can I please have Jannie's goldfish to dissect for my microscope?"

"No."

"But how'm I ever going to use my microscope if you won't let me *dissect* anything and it's just an old goldfish?"

"No."

"But I can't play—"

An idea came to me. "Sally," I said.

"Dissect Sally? You tipped?"

"No." I threw unnecessary words far and wide. "I want a sheet of her big drawing paper and a black crayon."

"What for?"

"Never mind."

He stared at me for a minute and then he said, "I got a picture upstairs she made me take, of a prince killing a wicked dragon and you can use the back."

"Get it."

Looking back at me over his shoulder, he went to the stairs and up to his room. He came back with the picture and a heavy drawing pencil. I spread the paper out on the kitchen table and with Laurie breathing heavily on my neck I wrote in big letters:

ULTIMATUM

"What does that mean?" Laurie asked.

"It means I have a headache," I said, and wrote:

BECAUSE OF GENERAL CONDITION OF BED-
ROOMS, WHINING, AND ALTOGETHER DIS-
TASTEFUL AND INFURIATING HABITS, ALSO BE-
CAUSE I AM TIRED OF HOUSEWORK AND
CLEANING AND PICKING UP AFTER EVERY-
BODY:

No movies for anyone until further notice.
No guests for ANY meals, including ballplayers, even
when it's too far to go home for lunch.
All allowances cut in half.
Television one hour per person per day.
Bedtime for everyone until further notice is 8:30. EIGHT-
THIRTY.
The system of fines will be rigidly enforced for:
disorderly rooms
uncared-for clothes
shutting cats in rooms unless hiding
teasing Barry
properties left on stairs
All goldfish to be kept under lock and key.

"Hey," Laurie said. "Hey."

Jannie was home from the library. We could hear her
out in the driveway saying goodbye to her friend Carole.
"And I'm not ever going to speak to *you* again, either,"
Jannie was saying, "and you can go swimming this afternoon with someone else, see if *I* care." She came up onto
the porch and called loudly, "And I'm going to tell Char-
lie Johnson every single word you said, and tell him who

said it, too. Hi," she said, opening the door, "what's for lunch? Daddy's company here yet?"

"I bet *you* sure thought you were going to see a baseball game today, I bet. I bet you're sure going to see some baseball game *today*."

"I was going swimming anyway," Jannie said unsympathetically, "except it's raining real hard out. What're you doing?"

"I am reforming this household," I said.

"Yeah," Laurie said.

I took my ultimatum and tacked it up on the kitchen wall where it was clearly visible to anyone sitting at the table for lunch. "That just makes this just a perfect day," Laurie said.

"What's the matter with *her*?" Jannie asked Laurie.

"She's tipped," Laurie said with conviction.

"I think it's Dad's company coming," Jannie said perceptively. "I think she's sore because Dad's got company coming and she hasn't got any."

"It is not," I said. I had forgotten to get lemons.

"But *eight-thirty*," Laurie said.

Sally came into the kitchen and stopped, looking at me plaintively. "You know that big doll of mine that Jannie wrote all over with crayon?"

"I didn't, it was Laurie and he wrote my name."

"You did so write on it, I saw you. Because it was the day Mommy said she would take you to get new shoes if you didn't do one single more thing bad all day and you did and she didn't take you."

"She did so take me and I got sneakers."

"Because anyway," Sally went on, addressing me, "you know that big doll? Because I was making a house and playing very nicely for Dikidiki Bear's birthday." She turned to Jannie. "We're going to have a party and no bad girls can come if they write on dolls."

"See if I care."

"What is it?" I turned to Laurie, who was poking me urgently.

"—goldfish?"

"No."

"So *any*way I *told* him not to and he did anyway. So," Sally went on insistently, "I think you better come and get him out."

"Who?"

"*Barry*. I been *telling* you."

"Barry?"

"Yes, because he's *stuck* in the *toy* box."

As I headed wearily for the stairs Laurie was saying with heavy disgust, "You see what she's gone and done, there on the wall? All because you girls leave your room in a mess, my goodness, and always fighting, and *now* look."

Barry was head down in the toy box, feet waving cheerfully. I picked my way carefully through thousands of little plastic cars and trucks, unwedged Barry, breaking a fingernail on the top of the toy box, and promised Dikidiki Bear an extra cookie if Barry would give me five minutes of his time to pick up the playroom. There was a sudden great shout of laughter from the kitchen below. With Barry's unwilling co-operation I scooped up handfuls of little cars and trucks and dumped them into the wooden box where they belonged. By the time I had the floor almost cleared Barry had uncovered a box of jigsaw puzzles and poured puzzle pieces in a heap; while I was gathering up the puzzle pieces, he went and got Jannie's doll house.

I picked up Dikidiki, retied his pink ribbon, and sat down on the toy box with him in my lap. Gato came to the doorway, moving fast, saw me, and veered toward Laurie's room and safe cover.

"Barry," I said, "you know what I would like to do more than anything?"

Barry bent over the doll house. "Here is the baby doll named Barry," he said. "And his mommy is putting him to bed. He is *already* in his pajamas."

"Mexico, maybe," I said. "Someplace where it's hot and I don't need to talk to anyone because I can't understand a word they say."

Far away the phone rang. "I'll get it," Laurie shrieked; Jannie howled, "It's for meeeee"; "*I* want to," Sally yelled.

"Hello?" Barry said into the doll-house telephone.

Downstairs, the study door opened. "Company here?" my husband inquired.

Then, without warning, a great shout arose, from Jannie in the kitchen, Laurie at the phone, my husband in the study, Sally somewhere out front. Barry lifted his head and nodded wisely. "Sunshine," he pointed out. The rain had stopped, the clouds were blowing off, and the sun was out, in that unbelievable unexpected brightness which makes the electric lights look faded. Barry and I started downstairs and we could hear Laurie in the study saying, "Signed Sylvia, and it said very sorry car broke down Albany must return maybe next year."

"Car broke down Albany?" My husband sounded puzzled.

My ultimatum on the kitchen wall was gone, hidden now behind a second sheet of Sally's big drawing paper, on which was written in black crayon:

OUR TERMS. If preveleges are returned we agree to—
   take care of our rooms except Barry
   wip feet
   brush all teeth dayly
   pick up things except not in rooms like clothes
   read to Barry and put him to bed and dress him unless
     he bites
   praktice music lessons
   remeber to set table
   only Barry has got to leave other peoples things alone
   also if Barry bites we can bite back
   and after this if Dad has got company coming Mommy
     has got to have a guest too because otherwise she gets
     grouchy

This document was signed by the three older children and gave Barry a good deal of honest amusement because, as he pointed out, he only bited when other people bited him first. My husband came to the lunch table, informed me of the telegram and the cancellation of our guests, and I told the children magnanimously that all privileges would be restored and they could have one more chance on keeping things neat. Sally and Barry decided to postpone Dikidiki's birthday party to the next rainy day. Jannie telephoned Carole and they decided to go berrying, so I said I would make a raspberry shortcake for dessert. Laurie came downstairs in his uniform and invited us all to come and see him play baseball, and my husband said we would, if Mother was not too tired from doing all that housework.

Laurie's ball team won easily. In the bottom of the fourth inning, when Laurie hit a double with the bases loaded, I turned to my husband and said in a forgiving kind of voice, "I'm sorry that your friends couldn't make it."

"Maybe it's just as well," my husband said. He broke off to address Laurie. "Slide, you lunatic, *slide*," he yelled. "Thinking about it," he went on to me, "I'm not so sure you *would* have liked her, after all."

Laurie's baseball team came in second for the summer, and Laurie and Billy and Artie and a dozen others graduated officially from the Little League because they would be too old to play another year. Everyone went off for the first day of school, bright in new shoes and jackets. After the first few mornings of fruitless railing at the alarm clock I became reconciled to getting up at seven again. One evening at the end of the first week of school I was sitting in the study unhappily fidgeting with a tooth which had contained a gold inlay until an entanglement with a salted peanut about five minutes before. My husband, who has no gold inlays, was eating salted peanuts and trying to read the evening paper. Laurie was up in his room with all the doors shut between him and us, practicing "When the Saints Come Marching In" on his trumpet. Jannie was playing the first line of "Flow Gently, Sweet Afton" over and over on the piano, making the same mistake each time. Sally was in the front room off the study watching a children's program on television; every now and then a hoarse, inhuman voice would rise in a shout of demonic laughter and announce, giggling, that all the little girls and boys watching the program must be sure and tell their mommies that they wanted only some crispy crunchy oh-so-good delicacy at the store. A little red caboose named Barry passed through the study regularly on his bicycle route, which went from the kitchen through the dining room through the hall through the study and back to the kitchen again.

I took my tongue out of the hole in my tooth, and said to my husband, "What I would like more than anything else in the world is about three days in a hotel in New York City. Where it's quiet."

I spoke in the low, vibrant voice which will carry best at that hour of the evening, and my husband answered me in the same tone. "You probably ought to get to the dentist," he said.

"If I went to New York I could go to the dentist, because the dentist who put that gold inlay in in the first place is in New York."

Jannie lifted her hands from the piano keys, the trumpet stopped, the television set snapped off, the bike crashed into the kitchen table and stalled, and my voice rose clearly through the sudden silence. "In a hotel in New York—" I was saying, before I stopped.

"What was that?" Laurie called down from upstairs.

"Hey," said Jannie, swinging around on the piano bench.

"Mother was only talking," my husband said hastily, but Laurie was leaping down the last five steps and Jannie had reached the study and Barry, hopping, came in from the kitchen and Sally was already hanging over the back of my chair.

"We can see some movies, and maybe Dad and I can get to one of the last ball games if we write for tickets now, and never mind about the first few weeks of school, because we don't get report cards until—"

"And Mom and I can go shopping—"

"We'll get a big room in the hotel, because six beds—"

"Wait, wait," I said.

"What about Sally and Barry?" Jannie asked Laurie.

He considered. "They're pretty young," he said. "The dog can go stay at the kennel, and I'll ask Rob to come over and feed the cats, but I suppose Sally and Barry—"

"Sally will have to get a new hat."

"Oh, we'll *all* have to get *clothes*. But never mind about *clothes*. Mom can just stay in the hotel room until *she* gets something to wear, and Dad and I don't need much for ball games and things, and the little kids must have a lot of junk to wear. But the Statue of Liberty—"

"It's too cold," I said. "And in the first place I was only speaking to your father, and in the second place any mention of New York was with reference to my going to the dentist, and in the third place—"

"We can't afford it," my husband said.

"And maybe we can get in to see a television show being broadcast," Jannie said to Laurie.

"Mom can't drive down, that's for sure," Laurie said. "Not with all of *us* in the car."

"Barry," Jannie cooed, "would you like to *ride* on a *train*?"

"Yup," said Barry.

"I'm going to have sirloin steak and chocolate ice cream every night, boy."

"Hah," said my husband.

"Sally, would *you* like to go to New *York* and *stay* in a *hotel*?"

Sally lifted her chin sleepily from my shoulder. "Go where?" she said.

In terms of actual physical transportation, getting to New York from our home in Vermont is almost unsurmountably difficult. Even if I could drive to New York with the children in the car, I could certainly not drive *in* New York, due to an uncontrollable tendency toward wiggling the wheel back and forth when I find myself surrounded by cars traveling in different directions. Naturally people are leaving our town all the time, going everywhere, and even sometimes coming back again, but none of them, we found, will answer a direct question about transportation. There is no train coming or going from our town; the nearest train is in Albany, fifty miles away. There is a bus which goes from our neighboring town, which is only six miles away, but that bus only goes farther into Vermont; occasionally a rogue bus gets off toward Albany, but of course it would be pretty silly for six of us to go sit in the bus station hoping that a bus might be going to Albany that day. Our local taxi would take us to Albany, but then, after we got to Albany, we would have to turn around and come home again, having run out of money. Finally, after a good deal of family discussion, in which the only fact that emerged clearly was that Barry was going to ride on a train, my husband remembered a fellow coin-collector who was desperately anxious for an 1877 Indian Head penny, and who agreed to drive us to Albany in return for the one in my husband's collection. All of us except my husband were amused at the notion that it was only going to cost us a penny to get to Albany. Laurie suggested that the coin collection be doled out, coin by coin, to pay our expenses in New York, and his father said gloomily that it was probably going to turn out to be like that, anyway.

Although none of us had any clothes to wear in New York, we took five suitcases. I also had a little black bag holding candy, handkerchiefs, crayons, coloring books, six volumes of fairy tales, the latest handicraft magazine, two jigsaw puzzles, and a bottle of cough medicine. Barry had Dikidiki. Sally had a new gray knitted hat with a fringed tail hanging down the back. Laurie and Jannie had looks of pleased anticipation.

It has long been my belief that in times of great stress, such as a four-day vacation, the thin veneer of family unity wears off almost at once, and we are revealed in our true personalities; Laurie, for instance, is a small-town mayor, Jannie a Games Mistress, Sally a vague, stern old lady watching the rest of us with remote disapproval, and Barry a small intrepid foot soldier, following unquestioningly and doggedly. The two nervous creatures hovering in the background, making small futile gestures and tending to laugh weakly, are, of course, unmistakable. They are there to help with the luggage. These several personalities began to emerge in the car driving to Albany, and Sally's hat began to unravel.

So long as we were within familiar territory, the circle of about ten miles which I cover regularly and of which I know every path and house, I was fairly comfortable, re-marking at intervals, "I'm sure no one will get into the house," and, "Does anyone remember whether we finally put in the little black bag?" When we got out into the world, and the hills were no longer at the same angle and the road turned past bewilderingly strange trees and houses, my hands began to tremble, and I said things like, "Hadn't we just better go back and see if—" and, "I'm almost sure I forgot to—" My husband kept asking Barry, "Well, are you going on a *train*?" and Barry kept saying, "Yup," and clutching Dikidiki tighter. "Are you going to ride on a *train*?" I asked him, and Barry said, "Yup," but Dikidiki turned pale.

Jannie and Laurie, smooth and sleek in their best clothes, devoted themselves to reassuring the rest of us; halfway to Albany my husband stopped asking Barry if he was going on a train and started asking me if I had remembered to find out what time the train left, and I kept telling him that I thought I had left the light on in the cellar. "Don't worry," Laurie said repeatedly, "it doesn't *matter*; *is* this a vacation or *isn't* it?"

"Now everybody *smile!*" Jannie cried gaily.

Sally is so often silent that no one thought to watch her particularly; if I noticed the little slip of gray wool in her hand it made no impression on me. As a matter of fact, I *had* gotten the time of the train wrong, but we made it, and the conductor was very nice about catching my husband's arm. We put Barry and Laurie in one seat, Sally and Jannie in the next seat, and then Barry had to move to sit with Jannie so Dikidiki could sit between them, and by the time Laurie had his coat off and up on the rack Sally had gotten herself somehow wedged between the two seats with her coat half off. While I was untangling Sally, Jannie and her father were taking off Barry's coat so I took off my own coat. There was by now no room to put it up on the rack over our seats, so Laurie took it across the aisle to where there was an empty space on the rack, and when he tried to put it up, it fell down on an old man reading science fiction. When everyone was sitting down again, Dikidiki decided that he had to sit next to the window, so Laurie changed with Jannie and then Sally thought that she would like to look out of the window, too, so Jannie changed with Sally. Then the old man reading science fiction got up and went and sat down at the other end of the car, so Sally thought she would sit over in his empty seat instead. "Are you on a *train?*" my husband asked Barry; "Is this a *train?*" Laurie asked, and I put in, *"Look,* we're all on a *train."* "Yup," Barry kept saying. "Yup."

"Listen," Laurie said, leaning forward to talk to his father and me. "Now, the diner's three cars up and I figure we better get into the diner early because there are such a lot of us. Jannie and I will sit at a table by ourselves because they only have tables for four, and you two can take care of the kids. And I better have the tickets, because if they get lost . . ."

We were really on the train, with our children, our suitcases, and Dikidiki; we were going to New York. That was, I believe, my last clear, co-ordinated thought. From that moment until I came back through our own front door again, four days later, nothing happened in any kind of reasonable or logical order; nothing made sense. I know that we reached Grand Central Station, and it was my fault that Barry fell down the crack between the train and the platform; I was looking back over my shoulder counting heads and Barry stepped into the crack, but the porter unwedged him. Then the porter vanished as we assembled on the platform with our suitcases, so that, at last, my husband carried two suitcases, Laurie carried two, Jannie carried one, and Sally carried the little black bag. Barry carried Dikidiki and I was supposed to lead Barry with one hand and Sally with the other; Laurie and Jannie followed us, and my husband brought up the rear, stopping every few feet to put down his two suitcases and pick up Dikidiki.

"Look at all the cars there were on our train," I told Barry, and Barry said, "Yup."

Sally giggled. "I bet *that* train doesn't get very far," she said, and showed me the long thread of gray wool following us. "I tied the end to the seat in the train," she said. "I'd like to see *that* train get away."

In Vermont we do not have revolving doors. Laurie finally had to go in and get Sally out; we estimated that with the expanse of the station and the length of the train platform and the number of times she had been around in the revolving door we had lost nearly three miles of gray thread. The hat was by now only a little beanie-type which sat on top of Sally's head. Because the end of the thread was caught in the revolving door, Barry and Jannie and I stood in fascination while Laurie and my husband tried to get a taxi, watching the hat unraveling off Sally's head. The last knot disappeared out the taxi window when we were about halfway to the hotel.

I remember the hotel because we had a suite of three bedrooms and a kind of foyer in the middle; nothing was where it is at home. "I guess we're here," my husband said. "I wish I could remember whether I left the study window open," I said. I had carefully put Barry's pajamas in the top of one of the suitcases, but he and Dikidiki were asleep before I could get it open. Sally and Laurie and Jannie went around and around the three rooms, moving restlessly, surveying beds and dressers and pictures and admiring the array of towels in the bathroom and reading all the little notices out loud.

We were awakened bright and early in the morning by the chambermaid, who had found Barry in the hall, clad in the top half of his pajamas. He had locked himself out of the room, and when the chambermaid came by he was standing there pounding furiously on the door. "Monsters," he was screaming, purple-faced, "monsters, monsters!"

At breakfast Laurie and Jannie endeavored to map out our plans for the time in New York. "I don't want to take the kids into any more restaurants than we can help," Laurie said. "Maybe from now on we could get some bread and peanut butter and milk and stuff and Mom could kind of fix some meals here in the hotel room."

"Indeed Mom could not," I assured him earnestly. "One of the things I came to New York *for* was to go to restaurants and have steak and pork fried rice and hot tacos and shishkebab and veal cutlets parmigiana and wiener schnitzel and shrimp curry and—"

"Don't you want to do anything except *eat?*"

"No," I said, with my eyes shut. "And cheese blintzes and sukiyaki and—"

Laurie said to Jannie, "Well, if Dad and I go to a ball game, you'll have to take Sally and Barry and Mom and go shopping or something. *You* know, clothes and stuff. Maybe take Barry on buses."

"Mother has to go to the dentist," my husband said.

"Oh, *Dad*—she can do that at *home.*"

"Certainly," I said. "So then it's settled; Jannie and Sally and I will go shopping and I will get myself a new housecoat, black, and I think a pair of lizard shoes. Or snakeskin."

"No," my husband said.

"And Laurie and Dad can go to the ball game."

"Sally will need a new hat," Jannie said. She turned to Barry, and said lovingly, "Now I want you to be *sure* not to fall out the window of the bus."

"What do *you* want to do in New York, Perfessor?" Laurie asked Sally.

Sally lifted her head from her coloring book. "Where?" she said.

The children retired to their several rooms to dress, and a spirited argument began between Jannie and Sally. Jannie injudiciously pointed out that Sally would sure be excited when she saw the big stores. And the tall buildings. "New York," Jannie said, "has the tallest building in the world."

That was precisely the kind of statement to arouse Sally, in whose world nothing was ever so stable as to warrant a superlative. "I just *bet*," she said.

"Laurie?" Jannie called. "Isn't the tallest building in the world right here in New York?"

"Empire State," Laurie said.

"I *bet*," Sally said. "I better just *see* this tallest building in the world, I just guess."

"Daddy?"

"Indeed, yes," my husband said. "The very tallest. Mother," he said, "will take you in an elevator right to the top."

"No, she won't," I said, shuddering.

"I don't need to go to the *top*." Sally was amused. "If it really *is* the tallest there's no sense going all the way to the *top*. But even from the *bottom* I just bet it's not the tallest."

"Well," said Laurie, nettled, "the people in New York certainly *think* it is, anyway. They tell *every*body."

"I just *bet*," Sally said direfully.

It turned out, Jannie and I subsequently discovered when we were shopping, that Sally was also not prepared to believe in escalators. "No," she said, standing at the bottom and clutching Barry firmly. "No. Not for me or for Barry neither. Stairs are hard enough by theirselves, not moving."

"I'll carry you," I said desperately. "I'll carry you up and then come back down and get Barry."

"It's *easy*," Jannie insisted. "I've done it lots of times."

"Nope." Sally pressed back against the crowd around us. "I don't know where it goes," she said.

"Just to the top—see the people getting off?"

"But," Sally said, "those are not the same people as the ones getting on down here. The people get on and go somewhere but the people who get off are just the ones that old staircase *lets* get off. And look coming down over there—all different."

I am afraid of elevators. "Look, Sally," I said, "I *promise* you—"

"*You* can get on if you want to," Sally said. "Me and Barry will go back and tell Daddy where you went."

I think that was the day that Jannie wanted to look at wedding gowns, or perhaps that was the day after. One day Laurie and Jannie went to Radio City with their father, so that must have been the day I took Sally and Barry to the zoo, and Barry and Dikidiki stood and looked silently at the polar bear and the polar bear stood and looked silently at Barry and Dikidiki. Sally was perplexed because the animals were not in cages when so many of the people in the city *were*. "*Why* are they all in cages," she asked insistently, moving along beside me, "in stores and restaurants and movies and everything, they have someone in a cage? But the big stone lions we saw are just standing right out there and the people in cages?"

"Look at the rhinoceros," I said.

"And in the hotel, in cages? Do they eat people, like

children? Is that bear going to eat Dikidiki? Do baby birds have tiny toy eggs to play with?"

It must have been the same day, because I had Barry and Sally, that we stood, craning our necks, with people passing by smiling at us, three country innocents gaping at the topless towers of the Empire State Building.

"See?" I said to Sally.

She shook her head mournfully. "Poor New York people," she said. "Going around saying *this* is the tallest."

"Well, it *is*," I said.

Sally sighed. "When even a little girl like me can come here and see lots taller right in the same city."

"It says in the books—"

"How do books know? Just looking around *any*one can see lots taller, and wider too."

"Well," I said compromisingly, "maybe you better just not say anything about it. It's not polite to come here from Vermont and start finding fault. And if the people here want to think this *is* the tallest, it's not up to a little girl like you to get them all upset about it."

"But if I tried to tell someone that Daddy was the smartest man in the world and it said so in a book, you would say I was not telling the truth? Why do they have all those cars in the street but everybody walking? Can Barry and I each have a present because we've been good? Can Barry have a little firetruck?"

I had Sally with me most of the time because it made her father very nervous when she was talking because he had no answers for her questions, but when she was not talking he was always worrying over what she was probably thinking. Consequently, it must have been on the third day of our visit that Laurie and his father and Barry were on a ferryboat, and I agreed to Jannie's eager proposal that we take Sally to lunch in the Automat. Once, for a very brief period of my life, I worked selling books in Macy's, and although they have remodeled the book department since my time, and I can no longer direct anyone to the section devoted to books on psychiatry and reincarnation, I can still recall, poignantly, the rare flavor of the cafeteria lunch. I was able to explain to Sally, standing before the cafeteria rail in the Automat with the usual little group of amused cynics listening, how you got something to eat in a cafeteria. Sally accepted the concept of a cafeteria, with reservations, but when I then directed her to the little cubbyholes with their glass fronts she balked absolutely. "No," she said.

"I'll show you," I said.

"No," Sally said flatly, regarding a nesselrode pie. "It won't work."

"*Other* people—"

"Like that tall building. They just *think* so, is all."

"But look at Jannie." Jannie's tray held a little pot of baked beans and a glass of milk; she was going slowly back and forth before the fairyland of desserts, eyes bright and nickels clutched firmly.

"Jannie's just lucky," Sally said. "They didn't grab it first."

"Who didn't grab what?"

"The people in the cages," Sally said. "On the other side of that glass where the people are, in the cages."

"There *are* people back there, surely. But they put things *in*. *We* take them *out*."

"Well, they're not going to get any of *my* nickels,"

Sally said. She reached up and opened the little glass door and took out the piece of nesselrode pie.

"No," I said. "Sally, no, that's *not* the *way*. You *have* to put the *nickels* in." I flapped my hands helplessly at the little glass door, swinging open. "Put it back," I said.

"No," Sally said. "On the other side, in the cage, they put *their* nickels in, and I just reached and grabbed fast. If I," she added complacently, "had of put *my* nickels in first, and if *they*'d been quicker, then *they*—"

"Jannie," I said, and skidded down to where Jannie was trying to balance a piece of chocolate nut cake and two cinnamon buns on her tray. I took the tray away from her and got it to a table, and she followed me, insisting, "Wait, wait, I didn't get *half* the things there were, I got to get—"

I told her to stay right at the table and not move, and went back for Sally, who was remarking patronizingly to a gentleman trying to get to a parkerhouse roll, "—might *think* it's the tallest, but even a little girl—"

There came one moment in our New York visit when we all sat wearily in the hotel room together. I had taken my shoes off, and my husband was trying to read his paper by the bedlight. Laurie, flung over the desk chair, observed suddenly that, golly, tomorrow night was band rehearsal at home. Jannie said that she hadn't practiced "Flow Gently, Sweet Afton" for days and days and *days*. Sally lifted her head from her jigsaw puzzle to ask if people in New York stayed there all the time, or only came when we did, and Barry, on the floor pushing his fire engine half-heartedly, said, "You know there was a big white house where we used to live before we lived here and maybe sometime we can go and visit *there* again for some days in a little while."

My husband telephoned his coin-collector friend that night and offered him an ancient silver dollar if he would meet us in Albany the next afternoon.

When I walked in through our own front door and Yain and Gato came to cross back and forth between my ankles I put my little black suitcase down on the floor and said to my husband, "You know, I didn't get to the dentist after all."

In the morning, at my own breakfast table, where the coffee was decently strong and the toast was hot and crisp, I told my husband that we had come off pretty well, considering. "We lost Sally's hat, of course," I said, "and that glove of mine and the bottom half of Barry's pajamas in the hotel room."

"I forgot to mail the postcards," my husband said. "You'll have to drive around today and deliver them."

"Dikidiki went on a train," Barry said.

"We only saw two movies," Laurie said. "I figured we'd see more."

"Sally," I asked, "did you have a good time in New York?"

Sally lifted her chin from the edge of the table. "Where?" she said.

The next morning was Monday and everyone went off to school again, world-bemused travelers. I picked up Toby at the kennel, which of course meant that on Monday we had two cats and one dog. Toby is actually the second oldest child in the family, being, we estimate, one year younger than Laurie. He has been Laurie's personal dog ever since the bright spring morning when Laurie was four and a half and we were still recovering from the impact of our first Vermont winter. When Laurie came through the back door that sunny morning, asking as he came, "Can I have a dog?" my husband and I both, staring at the great embarrassed creature trying to edge through the door behind him, said, with one voice, "No." "Don't let that beast in here," my husband said, putting down his coffee cup; "Shoo," I said. The dog, horribly upset, tried to curtsy ingratiatingly, put his left hind foot into an empty milk bottle, mistook the dining room doorway for a way out, and, hurrying, sideswiped a dining room chair, skidded on the milk bottle, and brought up sprawled flat against the buffet, wagging his tail and smiling in a sheepish manner.

"I want to name him Toby," Laurie said, regarding his dog with pride.

When my husband attempted to herd the dog outside again, the dog clearly interpreted the anxious, brushing motions as friendly overtures; with a wriggle of pure delight he rose, put his front paws on my husband's shoulders and put his head down and licked my husband's ear.

"Go away," my husband said, looking up into the dog's face. "Heel. Play dead."

"Down, sir," I offered.

"Come on, Toby," Laurie said. "I'm going to teach you some tricks."

After nearly ten years, Laurie was still trying to teach Toby some tricks. Toby was amiable, sentimental, and desperately anxious to please, but the simplest command got lost somewhere in that big head. We had a neighbor with a female dog and a glass-paned back-porch door, and one night my husband figured out that what with the amount Toby ate, and replacing the glass panes in our neighbor's back door twice a year, Toby's mean annual cost was only slightly less than Laurie's, even figuring in Laurie's allowance.

When I got Toby back from the kennel on the Monday after we came home from New York, I had to pay for the wire fence he had broken down, and the vet remarked wanly that although Toby was getting on in years he really seemed to be getting bigger. I disengaged myself from Toby's welcoming embrace and said tartly that we were none of us getting any younger, although when I got Toby home I could not help noticing that he was getting to be a venerable old man, with touches of gray at his temples and a little extra weight around the middle. I pointed this out to my husband and he put back his shoulders and pulled in his stomach and said that you had to figure that every year of a dog's life was equal to seven years of a person's life, so that Toby was nearly seventy. I said that Toby had followed the car when I went shopping one afternoon recently. Just out of curiosity I had checked him going up the big hill and he could still run thirty-five miles an hour, and I just hoped that when I was seventy *I* could run thirty-five miles an hour going uphill. My husband said it would probably depend on what I was chasing.

On Tuesday the senior cat, Yain, absent-mindedly turned his back on the spaniel from across the street, and Laurie and I took him to the vet's to be hospitalized for a mangled ear. Laurie swore that he saw the junior cat, Gato, walk down to the end of the driveway and shake hands with the spaniel, but I was inclined to doubt this, since Gato did not usually trouble himself to walk any farther than the distance between wherever he happened to be sleeping and the dish where he got his food.

On Wednesday, Toby was badly frightened by the last grasshopper of the season and took the back screen door off its hinges trying to get in fast and crawl under the piano, where he hid whenever he was attacked by fiends, such as grasshoppers, wedging himself in head first with his eyes tight shut, hoping that no one would notice the piano shaking and the great dog feet tucked in under the pedals.

On Thursday I went into the kitchen and opened the drawer where I kept hair barrettes and odd buttons and skate keys; I was looking for a pair of shoelaces for Barry, and when I opened the drawer a mouse jumped out. I was considerably startled, probably because it had been so long since I had seen a mouse in the kitchen, and I gave a kind of a howl and slammed the drawer, catching the mouse by the tail so that he hung head down, cursing and waving his fists at me. Although a mouse hanging upside down by the tail and calling names was not something I saw every day, I left the kitchen in some haste, reeling through the dining room and crying out something incoherent which may very well have been "Help, help!" as Laurie maintained. It sent Toby scuttling under the piano and brought my four children, armed with baseball bats, parasols, and rocket guns, into the kitchen.

"Get a *cat*, for heaven's sake," Laurie yelled, and while he stood with his baseball bat raised menacingly, I tiptoed across the kitchen—there was actually no need to tiptoe, as I realized later, since of course the mouse could see me perfectly well; he was by then smiling tightly and tapping his fingers irritably against the drawer—and poked around in the washing machine until Gato put his head out, yawning, and looked at me inquiringly. I pulled him out and, still tiptoeing, carried him over to the drawer, told him, "Look, Gato, mouse, *mouse*," and set him down on the floor. Laurie opened the drawer, I howled, and the mouse fell on Gato's head. There was a musical crash as Jannie's first-year exercise book fell off the piano rack onto the keys. Barry giggled, Sally and Jannie clung to one another wordlessly, and Laurie put his baseball bat down very gently onto the kitchen counter.

"Boy," he said at last, turning to look at Gato fastidiously washing his head on top of the refrigerator. "Boy, what a cat, a positive carnivorous wild beast. Get down off that chair," he said to me. "You look silly."

"I was just standing here," I said, coming down much slower than I went up. "Where's the mouse?"

Laurie gestured at the kitchen cabinets, where there was a great stirring and squeaking, as of some smart-aleck mouse telling his guffawing friends about the funny thing that happened to him a few minutes ago. "Boy," said Laurie helplessly, and he took up his baseball bat and went out to hit practice grounders.

On Thursday evening I went into the kitchen about eleven o'clock to make my husband a cold pot-roast sandwich and when I reached for the light cord a mouse ran down my arm and my husband had to come into the kitchen and lead me out. Gato, who had been sleeping on the waffle iron, arose in great indignation and went upstairs to sleep on Jannie's doll bed, after several pointed remarks about people who kept decent cats awake all night with their mice.

On Friday morning there was a mouse in the breadbox and around lunchtime on Friday my husband discovered a mouse on the dining room buffet eating a dish of salted almonds my husband had been saving for himself. It was at that time that the question of a new cat first arose. My husband announced shrilly that he personally would be prepared to pay any amount of money for a cat who was a *cat* and caught mice instead of spending all his time sleeping in the oven and eating his head off. This provoked Gato into coming out of the oven with icy courtesy and going across the kitchen and upstairs without even a glance at any of us. He spent the rest of the day sulking in Sally's toy box and therefore did not attend the animated family meeting which began almost immediately.

"A cat," my husband said over and over. "A cat that will catch and kill and get rid of mice. A *cat*, not a furry lounge lizard." He shook his fist wildly after Gato.

"Well, how about a dog, then?" Laurie asked.

"Oh, *yes!*" Jannie clasped her hands ardently. "He could help Toby guard the house, and we could teach him cute little tricks—"

"A tiny puppy," Sally said with joy.

"A tiny puppy," Barry confirmed, "and *I* will teach him to play baseball."

"Females are the best mousers," I said, as one who has spent years of study on the subject. "Besides," I went on, "maybe a pretty lady cat would be so gentle and nice she would influence Gato and Yain and they would stop quarreling all the time."

"Well, a *dog*, now," Laurie said.

My husband was looking at me curiously. "Is it your opinion—" he began.

"—tricks?"

"—that females of any species whatsoever—"

"—and dress him in doll clothes and a little bonnet—"

"—have *any* such effect?"

"—and name him Pal."

Discussion continued through lunch. Then, as the result of a wholly dispassionate vote in which my husband and I were inevitably outnumbered four to two, I drove in to the local newspaper office and left two advertisements for the paper. The first ad read:

> Wanted to buy: female cat, kitten or half grown, good mouser. Call 5679.

The second ad read:

> Wanted to buy: puppy, mongrel large breed preferred. Call 5679.

The paper came out at two o'clock on Saturday afternoon. At about two-fifteen Laurie's friend Rob came by on his bike and dropped off our copy of the paper. While we were all gathered around the kitchen table, admiring the appearance of our ads in print, the phone began to ring.

On Saturday evening, then, we had two dogs and three cats. One dog, Toby, was under the piano. One cat, Yain, had been unexpectedly returned, convalescent, by the vet, who said he was to be kept warm and quiet and away from other animals, since he was still extremely touchy on the whole subject of ears and spaniels. Yain, then, was down cellar, where I had hurried him without attracting Gato's attention. Gato was pacing ceaselessly back and forth, talking to himself, in front of the door which led to the back apartment. In the back apartment was an elegant gray golden-eyed lady cat. In the barn, howling remotely, was a great wriggling grinning brown puppy who gave irresistible evidence of planning to grow up to be exactly like Toby. Laurie had put a sign on the barn door saying "Do not open!! Dog!!" and Jannie had put a sign on the kitchen door into the back apartment saying "Do not open cat" and Sally had put a sign on the cellar door saying "DO K SALLY THIS IS FROM ME."

The next morning the children were up early, to take the puppy his breakfast, and they got me out of bed rather before my usual Sunday morning hour of arising to report that the puppy would not eat cornflakes. When I came unwillingly downstairs Gato was lying in a great black heap on top of the broom closet, which commanded a full view of the door to the back apartment; he glanced at me with a look that said clearly that after he had taken care of the gray cat he would have a word or two to say to the rest of us, and it crossed my mind that Gato did not know, yet, about either the puppy or Yain's return.

I put milk into Gato's dish and into Toby's, and then took down three more bowls and filled them with milk. While Gato and Toby were drinking their milk I gave Laurie one bowl to take out to the puppy in the barn, and eased the cellar door open a crack so Jannie could squeeze through and take a bowl of milk down to Yain. However, when I opened the door of the back apartment to let Sally go in there with the third bowl of milk the gray cat slipped through and into the kitchen, where she went directly to Toby's dish and began to drink his milk while Toby stepped back, looking with indignant anger from me to the gray cat and back again. Gato lifted his chin and stared incredulously, and the gray cat began a growl that started somewhere near the floor and broke off in a high register as I grabbed her up and carried her, struggling, back into the back apartment to her own bowl of milk. The barn door slammed as Laurie backed out, and down cellar Yain began to howl dismally.

"*That* was a dirty trick," Jannie said, shocked. "That cat *scared* Toby." Toby sniffled in corroboration.

"Why'd we *get* all these cats and dogs, anyway?" Sally asked. "Seems like it would be easier just having *mice* for pets."

During breakfast, while Yain wailed down cellar and the puppy yapped in the barn and Gato prowled back and forth before the back apartment door and my husband said half a dozen times that he personally planned to spend the entire day in the study with the door shut, the children and I mapped out a kind of plan whereby our several pets might become acquainted and enjoy a morning's lighthearted play together. It went without saying that this must happen outdoors; aside from the probably harrowing effect upon the mice of sitting in upon the introduction of three cats to two dogs, I keep my French salad plates and my grandmother's Italian decanter set and the ashtray Sally made in kindergarten on shelves in the kitchen. In any case the children ought to be out enjoying the sunlight instead of wasting away indoors. Therefore, I sent Sally and Barry out to settle in the sandbox, on the lawn near the back door. I planned to run Yain directly outside, from the cellar through the kitchen through the side hall to the side door, with no stopoffs, and Jannie was posted at that side of the house with the particular aim of herding Yain away from all other animals. Laurie was to ride around and around the house on his bike, doing courier service, and I was to be stationed on the back porch with the back door open behind me to serve as a retreat or as a temptation in case the sunny weather lured any mice out for a morning stroll.

I began by letting Toby out the front door onto the front porch; he was mildly surprised, since it is not his usual door, but there seemed to be nothing outstandingly menacing on the front porch, so he went out and sat down on the steps. Gato was established on the kitchen table and refused to move, which barred the way of exit for Yain from the cellar. I went first into the back apartment and let the gray cat out of that outside door, which aimed her directly toward the back of the house, around the corner from the sandbox and directly opposite Toby on the front steps. Then, after another attempt to unwedge Gato from the kitchen table, I was forced to fall back on guile and to use a piece of cantaloupe, of which he was passionately fond, to lure him out of the kitchen and into the study, where my husband was peacefully reading his morning paper. "I just want to leave Gato in here for a minute while I get Yain out of the cellar," I explained.

My husband nodded, I dropped the piece of cantaloupe and raced for the study door, slamming it just as Gato flung himself against it from the inside. "Eat your cantaloupe," I heard my husband saying.

I opened the cellar door to catch Yain and get him out the side door, which would put him on the fourth side of the house, with Toby at the front, the gray cat at the back, the children in the sandbox by the back porch, waiting to bring out the puppy, Jannie on the side front, and Laurie riding swiftly past shouting, "Toby okay on front steps!" or, "Gray cat washing face by back apartment door!" or, "Barry shovelful sand down Sally's back!"

I opened the cellar door and Yain hesitated. I called and

called, and Toby, hearing my voice, began clamoring to get in the front door. Just as Yain came easing through the cellar door into the kitchen I heard my husband come out of the study and go to let Toby in the front door—a gesture so automatic and frequent with all of us that we can, and often do, manage it sound asleep. "No, no," I yelled to my husband, diving for Yain, who doubled sideways and headed up the back stairs.

"Gato came out of the study. What shall I do?" my husband asked, coming into the kitchen with Toby following him.

"Where?"

"Up the front stairs. His cantaloupe—"

I thought quickly. "Put Toby out the back door so the children can watch him. I'll head off Yain before he meets Gato upstairs, so if you can get Toby outdoors I'll put Gato back in the study."

My husband, looking perplexed, went to the back door and Toby, looking perplexed, followed him. My husband said, "The gray cat's here. Shall I let her in?"

Just then Laurie opened the front door to shout, "Toby gone; gray cat heading back door!"

I scurried up the back stairs and found Gato, moving with measured steps across the jungle of the playroom toward Yain under Jannie's bed. With a fast racing dive I captured Yain just as he moved, wheeled, and hurled myself down the back stairs again, Gato following yearningly. My husband and Jannie and Toby were at the back door. "Put Toby out the front door," Jannie was saying urgently.

"He just came *in* the front door," my husband said.

"Then shut him in the study," Jannie said. "I can't catch the gray cat with Toby because he's scared of her."

"Don't put Toby in the study, because I want to put Gato in there," I said. "Don't let Gato out the back door if the gray cat's out there." I turned wildly, holding Yain. "I'll put Yain in Toby," I said.

My husband went into the study and slammed the door and I came right after him. "I'll put Yain in here for a minute now," I said. "We're just having a little trouble keeping them all straight."

"It's like the old League of Nations," my husband said obscurely, and picked up his newspaper.

Laurie rode by to report that the gray cat had gone back around the house and was meowing at the back apartment door to be let in, so I took Toby by the collar and put him, bewildered and evidencing a strong desire to get under the piano, out on the front steps again. Gato followed and I picked him up and put him on the front steps with Toby. "Stay there," I said severely. Then I started for the back apartment to let the gray cat in but my husband opened the study door and said I simply had to get Yain out of there because he was sitting on the desk in a fury chewing pencils, so I gathered up Yain and put him out the back door, which was of course the wrong door for Yain, but by then it hardly seemed to matter.

A quick inventory showed that everyone was outside except my husband who was now, judging from the sounds, engaged in pushing his desk across the study door. I went out onto the back porch, leaving the door open behind me. Sally had knocked over Barry's pail of sand and then left the sandbox to establish herself on the swing beyond the driveway. Barry was irritably refilling his pail, talking to himself about bad bad bad girls. Jannie had come around the house and stood in the driveway with Toby pressed nervously against her. The puppy was wailing hideously from the barn, so when Laurie passed the next time I stopped him and said he might as well get Toby's old leash and start getting the puppy ready to come out, and Laurie got the leash and headed for the barn. After a minute the gray cat slipped, smokelike, around the corner of the house and leaped to the second porch step where she settled uneasily. Gato leaned insolently against a tree, the tip of his tail twitching. One single evil snarl betrayed Yain under the hedge. I sat down on the porch rail and lighted a cigarette, trying to look casual; I had an uneasy sense of baleful eyes regarding me and I was acutely aware that I did not know who was going to jump first, or when, or from which direction. Barry began to make a noise like a dump truck, Sally sang, and the spaniel from across the street turned in through the gateposts and started up our driveway.

I jumped to my feet and shouted, "Get that dog *out* of here, someone!" Toby, confused—or perhaps the hijacking of his milk still rankled—wheeled sharply and made for the gray cat, who stood for a moment dumfounded and then, leaving one long scratch across Toby's nose, disappeared under the porch. Jannie started across the driveway, yelling and waving her arms, and the spaniel skittered sideways toward the hedge where Yain was waiting; with one great triumphant halloo Yain cleared the hedge and followed the shrieking spaniel down the driveway. Wild with success, Toby turned on Gato, who, still leaning against his tree, looked Toby straight in the eye and spoke once; skidding, Toby turned and without losing speed went in through the open back door and across the dining room and the living room and under the piano. From the barn came a single mournful yelp. "Any mice come out yet?" Sally called.

Jannie came back, panting, and I asked her to go under the porch and get the gray cat out so that I could put her back into the back apartment, but Jannie said that the only cat at present under the porch was Yain, who had apparently circled around the house and seemed to have eaten something large and satisfying, because he was half asleep and purring. Gato, humming to himself, trotted up the back steps and into the kitchen and up to the kitchen counter, where he ate the half cantaloupe I had left there.

Laurie called that he was coming out of the barn with the puppy, and Sally decided that since the barn door was going to be opened this would be a good time to go in and get her tricycle to ride, and Barry agreed. Jannie thought that at the same time she would get her stilts, so when Laurie was sure he had the puppy firmly leashed, Sally and Barry went in and came out riding their bikes and Jannie followed them, very tall and unsteady. Laurie came last with the puppy, who had clearly never been on a leash before. The two bikes went down to the end of the driveway, turned, and started back up again, and Gato stepped out onto the porch, where he settled to wash after his breakfast. Toby heard the puppy barking and hurried out to see what was going on; he and Laurie and the puppy began a sort of minuet up and down the driveway, with the two bikes turning and following them and Jannie stalking along beside. While Laurie held the leash in both hands, Toby came gravely forward and bowed to the puppy, and the puppy did a little tango step. Toby then crossed over and the puppy crossed under, taking the leash between Laurie's legs. While Laurie turned in a half circle, Toby and the puppy, *andante maestoso*, bowed and crossed again, then reversed in an allemande left, leaving Laurie perilously balanced on one foot. Gato watched, grinning, from the porch.

Then, without warning, the gray cat came down from the porch roof and charged Toby; Toby went "blip" and cleared the steps in one bound on his way to the piano, he jostled Gato, who went after the gray cat, who went under the porch and Yain came out, rudely awakened, and saw the puppy, whom he clearly mistook for the spaniel. Yain's charge upset Laurie completely and the puppy went through the stilts as through a doorway and down the driveway with Yain after him. The puppy lost a little ground because he cut sideways to go around the bikes, but Yain went clean over Sally and then, hardly touching the ground, clean over Barry, and we watched in silence as the puppy and Yain went up the hill and then off into the fields.

"He runs good, that puppy," Sally said at last. "We better call him Speedy."

Gato slouched lazily into the house and went to the washing machine for his nap. Jannie volunteered to search the yard for the gray cat, so I put Sally and Barry into the car, and Laurie took his bike, and we went off to look for the puppy. After hours of wandering and calling and knocking on strange doors we found our several ways back home, to discover that not only had Jannie failed to find any trace of the gray cat, but Yain had not come home, although Gato and Toby showed up for their dinners exceedingly chipper and affable. We spent that evening telephoning neighbors and speculating uneasily upon the probable fate of a four-month-old puppy lost in the country at night, and reminding one another that we had promised to give him a good home.

The next morning, which was Monday again, I sadly delivered three more ads to the local paper, and on Monday evening we were slightly embarrassed to discover that, since our first ads had been scheduled to run for a week, we now occupied the entire want-ad page except for the personals. Our ads now read:

Wanted to buy: female cat, kitten or half grown, good mouser. Call 5679.
Wanted to buy: puppy, mongrel large breed preferred. Call 5679.
Lost: female cat, gray tiger. Call 5679; reward.
Lost: shepherd puppy, brown and white. Call 5679; reward.
Lost: male cat, black, bandaged ear. Call 5679; reward.

On Tuesday morning the phone rang and when I answered it a man said, "You the person advertised for a pup?"

"I certainly am," I said. "Why, have you found him?"

There was a silence. Then the man said, "What reward you giving?"

"I thought two dollars," I said. "You see, we only paid five dollars for him in the first place, and—"

"That your ad to *buy* a dog, too?"

"Well, yes. You see, we put in the ad to *buy* a dog, and then we lost the dog we bought, so we put in another ad—"

"You must have quite a hand with dogs, lady," the man said.

"Look," I said, "this phone has been ringing steadily for four days. So if you have found—"

"Way *I* see it," he said, "you're paying five for a new dog? And only two if I found the one you already got?"

"Not at all," I said sharply. "Have you found—"

"Nope. What *I* got, lady," he said, "is a dog to sell." There was another pause and then he added reflectively, "Must look *some* like the one you lost, though."

I thought about it for a while and then I took the odd three dollars out of my housekeeping money and went off to get the dog. It took me most of the morning to find the farm where the puppy was and when I did I was not particularly surprised to see how strongly the new dog resembled the puppy we had lost. I remarked on this to the farmer, holding my five dollars uneasily in my hand, and the farmer laughed and took the five dollars and said it was a caution sometimes how two dogs could get to look alike. He put the five dollars into his back pocket and pointed out that naturally I didn't need to buy this dog unless I wanted to, but it was an uncommon good breed of dog for the price. I said I certainly hoped that *this* dog wasn't going to get lost, or, if he did, that I could find *him*, because it was quite a drain on my housekeeping money to have to go buying new dogs all the time. The farmer said soberly that well, a dog was man's best friend, especially children, thanked me for the five dollars without turning a hair, and helped me get the puppy into the car to bring home.

The children were just coming home from school for lunch, and they were delighted with the puppy, whom they clearly regarded as the one they had lost, and I did not feel that it was necessary to tell them or my husband that I had had to buy a new dog. I canceled all the ads in the papers, because the next morning Yain and the gray cat, whom we named Ninki, wandered up onto the back porch to share a bowl of milk and a good laugh with Gato. The gray cat was covered with burrs and Yain had lost his bandage somewhere. The spaniel from across the street did not come home for three days. On Tuesday morning there was a mouse in the sugar canister.

Gray Ninki was the first non-black cat we had ever owned, and for a while it used to give me quite a turn to see her moving soundlessly through the house; I kept thinking she was a ball of dust. When it became clear that she was going to have kittens we were all very much excited over the probable colors to be produced, fondly supposing that the father of the kittens was either Yain or Gato. However, when the kittens were born, four of them were gray, like Ninki, and the fifth one was green, a kind of olive drab shade. We gave away the four gray kittens and Ninki, who had never liked any of us much anyway, moved into a house about two blocks away and refused to come home, so we had Yain and Gato and the green kitten, whom we named Green Shax. Because our kitten was green we had less difficulty in reconciling ourselves to the local insistence that our puppy was not brown, but red, and that referring to such a fine red dog as "brown" was both offensive and misleading. The question of a name for the puppy was a matter of high dispute, and was only solved when my husband one morning cut out of the newspaper an account of a dog show in New York.

"*Here* are some good names," he said, at the breakfast table. "Now we can find something to call it by."

"He doesn't come *any*way," Jannie said. "We might as well go on calling him Puppy."

"But he won't *be* a puppy forever," I said. "After a while it will begin to sound silly, especially the way he's growing."

"Well," said my husband, consulting the paper, "how about Clifford Eidelweis? Quibble Baby? Tiny Trinket?"

"Clifford is nice," Jannie said. "I like Clifford."

"Won Ton Pearmain? Kreplach MacIntosh? Those all seem very fine dogs," my husband said. "In the paper."

"Why not Pal?" Jannie asked. "I thought we were always going to name him Pal."

"Why name him Pal," my husband asked, "when there are names like Hasty Pudding Put and Take? Or Silver Reuben of Iradell?"

"Pudding," Barry said eagerly. "A dog named Pudding."

"Squirrel Run Kentucky Boy? Shagbark Gimmel? Merriebert Ethelbeast?"

"Seems to me," Laurie said critically, "that a family with one cat named Yain and one cat named Gato and one cat named Green Shax had better get a dog named something like, maybe, Spot. Or Prince. Or Rover."

"Or Pal."

"I used to have a dog named Jack when I was a little girl," I said. "I'd like to have another dog named Jack."

"Champion Red John of Green Shax Farm," my husband said.

"Pal?"

"Jack. Red Jack."

"Red Pudding," Barry said softly.

It was very late, and I came in very quietly through the back door and closed it behind me without a sound. I went through the kitchen and dining room and living room and into the hall, guided by the hall light my husband had left on, took off my coat and left it on the stair rail, turned off the hall light and made my way upstairs softly in the dark.

Toby, on the living room couch, lifted his head as I went by, and thumped his tail once. Upstairs, I slipped off my shoes and in my stocking feet went through the guest room and down the hall to Laurie's room, saw that he was covered, and then into Jannie's room, where Gato lay hugely on the foot of her bed. Jannie stirred and said "M?" when I covered her, and I slipped out quickly before she woke. By the thin glow of the nightlights I found my way back through the guest room and into Sally's room; Sally's blankets were all heaped at the foot of her bed and she was sprawled over them. I took her extra blanket and put it over her, and she said "Hey!" indignantly. A small protest made me realize that Green Shax had been curled next to Sally and I had covered him, too; I moved the blanket and he poked his head out and closed his eyes again. Yain was sleeping on the hall chair, and purred once as I went past. Barry lay exquisitely asleep, blanket smooth, pillow straight. Jack was lying asleep across the doorsill of Barry's room, and Dikidiki was in bed with Barry, which argued that Barry had gone unwillingly to bed. Dikidiki stared at me unwinking, Jack groaned and sighed deeply.

I had thought to get undressed without turning on the light, and I found my dresser, where there was supposed to be a package of matches. I found my comb and a pair of earrings and what seemed in the dark to be some small furry animal; after a gasping minute I succeeded in identifying it as one of Sally's slippers, although I could not imagine what it was doing on my dresser unless Sally had been dancing up there in front of the mirror again.

"Who's that?" said my husband suddenly in the darkness.

[270]

"It's the Good Fairy," I said. "Didn't you leave a tooth under your pillow?"

"Oh," he said. Then, after a minute, "How was the poker game?"

"If you're going to chatter," I said, "I'll turn on the light and stop falling over the furniture." I turned and tossed Sally's slipper to him. "Here," I said.

"Ark," said my husband, thrashing.

"It's only Sally's slipper," I said. I turned on the light. "You don't have to kill it," I said. He had the slipper under his pillow and was beating it with his fist.

"Why aren't you asleep?" I asked. "It's late."

"I *was* asleep," he said. He doubled his pillow, put it against the headboard, and sat back comfortably. "How was the poker game?"

"We had the most *marvelous* food," I said. "Peggy brought some of those little hot sausage rolls, and Helen brought that shrimp stuff she makes, of course, and—"

"Did you win?"

"And everyone *loved* that cucumber mix *I* took, and I had to give Jean the recipe because she was so crazy about it, and Linda brought a kind of sour cream and clam soufflé stuff but I thought it had too much horseradish in it."

"Did you *play* poker?"

"Don't be silly—why would we have a ladies' poker game and not play poker? I *like* horseradish, ordinarily, but when you've got other things with it, it shouldn't be so strong, even though of course you can *always* taste clams."

"Did you win?"

"Shh," I said. "You'll wake the children."

I was brushing my hair, and he went and got a drink of

water and when he came back I said, "Listen, does three of a kind beat a flush?"

"What?" he said. "Oh. Well, no, it doesn't."

"Well, that's what I *said*," I told him, "and I kept arguing and arguing, but Helen said *she* knew perfectly well, and we were going to call up you or one of the other husbands and ask *them*, but you know how Linda always gets to crying at the least little thing? So of course there was nothing we could do, but anyway I'm glad to know I was right."

"Did you win?"

"Listen," I said, "when you come home late from a poker game and you're tired and the house is all dark and you try to get undressed in the dark and you're all worn out, do I—"

"Okay," he said. "Good night."

"Good night," I said.

Day after day after day I went around my house picking things up. I picked up books and shoes and toys and socks and shirts and gloves and boots and hats and handkerchiefs and puzzle pieces and pennies and pencils and stuffed rabbits and bones the dogs had left under the living room chairs. I also picked up tin soldiers and plastic cars and baseball gloves and sweaters and children's pocketbooks with nickels inside and little pieces of lint off the floor. Every time I picked up something I put it down again somewhere else where it belonged better than it did in the place I found it. Nine times out of ten I did not notice what I was picking up or where I put it until sometime later when someone in the family needed it; then, when Sally said where were her crayons I could answer at once:

kitchen windowsill, left. If Barry wanted his cowboy hat I could reply: playroom, far end of bookcase. If Jannie wanted her arithmetic homework, I could tell her it was under the ashtray on the dining room buffet. I could locate the little nut that came off Laurie's bike wheel, and the directions for winding the living room clock. I could find the recipe for the turkey cutlets Sally admired and the top to my husband's fountain pen; I could even find, ordinarily, the little celluloid strips which went inside the collar of his nylon shirt.

That was, of course, entirely automatic, like still remembering the home telephone number of my college roommate and being able to recite "Oh, what is so rare as a day in June"; if I could not respond at once, identifying object and location in unhesitating answer to the question, the article was very apt to remain permanently lost. Like Jannie's pink Easter-egg hat, which disappeared—let me see; it was the day Laurie got into the fight with the Haynes boys, and the porch rocker got broken—make it the end of October. We had many small places in our big house where an Easter-egg hat could get itself hopelessly hidden, so when Jannie asked one night at dinner, the end of October, "Who took my Easter-egg hat?" and I found myself without an immediate answer, it was clear that the hat had taken itself off, and although we searched halfheartedly, Jannie had to wear a scarf around her head until the weather got cold enough to wear her long-tailed knitted cap.

Laurie's sneaker was of considerably more moment, since of course he could not play basketball with a scarf tied around his left foot. He came to the top of the back stairs of a Saturday morning and inquired gently who had stolen his sneaker. I opened my mouth to answer, found my mind blank, and closed my mouth again. Laurie came halfway down the stairs and bawled, "Moooooooom, where'd my *sneaker* get to?" and I still could not answer. "I neeeeeed my *sneaker*," Laurie howled, "I got to play baaaaaaasketball."

"I don't know," I called.

"But I *need* it," Laurie said. He crashed down the stairs and into the study where I sat reading the morning paper and drinking a cup of coffee. "I got to play basketball, so I need my sneakers. I can't play on the basketball court without sneakers. So I need—"

"Have you looked? In your room? Under your bed?"

"Yeah, sure." He thought. "It's not there, though."

"Outdoors?"

"Now what would my sneaker be doing outdoors, I ask you? You think I get dressed and undressed out on the lawn, maybe, for the neighbors?"

"Well," I said helplessly, "you had it last Saturday."

"I *know* I had it last Saturday, you think I'm foolish or something?"

"Wait." I went and stood at the foot of the back stairs and called, "Jannie?"

There was a pause and then Jannie said, sniffling, "Yes?"

"Good heavens," I said, "are you reading *Little Women* again?"

Jannie sniffled. "Just the part where Beth dies."

"Look," I said, "the sun is shining and the sky is blue and—"

"You seen my sneaker?" Laurie yelled from in back of me.

"No."

"You *sure*?"

Jannie came to the top of the stairs, wiping her eyes with

her hand. "Hey," she said, "maybe some girl took it. For a keepsake."

"Wha?" said Laurie incredulously. "Took my *sneaker*? Who?"

"Like Mr. Brooke did Meg's glove, in *Little Women*, because he was in love with her and they got married."

"*Wha?*" For a minute Laurie stared at her, and then he turned deliberately and went back to the door of the study. "My sister," he announced formally to his father, "has snapped her twigs."

"That so?" said his father.

"I ask you." Laurie gestured. "Junk from books," he said.

"Well, he did," Jannie insisted, coming down the stairs. "He took it and hid it for ever so long and when Jo found out she—"

"Sally, Barry," I was calling from the back door. "Has either of you seen Laurie's sneaker?"

Sally and Barry were dancing on the lawn, turning and flickering among the last fallen leaves; when I called they circled and came toward the house, going "cheep-cheep." "We're little birds," Sally explained, coming closer. "Cheep-cheep."

"Have you seen Laurie's sneaker?"

"Cheep-cheep."

"Well?"

Barry thought. "I have unseen it," he remarked. "I did unsee Laurie's sneaker a day and a day and a day and a day and *many* mornings ago."

"Splendid," I said. "Sally?"

"No. But don't worry. I shall get it back for dear Laurie, dear Mommy."

"If you mean magic you better not let your father hear

you, young lady. No," I said over my shoulder to Laurie, "they haven't."

"But I will find it, Laurie dear, never fear, Laurie dear, I will your sneaker find for you."

"Yeah. So what'm I gonna do?" he asked me. "Play basketball in my socks or something?"

"Are you *sure* you looked under your bed?"

He looked at me in the manner his favorite television detective reserves for ladies who double-talk the cops. "Yeah," he said. "Yeah, lady. I'm sure."

"Daddy won't notice," Sally said busily to Barry. "All this will take is just a little bit of golden magic and Daddy will never notice and there will be dear Laurie's sneaker just right here."

"Can I do magic too?"

"You can be my dear helper and you can carry the shovel."

I went into the study and sat down and Laurie followed me. "And he kept it for weeks and weeks next to his heart," Jannie was explaining to her father, "and she was looking for it just like Laurie but Mr. Brooke had it all the time."

"How about that little dark-haired girl?" my husband asked Laurie. "The one who keeps calling you so much?"

"Nah," Laurie said. "She's tipped, anyhow. Besides, how could she get my sneaker?" He slapped his forehead. "A veritable madhouse," he said. "Lose a sneaker and they start criticizing your friends and trying to make out she stole it. Bah."

He flung himself violently into one of our good plastic leather chairs, which slid back across the floor and into the bookcase. "Bah," said Laurie. He threw his arms dramatically into the air and let them fall resignedly. "Never *find* anything around here, that's the *big* trouble," he explained. "Nothing's ever where you *put* it. If *she—*"

"If by *she* you mean *me—*" I began ominously.

"Always coming and picking things up and putting them away where a person can't find them. Always—"

"If you'd put things away neatly when you take them off instead of just throwing everything under your bed—" I stopped to think. "Have you looked under your bed?" I asked.

Laurie stood up and threw his arms wide. "Why was I ever born?" he demanded.

Jannie nodded. "In *Beverley Lee, Girl Detective*," she pointed out, "when the secret plans for the old armory get lost, Beverley Lee and her girl friend Piggy, *they* look for clues."

"A broken shoelace?" my husband suggested.

"Well, when did you see them last?" I asked reasonably. "Seems to me if you could remember when you had them last, you might remember where you put them then."

"Yeah. Well," Laurie said, scowling, "I *know* I had them last Saturday. But then I took them off and I remember they were on my bookcase because I had to remember to make that map for geography and that was for Wednesday when we had gym—say!" He opened his eyes and his mouth wide. "Gym. I wore them Wednesday to school for gym. So I had them on Wednesday."

"And Wednesday," I put in, "was the day you were so late getting home from school because you were hanging around Joe's with that pack of juvenile delinquents and—"

"I told you six times already, those girls just happened to come by there by *accident*, how'd I know they'd be around

Joe's? And anyway you got no right to go calling my friends—"

"And you never got your chores done and I kept dinner till six-thirty."

"That girl called, too," my husband put in.

"And I must of had my sneakers on all that time, because I never had time because *she* made me do my chores and then I had to rush through dinner because—because—"

"You were going to the dance," Jannie said, triumphant. "You got all dressed up, so *naturally* you put on shoes."

"Hey!" Laurie swung around and gestured wildly. "I got dressed—"

"You took a shower," I said. "I remember because—"

He shuddered. "I took a shower because *she* wouldn't let me have my good blue pants from the cleaners *unless* I took a shower."

"No gentleman escorts a lady to a public function unless he has bathed and dressed himself in completely clean clothes," my husband said.

"So I undressed in the bathroom because I always do and then when I went out I had this towel around me and I was carrying my clothes and the sneaker and I—"

"I saw it," I said suddenly. "I did see it after all. I came upstairs to get two aspirin after you had finally gone to the dance and I remember the way the bathroom looked; the floor was sopping and dirty towels all over and the soap and—"

"The sneaker," Laurie said impatiently, "keep on the subject. The sneaker, the sneaker."

I meditated. "It was lying just inside the door and one wet towel was half on top of it. And I . . . and I . . ." I thought. "What *did* I do?"

"Think, think, think." Laurie stood over me flapping his hands.

"Look," I said. "I go around this house and I go around this house and I *go* around this house and I pick up shoes and socks and shirts and hats and gloves and handkerchiefs and books and toys and I always put them down again, someplace where they belong. Now when I went upstairs and saw that mess of a bathroom I had to clean up I would have taken the soap and put it in the soapdish. And I would have taken the bathmat and put it over the edge of the tub. And I would have taken the towels—"

"And put them in the hamper," Laurie said impatiently. "We know."

"You do? Because I have often wondered what happens all the times I say to you to put the towels—"

"Yeah, so next time I'll remember, sure. What about the *sneaker?*"

"Anyway they were wet so I couldn't put them in the hamper. I would have hung them over the shower rail to dry so *then* I could put them in the hamper. And then I would have picked up the sneaker—"

"Laurie's sneaker is weaker and creaker and cleaker and breaker and fleaker and greaker . . ." Sally wound through the study, eyes shut, chanting. Barry came behind her, doing an odd little two-step. Sally had a pail of sand and a shovel and she was making scattering motions.

"Now *wait* a minute here," my husband began.

"It's all right," Sally said, opening one eye. "I'm just pretending. This is only sand."

"We're just untending," Barry explained reassuringly. "Bleaker and sneaker and weaker and deaker."

They filed out. My husband studied the floor morosely.

"That certainly looked like magic to *me*," he said, "and I don't *like* it. Going to have footwear popping up all over, right through the floor, probably wreck the foundations."

"Reconstruct the scene of the crime," Jannie said suddenly. "Because Beverley Lee Girl Detective and her girl friend Piggy, that's what *they* did. In *The Mystery of the Broken Candle*, when they had to find the missing will. They reconstructed the scene of the crime. They got everybody there and put everything the way it was—"

"Say!" Laurie looked at her admiringly. "You're charged, girl. Come on," he said, making for the stairs, and stopped in the doorway to look compellingly at me. "Come *on*," he said.

"And creaker and beaker and leaker and veaker."

"Gangway, birdbait," Laurie said. He stopped to pat his younger sister on the head. "You keep sprinkling that there magic, Perfessor. Size six and a half, white."

"Kindly do not poke the Sally," said Sally, drawing away stiffly.

"Unpoke, unpoke," Barry said.

"Come *on*," Laurie said to me. He called ahead to Jannie, "You get the towels wet and throw them on the floor. I'll get the other sneaker and when she comes we'll have it all ready."

"You might as well take two more aspirin," my husband said.

"I might as well," I said.

Wearily I headed up the stairs, sand grinding underfoot. The bathroom is at the head of the stairs, and by the time I was near the top I could see that everything was prepared. Rigorously, I put my mind back three days. It is eight-thirty in the evening, I told myself. I am coming upstairs to get myself two aspirin. Laurie has just gone to the dance, I have just told him goodbye, get home early, behave yourself, be careful, do you have a clean handkerchief? Jannie is reading. Sally and Barry are asleep. It is eight-thirty Wednesday evening, I am coming to get two aspirin. I came to the top of the stairs, and sighed. The bathroom floor was sopping, the bathmat was soaked and crumpled, wet towels lay on the floor. In the corner, half under a wet towel, was one white sneaker. I asked myself through my teeth how old people had to get before they learned to pick up after themselves and after all our efforts to raise our children in a decent and clean house here they still behaved like pigs and the sooner Laurie grew up and got married and had a wife to pick up after him the better off I would be and maybe I would just take his allowance and hire a full-time nursemaid for him. I picked up the bathmat and hung it over the edge of the tub. I put the soap in the soapdish and hung the towels over the shower rail. I picked up the sneaker and resisted the temptation to slam it into the wastebasket. Then, with the sneaker in my hand, I went to the other side of the hall to the linen closet to get clean towels and a dry bathmat and Laurie and Jannie burst out of the guest room shouting, "You see? You see?"

Jannie said excitedly, "Just like Beverley Lee and it turned out it *was* the caretaker all the time."

"Look, look," Laurie said, pointing. I had the door of the linen closet open and I reached up onto the towel shelf and took down Jannie's Easter-egg hat.

"What?" I said, surprised.

"That's my hat," Jannie said.

"Why would I want to put your hat in the linen closet?" I demanded. "Don't be silly."

"My nice pink Easter-egg hat," Jannie said, pleased.

"Craazy," Laurie remarked. "Opens the closet and there's the hat. Craazy." He pushed past me and began to paw through the towels.

"Ridiculous," I said. "I *never* put hats in linen closets. Linen closets are where I keep towels and sheets and extra blankets, not hats."

"Not sneakers, either." Laurie stood back and dusted his hands.

"You pick up every one of those towels," I said, annoyed. "And then you and your sister can get right in there and clean up that bathroom. And the next time I find that pink hat lying around I am going to burn it. And you can tell Beverley Lee Girl Detective—"

"Any luck?" my husband called from the foot of the stairs.

"Certainly not." I started down. "Of all the idiotic notions and now it's too late in the year *any*way for a little hat like that."

"Sneaker sneaker sneaker!" It was Sally and Barry, in glory. Laurie raced past me down the stairs. "Got it? Sal," he yelled, "you *got* it?"

Proudly the little procession wound around to the front hall. Sally was still scattering sand but Barry was bearing the sneaker on high. "Gee," Laurie said. "Hey, kids, thanks. Where was it?"

"Under your bed," Sally said. "We did a lot of—" she glanced at her father "—blagic," she said. "And then we went up and looked. Very good, Barry."

"Very good, Sally," Barry said.

"Gosh." Laurie was pleased. He turned and gave me an affectionate pat on the head. "Boy," he said, "are *you* ever a tippy old lady." Then, in a burst of gratitude, he added,

"I'm going to go down right now on my bike and get you kids each a popsicle."

"Well, me, too, I should *think*," Jannie said indignantly. "After all, it was me thought of reconstructing the crime, and in *Elsie Dinsmore* when Elsie—"

"What is this crime talk?" I said. "Anyone would think that instead of spending all my time picking up and putting away—"

"The sneaker," Laurie said to me, gesturing. "The other sneaker. I got to get down and get those popsicles, so let's have it."

"What?" I said.

"The sneaker, dear. The one you just had upstairs, for heaven's sake."

Uncomfortably I looked down at my empty hands. "Now let's see," I said. "I had it just a minute ago. . . ."

I was sitting at the kitchen table grating potatoes for potato pancakes and was thus a wholly captive audience when Jannie came in from school with her arithmetic and spelling books, and, of course, *Little Women*. She put the books down, hung up her jacket and hat, took an apple, and sat down at the table across from me. "I been meaning to ask you for a long time," she said. "Suppose I wanted to write a book. Where would I begin?"

"At the beginning," I said smartly; I had just grated my knuckle.

"I wish Laurie and Barry were girls," she said.

"Why on earth?"

"And Sally's name was Beth."

"Why put the whammy on Sally? Why don't *you* be Beth?"

"I'm Jo."

"And Laurie is Meg? And poor Barry has to be Amy?"

"If they were only *girls*."

"And does that make me Marmee? Or can I be the old cook?"

"Hannah? When *I* write *my* book—"

"I'd rather be crazy old Aunt March, come to think of it. Who do you like for Professor Bhaer?"

Jannie turned pink. "I didn't really think about that yet," she said.

Charitably, I changed the subject. "Don't you have any homework to do?" I asked.

She sighed. "I got to write a book report," she said. "That's why I'd like to write a book, so then I could write a book report on *that*, and save all that time."

"I see." Resolutely I took up the first onion and began to grate. "What I always wondered," Jannie went on, "was when they went on the picnic in the book and they played Authors. Because in *my* game of Authors there's Louisa May Alcott and she *wrote Little Women*." She looked at me inquiringly and I smiled bravely, tears running down my cheeks. "Well," she said, "in her own book did they play Authors with their own book on the cards? And if Louisa May Alcott had to do a book report for school then could she—"

"I see what you mean," I said, weeping.

She laughed. "You're crying like a fish," she said. "Now, what I wondered, if Louisa May Alcott wrote a book. Because she had to write *that* book because it was already on the Authors cards, you see? And *Eight Cousins* and *Rose in Bloom* and *Little Men*."

I sniffled. "*Jo's Boys*," I said. "Don't forget *Jo's Boys*."

"But if they were already playing Authors in the book how did they know she was going to finish it? Because suppose she got halfway and she didn't like it and threw it away how could they play Authors in the book with *Little Women* on the Authors card? Or if she changed her mind and decided to call it—"

"Suppose," I said, "she decided to have them play pinochle? Then she wouldn't have to write *any* books."

"But she would have to write *one* book anyway because otherwise she couldn't be in the Authors game."

I got up and went to the sink to rinse out the grater. "But if she weren't in the Authors game—" I began and then stopped myself, shaking my head violently.

Jannie giggled. "I suppose you *did* read the book?" she asked.

"I did."

"Then who," Jannie asked triumphantly, "said, 'That boy is a perfect Cyclops, isn't he?' "

"Amy," I said. "Who said, 'I never enjoyed housekeeping, and I'm going to take a vacation today'?"

"Marmee, but she didn't mean it. Who said, 'Birds in their little nests agree'?"

"Beth, on the first page." I took down the flour. "Who said, 'You can never get too much salt in potato pancakes'?"

"Who?"

"Your grandmother. Now go and write your book."

My husband is always making little remarks about money. Sometimes he says that it doesn't grow on trees, and sometimes he says that I must think he is made of it. When he buys a Greek drachma he says that we can't take it with us, and when I take the children to get shoes for school he says in a kind of high voice that there isn't enough of it in the world for this family. I once passed the door to the dining room when he and several friends were playing poker and I heard him laughing and saying it was a shame to take it away like this. When he pays the children their allowances he says that it is a great responsibility, and whenever any of us asks him for some he says he can't afford it. However, although the discussion of money in general is a constant and urgent theme in our family, I do not think I ever heard my husband say so many different things about money as he did when the man came from the income tax department. As a matter of fact, during the twenty-odd hours between the telephone call and the man's departure I do not think my husband spent more than a second or two reflecting on any other subject.

He was not pleased with the telephone call. It was a Wednesday evening, and our family was assembled at dinner. It was the kind of dinner I think of as a Wednesday evening dinner, because on Wednesday I always begin to think of economizing so we can have dinner on Thursday and Friday. As a result—although it hardly mattered, anyway, since my husband never did eat any dinner that night—we were having Monday night's meat loaf warmed over. Laurie had seized control of the conversation as we sat down, and I was trying to serve the meat loaf and gesture to Jannie to put her napkin in her lap and gesture to Sally to take her napkin ring out of her lap and gesture to Barry that he would not be served any meat loaf unless he put away his space gun and sat in his chair correctly and at the same time I was trying to ask my husband if he wanted noodles.

"Isn't it?" Laurie demanded of the table at large. "Because

suppose I did and then no one but me danced with her, what could I do?"

"Certainly," his father said.

"Noodles?"

"Besides," Laurie said, waving his fork, "you figure it's forty cents if I go stag, and sixty cents I take a girl—I don't know any girls *worth* twenty cents. And I'd have to dance with her, maybe every dance except if she wanted to sit down or something."

He stopped for breath, and I opened my mouth, but Jannie said, "But if no one took any girls there wouldn't be any girls there and who would you dance with at all?"

"There's *always* girls there," Laurie said drearily. "And Mrs. Williams always coming up and saying whyn't you go ask that nice girl over there if she wants to dance. Yeah."

"Elbows off the table," I said.

"Why go at all?" his father asked. "Why not stay home and save forty cents?"

Laurie sighed impatiently. "Because I already save twenty cents by not taking a girl, and I need the money. Anyway, they match pennies in the cloakroom."

His father frowned. "Young man," he said, "I will not have you gambling. Other people's money—"

The phone rang. "Stop her!" Laurie yelled, and I made a fast grab, but Sally had gotten away in a nice running start and was out in the hall before anyone else could move. Sally can move with unbelievable speed from a sitting position, and also she is the only one in the family except Barry, who is slow, who can fit under the telephone table.

"Hello?" she said in her sweet clear voice, and Laurie sighed irritably. "It's a wonder anyone bothers to call here any more at *all*," he said. "Rob tried to call me all day yesterday and Sally answered every time."

"Well, whose daddy did you want to speak to?" Sally asked.

My husband looked up, alarmed.

"How do you know it's my daddy you want to speak to if you don't know my name?" Sally asked shrewdly.

I got up and followed my husband out to the hall. Sally, eying us, retreated still farther under the telephone table and sat hunched up around the phone. "Because if he doesn't want to talk to you I have to say he's taking a shower," she explained.

"Sally," I said, "give me that phone."

"Do you have a little girl six years old named Sally?" Sally asked into the phone.

"Sarah," said her father.

She poked her head out and looked up innocently. "Will I say you're taking a shower?" she asked. "It's just some man who hasn't got any children."

My husband started to speak, checked himself, and held out his hand. Unwillingly Sally put the phone into it and crawled out between his legs. "No one ever telephones *me*," she said sadly.

"Hello?" my husband said into the phone. I took Sally by the wrist and led her back to the table and sat her down firmly. "No dessert," I said, and she snarled. "Stop it," I said, and she giggled.

"Fifteen cents?" Jannie said to Laurie.

"Half a buck?" Laurie countered.

"Twenty cents?"

"Forty?"

"What?" I said.

"If Laurie clears the table tonight and scrapes the dishes and stacks them," Jannie asked me, "is it worth any more than fifteen cents if I pay him from my allowance?"

"That's a lot of dishes," Laurie said. He poked scornfully at his butter plate. "Look at all this stuff," he said. "Thirty cents."

"If you practice my piano lesson for me I could make it twenty-five," Jannie said.

My husband came back to the table. He sat down in his chair and stared straight ahead of him. The children looked at him curiously, and then Jannie said, "Every time we let Dad talk on the phone something happens. Remember when it was the man about the dogs stealing deer hides?"

"Or the library with the books overdue," Laurie said.

"Or that lady," Jannie said, "the one who keeps calling to find out if the phone is working all right and Dad never knows."

"Or girls for Laurie," Sally said.

Laurie turned to look at her balefully. "Yeah?" he said. "Yeah?"

"At least," my husband said to me suddenly, "we still have the children. Our dear children, and a roof over our heads." He thought. "I hope," he said.

"You always worry about every little thing," I said. "The man told us clearly that the roof would last through this winter and maybe even on into spring."

"Trusting little creatures," my husband said, reaching one hand out toward Sally, who looked as though she might bite it. "An affectionate family, a warm hearth, a scrap of bread on the table—a man needs little more than that."

"*I* don't know," I said to Laurie, who was making faces

of astonishment at me. "Yes, dear?" I said to my husband. "Go on."

"I want you all to be brave," my husband said, looking around the table at us. "When misfortune strikes, a family must face the world together."

"Twenty cents?" Laurie whispered across at Jannie.

"Son," his father said, "I am afraid that your dancing days are over. All allowances will very likely be cut, if not withdrawn altogether. There will be no color television set this year. Your mother will stop squandering all that money every week and learn to make simple nourishing meals out of rice and perhaps oatmeal. On gala days we will share an egg. Laurie can perhaps take a newspaper route—"

"Jannie can support us with her needle, as far as that goes," I said.

"Where are *you* going to be?" Laurie asked. "In jail?"

His father turned pale. "Please don't *talk* like that," he said.

"You might as well tell us," I said. "So we can start facing the world together. Who was on the phone?"

My husband sighed. "The Department of Internal Revenue," he said. "A question has arisen about our income tax returns. The man will be here in the morning. I am to be ready with my books."

"Well, that doesn't seem very bad," I said. "It seems silly for them to check up on *you*, but of course you just have to tell them . . ." I looked at my husband and stopped talking abruptly.

"We learned in Social Studies class how to make out an income tax return," Laurie said. "After dinner I'll be glad to help you, Dad."

"I've *already* made out our return, thank you," my husband said. "That's why the man is *coming*. And I don't think I want any dinner, thank you." He got up and went into the study.

"Gosh," Laurie said. "What's *he* so bothered about, anyway?"

Sally nodded wisely. "That man on the phone sounded pretty mad," she said.

I saw the children through their dinner and then took my husband's coffee into the study. He was walking around and around in a little circle, carrying his checkbook. "Look," I said, "I just can't see what you're so *worried* about. Here's your coffee. Why, that man probably checks income tax returns all the time, it's his job. Are you going to get all upset just because he's coming here to ask a question or two?"

"Yes, indeed," my husband said.

"But we're honest citizens, aren't we? We're law-abiding, we pay our taxes—"

"Yes, indeed," my husband said.

"Well, then," I said, "all you have to do is tell this fellow that there's nothing to check over, all your deductions are in order, and everything will be—"

"Yes, indeed," my husband said.

"Well," I said helplessly, "I just don't see what you're so *worried* about."

"Don't you?" said my husband.

I stopped following him around with the cup of coffee and sat down instead. He turned suddenly and looked at me. "When you drive the car into town, what do you think about?" he asked me.

"What?"

"When you *drive* the *car* into *town*, what do you *think* about?"

"Money," I said. "Whether I have enough, or maybe even a little bit extra so I can maybe buy myself something. Shoes, maybe. I could certainly use a pair of shoes."

"I took off a lot for business expenses for the car," my husband said. He turned and waved the checkbook at me. "From now on," he said, "you don't ever drive that car into town, see, unless it's on business."

"What possible business could I have—"

"I don't care what you do when you're *there*, just so when you're driving the car into town you have in mind some business expense you're doing it for. Typewriter ribbons, maybe. If you went all the way into town to get typewriter ribbons, that would be going on business, see? Because I use a typewriter ribbon in my typewriter. And then once you got there for a typewriter ribbon, then you could do any fool shopping you wanted, and it would be a business trip anyway. See?"

"Not really," I said. "If I buy a typewriter ribbon for you every time I go into town then pretty soon you'd have more typewriter ribbons than—"

"You don't really have to *buy* one," my husband said impatiently. "You just *think* about buying it on the way into town. As though you were really only driving into town just to get a typewriter ribbon and planned on kind of sneaking off to do your other shopping, but it was really just a trip to get a typewriter ribbon, a *business* trip. See?"

"But they'd get to thinking I was pretty silly, around the stationery store," I said. "Seeing me come in every day nearly for another typewriter ribbon, or else coming in *pretending* I was going to get a typewriter ribbon, because I have enough trouble now with running out of money all of a sudden and having to give things back." He opened his mouth again and

I said hastily, "All right, though. I'll put it on my shopping list right away, and then I won't forget."

"Canceled checks," he said. He sat down at his desk and began to open drawers. I sighed.

"I just don't know what you're so *worried* about," I said.

"Four children?" he asked.

"Four."

"I wish . . ." he began, and then stopped. "Look," he said then, "I work in here, don't I? In this study?"

"I guess so," I said.

"So I was certainly justified in taking off the rent for one room in the house which is like an office for me. Couldn't I?"

"I guess not," I said, bewildered.

"And you better get Barry's train and stuff out of here before that fellow comes tomorrow. And I'll kind of leave my typewriter out and some papers lying around."

"I could go right into town tomorrow and think about a typewriter ribbon," I offered hopefully.

"I wish I felt better about that car," he said.

"Well, after all, four days a week I drive you up to your classes at the college, and then I come and get you. *That's* a lot of wear and tear on the car."

"No," he said. "Commuting to and from your employment is not business driving."

I stared at him. "You mean," I said, and gasped, and caught my breath, "you mean I get up in the morning and I drive Barry to nursery school and then I come back and I get you and I drive you to the college and then I go back and I get Barry and bring him home and then I go back and get you and I bring you home and then I take you up again in the afternoon and then I go and get you again and they call that *pleasure* driving? Now, listen." I got up and began to walk around and around the study. "Now, listen. There are a lot of things we have to put up with, like prices going up on everything and the children's overshoes nearly triple what they were last winter and even the laundry raising prices again and the turn-in they gave us on the old car, and the way the mail is getting slower every day, but I can tell you right now that no G-man covered with badges is going to come walking right into my own house and stand there with machine guns and tear gas and whatever else they carry and abuse his authority pushing me around and trying to tell me that this amateur taxi service I run has got to be called *pleasure* driving. Now you listen to me—"

"I don't *want* to listen to you," my husband said. "And now I think of it, I would like you to go out somewhere while the man is here tomorrow. Maybe you better stay away for the whole day, because it says right on the tax blank in the small print that commuting back and forth to your place of employment is not a legitimate deductible expense for your car. Look," he said. "If you drive me to the college, that's not deductible. But if I walk to the college and you drive along behind me with my brief case in the car, well, *that's* deductible."

"Drive your brief case? Why can't it walk?"

"No," my husband said. "No, no." After a while he went on in a very quiet voice, "I really can't see that it will do any good for both of us to be worrying about this. I'll just look over these old checks, and you go count the children again."

I bribed the children into bed, and read a story to Sally and Barry, and got the dishes done and the dogs and cats fed. When the kitchen was in order I went and knocked on the study door and my husband said to go away and not bother him. I watched television for a while, and read a mystery story, and about eleven I went and knocked on the study door and my husband said to go away and not bother him. I said I just thought he might like a little something to eat and he said that later he might have a glass of milk but not to wait up for him. I read for a while longer and then knocked on the study door and said good night, and my husband said to go away and not bother him and good night. Sometime around two in the morning Barry had a nightmare and I went in to quiet him, and then downstairs where I knocked on the study door and said did he know it was two in the morning. My husband said *please* to go away and not bother him; didn't he have enough on his mind without my coming to pound on the door every two minutes just to tell him what time it was?

When I came down in the morning he was asleep in the study chair. All his old checkbooks were lined up neatly on the desk, along with a stack of old bills. I covered him with a blanket and went into the kitchen and made breakfast for the children and got them dressed and fed and washed and off to school. I put Barry into his snowsuit and drove him to nursery school, and on the way home I picked up the morning papers. When I had the coffee made and the paper all ready by my husband's plate I went into the study and woke him and he opened his eyes and said, "I forgot the depreciation on the pencil sharpener."

The man was supposed to come at ten. Between ten, when he was stationed in the study, and five past ten, when the doorbell finally rang, my husband came into the kitchen four times, once to ask if I thought he ought to change into another shirt, the one with the darns on the elbows, once to ask if I had any idea what our garbage disposal came to by the year, once to ask if there was any aspirin in the kitchen, and once to complain that it was positively heartless to leave a victim like this, kicking his heels and waiting in agony.

When the doorbell rang I heard him go down the front hall with a dignified, measured step, as of one going manfully to his fate, and I closed the kitchen door and sat down on the kitchen stool and wondered what to do. I do not ordinarily find much difficulty in disposing of my morning time, which frequently seems too short for any reasonable occupation, but this morning the dishes were done and the table was set for lunch and I had made brownies and a nut cake the day before, and all that was left was the study rug, which needed vacuuming, but I thought my husband might not like having me coming through with the vacuum while he was talking to the man from the income tax. I heard his voice raised once; he was shouting "Depreciation," and then he was quiet, and I could hear the low reasonable murmur which was the man from the income tax.

My husband told me afterward that the man's name was Mr. Kelly and that, all things considered, he was quite an agreeable fellow, but I never saw him. I sat on the kitchen stool for about fifteen minutes and then I gathered up all the library books and went out and got into the car and drove down the street to the library. A couple of new mystery stories had come in, and I read one of them sitting at the library table, and I watched the library desk for a few minutes while Mrs. Johnson went out for a cigarette, and we talked about the P.T.A. and the Starlight 4-H Club food sale. After I left the library I picked up the mail and sat in the car for a few minutes reading a letter from my mother, and then it was almost time to pick up Barry at nursery school, so I stopped in the grocery and asked the grocer if he had a typewriter ribbon. He said no, but they had some pencils, so I bought four pencils.

When Barry and I got home a few minutes later the voices were still going on in the study. Barry headed directly for the study door to show Daddy the airplane he had made in nursery school, and I caught him and gave him a piece of paper and the four pencils to play with. By the time the other children came home I had vegetable soup ready, and grilled cheese sandwiches. As each child came up onto the back porch I opened the kitchen door and said "Shh." They came in quietly, casting uneasy glances at the study door, and sitting in silence at the table.

Finally Laurie burst out "Golly!" and I said "Shh," and he whispered, "I can't *stand* it. Golly, poor old Dad."

"I asked my teacher did she think my daddy would get arrested by the policeman if he took that man's money," Sally remarked, looking darkly into her vegetable soup. "She said she certainly hoped not."

"Shh," I said.

"Where's Daddy?" Barry asked.

"Shh," I said. "Eat your lunch."

"Shh," Laurie said.

"Poor old Dad," Jannie said.

"Shh," I said. We all heard the door between the study and the front hall open, and then footsteps going along the hall to the front door. We could hear the man from the income tax saying clearly, "Of course, you know by now it doesn't mean a thing to me. It's only a word, that's all. A hundred dollars—five hundred dollars—ten cents; it doesn't really *mean* anything to us fellows; it's just a word."

"Well, I can see where it might be," my husband said. "Goodbye."

"No, no," said the man from the income tax. "In our business we *never* come right out and say 'goodbye' to a victim. We always figure we'll be seeing him again some time." He laughed uproariously, and we could hear the front door close.

After a minute my husband's footsteps sounded again in the hall and he came through the dining room and into the kitchen. We all sat around the kitchen table looking at him.

"Well, well, well," he said. "What's for lunch?" He pulled out his chair and sat down.

There was a silence and then Laurie said, "How is everything?"

"Fine," my husband said, surprised. "Why?"

"We just thought you might be tired or something," I said. "You had so little sleep."

"Never felt better," my husband said. "That was a nice fellow, by the way. He gave me a few pointers on next year's income tax. Giant fan," he said to Laurie.

"That's too bad," Laurie said politely.

"Did he come all this way just to ask you to play for the Giants?" I asked.

"For the *Giants*?" He was astonished.

"I only thought," I said elaborately, "that there was some difficulty about your income tax. Some question. I thought he came all this way to ask you some questions about your income tax."

"Oh, that," my husband said. "Yes. Got my figures wrong, as a matter of fact. I put it down eight times nine was fifty-six."

"Dad." Laurie put down his soup spoon. "For *gracious* goodness sakes. Oh, Dad, for gracious goodness *sakes*."

"It's seventy-four," Jannie said helpfully.

My husband leaned back and took out one of the cigars he ordinarily saves for after dinner. "It never pays to worry about money," he said. "After all, money isn't everything."

Suddenly it was only two weeks to wait until Christmas, and the temperature was twenty-two below the night of the school Christmas pageant. Then it was only eight days to go; formally, the children and I hung a Christmas wreath on each gatepost. Then, some hours less than a week, and my husband's present, ordered from that place in Seattle, might not come in time; then it was five days and then sixty hours and fourteen minutes, and we brought the Christmas tree home and stood it on the back porch. The store in Seattle was criminally slow, perhaps even forgetful; it was only thirty-seven hours before Christmas. Then, the morning of Christmas Eve I stuffed the turkey and decided on apple pie, after all, because last year no one had touched the pumpkin. All afternoon the children and I drove around town to the houses of their friends, leaving little packages of candy, and chocolate apples, and all afternoon their friends had been stopping off at our house ("Can't stay; just want to leave this, and Merry Christmas!") and leaving little packages of Christmas cookies and fruit cake. Then at last it was five o'clock in the afternoon, and the special delivery truck pulled up outside with the package from Seattle. Laurie and his father went to bring in the tree and I signed for the package and Jannie stirred the eggnog and Sally salted the popcorn and Barry sat in a corner of the kitchen, wide-eyed and still.

"Deck the halls with boughs of holly," Jannie sang, and Sally chanted, "Christmas, Christmas."

"You'll have to get the ax," my husband told Laurie.

"Unless your mother would prefer a hole cut in the ceiling."

"You say that every year," I said, going past him sideways so he would not see the package I was holding behind me. "If you would only measure the tree before you bring it in—"

"You say that every year," he said. "Why are you walking like that?"

"Because I have your Christmas present behind me and I don't want you to notice," I said with dignity, and scurried into the kitchen to put the package behind the washing machine.

It takes three enormous cartons to hold all our Christmas decorations, and all during the green spring and the hot summer months and the long sunny days and the gray rainy days the cartons sit on a shelf in the far corner of the barn. Then, at last, Laurie and Jannie lift them down and carry them together through the snow to the house, going very slowly, cautioning one another, coming indoors with snow on their boots. I never look at the cartons labeled CHRISTMAS: LIGHTS, ORNAMENTS, DECORATIONS without remembering the sadness of putting them away last year, assuring the children that Christmas would come again, it would surely come again, they would hardly notice the length of the year before Christmas came again. Then Christmas comes again and I perceive that I, at least, have certainly not felt the year slip away; it has gone before I knew it.

Sighing, I lifted the carton named LIGHTS onto one of the dining room chairs to open it. "By the way," my husband asked Laurie very casually, "what *was* in that package, the one your mother just took into the kitchen?"

"Why, I wouldn't have any idea," Laurie said innocently. He called to me, "Did you remember to cut holes in the top so it could breathe?" he asked.

"Come on, you," his father said. "Get up on that ladder."

Jannie ladled eggnog into cups, Sally sat on the couch next to Barry with her lap full of popcorn, and spoke to him softly. "In the morning," she said, "when you wake up, what do you do?"

"I wake Laurie and I wake Jannie and I wake Mommy and I wake—"

"No, no," I said. "Tomorrow I plan to sleep very late."

"Eight o'clock by the playroom clock," Sally said.

"Eight-thirty," I said.

"Nine," my husband said.

"But *last* year it was eight o'clock," Sally said indignantly, "you know perfectly *well*. Last year and the year before that and the year before that and the year before *that* it was eight o'clock."

"Yeah." Laurie turned. "And no setting back the playroom clock, either, like you did that time."

Sally murmured to Barry, "So when you wake up tomorrow morning, what do you do?"

"I wake Laurie and I wake—"

My husband and Laurie had cut the tree down to size, and Jannie took the cut branches into the dining room and wreathed them around the punch bowl. She began to sing "Joy to the World," and my husband caught the tree as it toppled forward. "Hey," Laurie said, peering down between the branches, "you trying to knock me off this ladder or something? Entertain the kids seeing me go crash on the floor?"

"We need a new tree stand," my husband said.

"Don't be silly," I said. "We've *always* used that one."

We keep a spool of fine wire with the tree stand, and Laurie and his father contrived to secure the tree upright by fastening it with wire and thumbtacks to the frames of the bay window. "Look," Laurie called down, "last year it was maybe three inches farther over left; here's one of last year's thumbtacks."

I can remember, back in the dim time when I was a little girl, my father taking the strings of Christmas tree lights out of the flowered box, standing with his hands full, saying wistfully, "These lights again? No new ones?" and my mother, turning, frowning slightly, "But you said they were good for another year; last Christmas you said they were—"

"These lights?" my husband said. "You didn't get any new ones?"

A good deal of the tire tape which holds the light strings together was put on by my father, and some by my brother —kneeling on the floor, entangled, asking madly, "Why can't we get *new* lights, will someone please tell me?"—and of course my husband has put on tape of his own. He has taken off some of the tape my father put on and replaced it where it was getting ragged, and last year there was a new spot which Laurie taped. I went out one year (as I suppose my mother must have done at least once before me) and bought three new strings of lights, but somehow their bright green cord was so gaudy among the soft old ornaments, and there was nothing for my husband to do during the half hour when the rest of us were drinking eggnog and he would usually have been taping the light cords, so I put the new lights in the box with the old ones and they are still there; every year my husband takes them out of the box, looks at them, and puts them back again. "We ought to get new tree lights," Laurie said, unwinding the tire tape, "for heaven's sake, how long do you expect these will last?"

"They'll do for another year or so," my husband said absently. "Look, here's more of Grandpa's tire tape peeling off."

"—and Donner and Blitzen and Dasher and Prancer—" Sally told Barry. Jannie tugged at my arm. "Can you come a minute?" she asked. "I got to show you something." I followed her up the back stairs to her room, which had a sign on the door threatening the most dire vengeance on any who entered for any reason whatsoever. Jannie shut the door tight behind us and I sat down on her bed while with much pausing to listen apprehensively she took from her bottom dresser drawer a candy box. She set this down on the bed next to me and opened it carefully. Taking out one of the small packages inside, she set it on my lap. It was brightly wrapped, and the card on it read, "To Daddy from Jannie."

"It's fine," I said. "What is it?"

"Not so loud," Jannie said, whispering. "It's a potholder."

"A potholder?"

"Yes, we learned how to make potholders in Starlight 4-H Club. And this is for Sally."

"A potholder?"

"Yes, and this is for Laurie, and this is for Barry."

"A potholder for Barry?"

"Yes, because in the mornings when his cereal's too hot. Oh, golly." Hastily she snatched the bottom package from

the box and put it under her pillow. "You weren't supposed to see that," she said.

"I didn't see it," I told her. "I never even noticed it."

"Good," she said, "because that's a secret, that one. I
won't even tell you who it's for."

Voices called from downstairs, and I helped Jannie get
the packages back into the box and the box back into her
dresser drawer and her dresser drawer shut and then we
closed the door of her room behind us, with its forbidding
sign, and hurried downstairs. The tree burst into light as
we came into the living room, turning itself suddenly from
an alien, faintly disturbing presence in the house into a
thing of loveliness and color. "Ooh," said Sally, and Barry
nodded, smiling.

I took up the box named ORNAMENTS and opened it.
On top was the stuffed Santa Claus doll which is always
the responsibility of the youngest child, who must see that
it is put under the Christmas tree and then put safely away
again when the Christmas tree comes down. The Santa
Claus doll is always on top of the last box because it must
always be wrested at the last minute from the youngest
child ("Christmas will come again, *really* it will") and
gotten hastily into the box and hidden. Now, just as I had
promised last year, I took the Santa Claus doll and handed
it into Barry's waiting arms. "Santa Claus," Barry said in
confirmation, and returned to his place on the couch, holding the Santa Claus doll tight. Jannie began to sing "O
Little Town of Bethlehem" and Laurie said sharply, "No,
Dad, please. Let *me* do it; you'll fall."

Sally sat on the floor as close to the tree as she could get
and chanted musically, "When *I* was youngest child it was
the year of two trees, because when Mommy came to the

man he had forgotten and our tree was gone for someone else. So Mommy said to the man where will I get a Christmas tree for my little children and for my little child Sally and the man said here are two thin trees with almost no branches will they do and Mommy said yes, I will take these two thin trees for my little children and for my little child Sally and we made red chains and golden bells and frankincense and garlands of red flowers and we put them around and about the two thin trees and it was Christmas and the loveliest Christmas there ever was. . . ."

"And the Christmas when Laurie was covered with spots," Jannie said. "That was before you were born," she told Sally.

"But I know it was because they gave him a paintbox and they thought *that* was why he was spotty," Sally said.

"Remember the Christmas the furnace went off and we opened our presents all wrapped in blankets?" Laurie peered out from under the star he was fastening on top of the tree. "Boy, *that* was a real cool Yule."

"Did you notice that I put 'fur coat' on my Christmas list again this year?" I remarked to my husband. "Not that I really expect—"

"Here it is, here it is," said Jannie breathlessly. "The one I am going to give to my own dear daughter someday." She had taken out her own particular treasure, a little china lady with a wide spun-glass skirt. "My own little daughter," Jannie said.

"And you will tell her," Sally continued smoothly, "how you used to hang it on *your* Christmas tree when you were a little girl, and how your mommy used to hang it on *her* Christmas tree when *she* was a little girl—"

"Mommy?" said Barry, perplexed. He turned to look at me curiously.

"When *Mommy* was a little girl," Sally said, "they used to go in sleighs and sleigh bells and bring in a Yule log, but of course that was *very* long ago."

"Hey," I said, protesting, and Jannie started "God Rest Ye Merry, Gentlemen." Barry gave me a reassuring nod, shifted his Santa Claus to his other arm, and reached out for the popcorn.

I began to lift out the bright fragile ornaments. I handed them carefully to Jannie and Sally, who went back and forth from the tree, carrying the ornaments carefully with both hands and setting them with caution on the tips of the branches. Barry took the funny little wooden man, colored red and yellow, and hung him on a bottom branch, and then he came back for the little cardboard pictures of drums and soldiers and old-fashioned dolls which had come with my grandmother from England. He took them one by one and with great concentration, always holding the Santa Claus, tucked the little strings over the ends of the low branches and the little soldiers and dolls swung around and back, bending down the branches. Laurie came to the dining room table to select ornaments for the top of the tree. "Varnish dry yet?" I whispered.

"Shh." He turned to watch his father, who was helping Sally with an ornament. "I think so," he whispered. "You think he'll like it?"

"It's exactly what he's been wanting," I said.

"He's going to be so surprised I can't *wait*," Laurie said happily. "By the way," he added, "you just didn't happen to notice a .22 rifle tucked away in a closet somewhere?"

"I wouldn't even know what a .22 rifle looked like," I assured him. "You know perfectly well I'm afraid of guns."

"Brother," Laurie said. "When Sally sees that—"

"Shh," I said.

Laurie took up two ornaments and made for the tree. "Watch out here, you kids," he said grandly. "This is where the professionals go into action." He climbed onto his ladder again.

"—you will hear bells jingling and reindeers' feet on the roof," Sally told Barry confidentially.

I poured my husband a glass of eggnog and Jannie began to sing "The First Noel."

"And milk and crackers for Santa Claus," Sally went on busily, "and then we have breakfast, and you are all always *my* guests at breakfast and we sit on the floor in my room and eat cereal from the new cereal bowls green and red, red and green. And what do you do when you wake up?" she demanded suddenly of Barry.

"Wake Laurie and—"

I opened the last carton, labeled DECORATIONS. There on top was the cardboard candle Jannie had made in kindergarten. That always went on the dining room buffet and then there was the big Santa Claus face Sally had done in first grade and that went on the back door and the red and green paper chains Laurie had made when he was a Cub Scout went over the doorway. Not two weeks ago Barry had come home from nursery school with a greenish kind of a picture of a Christmas tree and that had somehow got itself established on the refrigerator next to the big chart Laurie always made early in December so we could all fill out our Christmas lists and keep them in plain sight. Here were the popcorn strings my mother strung when *I* was youngest child, and the paper bells Laurie and I made when he was so small it seems unbelievable now, and the jigsaw Santa my husband cut out that same year, and the painted candy canes and the red ribbons and the green paper wreaths. "Oh, my," I said, looking at all of it.

"Here, you just sit down," Jannie said. "You just don't remember, is all. You sit down and I'll do it."

She sent Sally with the paper bells for the front door and Barry with the Santa Claus face and Laurie got back on his ladder and put up the paper chains and Jannie put the candy canes on the doorknob and the paper wreaths on the kitchen cabinets and the popcorn strings went around the foot of the tree because they were so old and delicate by now that they broke if we tried to hang them. Jannie and Laurie together put up the paper bells and Sally set the jigsaw Santa in the center of the dining room table. Sally reached into the box and took out the string of bells and Jannie sang "Jingle Bells." Barry hung the bells on the nail by the front door where they hang every year. "Bells and reindeers and presents," Barry sang, and Jannie came over to drape a piece of tinsel in my hair.

"Tell me," my husband asked Jannie confidentially, "what *was* in that package?"

Jannie thought. "A lovely new tie," she said at last. "Colored red and green for Christmas and pink and yellow for Easter and red and white and blue for Fourth of July, and black."

"I been telling you and telling you and *telling* you," Sally said to Barry. "Now, do you peek?"

"No?" Barry said uncertainly.

"You get up in the morning and what do you do?"

Barry opened his mouth and said "I wake—" Sally sighed and said, "Well, then, who is coming tonight?"

Jannie began to sing "Silent Night."

The tree was growing; it was hung with tinsel now, and every possible corner of the house held some touch of Christmas. "If one more child makes one more decoration," my husband said, "we'll have to move out to the barn next year."

"You'd think some of it would fall apart from one year to the next," I said helplessly.

"Tomorrow morning," Sally said, "all under the tree will be presents."

"That reminds me," my husband said to Laurie, "you'd better get out the screwdriver and the hammer, for a couple of construction jobs we've got to do later. Last year I needed the wrench, too."

"—and an orange in your stocking," Sally said, and then at last it was time. Solemnly, reluctantly, Barry climbed down from the couch with the stuffed Santa Claus. He stood for a minute looking up at the lighted tree, his small face touched with reflected color, and then, bending low and wiggling, he crept underneath and set the Santa Claus against the trunk of the tree. "Now," he said to the Santa Claus, "make it be Christmas."

"He ought to say 'God bless us every one' or something like *that*," Jannie pointed out.

"Say," my husband said to Sally in a low voice, "how about that package hidden in the kitchen?"

"Mice," Sally said firmly. "Full of mice."

"Listen," Laurie said in my ear, "suppose he *doesn't* like it, after all? I mean, suppose he doesn't *like* it?"

"Don't worry about *that*," I said. "It's just beautiful."

Barry climbed up into his father's lap to look further at the tree and his father bent and whispered in his ear. "What package?" said Barry, turning.

"Careful," said Laurie warningly.

"Don't tell," Sally said.

Barry chuckled. "A elephant," he said.

Jannie sang "Hark the Herald Angels Sing," Laurie took out the cartons to stack them on the back porch until we took the tree down again, Sally sat cross-legged on the floor watching the tree. Suddenly Sally and Barry spoke at once.

"Last Christmas—" Sally said.

"Next Christmas—" Barry said.

SHIRLEY JACKSON was born in San Francisco in 1916, though she often gave the date as 1919, and spent most of her early life in California. She attended Syracuse University, where she met fellow student and future critic and teacher Stanley Edgar Hyman. They married in 1940 in New York City and moved to Bennington, Vermont, five years later. The mother of four children, Jackson was at once the perfect professor's wife—a successful writer, an engaging conversationalist, an energetic hostess—and a troubled woman—addicted to drinking, smoking, amphetamines, and chocolate. Jackson published six novels and countless short stories, including "The Lottery," which generated the largest volume of mail ever received by *The New Yorker* after its appearance there in 1948. In subsequent years it has continued to spark controversy and inspire admiration—and terror—becoming perhaps the most famous short story of our time. Afflicted by weight and health problems, in later years Jackson was increasingly afraid to leave her house. In 1965 she died suddenly of heart failure during an afternoon nap. She was 48 years old.